The U

The Ungovernable Society

A Genealogy of Authoritarian Liberalism

Grégoire Chamayou

Translated by Andrew Brown

polity

Originally published as *La société ingouvernable* © La Fabrique Éditions, 2018

This English edition © 2021 by Polity Press

This book is supported by the Institut français (Royaume-Uni) as part of the Burgess programme.

This work received the French Voices Award for excellence in publication and translation. French Voices is a program created and funded by the French Embassy in the United States and FACE Foundation (French American Cultural Exchange). French Voices Logo designed by Serge Bloch.

Illustrations from R. Edward Freeman, *Strategic Management: A Stakeholder Approach* © Cambridge University Press, 2010, reproduced with permission of Cambridge University Press through PLSclear.

Polity Press
65 Bridge Street
Cambridge CB2 1UR, UK

Polity Press
101 Station Landing
Suite 300
Medford, MA 02155, USA

ISBN-13: 978-1-5095-4200-0
ISBN-13: 978-1-5095-4201-7 (pb)

A catalogue record for this book is available from the British Library.

Library of Congress Cataloging-in-Publication Data
Names: Chamayou, Grégoire, author. | Brown, Andrew, translator.
Title: The ungovernable society : a genealogy of authoritarian liberalism / Grégoire Chamayou ; translated by Andrew Brown.
Other titles: Société ingouvernable. English
Description: Medford : Polity Press, 2021. | Includes bibliographical references and index. | Summary: "A brilliant work that shows how the political contours of our contemporary neoliberal societies took shape in the crisis-laden decade of the 1970s"-- Provided by publisher. Identifiers: LCCN 2020032896 (print) | LCCN 2020032897 (ebook) | ISBN 9781509542000 (hardback) | ISBN 9781509542017 (paperback) | ISBN 9781509542024 (epub)
Subjects: LCSH: Free enterprise--History. | Capitalism--History. | Liberalism--History. | Labor discipline--History.
Classification: LCC HB95 .C47613 2021(print) | LCC HB95(ebook) | DDC 330.12/2--dc23
LC record available at https://lccn.loc.gov/2020032896
LC ebook record available at https://lccn.loc.gov/2020032897

Typeset in 10.5 on 12pt Sabon by
Servis Filmsetting Ltd, Stockport, Cheshire
Printed and bound in Great Britain by CPI Group (UK) Ltd, Croydon

For further information on Polity, visit our website: politybooks.com

CONTENTS

FOREWORD

Grégoire Chamayou's book should be read as an important contribution to the study of neoliberalism – or whatever we are to call
the great renewal of reactionary thought that emerged in the 1970s
and still dominates our society today. In fact, he contributes to the
literature on neoliberalism while simultaneously rejecting that term
neoliberalism itself – or, rather, fundamentally reorienting our understanding of it.

Chamayou accomplishes this reorientation, in part, by giving voice
and priority to intellectual and political figures that have largely
been left out of the standard accounts. He orchestrates wonderfully
the conservative and reactionary chorus in the United States in the
battle of ideas that in the 1970s arrived at a new hegemony. He
does, of course, engage with and give insightful interpretations of the
well-known protagonists of neoliberal economics, such as Friedrich
Hayek, Milton Friedman and James Buchanan. But the standard
focus on such figures leads too often to a conception of neoliberalism
as a single, coherent project. Chamayou demonstrates, instead, that
the movement was profoundly heterogeneous.

In fact, one of the most innovative aspects of the book is, in my
view, the way Chamayou delves deeply into the literature emerging
in the 1970s on management and managerialism, which in many
respects diverges significantly from neoliberal economics. Managers,
business leaders and management theorists, rather than thinking
only in economic terms, constructed a political project, opposing
workplace democracy, for instance, in order to preserve the authority of the 'private government' of the firm. Management theorists
developed a practical, strategic conception of governance, no longer
aimed internally within the individual business but instead oriented

outward: an expansive notion of strategic management intended to govern also the social world outside of the firm, ruling over workers, shareholders, consumers and other social forces, as if in concentric waves. These lesser known authors of management theory are in Chamayou's argument just as important as the well-known neoliberal economists, if not more so, in developing the new paradigm. By highlighting their perspective and their importance, he casts the entire project in a new light.

A second way that Chamayou reorients our understanding of this movement is by emphasizing its internally varied and political character. This is particularly apparent from the analyses of strategic management. Rather than analysing neoliberalism as a solely or even primarily economic project, we must grasp this heterogeneous project that is political at its core. Many authors have highlighted how neoliberalism is intimately tied to authoritarian state policies, for instance in the Pinochet, Reagan and Thatcher governments. For Chamayou, however, the authoritarian rule that accompanies neoliberalism is not only or even primarily based in the state but instead the power of managers and the firm. Authoritarian liberalism is Chamayou's preferred term to grasp the range of strategic deployments of power extending from state to business.

The political nature of the movement is made particularly evident by the repeating lament that Chamayou traces among management theorists: that the firm and society as a whole have become ungovernable. This plaintive cry echoes the evaluations of neoconservatives and neoliberals of the era. The management discourse against workplace democracy, for example, parallels Samuel Huntington's well-known claim that democracy has gone too far and is no longer sustainable because it has allowed too many 'minorities' to make demands on the state and on social resources. It is fascinating (and chilling) to see how in these conservative and reactionary circles in the 1970s, democracy is so willingly sacrificed in the name of governability, which takes the place of supreme value. In fact, the theorists, business leaders and politicians involved in these debates wield the fear of ungovernability as a weapon. Merely the threat of it served to legitimate and make appear inevitable the deployment of new structures of authority at all social levels. But that is not to imply that cynical business leaders and management theorists simply invented the threat to legitimate authority. No, it is important to keep in mind that pressures of social antagonisms, insubordination and indiscipline were very real in the 1970s.

The question of ungovernability, in fact, can serve as a pivot to look back on Chamayou's argument from a different perspective. He tells us that his book is a history from above, and, indeed, the dramatis personae who populate centre stage are primarily those on top or, rather, those who serve the interests of the ruling class, preserving the power and wealth of business and élites. It might seem, looking only at this well-lit stage, as if these thinkers, through debates with each other and through the forward march of ideas, were autonomously inventing a new paradigm and driving forward historical development. And yet, incessantly in Chamayou's book one hears the clamour off stage of social antagonism and contestation, and it is not hard to see that the pressure of those forces is the real motor of the development. He does, in fact, give an excellent account of the rising insubordination of young workers, the threats to corporate profits of consumer movements and environmental movements, and the anti-corporate thrust of the Vietnam War protests. Business and political leaders, economists and theorists were keenly focused on and trembled at the thought of these rising powers. Faced with the rising crisis of governability, they were forced to invent new mechanisms of governance. The development of strategic management and liberal authoritarianism, then, were really a *response* to the way these forces had made society ungovernable. Chamayou's history from above, then, has to be read at an angle, because all the drama on stage is really seeking answers to threats of those forces off stage, from below.

Although it is firmly rooted in the 1970s and the debates of the era, this book is also profoundly about our present. It demonstrates, in fact, some of the myriad ways in which the structures and strategies of power developed then still rule over us today. And understanding better the birth of these forms of rule will allow us better to contest and eventually overthrow them.

Michael Hardt

INTRODUCTION

Governable. Adjective (neologism): that can be governed.
Example: 'This people is not governable'.
    Supplement to the *Dictionnaire de l'Académie française* (1839)[1]

This type of period is familiar. The signs never lie; the same omens had been observed on the eve of the Protestant Reformation or the Russian Revolution. So says the Californian engineer and 'futurologist' Willis W. Harman, for whom all the indicators of a major earthquake are now flashing red. They include: 'Increased rate of mental disorders. Increased rate of violent crime, social disruptions, use of police to control behavior. Increased public acceptance of hedonistic behavior (particularly sexual). [. . .] Signs of anxiety about the future [. . .], decreased trust in institutions of business and government. Growing sense that old answers no longer work.'[2] In short, it is 'the legitimacy of the present social system of the industrialized world' that is crumbling, as he warned us in 1975.

And indeed, widespread rebelliousness was in the air. No relationship of domination was left untouched: insubordination in the hierarchy between sexes and genders, in the colonial and racial orders, in the hierarchies of class and labour, in families, on campuses, in the armed forces, on the shop floor, in offices and on the street. According to Michel Foucault, we were witnessing 'the birth of a crisis in government' in the sense that 'all the processes by which men govern each other were being challenged'.[3] What happened at the beginning of the 1970s, as people have since remarked, was a 'crisis of governability that preceded the economic crisis',[4] a 'crisis of governability' at the levels of society and business,[5] a crisis of 'disciplinary governability'[6] that foreshadowed major changes in the technologies of power.

1

Before being taken up by critical theory, however, this idea had already been put forward by conservative intellectuals. It was their way of interpreting current events, of problematizing the situation. Democracy, as Samuel Huntington stated in 1975, in a famous Trilateral Commission report to which we will return in detail, was affected by a 'problem of governability': a universal surge of popular feeling was undermining authority, overburdening the state with its boundless demands.

The word 'governability' was not a recent invention. In French, *gouverner* can mean both 'to govern' and 'to steer'; *gouvernabilité* had already been used in the nineteenth century to refer, for example, to the 'properties of governability or steerability' of a ship or the 'conditions of stability and governability' of an airship, but also the governability of a horse, an individual or a people. In this sense, the term refers to a disposition within the object to be led, its propensity to be guided, the docility or the ductility of the governed. Ungovernability is therefore conceived as its polar opposite: as a restive counter-disposition, a spirit of insubordination, a refusal to be governed, at least 'not like that, not for that, not by them'.[7] But that's just one facet of the concept, just one of the dimensions of the problem.

Governability is indeed a *compound capacity*, one which presupposes, on the side of the object, a *disposition* to be governed but also, on the other side, on the subject's side, an *aptitude* to govern. Mutiny is just one hypothetical instance. A situation of ungovernability can also be the result of a malfunction or failure in the governmental apparatus, even when the governed are perfectly docile. A phenomenon of institutional paralysis, for example, may result from something other than a movement of civil disobedience.

Schematically speaking, a crisis of governability can have two great polarities: at the bottom, among the governed, or at the top, among the governors, and two great modalities, revolt or breakdown: the rebellious governed or the powerless governors (the two aspects can of course be combined). As Lenin theorized, it is only when 'the *"lower classes" do not want* to live in the old way and the "upper classes" *cannot carry on in the old way*' that a 'governmental crisis' is likely to turn into a revolutionary crisis.[8]

In the 1970s, conservative theories of the crisis of governability also linked these two aspects. Without imagining they were on the eve of a revolution, these writers were worried about the current political dynamic that seemed to be leading to disaster. The problem was not only that people were growing rebellious, nor just that the apparatuses of government were congested, but that these failures and revolts overdetermined each other, weighing down on the system to the point of bringing it close to collapse.

Foucault, who knew the Trilateral Commission's report on 'the governability of democracies', mentioned it to illustrate what he preferred to call a 'crisis of the apparatus of governmentality':[9] not a mere movement of 'revolts of conduct',[10] but a blockage in the 'general system of governmentality'.[11] There were endogenous reasons for this, irreducible to the economic crises of capitalism, although connected with them. What he thought was starting to seize up was the 'liberal art of government'.[12] We must not anachronistically take this to mean the dominant neoliberalism, but rather what has since been called 'embedded liberalism', an unstable compromise between a market economy and Keynesian interventionism. Having studied other similar crises in history, Foucault made the prognosis that, from this blockage, something else was about to emerge, starting with major redevelopments in the arts of governing.

If society is ungovernable, it is not so *in itself*, but, in the words of the Saint-Simonian engineer Michel Chevalier, 'ungovernable in the way that people want to govern it at present'.[13] This is a traditional theme in this kind of discourse: ungovernability is never absolute, only relative. And it is in this gap that we find the raison d'être, the real object, and the constitutive challenge of any art of governing.

In this book, I study this crisis as it was perceived and theorized in the 1970s by those who strove to defend the interests of 'business'. This is therefore the opposite of a 'history from below'; instead, it is a history 'from above', written from the point of view of the ruling classes, mainly in the United States, at that time the epicentre of a far-reaching intellectual and political movement.

Karl Polanyi explained that the rise of the 'free market', with all its destructive effects, had historically triggered a vast countermovement of self-protection on the part of society – a countermovement which, he warned, 'was incompatible with the self-regulation of the market, and thus with the market system itself'.[14] But this was just the kind of conclusion that the organic intellectuals of the business world in the 1970s were coming to: things were going too far and, if current trends continued, they would entail the destruction of the 'free enterprise system'. What was starting to gather pace in this decade was a *third movement*, a great reaction from which we have not yet emerged.

3

I will here be studying the formation of this countermovement from a philosophical point of view, by tracing the genealogy of the concepts and modes of problematization that underlay it rather than setting out the factual details of its institutional, social, economic or political history. The unity of my object, however, is not the unity of a doctrine (this book is not a new intellectual history of neoliberalism), but the unity of a situation: starting out from identifiable points of tension, from the conflicts which broke out, I shall seek to examine how they were thematized, and what solutions were considered. I will try to examine the ideas that were put to work, their endeavours and the intentions behind them, but also the dissensions, contradictions and aporias they encountered.

The challenge of the new thinking was not just to produce new discourses of legitimation for a capitalism under scrutiny, but also to formulate programmatic theories and ideas for action aimed at reconfiguring the current order. These new arts of government whose genesis I propose to relate are still active today. If it is important to carry out this investigation, it is because it may help us understand our present.

This third movement is not reducible to its doctrinaire neoliberal component – far from it. Many procedures and *dispositifs* that have become central to contemporary governance did not figure in the texts of the founding fathers of neoliberalism, unless they were introduced and defended in complete opposition to their theses. Our era is admittedly neoliberal, but with a bastard neoliberalism, eclectic and in many ways contradictory; its strange syntheses can be explained only by the history of the conflicts that marked its formation.

This crisis of governability has had as many facets as there are power relationships. They were met, in each field, with specific backlashes. I here focus on the crisis that affected business insofar as it was a form of *private government*.

In addition to the issues that are still with us and that will emerge over the course of this book, my choice of topic was motivated by a more specific preoccupation. At the very time when big business is one of the dominant institutions of the contemporary world, philosophy remains under-equipped to understand it. From its traditional corpus, it has mostly inherited theories of state power and sovereignty dating back to the seventeenth century. It has long had its treatises on theologico-political authorities – but nothing of the kind for what we might call 'corporato-political' authorities.

When philosophy finally approaches this subject, for example by belatedly incorporating it into its teaching, this often happens in the worst possible way, by regurgitating a naive discourse on business ethics or corporate social responsibility, of the kind produced in business schools. Philosophy these days is no longer the handmaid of theology, but of management.

It is now time to develop critical philosophies of business corporations. This book is just a preparatory work in this direction, a historico-philosophical inquiry into some of the central categories of dominant economic and managerial thought – categories that are now prospering, while the conflicts and objectives that led to their development, and continue to guide their meaning, remain forgotten.

This book is organized along the various axes which, in their interaction, comprised the crisis of governability in business as it was thematized at the time. For the defenders of the business world, each axis corresponded to a new difficulty, a new front on which to mobilize.

1. A corporation, first and foremost, governs workers. At the beginning of the 1970s, management faced massive indiscipline from the workers. How could it square up to these? How could it restore the former discipline? If the old procedures were obsolete, what form could a new art of governing take? Various strategies were envisaged and debated. (Part I.)

2. But if we go higher up the vertical axis of subordination, a second crisis appears, this time in the relation between shareholders and managers. Noting that, in companies run by shareholders, managers simply become the managers of *other people's* business, and do not have the same interest as the former bosses and proprietors in maximizing profits, some people worried about a possible lack of zeal on the managers' part, or even worse, a 'managerial revolution'. How were managers to be disciplined? How could they be brought back into line with the shareholders' values? (Part II.)

3. At the same time, on the horizontal axis, in the firm's social and political environment, unprecedented threats were emerging. Against a growing cultural and political rejection of capitalism, new movements directly attacked the way major business groups were led. How were people to react to what appeared as 'an attack on the free enterprise system'? They were torn as to the strategy to adopt. (Part III.)

4. These 'attacks' intensified and spread from country to country, especially with the first big boycotts launched against multinationals; firms now turned to new consultants. How were they to manage not only their employees, but protestors from outside their firms, and,

beyond them, a 'social environment' that had become so turbulent? New approaches and new concepts were invented. (Part IV.)

5. At the behest of the emerging environmental movements in particular, new social and environmental regulations became necessary. As well as the horizontal pressure of social movements there was now, in addition, the vertical expansion of new forms of public intervention. How could these regulatory projects be defeated? How could they be opposed, in theory and in practice? (Part V.)

6. What, more fundamentally, did this twofold phenomenon of generalized protest and growing government intervention stem from? One answer was the flaws of welfare democracy which, far from ensuring consent, was digging its own grave. In the eyes of neo-conservatives as much as neoliberals, it was the state itself that was becoming ungovernable. Hence these questions: how could politics be dethroned? How could democracy be limited? (Part VI.)

For my investigation, I have gathered various heterogeneous sources from different disciplines; I have taken the decision to intertwine 'noble' and 'vulgar' sources when they have the same object – thus a Nobel Prize-winning economist may rub shoulders with a specialist in 'busting' trade unions. Their writings are all strategic texts in a struggle, and they all provide answers to the question 'What should be done?' They are texts that set out procedures, techniques and tactics – either very concretely, for example in practical guides or manuals for managers, or more programmatically, through reflections on discursive strategies or overall practices. This corpus comprises mainly English-language sources: as far as managerial thinking and economic theories of the firm are concerned, the United States has been the birthplace of new notions that have quickly spread worldwide.

I often keep myself in the background in this book, so as to reconstitute, by cutting and editing quotations, a composite text whose assembled fragments are often worth less individually, through their attribution to a singular author, than as characteristic utterances of the different positions to which I strive to give a voice.

Part I

Indocile workers

— 1 —

INDISCIPLINE ON THE SHOP FLOOR

Put thirteen small bits of card into thirteen small holes, sixty times an hour, eight hours a day. Solder sixty-seven pieces of sheet metal per hour and then find yourself one day placed in front of a contraption that needs 110. Work amid noise, [. . .] in a fog of oil, solvent, metal dust. [. . .] Obey without answering back, be punished without right of appeal.

André Gorz[1]

Tommy passes a joint to Yanagan who draws the smoke deep, then hands it to me. [. . .] The smoke striking into my lungs sends my blood leaping. And soon the flying sparks, the hot steel, the raging, exploding furnaces above us seem like frivolities on carnival night.

Bennett Kremen[2]

'The younger generation, which has already shaken the campuses, is showing signs of restlessness in the plants of industrial America', warned the *New York Times* in June 1970. 'Many young workers are calling for immediate changes in working conditions and are rejecting the disciplines of factory work'.[3] 'Labour discipline has collapsed', observed an internal report at General Motors the same year.[4]

If discipline means gaining 'a hold over others' bodies',[5] Indocile behaviour is manifested by an irresistible longing for disengagement: don't stay where you are, run away, get out of the business, take back your own body and make off with it. But this was exactly the set of feelings that factory life was starting to generate on a large scale at the time, as there was among the younger generation of workers a 'deep dislike of the job and [. . .] a desire to escape'.[6]

In the US automobile industry, turnover was huge: more than half of the new unskilled workers were leaving their positions before the end of the first year.[7] Some were so repelled by their first contact with the assembly line that they took to the hills after the first weeks. 'Some assembly-line workers are so turned off', managers reported with astonishment, 'that they just walk away in mid-shift and don't even come back to get their pay for time they have worked'.[8]

At General Motors, 5 per cent of workers were absent without any real justification every day.[9] On Mondays and Fridays this rose to twice the figure. In summertime, in some factories, it could reach 20 per cent. 'What is it like on a Monday, in summer, then?', one factory worker was asked in 1973. He replied, 'I don't know, I've never been in for one'. Another worker, when asked 'how come you're only working four days a week?' replied, 'because I can't make enough money in three'.[10] A third was asked what exactly he was looking for, and replied 'for a chance to use my brain', a job where 'my high school education counts for something'.[11] Factory life? 'You're like in a jail cell – except they have more time off in prison', replied another.[12]

In factories, your body was ruined and your mind was exhausted, you felt dead: 'I sing, whistle, throw water at a guy on the line, do anything I can to bust the boredom'.[13] Unable to endure the infinite repetition of the same any longer, you aspired to create rather than to produce: 'Sometimes, out of pure meanness, when I make something, I just put a little dent in it. I like to do something to make it really unique. Hit it with a hammer; deliberately to see if it'll get by, just so I can say I did it'.[14]

Ordinary acts of indiscipline, just like the disciplines of which they are the counterpart, involve an art of detail. They require just as much meticulousness and obstinacy in producing their transgressions as the opposite side does in enacting its regulations. Operating on the scale of the smallest gesture, they recover moments of respite, in a fierce and intimate struggle whose booty can be calculated in the few dozen seconds you can grab for yourself from the rhythms of the assembly belt. 'But eventually the main problem is *time*'.[15] You slow down on purpose, you put on the brakes, alone or collectively, or conversely you sometimes accelerate so you can later enjoy a brief stretch of time out. 'I'm not the only worker playing this game: almost everybody does it'. You steal a handful of moments for yourself, just to breathe, to exchange a few words, to do something else: 'I'm good enough at my job now that I can do two or three cars in a row fast and then have maybe 15 or 20 seconds for myself in between. The main thing I do with these interludes is read. I read the paper every day and I read books. Some of the books are quite complex. The main thing I've had to learn in order to read under these conditions is to remember what I've read and to be able to quickly find where I've left off'.[16] If discipline is a rhythmopolitics or a chronopower, indiscipline is too, but in a diametrically opposite direction, a fight against the clock of a particular kind. 'I actually saw a woman in the plant running along the line to keep up with the work. I'm not going to run for anybody. There ain't anyone in that plant that is going to tell me to run'.[17] The first main refusals of *acceleration* were workers' struggles. The Indocile are time thieves.[18]

At General Motors, one trade unionist reports, the staff 'uses its powers as a dictatorship'.[19] The authoritarianism of the little bosses, close supervision, pernickety instructions and absurd orders, insults and continued pressure – all of this was now unacceptable. 'The foremen', says one Black worker from Baltimore soberly, 'could show more respect for the workers – talk to them like men, not dogs'.[20]

The state of social tension, said an alarmed *Wall Street Journal* in 1969, is the 'worst within memory'. Everything suggested that an 'epic battle between management and labor' was imminent, announced *Fortune*.[21] In fact, in the year 1970 alone, nearly two and a half million workers went on strike in the United States.[22] This was the biggest wave of work stoppages since the immediate aftermath of the Second World War. With the high number of strike actions came more radical forms of struggle. Over and above wage demands, the complaints concerned the forms of labour organization and were aimed at the authorities that were imposing them.

Bill Watson, a worker at a Detroit car factory in 1968, recounts a widespread wave of sabotage that he witnessed. The engineers had introduced a new six-cylinder engine model that workers judged to be poorly designed. They had expressed their criticisms to the management, in vain. Faced with this flat refusal, some teams started to 'forget' to mount certain parts. Soon, others followed, sabotaging the work in their turn. Mountains of unserviceable machines rose up in the workshops: 'At that point there were so many defective motors piled around the plant that it was almost impossible to move from one area to another'.[23] This phenomenon, says Watson, was not isolated. There were, pretty much all over America at the time, conflicts of the same kind: they expressed a desire on the part of workers to take over production, to gain control of their work, of the way they did it, of what was being *manufactured* in the factory.

In 1970, the CEO of General Motors sent a warning to his employees: 'we cannot tolerate employees who reject responsibility and fail to respect essential disciplines and authority. [...] GM increased its investment [...] to improve both productivity and working conditions, but tools and technology mean nothing if the worker is absent from his job. We must receive a fair day's work for which we pay a fair day's wage'.[24]

How was discipline to be restored? GM management opted for the 'hard line':[25] speed up the work rate, automate unskilled tasks, downgrade the remainder, make cuts in wages, and strengthen surveillance and control. The automobile factory in Lordstown, Ohio, with its assembly line described as 'the fastest in the world', was the firm's technological flagship, the incarnation of the employers' solutions to productivity problems. In 1971 it was placed under the control of the 'General Motors Assembly Division', a managerial shock force, described as 'the roughest and toughest' of the group.[26] Under this harsh regime, many jobs were scrapped and the production rates, already very fast, were accelerated: from sixty cars per hour to almost double that amount. Now, 'in 36 seconds the worker had to perform at least eight different operations'.[27] 'You just about need a pass to piss. That ain't no joke. You raise your little hand if you want to go wee-wee. Then wait maybe half an hour 'till they find a relief man. And they write it down every time too cause you're supposed to do it in your time, not theirs. Try it too often and you'll get a week off'.[28]

In Lordstown, the workforce was particularly young, twenty-eight on average. It took young bodies to keep up with such a work rate – but the young minds that guided those bodies were also the least ready to submit to it. One day, a car arrived at the end of the assembly belt with all its parts unmounted, lying in a tidy pile in the frame. The managers accused the workers of sabotage. 'Sabotage? Just a way of letting off steam. You can't keep up with the car so you scratch it on the way past. I once saw a hillbilly drop an ignition key down the gas tank. Last week I watched a guy light a glove and lock it in the trunk. We all wanted to see how far down the line they'd discover it. [...] If you miss a car, they call that sabotage'.[29]

The management, which reckoned that the losses due to 'indiscipline' amounted to 12,000 cars per year not being produced on the site, reacted with increased firmness, launching hundreds of disciplinary proceedings: one worker was sacked for arriving a minute late; another was suspended for having farted in the passenger compartment of a vehicle; a third for singing *tralala* on the shop floor.[30]

At the beginning of March 1972, faced with this tightening of screws, the workers resorted to a wildcat strike. The fighting spirit of the Lordstown workers made an impression. 'These guys have become tigers'.[31] They were 'just not going to swallow the same kind of treatment' as their fathers; they were not afraid of the management – this was what was at stake in the strike.[32] The press talked of a 'Lordstown syndrome', an 'industrial Woodstock'.[33] After a month of conflict, the management backed off and reinstated the previous pace of production.

Thus, when confronted with acts of worker indiscipline, the management could find no better solution than to respond by intensifying the disciplinary regime that this indiscipline had rejected in the first place, then fanning it to such an extent that it was radicalized and turned into open revolt. Managers were caught in a contradiction. They knew for a fact that worker indiscipline expressed a visceral rejection of the organization of industrial work and, 'especially among the younger employees, a growing reluctance to accept a strict authoritarian shop discipline'.[34] They were also aware that 'the conditions for work in the new factories are such that discontent and rebellion are not exceptional reactions but rational',[35] that there was 'a link between fatigue and repetitive work, between discontent and absenteeism'. And yet they continued to act as if discontent 'constituted an "abuse" to be punished',[36] and to respond with 'techniques of fear and relentless pressure' that were a 'source of unending conflicts'.[37]

Hence this worry: if it continues like this, where are we going? Right to the wall, some answered: 'dark days are coming for GM if, as the management has often stated, Lordstown represents the future of the automobile industry'.[38]

Even among specialists in management, perplexity spread. Deeming the old procedures to be obsolete, some hatched plans for reform. Faced with the crisis of disciplinary governability, a new art of governing labour would need to be invented.

— 2 —

HUMAN RESOURCES

[The alien character of labor] emerges clearly in the fact that as soon as no physical or other compulsion exists, labor is shunned like the plague.

Karl Marx[1]

In the 1950s, conservative intellectuals had believed they were in a position to announce 'the end of ideology' – already! – and the extinction of the class struggle with it. The 'American worker', claimed Daniel Bell in 1956, had been 'tamed'. Not, admittedly, by the means that Marx had criticized in his time, nor by impoverishment, nor through 'the discipline of the machine' but 'by the "consumption society," by the possibility of a better living which his wage, the second income of his working wife, and easy credit all allow'.[2] Even when he suffered from his working conditions, the worker's thoughts led 'not to militancy, despite occasional sporadic outbursts, but to escapist fantasies – of having a mechanic's shop, a turkey farm, a gas station, of "owning a small business of one's own."'[3]

Everything was quiet, and then – crash, bang, wallop! At first, people were stunned, unable to understand anything. We need to try and imagine the immense and painful surprise represented by the movements of the 1960s for those who were firmly convinced of the withering away of social conflict in the 'consumer society'.[4]

Some, revolted by this revolt, accused the troublemakers of ingratitude. General Motors Vice-President, Earl Brambett, 'deplores the younger workers' insistence on even more benefits and improvements, [and] thinks instead they should show more appreciation for what they have'.[5] But what more did they want, exactly? That was the scandal. And how could they still revolt? That was the mys-

14

tery. Explanations were sought; people concocted theories about the revolt, and sought out its causes.

This unrest was first understood as arising from the generation gap. New workers were 'younger, more impatient, less homogeneous, more racially assertive and less manipulable'.[6] They 'bring into the plants with them the new perspectives of American youth in 1970'.[7]

What else happened? Psychologists made their contribution to the ongoing debate. Once the primary needs of human beings have been satisfied, they do not stop there: once their stomachs are full, then it is the turn of their minds to cry famine, as Abraham Maslow explained, pointing to his famous diagram of the 'pyramid of needs'.[8] Beyond their salaries and their careers, new generations aspired to something else, to more intense human relationships, as we see from reports in the *Harvard Business Review*, 'as provided by commune living experiments'.[9] Similarly, workers' expectations were being fleshed out, taking on a more qualitative dimension. They were demanding of their jobs something more than an income: interpersonal relationships, something substantial, a 'meaning'. A transition to a 'post-materialist' state of mind.

It is clear that the more such subjectivity asserts itself, the less it will tolerate being subjected to alienating work. Max Weber had warned: 'The capitalistic system [. . .] needs this devotion to the calling of making money', to that 'incomprehensible', 'mysterious' idea that a human being 'should be able to make it the sole purpose of his life-work to sink into the grave weighed down with a great material load of money and goods'.[10] If other appetites take over, the 'work ethic' suffers. 'Who Wants to Work?' was the headline in *Newsweek* in March 1973.[11] The question answered itself.

In this analysis, it was relative material prosperity, of the very same kind that Bell claimed had endorsed an enduring consent to the exploitation of wage-earners, that was identified as the source of new dissent. This entailed a major shift in theories of revolt. Why does anyone rebel? One answer had been: out of necessity. But now people started saying: because it was a luxury they could afford.[12]

The factory is one of the sites where new aspirations collide most brutally with old structures. But we need to be careful, as 'an anachronistic organization of work can create an explosive and pathogenic mix'.[13] According to Management Professor Richard Walton: 'In some cases, alienation is expressed by passive withdrawal-tardiness, absenteeism and turnover, and inattention on the job. In other cases, it is expressed by active attacks – pilferage, sabotage, deliberate waste, assaults, bomb threats, and other disruptions of work routines'.[14] But 'dramatic increases in these forms of violence are taking place at the plant level'.[15] The danger is political: the worker may resort to 'displacement of his frustrations through participation in radical social or political movements'.[16]

Echoing the Lordstown strike, the question of 'quality of life at work' became central, for a time, in American public debate. In 1972, using the terminology of the young Marx, the *Harvard Business Review* asked: 'How to counter alienation in the plant?' And Congress, the same year, organized senatorial hearings on 'worker alienation'.[17] But if alienation is problematic, this is above all for economic reasons, because of its negative impact on productivity. If there is a lesson to be learned from the Lordstown episode, it is that it showed a 'disregard for the interaction of human resources with capital and technology'.[18] What advantage is it for a manager 'to have a perfectly efficient assembly-line if [. . .] workers are out on strike because of the oppressive and dehumanized experience of working on the "perfect" line?'[19]

If you could start your professional life again from scratch, would you choose the same job that you are currently doing? To this question, in the middle of the 1960s, 93 per cent of the university professors and 82 per cent of the journalists canvased replied 'yes', compared to 31 per cent of textile workers and 16 per cent of automobile workers.[20] The authors of the study concluded that, in addition to the least physical demand, *autonomy* was the main factor in job satisfaction. Conversely, 'alienation exists when workers are unable to control their immediate work processes'.[21]

Lauding the virtues of 'autonomy and self-control',[22] and judging that 'industry today is over-managed and over-controlled',[23] the managerial reformers of the 1970s recommended stimulating the 'participation' of workers to increase their productivity as well as their satisfaction. Instead of the old strategy of 'control' they recommended a strategy of 'commitment'.[24] While the previous, intensive strategy had still aimed to pressure workers by submitting them to intensified discipline, the later, extensive strategy proposed to 'use effectively the capacities of a major natural resource – namely, the manpower they employ'.[25]

Several pilot projects involving participative management thus emerged in the United States.[26] If the French Left had, as fuel for its ideas about self-management, the experience of the Lip factory (occupied by its workers in Besançon in 1973), American managers, for their part, could assess the benefits of participation by pointing to the case of the General Foods dog kibble factory in Topeka (Kansas) in 1971. This was the countermodel of Lordstown: the rules were set collectively and the activity was organized into 'autonomous working groups', with 'self-managed' teams responsible for large swathes of production.[27]

The conclusion was very definite: 'productivity increases [. . .] when workers participate in the work decisions that affect their lives'.[28] The enrichment of tasks, said psychologist Frederick Herzberg, pays.[29] With this in mind, the good news could finally be announced: there was a 'a felicitous congruence between worker satisfaction and the securement of managerial objectives'.[30] For the workers, more satisfaction; for capital, increased productivity. In the end, it was win-win.

However, there was at least one social group that felt it had something to lose: management, which feared being deprived of a significant number of its prerogatives.[31] Activist worker Bill Watson recounts the following anecdote: in the factory where he worked, the management had, during a period of high lay-offs, planned to make an inventory of their stock, planned to last six weeks. The task had been entrusted to some fifty workers. To save time, they cobbled together a system of their own, a self-organized inventory, which proved more effective than the original procedure provided by the management. The management abruptly ended this spontaneous experience, on the grounds that 'the legitimate channels of authority, training, and communication had been violated'.[32] 'Management', says Watson, 'was really determined to stop the workers from organizing their own work, even when it meant that the work would be finished quicker and, with the men quickly laid off, less would be advanced in wages'.[33] Managers could therefore set the preservation of their own power higher than strict considerations of economic efficiency.

As *Business Week* also put it: 'Attempts to introduce plant democracy at one model General Foods (GF) plant in Topeka, Kansas have failed because managers felt their positions threatened by the success experienced when workers started taking some initiative in making decisions'.[34] 'In reality', says André Gorz, 'the hostility of the employers was not based on essentially technical or economic factors. It was political. The enrichment of tasks marked the end of the despotic authority and power of bosses great and small. [. . .] In short, once they went down this road, where would it all end?'[35]

Could the productivity gains associated with participation be assured without losing control, without triggering dangerous new trends? The reformers were betting that one could give workers a limited autonomy without things going bad; others were much more sceptical. The problem with autonomy is that, once granted, it is not satisfied with half measures. There was fear of a 'domino effect'.[36]

In fact, from the employers' point of view, the room for manoeuvre was narrow. What were the options available? One strategy involved keeping the status quo, and even hardening the existing disciplinary regimes, but at the risk of intensifying indiscipline and social conflicts, with the shortfall this implied. The second option was to introduce 'participation', with the promise of a harmonious convergence of interests, less alienation and more productivity – except that in this irenic picture, it was feared that even limited forms of empowerment might bring the wolf into the fold.

This was the dilemma: either to renew a disciplinary regime that was known to be counterproductive, or to promote an autonomy which, although factitious, could be dangerous. The result was a dead end. Another solution, however, was coming into view.

— 3 —

SOCIAL INSECURITY

What cause have they to fear, when they are assured, that if by their indolence and extravagance, by their drunkenness and vices, they should be reduced to want, they shall be abundantly supplied, not only with food and raiment, but with their accustomed luxuries, at the expense of others. [. . .] In general it is only hunger which can spur and goad them on to labour; yet our laws have said, they shall never hunger.

Joseph Townsend[1]

In 1970, a *Wall Street Journal* reporter visited a factory. At the assembly belt, he saw long hair, beards and, sometimes, pinned to a T-shirt, a peace badge. And then, 'above all, young faces, curious eyes. Those eyes have watched carefully as dissent has spread in the nation'. He scrutinized these eyes; he found their expression surprising and concluded: 'They do not look afraid'.[2] This, for employers, was the main problem.

Where did this new intrepidity come from? These young people knew nothing of 'the harsh economic facts of earlier years'.[3] Previously, even if they had not lived through the dark years of the Wall Street Crash in 1929, they had heard about it in their families. But this social memory, some theorized, had finally dried up: 'It took that long – almost two generations – for the motivation by economic fear to fade'.[4] Many current workers 'have never experienced economic want or fear – or even insecurity. In the back of their mind is the knowledge that public policy will not allow them to starve, whatever may happen'.[5]

The source 'of our present difficulties with the workforce might be termed a general lowering of employees' frustration tolerance', as one Ford executive, Malcolm Denise, put it'.[6] This idea that there are variable levels of 'frustration tolerance' came from the psychology

19

of behaviour. At the end of the 1930s, American researchers had conducted experiments on chimpanzees, from which it emerged that, in individuals with little experience of frustration early in their life, 'insufficient frustration tolerance will be developed for meeting the frustrations of later years'.[7] These psychologists concluded that the cardinal task of education properly understood was not so much to enable a young person to blossom as the 'building up of frustration tolerance' through discipline. This theory of punitive disciplining by an ogre figure explained 'deviant behaviour' in a similar way. An indocile individual is a subject whose level of tolerance to frustration is pathologically low. To cure him, he must be taught to rein in his desires: 'Re-education or psychotherapy is [. . .] a process of building up frustration tolerance by allowing the patient, [. . .] to experience small or tolerable doses of frustration until resistance is gradually developed and the areas of low frustration tolerance disappear'.[8]

Applying this interpretation to worker revolts boiled down to presenting them as manifestations of psychological immaturity, like the whims of spoiled children. To state that the problem lay in subjects having *too low a degree of tolerance to frustration* was to deny that the relevant question was one of *too high a degree of dissatisfaction* inflicted by alienating forms of work. The workers, the general conclusion ran, had become just too comfy.

As one executive from General Motors said, 'absenteeism occurs not because the jobs are dull, but because of the nation's economic abundance, and the high degree of security and the many social benefits the industry provides'.[9] The problem was nicely reproblematized: rather than remedying blue-collar worker blues, it was seen as advisable to take an interest in the advantageous social conditions that afforded them the luxury of appearing so bold. The problem was not that work was too hard, but that society was too soft.

From the end of the 1960s – well before the famous 'oil shock' of 1973, which is often taken as a historical turning point – the profit rate began to fall in the United States.[10] The business community realized this, and worried about it. How could this slump be explained? The mainstream economic press hastily pieced together a theory, or rather an ideology of the crisis in profitability.

In March 1969, *Fortune* reported a drop in profit.[11] In July, the magazine found the culprit: rising labour costs,[12] themselves fuelled by worker militancy. In a context of galloping inflation, faced with rising prices, unions were still managing to negotiate wage increases.[13] At the same time, labour productivity, which had previously been progressing at a steady pace, was stalling. If profits were declining, it was claimed, this was only because of these two phenomena combined: while wages were rising under the pressure of social struggles, rising labour costs were no longer offset by sufficiently vigorous growth in productivity. However, 'our productivity curve begins to flatten [. . .] because some of the motivations – the spirit and the fear – have gone out of the producers. And maybe our inflation is persistent'.[14]

Debates on the causes of the 'profit squeeze' and the 'strangulation of profits' divided the economists. Keynesians, as usual, pointed to the weakness of demand, a phenomenon of under-consumption. Some Marxists, rather strangely, echoed the theory of the editorial writers of *Fortune*, while others formulated alternative explanations.[15] Whatever the decisive factor behind the falling rate of profit – the strength of the working class (Boddy and Crotty), overaccumulation (Sweezy), increased international competition and the effects on prices (Brenner) – 'the solution to the crisis was, as we shall see, to attack labor'.[16]

The dominant theory of the crisis – let's call it the 'theory of power relations' – placed the blame on a socio-economic situation that was too favourable to the workers and their struggles. Rather than focusing on psychological considerations, it attributed the crisis to three main factors: (1) the Keynesian commitment to the maintenance of full employment, (2) the social protection systems of the welfare state, and (3) the power of the unions. If the tide was to be turned, none of these pillars should be left standing.

In fact, until the first third of the 1970s, the US labour market had experienced almost full employment. In this context, the supreme threat a boss could resort to, namely dismissal, was no longer perceived as so terrible. As one Detroit teamster recalls, 'We could just walk in and get a job at any warehouse or dock. We didn't care if we got fired'.[17] Hence, also, the ability to say no, a freedom, a strength that triggered alarm on the opposite side.

'In a nation where the government is formally committed to maintain full employment, what forces will restrain the perfectly human demand of labor for more money and more power?' asked *Business Week* in 1970.[18] If it was true that worker indiscipline was the daughter of full employment, people in the business community told themselves, then they would have to think seriously about putting an end to the latter. 'Mass employment is not a politically viable option [. . .] in short: what this country needs to block this band of madcats is a good depression' – so wrote an economic chronicler of the early 1970s who allowed himself to be all the more provocative in that he signed his texts with a borrowed name, a revealing pseudonym: 'Adam Smith'.[19]

When the spontaneous cycle of crises in capitalism does not offer this kind of opportunity, people can always devote their efforts to bringing it about artificially. And this is what they did, while waiting for a better solution: 'between 1969 to 1970, the Nixon administration engineered a short recession in order to cool the economy, a euphemism for putting labor in its place'.[20] In August 1971 it announced it was going to control prices and wages. The objective of a wage freeze, said one White House adviser, was to 'zap labor, and we did'.[21]

As this policy started to bear fruit, an editor at *Fortune* finally foresaw, in 1971, reasons for hope: if a rise in unemployment were indeed to occur, 'labor attitudes could change quite rapidly'.[22] People had to realize that 'even a few layoffs can have a dramatic effect'[23] in cooling the ardour of protestors.

But as long as social welfare measures were in place, the threat of unemployment could not play its full role, given that the existence of unemployment benefits reduced 'the "penalty" associated with being fired'.[24] Publicly, however, the attack on welfare was justified by another kind of discourse. Neoconservative ideologues, headed by George Gilder, developed an anti-welfare discourse stigmatizing the 'culture of poverty': 'the poor must not only work, they must work harder than the classes above them. [. . .] But the current poor, white even more than black, are refusing to work hard'. But 'the poor chose leisure not because of moral weakness, but because they are paid to do so'.[25] For Gilder, the welfare state represented a *moral* threat, one that perhaps menaced civilization itself: by setting up relief, the welfare state meant that the poorest needed no longer comply entirely with market imperatives that were presented as powerful prods to virtue. Thus, unemployment benefits encouraged laziness; the right to retire dissolved filial duty towards one's elders; disability benefit exaggerated the drawbacks of superficial physical defects, etc.

This marked a major comeback for some old doctrines. In 1786, in his famous *Dissertation on the Poor Laws*, Joseph Townsend deployed similar arguments to oppose welfare measures which, in his view, made the mistake of filling the bellies of the needy and blunting that precious stimulus, hunger. To force the poor to work, there was no need to constrain them by law. It 'is attended with too much trouble, violence, and noise; creates ill will, and never can be productive of good and acceptable service: whereas hunger is not only a peaceable, silent, unremitted pressure, but, as the most natural motive to industry and labour, it calls forth the most powerful exertions'. Meanwhile, 'the slave must be compelled to work; but the freeman should be left to his own judgment and discretion'.[26] This is a valuable document in the genealogy of liberal morality: it tells us that its conception of 'freedom' presupposes the Damocles' sword of poverty, and that the destruction of established forms of social solidarity is the precondition for the emergence of the 'voluntary worker'.[27]

In the post-war period, however, there had been a heartfelt belief that these old ideas had had their day. If, in the earlier phases of capitalism, social insecurity could be considered 'useful because it drove men – businessmen, workers, the self-employed – to render their best and most efficient service',[28] in contrast, in the age of affluence, Galbraith concluded in 1959, it had become clear that 'a high level of security is essential for maximum production'.[29] Unemployment benefits, for example, far from entailing a slackening of activity, obviously played an essential role in stabilizing the economy by sustaining demand.

Now, thanks to a new swing of the pendulum, it was this consensus which was challenged in the early 1970s. What some people hoped to return to was a society of *social insecurity*. 'Government full-employment policies', wrote Gilbert Burck in *Fortune* in 1971, 'have practically extinguished old fears of being out of a job for a long time. Unemployment insurance and other cushions provided by a well-intentioned society take the hardship out of strikes and enable strikers to stay out in relative comfort until the employer surrenders'.[30] Hence the programme: get rid of those 'cushions' in order to revive the 'old fears' which the cushions seemed to have put to sleep.

How were the workers to be disciplined? The first option was, as we have seen, to exacerbate disciplinary power, at the risk of creating negative side effects. The second option, the one proposed by reformist managers, consisted in introducing forms of participation for self-discipline purposes. According to Stephen Marglin, 'managerial initiatives to "humanize" work must be seen in general as a response to the increase in labour costs associated with indiscipline born of prosperity'[31] – but such well-meaning plans faded away as soon as unemployment became a reality.

A third possibility then appeared: to discipline one's own workforce, one should give free rein to economic and social insecurity in the world outside. If people continued to work in conditions that they hated, explained the militant worker John Lippert in the late 1970s, at a time when the economic tide was turning, this was not 'because of any internal control the company has on the workers. The control is more external: the economic hardship would be too great if the workers did what their every instinct tells them to do: leave that place behind forever'.[32]

Discipline is not imposed in the same way in closed institutions, those which you can leave only by escaping, such as prisons, as it is in open institutions, those from which you can always resign, such as businesses. In the former, discipline reigns in a vacuum, preventing subjects from leaving; in the latter, it works by threatening you with forced expulsion. On the one hand, confinement, on the other, dismissal. In institutions that subjects are 'free' to leave, the rigours of internal disciplinary power are not enough to obtain docility. This requires in addition, in the absence of sufficient positive motivation, the negative incitement of external disciplinary effects. The notion is a disciplinary power inside and disciplining pressure outside, in a pattern where the intensity of the latter determines the degree of a tendency to submission in the former.[33]

The generations born after 1973, those who grew up in the era of perpetual 'crisis', successively internalized the idea that each generation would generally be worse off than the previous one. They learned, again, to be afraid. This was a historic reversal that could also be read as a kind of group psychotherapy, a mass re-education in 'frustration tolerance'.

— 4 —

WAR ON THE UNIONS

People of the same trade seldom meet together, even for merriment and diversion, but the conversation ends in a conspiracy against the public, or in some contrivance to raise prices. It is impossible indeed to prevent such meetings, by any law which could either be executed, or would be consistent with liberty and justice.

Adam Smith[1]

'The U.S. can't afford what labor wants' was the headline in *Business Week* in April 1970: 'new union militancy could skyrocket wages and trigger runaway inflation'.[2] The magazine denounced the trade unions for, as it saw it, their virtual control of the economy: 'a democratic society works on the assumption that no group within it can accumulate so much power that it can write its own ticket. [. . .] is collective bargaining still bargaining, or has it become something close to blackmail by the unions?'[3]

'The gravest economic problem facing the Western world in the early 1970s is cost-push inflation powered by excessive wage increases', claimed Gilbert Burck in *Fortune*. 'What is happening, throughout the Western world, is that organized labor is overreaching'.[4]

But the observation was paradoxical because, at the very same time that the abuse of union power was being denounced, there was also anxiety about their loss of authority. Union leaders, as Richard Armstrong pointed out in *Fortune*, no longer appeared able to control a base that was showing 'an acquisitive and rebellious frame of mind',[5] whose members were more and more obviously getting carried away 'by a tide of angry revolt, against management, against its own leadership, and in important ways against society itself'.[6]

Less and less able to control their troops, union leaders no longer seemed capable of fulfilling their role of social pacification. 'Have the

25

aging leaders of labor lost their grip?'[7] They too, in short, seemed to be facing a crisis of governability. 'Right now', said one executive from the automobile industry, 'our interlocutor is no longer the bureaucrat trade union', but 'the stubborn guy, the irresponsible local leader', with 'the power of the whole organization behind him'.[8] This seizure of power by the faceless rank and file seemed to herald a new era in labour relations, possibly marked by strikes of an unprecedented magnitude.[9]

In the post-war period, as the Marxist sociologist Michael Burawoy suggested in 1979, American unions had become part of the company's 'internal state': having fitted into the regulated system of collective bargaining while very broadly giving up on effective conflict, they did not so much help to question the order of domination as to reproduce it.[10] By collaborating with a form of 'private government in industry',[11] they not only maintained the productive order, but contributed to fabricating consent and ensuring the hegemony of the ruling system of production. However, at the very moment when Burawoy was setting out his ideas, demonstrating in plain and simple terms how robust this regime of domination was, the latter was starting to fall apart behind his back.[12]

From the employer's point of view, the diagnosis was twofold: the unions were both too strong and, in a sense, too weak. They were too strong in that they were still in a position to extract wage rises, no longer strong enough in that the union bureaucracies were no longer able to discipline their troops.[13] What was the point, they said to each other, of continuing to make concessions to the trade union leadership if this no longer meant they could buy social peace at the base?

People started to make preparations for a showdown, but only on one side of the bargaining table because trade union leaders had completely failed to foresee what was coming.[14] When they finally realized, it was already too late, and they reacted with bitterness. In 1978, Douglas Fraser, a great figure of American trade unionism, slammed the door of the Labor Management Group and wrote an open letter that sounded like a political testament: 'leaders of the business community, with few exceptions, have chosen to wage a one-sided class war today in this country – a war against working people, the unemployed, the poor, the minorities [. . .] The leaders of industry, commerce and finance in the United States have broken and discarded the fragile, unwritten compact previously existing during a past period of growth and progress'.[15] He took note of the end of nearly thirty years of cordial agreement, a period during which 'many big companies had come to depend on the unions as a primary force for stabilization'.[16]

26

This reversal had been foreshadowed in the theoretical field by an intellectual trend whose theses, formerly held by only a minority, would serve as the basis for an assault on trade unionism, which was now rejected in its very principles. Neoliberal economists had long been developing an aggressive critique of trade unions. As early as 1947, economist Fritz Machlup had characterized their action as an attempt to 'fix monopolistic wages'.[17] At the same time, Henry C. Simons, a fierce opponent of the New Deal and the mentor of the young Milton Friedman, denounced the 'anomalies of control by the voluntary association': faced with the threat of a kind of trade union government being set up, it was vital to 'preserve the *discipline of competition*'.[18] In the strategic debates which divided the Mont Pelerin Society on this issue, the cradle and vanguard of neoliberalism, Machlup defended a bellicose position: 'Industrial peace is something we should be afraid of, as it can only be bought at the cost of further distortion of the wage structure'.[19]

It was this position that prevailed among economic elites in the early 1970s. In 1971, *Fortune* castigated 'the power monopoly of work':[20] 'Allowed to organize like armies, they practice coercion and intimidation, and do not hesitate to disrupt a whole economy to gain their ends. [. . .] The question is no longer whether this force needs curbing, but how. The key to doing so lies in understanding that the power of unionism is not preordained. It derives from exemptions and privileges granted by government that give unions a special sanctuary in our society. The task is to break down this sanctuary'.[21]

This took the form of direct political attacks from above, but also of more local manoeuvres. From the middle of the 1970s a new kind of consultant started to flourish, the 'union busters'.[22]

Imagine you are a senior manager in a big American company, and you receive in your mailbox a brochure entitled *Trade unions: how to avoid them, defeat them and get rid of them*. Attached is an invitation to a three-day seminar in a big hotel. Arriving the night before, you meet the organizers. The unusual appearance of the first, a labour psychologist – beard, open shirt, rolled-up sleeves – initially takes you aback, until you realize that this casual demeanour is part of the dress code of a profession he has been working in for more than twenty years with large American companies, including IBM, Shell, Dupont and Texas Instruments. The second is a New York lawyer wearing the obligatory outfit: dark suit and tailored shirt.

The seminar takes place in three stages: (1) How to prevent

unionization? (2) How to stop a trade union organization gaining a foothold? (3) How to 'de-unionize' a company?

The first day is reserved for the 'industrial psychologist', who is going to teach you 'how to make unions redundant'. When a management team ends up with union members in its company, he tells you, it has only itself to blame. 'In fact, there are really only two approaches to unions which I call the cactus and the plum. The plum is an easy target. [. . .] The cactus is tough and prickly – creating an environment clearly opposed to unions'.[23]

It starts at the job interview. You have to learn how to grill the candidates. Since the law prohibits asking too direct questions about personal beliefs, you will need to be indirect: 'Find out if they are involved in liberal causes; tenant organizations, consumer rights organizations or other activities which would reveal a pro-union tendency'.[24]

Once they have been recruited, make it clear to the newcomers that 'the company operates without unions, and has for a long time. [. . .] Now we are not saying that unions are good or bad, what we are saying is that we don't feel there is a need for them here, and no one has evidently ever felt the need for them because we don't have any'.[25] QED.

You must also familiarize yourself with the art of 'management without interference': 'Don't drive to work in a fancy car. Don't call people workers or even employees and don't call bosses, bosses. Everyone should be considered part of the same firm. [. . .] Give people titles they respect like technician or engineer'.[26]

To give you a better understanding of what makes your subordinates tick, the psychologist then introduces you to the basic principles of the psychology of learning. If, while driving through Yellowstone Park, you come across a bear and feed him sweets through the window, 'it is natural for him to expect a second jelly bean. [. . .] If we continue this process long enough, we will run out of jelly beans, at which time the bear will take not only the empty sack, but an arm and a leg. We are likely to wonder why that lovable bear has suddenly turned into a hostile animal. The answer is simple: The bear has been rewarded and reinforced by his aggressive activities in much the same manner that employees of some organizations have been rewarded for collective activity'.[27]

After the lunch break, the psychologist presents his 'early warning system to spot unionization' – a bundle of questionnaires. Employees will be required to complete personality tests, officially intended to 'anticipate and solve employee relations problems',[28] but actually serving to establish a 'psychological profile of the workforce' aimed at evaluating the 'loyalty of the employee' and to detect, even on the basis of weak signals, the individuals most likely to join a union.[29] 'Think for a moment who are the people who are going to be the most vulnerable if the union knocks on your door. Are these people really meant for us? Maybe they'd be more happy someplace else. Weed 'em out. Git rid of anyone who's not going to be a team player'.[30]

And have no compunction in doing so, for it is your *freedom* that is at stake. For, when there is no union,

> you hire whom you wish, pay them whatever you have to pay them or you wish to pay them and terminate their employment as you wish and lay them off. You assign them to any kind of job you want. Those things are all going to change. [. . .] If a union comes into the plant, who do you think is going to be affected most? It isn't the president, or the vice-presidents of the company. It's you. Mr. and Mrs. Supervisor. You're the ones who are going to be up against the union every day. You're going to have to deal with the shop steward, with the grievances, with the complaints, with the slowdowns, with the harassment. [. . .] Having a union in your shop is going to affect how you operate in many personal areas. It will affect your ability to control promotions, transfers, job assignments, trial periods, discipline, discharge, retirement, layoffs, and recalls.[31]

With these fine words, the psychologist closes the first day of the seminar.

The next day, the lawyer sets out a series of manoeuvres to obstruct the formation of a union and delay the convening of professional elections – these are obstruction tactics and verge on illegality. Anti-union arguments, standard letters and patterns of pre-written speeches are handed out for you to distribute among your subordinates.

The third day, finally, the lawyer divulges to you, under the seal of strict confidentiality, a whole range of tactics of 'de-unionization'. If you practise (as it is wise to do so) espionage on your employees, there is for example this advice: 'I know the union meeting is going to be held at the Holiday Inn. I park my car in the lot and watch everybody who comes into the parking lot. That is an act of surveillance. I may not do this. Now, if I just happen to be coming to the Holiday Inn to attend another function and I happen to see certain people go in – I have every right to do that'. Once the ringleaders have been identified, you must be able to sack them in all due form. Here, too, provided you have made advance preparations, nothing could be easier: 'If management keeps careful records of absences and reprimands, it can usually make dismissal of a pro-union worker look legitimate'.[32]

As a reminder, you will be able to leave this seminar with a signed copy of the book written by one or the other of these consultants – a practical guide in which you will find a detailed list of all the 'tactics and strategies needed'[33] to set up your anti-union guerrillas.

It is important to be always on your guard, this useful vade mecum reminds you, and to be attentive to any warning signs of emerging trade union activity: when 'groups of people who are deep in conversation suddenly clam up when supervisors approach', when 'graffiti hostile to the business appears on the restroom walls' (and these same restrooms start attracting a lot of people even when, as far as you know, there is no epidemic of 'gastro-enteritis'), you may well suspect that people are getting together well in the restroom to discuss *something*'.[34]

If the movement is confirmed, establish a 'war room' in the management offices, a command post that will act as 'a centre of activity'.[35] On the wall, you'll pin a big diagram listing 'the names of all employees by department with the designation "union," "company," and "?"' – which will give you an overview of the loyalty of your employees. All the relevant information will need to be taken up daily to the war room. Thus, informed in real time of how things are developing on the battlefield, management can 'determine the strategy and decide on effective counter-attack techniques'.[36]

It's your turn to campaign, distribute leaflets and put up posters – the manual provides you with templates, all you need to do is get them photocopied. One example of a slogan on a poster: 'Yes, you have something to lose in voting for a union: freedom to solve your own problems individually and directly with the management'.[37] In addition to posters and leaflets, the manual suggests you have made some anti-union 'fortune cookies' to hand out in the canteen, stuffed with relevant messages. The employee breaks open the cookie and reads: 'Union dues put rice in someone else's bowl', or 'Sorry, no luck with the union' or 'Beware of dragon in organizer's magic lamp'.[38] Other procedures of the same kind include organizing free cocktail evenings or even offering your employees a free turkey for Thanksgiving – a tangible economic reminder of the commitment of the employer to a happy and satisfied workforce.[39] On this occasion, between raising two toasts, 'the company will highlight the fact that the strong feelings of loyalty employees feel toward him would be disturbed by the presence of a union'.[40]

And, if, despite all these efforts, you still can't solve the problem, you will always be able to use the services of anti-union consultants who will come, in commando mode, to lend you a helping hand 'aimed at the areas of greatest worker vulnerability as divined by their psychological spade-work'.[41] One of these reformed 'union busters' testified in his autobiography to what was more concretely implied by this combined strategy of misinformation and personal attacks: 'as the consultants go about the business of destroying unions, they invade people's lives, demolish their friendships, crush their will, and shatter their families'.[42] As one unionist said: 'their weapons are emotional intimidation and the subversion of the law. Whenever and wherever working people seek to organize, this guerrilla army dressed in three-piece suits stands ready to resist'.[43]

When journalist Beth Nissen got a job incognito with Texas Instruments in 1978 so that she could produce a report on unionism, she felt the fear that was now prevalent among the employees. While discussing the issue of the union with a colleague, the latter replied: 'Please don't talk to me on break any more. [. . .] If the company finds out I'm listening, I'll get fired'.[44] For simply mentioning the possibility of joining a trade union, the undercover reporter was dismissed on some spurious context barely three weeks after being hired.

Part II

Managerial revolution

— 5 —

A THEOLOGICAL CRISIS

The capitalist process, by substituting a mere parcel of shares for the walls of and the machines in a factory, takes the life out of the idea of property. [. . .] Dematerialized [. . .] ownership does not impress and call forth moral allegiance as the vital form of property did. Eventually there will be nobody left who really cares to stand for it – nobody within and nobody without the precincts of the big concerns.

Joseph A. Schumpeter[1]

'It may not be saying too much to assert that the new thinking about collective enterprise, or managerialism, is about to be recognized as constituting *a great theological crisis*, on the order of the one that accompanied the introduction of Darwin's work, or even the social and political thought that followed the Reformation. For we are experiencing the collapse of the economic and political pillars of the ideology which has dominated Western thought for the past several hundred years'.[2] The decisive intellectual event in this respect, as the author of these lines said in 1962, had been the publication, three decades earlier, of a book co-authored by the lawyer Adolf Berle and the economist Gardiner Means, *The Modern Corporation and Private Property*.[3] This work, which John Kenneth Galbraith considered to be one of the two most important books of the 1930s, with the *General Theory* of Keynes,[4] did in fact polarize debates on the theory of firms for nearly half a century.

A few weeks after its release, however, its publisher, a small house specializing in tax issues, suddenly had second thoughts and withdrew it from sale. A General Motors executive, horrified by what he had read, had expressed his disapproval to the officials of the Corporation Trust Company, a business consulting agency whose publishing wing was one of the subsidiaries, and of which General

35

Motors just happened to be one of the big customers – the kind of customers that it is always a pity to lose. As Berle comments, looking back on the affair: 'Discovering the viper they had nourished in their corporate bosom, publication was promptly suspended after a few copies had been sold. (Copies under that rubric are – modestly – collectors' items now.) [. . .] Books questioning power systems – as did *The Modern Corporation* – often do have initial rough handling by the power system whose rationale and bases are analyzed'.[5] This attempt at censorship in fact produced the opposite effect. Reprinted by Macmillan Publishing, the book was able to benefit from a much wider circulation. 'Ironically, General Motors, [. . .] was responsible for launching Berle and Means's book', as a conservative intellectual lamented some years later.[6]

What was so disturbing about the work? Its authors highlighted an unnoticed transformation in property rights, a revolution that led to the undermining of the principles of the capitalist economy as it had been justified for almost three centuries by its defenders.

Imagine a horse and its master. 'The owner of a horse is responsible for it. If the horse lives he must feed it. If the horse dies he must bury it'.[7] What about another relationship, that between a shareholder and the company of which he owns shares? 'No such responsibility attaches to a share of stock'. The shareholder is not responsible for the company. Often, he has not even set foot on its premises. He has become, in the words of Thorstein Veblen, an 'absentee owner'.[8] He no longer has the physical possession of a property, only that of a 'title deed' – a dematerialized, abstract property, a paper property.

The old property-possession was solid. It immobilized the owner, who lived in the landscape of his 'thing'. The shareholder, however, is without ties. If his property no longer suits him, he liquidates it. This represents a dematerialization, a fluidification and also a splitting of shareholder ownership, with the shares of a corporation being scattered between thousands of shareholders.

But something else also happens: 'there has resulted in the dissolution of the old atom of ownership into its component parts'.[9] The functions that private property had traditionally brought into a whole were split into two: 'the power, the responsibility and the substance which have been an integral part of ownership in the past are being transferred to a separate group in whose hands lies control'.[10] The shareholder now has only a passive property, and it is salaried managers, non-proprietors, who are now responsible for the active control of the company, its concrete management. So we have, on the one hand. 'owners without real control' and, on the other, 'control

36

without real ownership'.[11] This is the main idea put forward by Berle and Means, that of the *separation of ownership and control.*

At the same time, the nature of business has been transformed. The big corporation with shares no longer has much in common with the business of the manager-owner. By freeing itself from the boundaries of individual and family ownership, by concentrating and social-izing capital from a large 'investing public',[12] the shareholder form allowed the development of giant firms, 'quasi-public' institutions where thousands of workers were under the leadership of a unified management.

Here, Berle and Means agree with the industrialist and German politician Walter Rathenau: 'The de-individualisation of ownership, the objectification of enterprise, the detachment of property from the possessor, leads to a point where the enterprise becomes transformed [. . .] into an institution resembling the state'.[13] Detached from any substantial economic anchoring in the ownership of capital, 'control by management' appears as a power of a governmental kind. Hence the way that, in describing it, political metaphors are used: managers are 'new princes' at the head of great 'industrial empires'.

The way this phenomenon was viewed was, from the start, highly ambivalent. While some celebrated the arrival of a disinterested man-agerial power, others feared the rise of a new managerial despotism. In the most pessimistic view, popularized in 1941 by James Burnham, in *The Managerial Revolution*,[14] the managers would, as Orwell sum-marized it in an account of these ideas, 'eliminate the old capitalist class, crush the working class, and so organize society that all power and economic privilege remain in their own hands'.[15]

The discovery of Berle and Means had many implications, one of which was particularly radical on the theoretical level: 'This dissolu-tion of the atom of property destroys the very foundation on which the economic order of the past three centuries has rested'.[16]

In their crosshairs was Adam Smith and his famous 'invisible hand'. The rich, explained the author of *The Wealth of Nations*, may have nothing to worry about but their 'vain and insatiable desires', but paradoxically they are working unintentionally, by their private greed, for the public good. Their selfish interest lies in getting the most profit from their property, so they are driven to manage it in an efficient way that will contribute to the growth of general wealth, and, in turn, to the wealth of everyone.[17] But, note Berle and Means, the economist was arguing in a context where 'the system of private enterprise has rested upon *the self-interest of the property owner*'.[18]

'To Adam Smith and to his followers, private property was a unity involving possession. He assumed that ownership and control were combined'.[19] But 'today, in the modern corporation, this unity has been broken'.[20] Shareholders may still be motivated by profit, but this does not mean that they do in fact make 'a more efficient use of the property, since they have surrendered all disposition of it to those in control of the enterprise'.[21] As for managers, as they are no longer owners, it is difficult to see what would impel them to sweat blood so as to maximize the profits of others.

Smith, they point out, noted that company managers – a form still rare in the eighteenth century – did not show the same eagerness to make the business entrusted to them flourish as did a boss who owned his own business; so 'he [i.e. Smith] repudiated the stock corporation as a business mechanism, holding that dispersed ownership made efficient operation impossible'.[22] The classical doctrine thus *itself* foresaw its own dysfunctioning, for the particular case of a form that has since become dominant. Without realizing it, one continues to justify this form by anachronistically resorting to a theory which actually demonstrates its flaws.

The least motivation of the managers is one thing, but nothing further guarantees that their interests will converge with those of shareholders. On the contrary, everything suggests a problematic divergence, especially if the former realize that the most profitable way to follow their selfish interests, after all – given that, as Schumpeter writes, 'personal gain beyond salary and bonus cannot, in corporate business, be reaped by executives except by illegal or semi-illegal practices'[23] – lies in dipping their hands into the till. Ironically, if managers comply with the maxim of the rational economic agent, the system starts to go off the rails, as it is true that 'the interests of ownership and control are in large measure opposed *if* the interests of the latter grow primarily out of the desire for personal monetary gain'.[24]

Berle and Means make no objection to classical theory. They do not say that Smith was wrong, but on the contrary that he was right – and right to foresee the possible obsolescence of his own theorem. The importance of their critique, which explains why it has led to the shedding of so much ink, lies in the fact that it was 'the first major effort to criticize the legal structure of the modern corporation in terms of the traditional economic notions upon which this structure was premised'.[25]

If the justifications provided by classical theory have become inoperative, it is not because they have been refuted intellectually, but because they have been rendered obsolete by a real transformation. This is the idea of 'the Inadequacy of Traditional Theory'.[26] Shareholder capitalism, by revolutionizing the forms of ownership, has moreover brought off the feat of undermining the foundations of its own legitimizing discourse.

The problem of Berle and Means, and conversely of the subsequent reductive reinterpretations of their work, was not that of knowing how to realign managerial conduct on the interests of shareholders, but of raising yet again the question of the motives and purposes of economic activity.[27] This was firstly a question of legitimacy: if a modern enterprise can no longer be thought of as 'the enlarged figure of the classical owner-enterprise',[28] wherein will reside the legitimacy of managerial power?

Berle and Means had spotted a huge gap in the dominant economic ideology. It remained to be seen how this gap could be sealed. Some thought that the best they could do in their search for a great saviour figure was to call on morality – better yet, a version of morality fished up out of the moat of a mediaeval *imaginaire*.

— 6 —

ETHICAL MANAGERIALISM

There is no theory of the firm that satisfactorily justifies the large modern corporation. Efforts are made to elevate the idea of social responsibility (or, synonymously, the corporate conscience or good citizenship) to the status of a theory of the firm.

Wilbur Hugh Ferry[1]

[. . .] they have not, like the medieval corporations, as yet created a corporate conscience in lieu of the individual responsibility which, by dint of their very organization, they have contrived to get rid of.

Karl Marx[2]

In the modern period, noted Charles Fourier, a new type of discourse had taken the place of morality and its sermons. The moralists did not realize soon enough that 'Political Economy [has] invaded the whole field of charlatanerie [. . .], the moralists have fallen into nothingness, and have been pitilessly enrolled into the class of novelists. Their sect died with the eighteenth century; it died politically'.[3] As for the economists, they had quickly become too strong to need allies, and had 'scorned any path of rapprochement and maintained all the more that what was needed was *great, no, very great wealth, with a huge trade and huge commerce*'.[4]

But, he added, 'the fall of the moralists harbingered the fall of their rivals. We can apply to those literary sects the words of Danton who, on the scaffold, already tied down with a strap, said to the executioner: Keep the other for Robespierre; he will soon be following me. So moralists can tell their hangman, and the public opinion that is sacrificing them: Keep the other belt for the economists; they will soon be following us'.[5]

What Fourier did not foresee, however, was that this predicted death would be followed by a singular rebirth. In the twentieth century, an unprecedented crisis undermined Adam Smith's doctrines. People were already working behind the scenes to update the theory, but the initial response was to exhume ancient idols. The economy succumbed in turn, and its fallen rival, morality, made a new entrance in the new guise of an *ethical managerialism* that presented itself in the 1950s as the grand solution to the problem of the legitimacy of managerial power.

In the vision of the world put forward by the old industrialist paternalism, the manager-owner reigned over his business as his own 'thing'. He was still viewed in the nineteenth century as a descendant of line of the old 'master, the *dominus*, that is to say, the owner of the workers he employs'.[6] He could always retort to those who questioned his power, 'Here, I am the one who commands because I am at home, and this belongs to me'. This was the basis for an authority to which the managers of large modern companies can no longer lay claim.

The separation of ownership and control has not only shattered the old managerial justification for authority,[7] but has also weakened the demands of the shareholders (who are now merely passive owners) that the 'corporation should be operated in their sole interest'.[8] The appearance of huge, 'quasi-public' companies, whose decisions have an impact on everyone's lives, have 'placed the community in a position to demand that the modern corporation serve not only the owners [. . .] but all society'.[9]

So what interests must be taken into account in the management of businesses? In 1932, Edwin Merrick Dodd asked 'for whom corporate managers are trustees'?[10] An American CEO replied: 'the social responsibility of management has broadened [. . .] Management no longer represents, as it once did, merely the single interest of ownership; increasingly it functions on the basis of a trusteeship which endeavors to maintain, between four basic interlocking groups, a proper balance of equity'.[11] Thus was formulated a new 'philosophy of management', 'the "trustee" philosophy or fiduciary administration', which presented managers as the trustees of several social groups.[12]

What happened in the wake of the book by Berle and Means, over several decades, was that an ideology of the social responsibilities of the businessman was attached to the problem of the separation of ownership from control. In what is considered to be the founding text of this paradigm, *Social Responsibilities of the Businessman*, published in 1953, Howard R. Bowen rejected the view that 'no rules for the individual would be required except those of following one's self-interest ardently and competing vigorously'.[13] True, businessmen must make a profit, but they are also obliged to 'to conduct their enterprises with concern for all the interests affected' by the business's activities.[14]

Where legitimate private authority was thought to be an attribute of property rights – it's because the business is *mine* that I am authorized to manage it – ethical managerialism now justifies it in a non-patrimonial way: the manager now draws his legitimacy from non-proprietary interests. It is precisely to the extent that I do not manage the business *for myself* that I am justified in doing so. As Hal Draper notes: 'In this approach, then, the new irresponsibility of the uncontrolled Institutional Leaders is no longer a thing to view with alarm but rather a necessary precondition to freeing them from the petty, distorting influences of short-range, profit-maximizing considerations'.[15] The empowerment of managerial power, the very same empowerment that led to anxieties about a drift into autocracy, now miraculously transfigures itself into moral autonomy. The turnaround is complete, since it could now be claimed, *pace* Burnham, that this new managerialism was not a new form of dictatorship and that 'the managerial ethic is inherently benevolent', precisely *since* 'the manager is in no sense an owner'.[16]

If the art of leadership is that of 'balancing interests', so the position of the 'almost anonymous managers' will be a 'point of convergence' between multiple claims that they will decide fairly, in accordance with the ancient virtue of the *juste milieu* (the middle ground).[17] If business thinks of itself as 'a system of private government',[18] the manager will change his spots and be transformed into a sort of 'statesman'[19] – '*L'État c'est moi, mais moi, je suis une corporation*' ('The state is me, but I am a corporation'), as one American commentator wrote at the time, resorting to French.[20]

Until the early 1970s, the thesis of Berle and Means on the separation of ownership and control was the object, as the sociologist Maurice Zeitlin pointed out, of an 'astonishing consensus' in the American social sciences.[21] This thesis was at the heart of a managerialist vision of capitalism based on a series of established truths. Here they are:

1) The main site of economic power has moved: 'the decisive power in modern industrial society', concluded Galbraith, 'is exercised not by capital but by the organization, not by the capitalist, but by the industrial bureaucrat'.[22]

2) The principle of profit maximization was rejected: 'Never has the imputation of a profit motive been further from the real

motives of men than it is for modern bureaucratic managers', claimed Dahrendorf.[23]

3) The capitalist class, divided between shareholding and managerial functions, has lost all consistency, giving way to an 'amorphous power structure'.[24] Berle went so far as to refer to a 'capitalism without capitalists'.[25]

4) Private property of the means of production, which was already being seen as liquid, evaporated for good: 'Ownership', announced Kaysen in 1957, 'is disappearing'.[26] 'Private productive property, especially in the United States', confirmed Bell in 1961, 'is largely a fiction'.[27] In short, it was now certain: 'Capital – and thereby capitalism – has dissolved'.[28]

As Daniel Bell concluded, there had once been 'a society "designed" by John Locke and Adam Smith and it rested on the premises of individualism and market rationality [. . .] We now move to a communal ethic, without that community being, as yet, wholly defined. In a sense, the movement away from governance by political economy to governance by political philosophy – for that is the meaning of the shift – is a return to pre-capitalist modes of social thought'.[29]

Here, I would make one remark. This idea of governance, the idea that prevailed before the great neoliberal shift, is what I propose to call, both as an echo of and in contrast with the notion of governmentality, 'manageriality'. Michel Foucault conceived 'liberal governmentality' as an answer to the cardinal problem of the arts of governing: how can the economy be brought within the remit of the state? How is power to be exercised 'in the form of the economy'?[30] As an extension of this project, neoliberalism sought to analyse 'non-economic behavior' (etc.) through 'a grid of economic intelligibility', leading to 'the criticism and appraisal of the action of public authorities in market terms'.[31] But its predecessor, the managerialism of the 1950s and 1960s, did the complete opposite, in both those aspects (practical and theoretical). Its problem was not that of introducing the economy into the state, but on the contrary of introducing an *analogon* of political government into the private management of economic affairs. It was not conceived as an art of exercising political power in the form of the economy, but on the contrary as an art of exercising economic power in the form of a certain politics, of a private politics. Manageriality does not have the economy as its 'major form of knowledge'; rather, its fundamental epistemic predilection gazes beyond ethics into politics and, as we shall soon see, strategy.

In 1954, in *The 20th Century Capitalist Revolution*, Berle depicts the magical image of a prince-manager administering business as an 'oracle of the public interest'. We can read this text as an anachronistic iteration, right in the middle of the American twentieth century, of the old genre of the *mirror for princes*.[32] Berle refers to Augustine and his *City of God*, where 'a moral and philosophical organization [. . .] ultimately directed power'.[33] He also mentions the Plantagenet court, where a man, often a priest, called the 'chancellor', played the role of 'keeper of the conscience of the king'.[34] The manager, the new prince, will likewise exercise his benevolent power with business ethics as a safety rail. The only limit placed on the power of the manager is his conscience, hemmed in by the informal sanctions of public opinion.[35] A few lines further on, without seeing any particular contradiction in this, Berle can argue that managers constitute 'tiny self-perpetuating oligarchies' and that the 'tacit philosophy of the men who control them' guarantees a 'real control' against the excesses of such power.[36]

But many, including those who followed the managerialist mindset, were sceptical: 'how could managers be trusted to advance social welfare when they could not be trusted with their own shareholders?'[37]

Rather than relying on the self-proclaimed virtue of the managers, some people proposed regulating the exercise of business power by a kind of internal constitution – a charter stating the rights and duties of management. This meant applying to managerial power 'the concepts of limited government which are the essence of Western constitutionalism'.[38]

In 1962, Richard Sedric Fox Eells, a General Electric executive, noted that wondering whether business possesses a 'constitutional structure' is tantamount to asking the 'question of business *governance*'[39] – note that Eells is one of the first to use this term, outmoded at the time, in this new sense. A company is admittedly 'a producer and a distributor, a supplier and a buyer of economic goods', but it is also something different, a 'decision-making centre', 'an instrument of power and authority'.[40] As such, one can ask it other questions than those raised by economists, questions of governance. 'Who really controls a company? What power does it exercise? To whom should the power-wielders be accountable, and how? Is the company a "self-perpetuating oligarchy," as some have charged, or is it a type of republic?'[41]

The difficulty, Eells pointed out, is that the private government of business 'is decidedly not a democracy, and yet, it is no longer possible for a really big business to be an autocracy'.[42] The path of corporate constitutionalism is narrow: what political space does it still have, on the basis of this dual diagnosis, between an autocracy that it considers untenable on the one hand and, on the other, a democracy it rejects? Actually, not much.

But we need to be careful, warned a 1958 report from the Rockefeller Foundation, for if we accept this, 'the same sort of question that can be asked of other governments can also be asked of these private governments', and if 'the democratic ideals by which the state is properly judged may also be applied to the ways in which the lives of men are governed in the private sector',[43] then we will soon face a major problem: 'Very simply, the corporation is an authoritarian form of industrial government in a purportedly democratic society'.[44] Or, if you apply the standards of political legitimacy to it, there will necessarily be a contradiction 'between the democratic tradition of government by consent and the inevitably hierarchical and authoritarian procedures of business'.[45]

There was even, some thought, a great danger in this. If you shout from the rooftops that 'management has the worker's best interests at heart', warned Peter Drucker in 1950, then 'management can be legitimate if only it tries'. But how far can it go? It is very unwise to make this kind of promise, as is 'proven by the one experience that is strictly comparable to modern industrial paternalism: modern colonial paternalism'.[46] By mistakenly adopting a rhetoric of 'government for the people', the colonialist discourse has placed itself at odds with its 'obligation to manage the colony in the economic, political or strategic interest of the home country'.[47] This kind of language was catastrophic because rather than achieving 'the one thing that mattered: acceptance by the natives as a legitimate government [. . .] it made the colonial peoples conscious of the split between the ideals of colonial government and its responsibility toward the economic interests of the home country'.[48] And this, says Drucker, is a constant in history: 'All Enlightened Despotisms have ended in revolution'.[49] And if people persist, 'Enlightened Managerial Despotism' will be no exception to the rule.

This was also what the neoliberals of the time feared. Milton Friedman pulled the emergency cord very early on. In March 1958, at a seminar held under the gilded mouldings with their griffon decorations in San Francisco's Drake Hotel, the Chicago economist adopted a solemn tone: 'If anything is certain to destroy our free society, to undermine its very foundations, it would be a wide-spread acceptance by management of social responsibilities in some sense other than to make as much money as possible. This is a fundamentally subversive doctrine'.[50] By dint of repeating everywhere that managers are 'civil servants rather than the employees of their stockholders then in a democracy they will, sooner or later, be chosen by the public techniques of election and appointment'.[51]

In the name of what, after all, are business leaders appointed by shareholders via the board of directors? There is, he replies, no justification for this state of affairs, except that the former are agents in the service of the latter, and if this postulate falls, everything collapses with it. If you accept that the business leader is a kind of private agent of the public, you will inevitably conclude that 'it is inadmissible that such public officials [. . .] be named as they are now. If they really serve the public, they must be elected via a political process'.[52] By admitting that they exercise governmental functions, managers are unwittingly exposed to criticism, and soon to much worse. For, under the deceptive charms of ethics, Friedman senses the tracks of a Soviet tank: 'the doctrine of "social responsibility" involves the acceptance of the socialist view that political mechanisms, not market mechanisms, are the appropriate way to determine the allocation of scarce resources to alternative uses'.[53]

Considered as a form of government, what does big business look like? It looks bad. It looks like a regime where a caste of unelected leaders exercises undivided power. As one British anarchist concluded in the early 1960s:

> The political system we find in industry is, on the contrary, one in which the government (the management) is permanently in office, is self-recruiting, and is not accountable to anyone, except formally to the shareholders [. . .]. At the same time, the vast majority of those who are required to obey this permanent government have not citizenship status at all, no right to vote for the leaders who form the government. The only rights that the masses have in this system are the right to form pressure groups (trade unions) seeking to influence the government and the right to withhold their co-operation (the right to strike). Such a political system [. . .] no more deserves to be called democracy [. . .], than does the oligarchical political system of 18th century Britain.[54]

Big business employees are not only deprived of political rights, but also of certain freedoms otherwise recognized as imprescriptible: 'For nearly two centuries', wrote a professor from Harvard Business School, 'Americans have enjoyed freedom of press, speech, and assembly, due process of law, privacy, freedom of conscience, [. . .]. But Americans have not enjoyed these civil liberties in most companies, [. . .]. Once a U.S. citizen steps through the plant or office door at 9 a.m., he or she is nearly rightless until 5 p.m., Monday through Friday. The employee continues to have political freedoms, of course, but these are not the significant ones now'.[55]

The fundamental problem, the major ideological aporia, is that liberal democratic theory provides no consistent justification for this asymmetry of treatment. 'Capitalism', said the economist of self-management Jaroslav Vanek, 'is based on property rights, and democracy on personal rights. [. . .] One of the main reasons why the western world is so schizophrenic is that we have political democracy and economic autocracy'.[56]

In the 1960s and 1970s, in response to the workers' revolts, philosophers and economists of a critical turn of mind developed theories of economic democracy. The form of authority still prevalent in business – the one that Marx described as being that of a 'private legislator' with 'autocracy over his workpeople'[57] – appears to them as a remnant of archaic power relations, a bastion of tyranny that escaped the democratic revolutions.[58]

In *Spheres of Justice*, Michael Walzer takes the example of Pullman, an American village founded in the late nineteenth century by a wealthy industrialist, George Pullman, who, because he was owner of the city walls and the soil on which it was built, claimed to have the right to 'govern' the inhabitants in the 'same way a man governs his house, his store, or his workshop'.[59] In his city, Pullman was a private autocrat. No elections, no civil liberties, no proper justice, let alone any right of assembly or right to demonstrate. Believing that the ownership of a city was incompatible with the theory and spirit of its institutions, the Illinois Supreme Court put an end to this state of affairs. Walzer's question: this kind of power, applied to the inhabitants of a city, is considered incompatible with the principles of liberal democracy, but was the power that Pullman exercised over the workers in his company really different? No, he answers. 'If this sort of thing is wrong for towns, then it is wrong for companies and factories'.[60] In both cases, the same standard of self-determination must prevail: 'with regard to political power democratic distributions can't stop at the factory gates. The deep principles are the same for both sorts of institution. This identity is the moral basis of the labor movement [. . .] of every demand for progress toward industrial democracy'.[61]

The ideas propounded by Berle and Means had thrown the traditional discourse of legitimization of the capitalist order into crisis. The problem was theoretical, but it was also thoroughly political. As Edward Mason put it: 'As everyone now recognizes, classical economics provided not only a system of analysis, or analytical "model," intended to be useful to the explanation of economic behavior but also a defense – and a carefully reasoned defense – of the proposition that the economic behavior promoted [. . .] by the institutions of a free-enterprise system is, in the main, in the public interest. It cannot be too strongly emphasized', he continued, 'that the growth of nineteenth-century capitalism depended largely on the general acceptance of a reasoned justification of the system on moral as well as on political and economic grounds. The managerial literature appears devastatingly to undermine the intellectual presuppositions of this system. And what does it offer in its place?'[62] Nothing, or almost. Worse than that, the ethical managerialism that has striven to fill the void is dangerous, giving a foothold to the demands for democracy in business, thus weakening the institution in its very principle.

Among the intransigent, calls were heard to repudiate such unnatural language and to extol capitalist values: 'Instead of fighting for its survival by means of a series of strategic retreats masquerading as industrial statesmanship', advised Theodore Levitt in 1958 in the *Harvard Business Review*, 'business must fight as if it were at war. And, like a good war, it should be fought gallantly, daringly, and, above all, *not* morally'.[63]

— 7 —

DISCIPLINING THE MANAGERS

The modern proxy contest is at best a device for tempering autocracy by invasion.

Bayless Manning[1]

For neoliberals, the question of the legitimacy of managerial power simply did not arise. Managers were shareholders' agents, *tout court*. Above all, one must never open Pandora's box. Once this embarrassing question has been ruled out, there was just one difficulty to be sorted, of a technical-practical order: if it is true that managers do not use all their care and efforts to maximize shareholder value, how can they be impelled to do so? For what was potentially a new aspect of the crisis in governability had loomed: after the case of unruly workers, there was now the issue of managers who shirked their tasks.

Economists who reformulated the problem of Berle and Means in this way initially focused on minimizing its magnitude. 'Clearly, the present managers of United States Steel could, if they are really in control of the corporation, pay themselves perhaps a hundred times their present salary without difficulty'. But they did not, which proved that their latitude was limited. A CEO can indeed, conceded Tullock, 'hire a beautiful secretary who is not the best and cheapest typist', but if managers 'decided to devote regularly half their profits to the Poverty Program. I take it that they would be removed with great speed by the stockholders'.[2] One can appreciate his judicious choice of example. At worst, then, there may be non-optimal management, a relative lack of zeal, little sexist favours – but we are far from the picture painted by some, of an all-powerful, freewheeling management, prepared to squander the dividends of the rich to give them to the poor.

Here indeed lies the rub: due to their remoteness and dispersion, shareholders are not 'perfectly efficient in supervising', so it may happen that managers do not fully comply with the imperative of 'making as much money as possible'.[3] In short, we here have what economists call a 'problem of agency'.[4] There is a 'relationship of agency' when someone (hereinafter referred to as 'the agent'), acts for someone else (hereinafter referred to as 'the principal'), in his name and in his place. This is the technical term for an ordinary question: how to get other people to do one's work?

'A key problem that principals in such relations face is that of insuring that the agent does in fact act for the principal'.[5] The problem, therefore, is – as Barry Mitnick eloquently puts it – one of 'policing agency'. The principal can use various devices to control the agent's activity, but these 'surveillance and police tasks have costs'.[6] Hence the question: how to reduce 'agency costs'? How to police things more cheaply?

This reduced Berle and Means' problem to a task of policing managerial work, the challenge being to discover processes for the efficient disciplining of opportunistic managers – and with them the whole chain of their subordinates – with the servicing of shareholder value as their sole aim.

This questioning is justified, however, notes one critic, 'if, but only if, it is assumed that shareholders when in power keep managers in line to the benefit of all society',[7] which comes down to admitting as a postulate what should instead be questioned: the fact that the rest of society need not worry about companies as long as it is their 'owners' who run them. But 'is there any evidence or argument that our society is more safe at the hands of the Ford Motor Company than at the hands of General Motors or AT&T?'[8] Certainly in the first case, the case of a proprietor-manager, the unity of patrimonial control remains, but 'to whom is such an individual or small family group "accountable?"'[9]

Ignoring such objections, neoliberal economists started looking for ways to 'align incentives'[10] so as to regulate the conduct of managers in line with the interests of shareholders. They were convinced that the solutions were already there, just waiting. Indeed, if unnoticed mechanisms had not already been working in the shadows to neutralize the dynamic brought to light by Berle and Means, the corporation would have long since disappeared from the face of the earth, fatally ousted by one that was more efficient on the competitive meta-market of forms of organization. If it has lasted, the real reason was thought to be that the loss of owner control was thwarted by a 'disciplinary role of the markets'.[11]

The Marxist Paul Sweezy, refuting the arguments of Berle and Burnham, had been among the first to point out, as early as 1942, one simple but crucial fact that explained the persistent alignment of managerial control over shareholder interest. Those who ran the leading companies, he noted, 'although owning an inconsequential proportion of stock, are nearly always owners of absolutely large amounts of stock, so that their interests are largely identical with the interests of the body of owners'.[12]

In the early 1960s, the British economist Robin Marris, who, for his part, persisted in believing firmly that 'management has considerable freedom of action'[13] in the age of 'managerial capitalism', did, however, wonder about the potential effects of a possible change in the structure of executive compensation. In the United States, he pointed out, some economists were advocating that sources other than wages should be encouraged, including various forms of 'financial rewards', including bonuses and stock options, with a view to 'more closely aligning the interests of the managers on those of shareholders'[14] and encouraging 'neo-classical behavior'.[15] Would such an 'institutional change' be able to 'remove some of the contradictions otherwise inherent in the neo-classical conception of capitalism?'[16]

For neoliberal economists, such, at least, was the hope. Jensen and Meckling recommended establishing 'incentive compensation systems for the manager or [giving] him stock options'.[17] By linking the incomes of managers to share price and performance, Easterbrook and Fischel predicted, the personal interest of managers could 'be aligned with that of investors through automatic devices'.[18] 'Mobilization', as Frédéric Lordon puts it, from the other side of the barricade, 'is a matter of collinearity: the desire of those enlisted needs to be aligned with the master-desire'.[19]

The other major process was negative, based on the stick rather than the carrot. In the 1960s, Henry Manne, the leader of the 'Law and Economics' trend, raised a decisive objection to Berle and Means' thesis: if the managerial teams exercise, as they claim, an absolute control of business, how is it that CEOs are regularly replaced against their will, ousted by others? For this, managerial orthodoxy provided no explanation.[20] But Manne himself did.

According to his colleague and friend Gordon Tullock, there were people and organizations whose business was to make money by taking control of poorly managed companies. And 'very large profits can be made by eliminating the incompetents'.[21] There is a whole range of processes for doing this: besides the tender offer, where the bearers are promised that their shares will be bought back on condition that they have succeeded in collecting a sufficient number by a given time, there is the 'proxy race' where a group of shareholders collects voting rights from others in order to take over a board.

Control of companies is in itself a coveted object, a resource that has its own value, and there is a market for this, a *market of power*. This represented the discovery of an aspect of financial markets hitherto ignored by economic theory, the existence of a 'takeover market' where 'management teams compete for the right to control – that is, to manage – corporate resources'.[22]

Introducing this notion of the 'market for managerial control'[23] in 1965, Manne highlighted the 'role that the stock market plays as an instrument for controlling and disciplining managers'.[24] He thus reinterprets the hostile takeover, usually perceived as strengthening one firm's managerial power over another, as a subordination of management as a whole to market performance in general.

When the management of a company is underperforming, he argues, the stock price tends to plunge, which incites other actors, who think they can put in place a 'better performing' management, to buy the falling stocks so as to take over the company. One of the most fundamental premises of this theory is that there is a higher correlation between 'managerial efficiency and the market price of shares'.[25] Any significant deviation from a behaviour of profit maximization automatically leads to a fall in the share price, making the firm a vulnerable target for hostile takeovers leading to the dismissal of the management team.

A top manager lives with a sword of Damocles hanging over him: he constantly incurs the 'risk of being replaced'.[26] Considerable pressure weighs down on him: the more money he makes, the safer he is, but 'the less money he makes, the more likely he is to be thrown out'.[27] It is this continual threat which already leads the manager, his heart taut with unease, to keep a close and anxious eye on share prices. 'Imagine that you are the president of a large billion-dollar corporation. Suddenly, another management team threatens your job and prestige by trying to buy your company's stock. The whole world watches your performance'.[28] What do you do?

As Alchian concludes, 'the policing of managerial shirking relies on across-market competition from new groups of would-be managers [. . .] who seek to displace existing management'.[29] 'An enormous amount of power and control is exercised by the owners of the corporation, albeit not in the fashion Berle wanted, i.e. not in a political fashion'.[30]

As long as we do not see this, 'so long as we are unable to discern any control relationship between small shareholders and corporate management', then Berle and Means' thesis retains all its credibility. But as soon as we understand this logic, everything changes. We realize that 'the market for corporate control gives to these shareholders both power and protection',[31] and that it guarantees by its own mechanisms 'the real identity of interests of owners and management'.[32] Manne was paving the way for 'a market-based theory of the firm',[33] soon called on to supplant the old managerialist conceptions based on the opposite assumption that managerial rationality would become independent of the market.

Another important discovery had occurred at the same time. In 1959, the managerial economist and Jesuit father Paul Harbrecht drew attention to a new economic phenomenon with major complications: managers of 'pension funds', he remarked, began investing heavily in equities, to the point of 'buying control of the most influential American corporations at a rather rapid pace'.[34] What would the situation be like, he asked, within a decade or two?

If 'socialism' is defined as 'ownership of the means of production by the workers', wrote Peter Drucker ten years later, 'then the United States is the first truly "Socialist" country. Through their pension funds, employees of American business today own at least 25 percent of its equity capital, which is more than enough for control'.[35] The paradox was stimulating, but Drucker was exaggerating – knowingly.

'Corporate shareholding on such a scale is power', acknowledged Harbrecht; but that power, he immediately noted, is held by 'pension trustees', not by the employees themselves.[36] This is thus a new case of a separation between ownership and control. Managerialism was adding a string to its bow. The managerialization of the company was accompanied by a managerialization of shareholding, and the problematics of social responsibility could be transposed to this new storey in the economic building: of whom are the managers of 'social funds' the agents?[37] Should not workers exercise control over the use that is made of their deferred wages? And so on.

Manne knew these texts and took the matter seriously. 'Institutional investors may be playing a far more important role than is commonly realized', he acknowledged in 1962. Indeed, such institutions have an unparalleled strike force, given that 'the effect of a sale of a large bloc of shares will be to depress the market value of the stock'.[38] However, rejecting Harbrecht's criticisms out of hand, he merely took note of the major role that pension funds could play in his model of the disciplinary control of managerial performance by the market.

Manne and his colleagues were not content to refute managerial theses by highlighting the existence of counter-mechanisms; they were also very active in intensifying the latter. For the disciplinary effect of the market for control to function fully, it was necessary to deregulate the stock markets – in particular to finish with antitrust laws that limited hostile repurchases.

Agency theories are both explanatory and prescriptive. They tell both how agency works and how it should work. However, in these theories, between these two regimes of discourse, lies a contradiction that has not been emphasized enough. While on one side, on their 'positive' side, they show that there is no real problem of misalignment, on the other hand, on their 'normative' side, they struggle to advocate solutions to solve this problem that they otherwise deny. 'Enthusiasts of laissez-faire capitalism', remarked Williamson, 'are sometimes schizophrenic [. . .] Focusing on any given time, they commonly deny the existence of managerial discretion. Taking a long-term perspective, however, these same enthusiasts point with pride to the development of new techniques that have brought managerial discretion under more effective control'.[39]

When he scrutinized the statistics, the economist Robert Larner, who had decided to settle the nagging question of 'managerial latitude' empirically, found no evidence of any significant difference between the performances of 'managerial' companies and 'proprietorial' companies: 'Although control is separated from ownership in most of America's largest corporation', he concluded in 1970, 'the effects on the profit orientations of firms, and on stockholders' welfare have been minor. The magnitude of the effects appears to be too small to justify the considerable attention they have received in the literature of the past thirty-eight years' (he was referring to the date of publication of Berle and Means' book).[40] This confirmed what Marxists and neoliberals had long been convinced of: the thesis of the new independence of managerial power, of its misalignment with the imperatives of profit, was a house built on sand.

Still, the programme of Manne et al. was actively promoted – but not so as to solve a problem that was well known to be a phantom, not to *realign*, but rather to *over-align* managerial management with shareholder value.

In 1981, US President Reagan handed over the department of justice's antitrust to William F. Baxter, a fervent opponent of antitrust laws, a supporter of Manne's theses on the virtues of the 'market for control'. It was he who, implementing a new competition policy, deregulated merger-acquisition operations.[41]

During the subsequent phase of speculative fever, where companies were bought up in hostile raids so as to tidy them up and sell them on at a profit', more than a quarter of the 'top 500'American companies faced hostile takeovers and nearly a third of the large industrial companies were bought or merged.[42] 'Manne's hypothetical market for corporate control [became] a reality'.[43] And with it came the inevitable consequences: restructuring and massive layoffs – and huge social violence.

The American working class, in its best organized, most unionized fractions (those which had – as the reader will remember – proved so active in the previous decade) had the stuffing knocked out of it. Combined with the recession and the effects of international competition, the economic discipline imposed by stock markets was much more effective in this area than all the union busters together.[44]

In this great race for stock profits in the 1980s, pension funds were not left behind. The tragic irony, in this case, was that the hedge funds that played a part in laying low whole sections of the American working class came in part from its own income, set aside for its retirement.[45] It was by conforming to the interests of workers as shareholders that the interests of these same shareholders as workers were trampled on. This was an illustration of the central contradiction of capitalism in general, and of *fondiste* capitalism in particular: it entailed a great antisocial diversion of social wealth.

In a series of late, unfinished texts, Marx had outlined his own theory of the separation of ownership and control. This was an alternative, anticipatory version, of subsequent managerialist theses.

Corporations, i.e. stock companies, he noted, 'have an increasing tendency to separate this work of management as a function from the ownership of capital'.[46] The former unitary figure of the capitalist-producer is fragmented. There are now, on the one hand, non-owner directors, and on the other, share owners, simple money capitalists. At the same time, the old individual private ownership of the means of production is duplicated in share capital on the one hand and in the private ownership of shares on the other. Capital then takes 'directly the form of capital (the capital of directly associated individuals) as opposed to private capital, and its companies appear as social enterprises as opposed to private enterprises. It is the overtaking of capital as private property within the limits of the capitalist mode of production itself'.[47] For Marx, this showed the ferment entailed by exceeding the relations of capitalist property: 'share capital as most accomplished form (turning into communism)',[48] he wrote one day in telegraphese to Engels, who luckily did not need further explanation. However, the dialectical nuance – 'within the limits of the capitalist mode of production itself' – is very important. For while we can already 'catch a glimpse of the opposite of the old form, where the means of social production appear as individual property', the 'metamorphosis into shares [. . .] still remains locked up in capitalist limits'.[49] The contradiction between social wealth and private property is perpetuated by assuming a new form.

But what form is it? Marx identifies it with the creation in France, under Napoleon III, of the 'Crédit Mobilier', the distant ancestor of contemporary investment funds. 'We see, as it were, kings of industry whose power is in inverse ratio to their responsibility – are they not solely responsible within the limit of their own shares, while they have the entire capital of the company at their disposal? They form a more or less permanent body, while the mass of the shareholders is subject to an incessant process of decomposition and renewal'. To characterize this phenomenon, Marx borrows from Fourier the notion of 'industrial feudalism'[50], but what has been invented, he adds, intensifies the phenomenon because 'the new idea is to make industrial feudalism dependent on stock market speculation'.[51]

Thus, on the basis of what he had barely had time to glimpse, Marx drew completely different conclusions from those later drawn by Berle and Means. Far from confirming the triumph of an almighty managerial power, the shareholder form, at the same time as having the *potential* to go beyond the relations of capitalist property (given the tremendous socialization of capital that it was setting in motion), was for now paving the way for its subordination to yet other masters. Not just to the new princes of finance, managers centralizing the control of vast socialized masses of capital money, but, more fundamentally, by them, through them and beyond them, to a new level – in terms of shares and finances – of government by capital.

— 8 —

CATALLARCHY

We shall see [. . .] how the capitalist, by means of capital, exercises his governing power over labor, then, however, we shall see the governing power of capital over the capitalist himself.

Karl Marx[1]

Powerful arrangements had been discovered for disciplining managers, closely tying their interests to those of shareholders, and for further subjecting the management of companies to the financial markets, even at the price of a drastic redefinition of 'economic efficiency' in accordance with the short-term criteria of shareholder value.[2]

This received the sweet name of 'governance'. We already have come across this notion. In the meantime, it had been subjected to profound modifications. The term 'governance' had been, as we have seen, revived in the 1960s by a 'constitutionalist' discourse that used it to apply to the private government of business the standards inspired by the principles of public government. Under the influence of theories of agency, this term began to be used in a different way in the late 1970s. As one writer significantly put it at the end of the 1990s: 'Our perspective on corporate governance is a straightforward agency perspective [. . .]. We want to know how investors get the managers to give them back their money'.[3]

Whereas the first notion of corporate governance served to pose the problem of managerial power in the form of politics, the second refigured it terms of an economics viewed in a particularly narrow way. By setting out to 'describe the internal and external devices purported to discipline corporate management and to orient them toward share price',[4] as the sociologist Gerald Davis summarizes it, 'the functionalist theory of corporate governance provided the intellectual foundation for shareholder capitalism'.[5] This represented a shift from ethical managerialism towards financial governmentality.

The key question of contemporary governance, it has been said, is knowing how to rule without rulers.[6] But this is exaggerated. Armchair agents playing the role of leaders are still necessary. The real question, rather, is knowing how to rule the rulers, how to institute forms of meta-control such that, whatever these rulers initially wanted, they have no other option, once in position, than to do what they are supposed to do. What Marx called the 'government of capital', contemporary newspeak has started to call 'governance'. Governance as the art of ruling the rulers involves mechanisms for the impersonal government of these rulers. If market governance prevails, then the pipe dreams of ethical governance will in any case be powerless to achieve anything of importance.[7]

If this idea was viewed as so important, it was especially, to begin with, in order to keep the alternative at bay. In the eyes of neoliberals, 'the greatest danger' represented by the demand for self-management or economic democracy rested 'in the very forms suggested for control',[8] a political, conscious and finalized control of the economy. This, basically, was what they aimed to counter with the ideal of control by the markets.

No one formulated this project more clearly than Friedrich Hayek. The fundamental issue was the very definition of economics. Etymologically, the term refers of course to the *oikos*, to the home, both the family's place of residence and the unit of domestic production – typically, a farm. Economics, originally, was the art of governing the *oikos*; it was a science of the master, his skill at exercising domination over his wife, children and slaves. There was an archaic synonymy between economics and the art of private domination.

It was this ancient notion from which Hayek sought – quite understandably – to distance himself. He preferred another, less repulsive and much more cheerful take on economics; one that could better be conveyed, in his opinion, by the neologism 'catallaxy',[9] based on a Greek term meaning exchange. In contrast with *oikonomia*, 'an economy, in the strict sense of the word in which a household, a farm, or an enterprise can be called economies',[10] catallaxy would refer to 'the system of numerous interrelated economies which constitute the market-order', or, more precisely, the 'market order that forms spontaneously'.[11]

While economics sees itself as a '*taxis*', a 'deliberate arrangement', catallaxy is presented as a '*cosmos*', a world. While the first is a 'teleocracy', a unit oriented by a hierarchy of ends set by a central agent, the second is a 'nomocracy',[12] an order where everyone pursues his own ends, following the rules of a universal game. On the one hand, there are organizations, on the other hand, markets; on the one hand, there is authority, on the other, exchange; on the one hand, there is centralized management, on the other, self-coordination without any apparent domination; on the one hand, there are orders given and received, on the other, a spontaneous order populated by free inter-actions; on one hand, there are orders as commands, on the other, orders as arrangements. On the one hand, there is the tyranny of the master, on the other, the law of the jungle.

In the neoliberal vision of history, *katallaxia* replaces and crushes *oikonomia*: the market model replaces the model of the hearth. Between the world of Aristotle and that of today, the old 'paradigm of economics', that of the subordination to a master, seems to have given way to the 'exchange model of economics', catallactics.[13]

In reality, however, the one has not ousted the other, but has taken it over in a subsumption of *oikonomia* into *katallaxia*, of the private government of the master to the cosmic order of the markets. But in doing so, catallaxy crosses a boundary. It becomes something new. It has changed, we might say, adding another neologism to Hayek's terminology, into a 'catallarchy' – a new regime of government, one that needs to be conceived as a *government of rulers by the markets*.

The market of control theorized by Manne answers the problem of the 'detection and policing costs' discussed by the theories of agency. What would have needed to be implemented by a laborious work of direct supervision is accomplished all by itself, as a side effect of speculation.

Who controls the managers? In the market, nobody, no shareholder in particular. This second-level control is exercised in a completely different mode to the first: not personal, but impersonal, not direct, but indirect, not conscious, but unconscious, not intentional, but automatic. Any deviation from the standard of shareholder value will instantly cause an adverse reaction impacting on the share price. In the long term, if people persist in following this route, it will mean the elimination of the management team. As sanctions are integrated into the operation of the market, shareholder value is no longer a mere ideological norm, but also something else: the operator of an automatically triggered police measure.

The stock market is linked to a certain mode of verification which evaluates productive activities according to the 'single metric' of financial performance.[14] But this production of 'truth' is also the instrument of a technology for governing behaviour. As variations in share price are supposed to provide information on management performance, everyone can react accordingly.[15] Thus 'the signals provided by the managerial labor market and the capital market [. . .] discipline managers'.[16] Stock exchange indicators are aptly named in French: they are *indics* (slang for 'informers').

In this rejigged apology for the market economy, the primacy of shareholder value is lauded as an efficient catallarchic principle of meta-government, the dogma of a new faith, where the *nomos* of the market spontaneously converts capitalist chaos into an orderly regularity. The real raison d'être for the stock exchange and profit, 'its ultimate justification' as the French neoliberal Henri Lepage wrote in 1980, is first and foremost to be 'an instrument of social "regulation"'. The 'social legitimacy of capitalist profit', he argued, is based on the 'principles of cybernetic regulation of the market economy'.[17]

While Berle and Means thought that shareholders had become almost helpless, the neoliberals were showing, on the contrary, that shareholding systemically exercised a 'great pressure on managers'.[18] But this does not imply that the managerial authority has evaporated internally. What managerial power loses in its latitude for decision, particularly in terms of investment choice, it certainly does not lose in its power over its own subordinates. We do not have just one or the other – either *katallaxia* or else *oikonomia* – we have both: submission to a managerial government that is itself subordinate to a shareholder government, each with its own modalities.

But who is submitting to what? New theories of the firm have so disfigured their object that the workers have almost disappeared from the landscape. You can read dozens of articles of this kind without the workers ever being mentioned, as if business were reduced to being a remote relationship between CEOs and shareholders. When it is repeatedly said that what is needed is to 'discipline the management', what is also meant, between the lines, is the workers, the same workers who were proving so recalcitrant at the time. Through this, beneath this, it was all about the workers, who needed, as ever, to be countered. Disciplinary pressure exerted at the top would cascade down each rank of the organigram from top to bottom; those at the bottom would assume in its own particular way the 'residual risk' – in its very body. This was another kind of 'trickle-down theory', different from the official version: while profits go up, what falls like drops of rain are the pressure tactics, the moral harassment, the accidents at work, bouts of depression, musculoskeletal disorders, social death – and sometimes, just death.

Shareholder value is not just an ideology vaguely hidden in the equations, it is also and above all a *programmatic theory*. It's not a performative, it's a *programmatic*. By uttering itself, it does not implement itself; it gives just the necessary instructions to whoever is authorized to make it happen. So its truth status is very special. A programmatic description may well be 'wrong' at the time of its utterance, but this inadequacy does not constitute an objection to it: the aim of such a description is to make its object conform to its description and not the other way around. The movement does not consist in making the utterances coincide with the real, but the real with the utterances. It changes the thing so that the notion will become true. This is a movement, not of verification but of true-ification (*vrai-ification*).

What Manne's theory proposed is, strangely enough, quite close to what Marx said about the government of capital: there is a meta-government, one which governs the governors. However, what the young Marx was still saying as a critical philosopher, Manne has stated as a technician of law and economics, not as a general truth, but as a project to be put into operation.

However, for this, in this area, it is not necessary to persuade the great mass of people. The strength of this kind of theory is not of an ideological order. At the limit, it does not have to make big speeches. It is enough for it to gain the ear of the project managers. Its effective-ness is more of the order of a concretized phantasmagoria than an internalized ideology.[19]

The market economy, Hayek wrote, is 'a spontaneous cosmos'. It is a world, perhaps; but spontaneous it certainly is not. Neoliberalism rests less on naturalism than on political engineering: it aims to build, by institutional architecture, artificial worlds.[20] Not only is this uni-verse, presented as automatic, nomothetic and impersonal, actively constructed but, more importantly, as its effects are inevitably chal-lenged, it needs to be tirelessly reimposed by conscious strategies. For capital does admittedly govern, but it could not continue to do so for very long if people did not constantly busy themselves, with pugnac-ity and determination, propping up its domination. Without that, it would not last very long. The 'government of markets' is far from being a self-sufficient order. This cosmos holds together only thanks to demiurges who somehow patch it up permanently and who defend it tooth and nail against the new enemies it makes for itself every day.

At the end of the twentieth century, business was affected by a multidimensional 'crisis in government'. One of the important aspects of the malaise was, we have just seen, theoretical. However, it took new social and political confrontations to make people really become aware of the danger.

Part III

Attack on free enterprise

— 9 —

PRIVATE GOVERNMENT
UNDER SIEGE

A corporation is government through and through. [. . .] Certain technical methods which political government uses, as, for instance, hanging,
are not used by corporations, generally speaking, but that is a detail.
Corporation activities often put people to death by carelessness or by
parsimony: this is not a judgment upon the corporations, but merely a
statement of fact.

Arthur Fisher Bentley[1]

What is a business corporation? To this question, in post-war
America, managerialism brought a completely different answer from
that imposed since by neoliberal theories of the firm. A big corporation, it was said, is admittedly an economic entity, but also, and
perhaps most importantly, something else: a kind of government, a
private government.

One could cite dozens of texts on this theme. Let's take one almost
at random – a minor text, little known but very representative of this
trend. An article written in 1951 by Beardsley Ruml, an economist
and former advisor to President Hoover and an ex-business leader (in
the 1940s he was CEO of Macy's chain of department stores). His
position is instructive in that he played the triple role of intellectual,
technocrat and manager. His text was titled 'Corporate Management
as a Locus of Power'.[2]

Ruml begins with a finding that many were already making at
the time: the omnipresence of business in 'modern life'. Business is
everywhere, in every aspect, every corner, every moment and every
place – or almost – of our lives: 'We depend on business for the things
we eat and wear, for the home we live in, for most of our amusements
and recreation, for going places and knowing what is going on in the
world. Most of us depend on business for the kind of jobs we have'.[3]

But, says Ruml, all these things that business does . . . how exactly does it do them? It does them by permanently fixing *rules*.[4] A business works by issuing rules. It is a prescriptive power, a power that continues to give instructions about how things should be done, business conducted and, ultimately, lives lived. Certainly these rules, self-dictated and particular, are not *laws*, but they are no less a form of governmental activity: 'It is in no sense a figure of speech to refer to a business company as a private government. A business is a government because within the law it is authorized [. . .] to make rules for the conduct of its affairs'.[5] In this sense, business enjoys a great 'private authority'.

But on whom is this authority exercised? 'If business is private government, who are the governed? We are the governed!'[6] As workers, the situation is obvious: all along the business's chain of command, they are governed by rules produced by the business – rules that are mainly dictated by their employers. 'These rules determine for the individual where he shall work, when he shall work, what he shall do, who will give him orders, who will take orders from him, his promotion and discipline, the amount he gets paid, and the time and duration of his holidays and vacations'.[7]

We are still subject to this private governance of corporations in another respect, namely as consumers. Certainly, consumers make choices, but the fact remains that it is 'the management who decides, here again, the supply, where and when this offer will be made to them, and at what price'.[8]

If the corporation is a private government, then, this is not just in the obvious but too restricted sense, where the management exercises power over the workers (i.e. as an internal government). Management as a locus of power governs much more than employees. It also governs *extra muros*. It governs individuals in almost all their social roles and almost all their dimensions, so true is it that everyone is caught in multiple arrangements established by the private authority of different managers. In short, the corporation thus conceived starts to appear as an immense and proliferating *private government of life*, much more finely-grained and much more invasive than state power.

There was certainly nothing new in thinking of the firm as a government. The 'corporation', its ancestor, had already long been called a 'Commonwealth in miniature' (Hobbes), or a 'little republic' (Blackstone).[9] But in the twentieth century the thing had assumed quite different proportions. Big modern corporations outperformed, by their gigantism and by the extent of their social impacts, all that had been known until then. Beyond their own members, they began to rule the world. But this unheard-of power was concentrated in the hands of small castes of managers constituting 'an autonomous center of decision'.[10] They are the ones who decide, on a discretionary basis, prices and investments, who choose the models to put on the market, who pilot innovation at will; they are also the ones who guide, through advertising or marketing, the desires and tastes of consumers – and management is thus in a position to exert a *stylistic domination* of society.[11]

But what were the implications of such a diagnosis? Ruml, we must emphasize, did not seek to criticize the power of business. He was, as an 'organic intellectual' of management, addressing his peers in a respected academic journal. His goal was to warn them of a danger that he saw coming, a political danger that flowed directly from the observation he had just made.

Such power, both omnipresent and discretionary, cannot long continue to be exercised uncontested. A huge mass of diverse interests is subject to an authority over which they have no control, and so it could well happen, Ruml prophesied, that 'someone, one day, and perhaps at the least opportune time, embarks on a crusade to convert these interests into rights'.[12] Then major protest movements will rise up against the private government of business.

'Fortunately', he added, 'there is no critical situation that presses for action'.[13] He advised taking the lead: business would do well, he advocated vaguely in the early 1950s, to put forward, while there was still time, 'new responsibilities'. As the historian Morrell Heald puts it, 'for the moment, there was no apparent threat to managerial initiative. No perceptible popular demand arose for the immediate implementation of a larger system of checks and balances'.[14] Until the mid-1960s, these debates took place in an 'atmosphere of relative peace'.[15] It was not going to last.

In Washington, one morning in March 1969, six Catholic priests gained access to the offices of Dow Chemical, one of the leading suppliers of napalm to the US military: 'They threw files out the window, hung pictures of Vietnamese peasants and children burned during a napalm attack, and poured blood on furniture and equipment. They left a statement declaring outrage at Dow: "You exploit, deprive, dehumanize and kill in search of profit. [. . .] Your product is death."'[16]

The managerialist conception of the private governance of corporations, the conception that we found in Ruml, highlighted a power that was being exerted on the *lives* of all. Radicalized by the protest movements of the late 1960s, this theme assumes a different hue – the denunciation of a power of death, of a necropower.

In the face of criticism, Dow's executives evaded the issue: 'simple good citizenship requires that we supply our government and our military with goods they need. [. . .] Dow does not make the policy on what materiel is used or for what purpose it is used by our military forces nor should attempt to decide on military strategy.'[17] As if napalm had any other uses than the use that is made of it. Howard Zinn replied at the time: 'Indeed, the government itself has ordered the napalm manufactured by Dow, and is using it to burn and kill Vietnamese peasants. Should private citizens [. . .] act themselves, by physical interposition, against Dow Chemical's business activities? To do so would be to "take the law into your own hands." That is exactly what civil disobedience is'.[18]

Honeywell was another of those 'merchants of death' indicted by the anti-war movement. It made the latest sensors for the 'electronic battlefield' deployed in Vietnam, as well as particularly sophisticated antipersonnel mines: 'people sniffers', 'spider mines' hurling thousands of steel needles around, 'gravel mines' packed with fibre optic logs, and 'silent button bomblets'[19] activated by a motion sensor camouflaged in a brown plastic gangue that, on the ground, made it look like animal excrement. The firm also produced an antipersonnel Cluster Bomb Unit which, once released, ejected from its metal pod several hundred mini-bombs scattered over the ground.

In 1970, some students from the University of Minnesota got together to stump up the money for thirty-nine shares in the company 'which they claimed were "tickets of entry" to the upcoming stockholders meeting'.[20] A few months later, several hundred activists flocked to Honeywell's Annual General Meeting. However much the CEO had given assurances that protesters 'ha[d] the right to attend the meeting and express their opinions', he adjourned it, amid booing, barely fourteen minutes after it had begun.[21]

The anti-war movement was changing its strategy. This new tack was discussed in 1969 by Staughton Lynd, a leader of the New Left, who asked: 'Why, then, do we continue to demonstrate in Washington, as if the core of the problem lay there?'[22] Since this war was the product of a military-industrial complex, why not also take on the arms industry directly? 'Our inevitable enemy in the coming years is the corporation'. Questioning the right 'ways to lay siege to corporations', he proposed to start by disrupting the AGMs of shareholders – a first step in the construction of a mass 'anti-corporate' movement.

These activists were carrying on a process invented at the beginning of the 1960s in another context: the 'tactics of proxies'. Saul Alinsky has told the story of this movement. Two years after the riots that had broken out in 1964 in the Black ghetto of Rochester, an organization, FIGHT, was created to constrain Kodak, the city's flagship industrialist, to hire Black workers. But how should they go about it? 'A boycott was out of the question. That would be like asking everyone to stop taking pictures. This called for a new kind of tactic'.[23] They imagined several, including this one: buying a hundred concert tickets at the Rochester Philharmonic Opera, the cultural holy of holies of the city's well-heeled White middle classes and the jewel in the crown of Kodak's philanthropic activities; the hundred or so activists invited would first be given a grand 'pre-show banquet in the community consisting of nothing but huge portions of baked beans. Can you imagine the inevitable consequences within the symphony hall?' As Alinsky says of Kodak: 'Demonstrations, confrontations and picketings they'd learned to cope with, but never in their wildest dreams could they envision a flatulent blitzkrieg on their sacred symphony orchestra. [. . .] Very often the most ridiculous tactic can prove the most effective'. Finally, they resorted to another process. FIGHT started to ask shareholders of the firm – including several American churches that had wisely invested money from the collection plate in the stock market – for proxy votes so they could attend Kodak's AGM and submit anti-discrimination motions. This other form of 'proxy tactic' caused a considerable stir and was greeted with considerable nervousness by the company's management: 'It scared Kodak, and it scared Wall Street'.[24] The firm finally gave way.

As Lynd has foreseen, the spring of 1970 saw tumult in several conference centres. Everywhere the CEOs of big American companies saw their sempiternal shareholder AGMs disrupted by militant intrusions. This new tactic 'compelled executives, who were faced with possibly total disruption at the normally staid-to-boring meetings, to put on war paint. The companies were forced to devise tactics in advance to counter the demonstrations'.[25]

In 1970, the NARMIC,[26] an activist research institute, had written a short practical guide outlining various tactics for breaking into shareholders' meetings.[27] In 1971, an employers' organization, the Conference Board, published its own anti-activism manual for firms. The brochure, *Handling protest at annual meetings*, gave valuable advice, including the need to carry out 'intelligence work to learn the intentions of the groups that would demonstrate',[28] controlling entry by creating a list of the names of those who could be admitted, providing big cans of water for leaching the soil in case of attacks from stink bombs,[29] managing speakers by centralizing the control of the microphones ('Placed strategically throughout the auditoriums, they could be switched on or off by the chairman'),[30] providing, if necessary, an audio output protected by armoured glass,[31] placing in the hall security officers to carry out 'prompt and firm action in removing unruly persons'[32] (dressed preferably in civvies rather than in uniform, to avoid creating 'a "police state" image'),[33] and prohibiting the presence of film cameras inside the hall so that the meeting did not turn into 'a circus'.[34]

When confrontation occurs, advised Carl Gerstacker, the CEO of Dow, the number one rule is not to overreact.[35] 'You may be outraged, and much of the time you should be, by such behavior but [...] the first and most important thing of all is to keep your cool, in spite of their efforts'.[36] In cases of this kind, nothing beats thorough preparation, which can take the form of 'training' for CEOs. Their collaborators will make cards that, in addition to the standard answers to be learned by heart, will also provide them with various 'procedures for dealing with emergencies that might arise'.[37] Always stick to the agenda, refusing, for example, any discussion of the war. In the case of untimely intervention, they can use formulas such as 'this is a business meeting and not a political meeting'[38] or 'this is not a forum for that kind of speech'. In some companies, CEOs could even be subjected to demanding real-life rehearsal sessions (though, one might well imagine, they were also quite enjoyable for some): 'Impersonating professional hecklers, student protesters, and cantankerous stockholders, staff members put the chairman to every verbal test they could devise. The company's secretary said the rehearsal was rougher on the chairman than any annual meeting had been ever'.[39]

Managerialists of the 1950s suggested that corporations be viewed as a private government. The New Left of the 1960s took them at their word. 'The corporate order is largely private *from* – from public accountability. [...] The privacy of this private government serves mainly to ensure its authoritarian nature'.[40] Large companies exercise public or quasi-public responsibilities: their activities have a considerable impact on society, including health effects and environmental issues that affect us all. The phrase 'private government' can thus be read as a contraction, of which the complete form, once unfolded, would be *the private government of public affairs*. 'Private government' then becomes the name of a scandal. The notion is transformed into a critical leitmotif, a controversial characterization, an untenable alliance of words that places its object in crisis.

This was exactly the basis for the movements in the United States at the end of the 1960s: starting from the premise that management exercises a private government, they aimed to challenge, in more or less radical forms and directions, this power.[41] In the mid-1960s, as the activist Philip Moore confirmed, the movement was 'redirecting its energies from institutions of government to institutions of private power'.[42] Unlike the trade union movements which the management was used to, these new conflicts no longer occurred along the classic axis of the wage relationship. The big surprise was that social movements 'outside' the firm were now addressing it directly from positions other than those of employees, by mobilizing other subjectivities than those of workers.[43]

The activists' strategy was to 'politicize the company'. They succeeded. The result was an unprecedented mobilization of the business world.[44] Business had got its fingers burnt: it anxiously launched into a multiform counter-offensive, one that would prove merciless.

—— 10 ——

THE BATTLE OF IDEAS

The anti-liberal conspiracy is a pure invention.

Karl Polanyi[1]

'No thoughtful person can question that the American economic system is under broad attack'.[2] Thus began a confidential note sent in August 1971 to the vice-president of the American Chamber of Commerce. It was entitled *Attack on American Free Enterprise System*. The author, Lewis Powell, who was soon to be appointed by Nixon as a Supreme Court judge, had previously drafted another memo, *Political Warfare*, in which he lavished his advice to the White House on the worldwide ideological struggle against communism.[3] But the enemy this time was not quite the same. The offensive in question was being waged in the United States itself, and was not limited to a few Moscow agents: 'We are not dealing with sporadic or isolated attacks from a relatively few extremists or even from the minority socialist cadre. Rather, the assault on the enterprise system is broadly based and consistently pursued. It is gaining momentum and converts'.[4] Among the leaders that Powell pointed out were the consumers' rights advocate Ralph Nader and the ecologist Charles Reich: the former called for the bosses who 'poison food' to be jailed, while the latter conspired to 'green' America.[5] In short, America was witnessing, without the slightest doubt, a 'frontal assault', a 'broad, shotgun attack on the system itself'.[6]

Powell fleshed out his report with a series of recommendations – in fact: a battle plan for the world of business to retake control of a society thrown into turmoil by the protest movements of the late 1960s. At the time, there was a flurry of writings of this kind in the United States: manifestos with bellicose titles, urging a counter-offensive. I would like here, drawing on this corpus, to highlight the main axes of this *discourse of reaction* – in the twofold sense that it was *reactive* (that which is expressed against something, opposed to what is not itself) and *reactionary* (that which aims to conserve or restore a dominant order threatened by change).

The diagnosis, widely shared, was that never in recent American history had capitalism and its institutions been as intensely criticized, never had the feeling of animosity towards them been so widespread. As the banker David Rockefeller put it in 1971: 'It is scarcely an exaggeration to say that right now American business is facing its most severe public disfavour since the 1930s. We are assailed for demeaning the worker, deceiving the consumer, destroying the environment and disillusioning the younger generation'.[7] James Roche, CEO of General Motors, took the same line, deploring 'an extremely critical climate hostile to free enterprise'.[8] 'Business legitimacy has suffered a precipitous decline over the past decade', noted one sociologist in 1977.[9]

According to Powell, this situation was primarily the result of an ideologically driven assault. At the forefront were the campuses of the big universities, with their social science faculties and their inevitably leftist 'bad masters', including Herbert Marcuse and other 'attractive and magnetic' figures; they were 'stimulating teachers, and their controversy attracts student following; [. . .] and they exert enormous influence far out of proportion to their numbers – on their colleagues and in the academic world'.[10] 'Members of the intellectual community', noted the neoliberal economist Arthur Shenfield, had launched an 'ideological war against Western society'. Things had moved on from being just a 'competition between ideas' and turned into 'a war *against* society itself', an attack based on 'deliberate use of ideas, [. . .] for the purpose of the destruction of that society'.[11]

All the same, one still needed to explain how a small clique of radical academics could, despite their convoluted prose and their numerical weakness, exert the influence attributed to it. For that, it was necessary to refine the analysis somewhat.

By the mid-1960s, one New York essayist had formulated a critical theory of modernism. In art, in literature, what exactly *was* modernism? Nothing else, as Lionel Trilling basically concluded, than a cuckoo's egg laid in the dull, cosy nest of the middle classes. Aesthetic modernity is viscerally driven by an *oppositional culture*, with hostile intent for the social milieu in which it had been born: 'the actually subversive intention that characterizes modern writing [. . .] [has the] clear purpose of detaching the reader from the habits of thought and feeling that the larger culture imposes, of giving him a ground and a vantage point from which to judge and condemn, and perhaps, revise the culture that produced him'. And yet, he continued, 'around the adversary culture there has formed what I have called a class'.[12]

Taking up the aesthetic intuitions of Trilling, neoconservative ideologues developed, in the early 1970s, the corresponding sociological thesis. The political and cultural hostility towards the business world, they decided, emanated from a new social group that broadcast it, the 'new class'. The protest movement, said Norman Podhoretz, 'is made up largely of educated, prosperous people, members of the professional and technical intelligentsia'.[13] Irving Kristol agreed: 'This "new class" is not easily defined but may be vaguely described. It consists of a goodly proportion of those college-educated people whose skills and vocations proliferate in a "postindustrial society"':[14] teachers, journalists, social workers, public sector employees, senior civil servants, and so on. 'From the very beginnings of capitalism there has always existed a small group of men and women who disapproved of the pervasive influence of the free market on the civilization in which we live. One used to call this group "the intellectuals," and they are the ancestors of our own "new class."'[15]

As to the question of 'the spring and origin of the ideological attack on Western society', Shenfield's answer was this: it lay in 'the character of the modern intellectual class' whose sense of elitism had been corrupted by 'democratization and the spread of education'. This had 'enormously extended the numbers of the intellectual class' and 'lowered the standards of intellectual life' – a putative lowering that the dismaying defects of his own text would tend to corroborate. In addition, there was a very sad inclination to 'care for the disinherited'. This explosive cocktail of 'mass' access to education, belief in the possibility of social transformation and excessive empathy towards the flea-ridden masses explains why the intellectual strata had become such a nest of 'enemies of society'.[16] The result, moreover, was that there were no longer any real intellectuals to deal with, but mere 'intellectualoids'[17] – in short, an enlarged intellectual class, relatively massified, and ipso facto degenerate.

According to Robert Bartley, an editorialist on the *Wall Street Journal*, 'a whole new industry of "public interest advocates" has sprung up to bedevil business over issues like pollution'.[18] But, on closer inspection, under cover of the general interest, these groups were also defending a caste interest. As Kristol asked: 'What does this "new class" want, and why should it be so hostile to the business community? Well, [. . .] they are not much interested in money but

are keenly interested in power. [. . .] The power to shape our civilization – a power which, in a capitalist system, is supposed to reside in
the free market'.[19]

Now this ongoing war – and this was the second part of the diagnosis
– was being lost. The enemy was making rapid strides forward. He
was constantly conquering new positions. The younger generation
had almost completely switched to his side already, and other social
strata were following suit. A report from the National Association of
Manufacturers warned in 1973: 'the system – the free society if you
will – which has been winning this impressive series of such battles is
in grave danger of losing the war'.[20]

Researchers David Vogel and Leonard Silk, who were then probing
the state of mind of American employers, discovered a deep crisis of
trust, a real loss of faith: 'Strikingly, businessmen today seem remark-
ably pessimistic about the future of the capitalist system. The only
group that is even more convinced that we are witnessing the twilight
of capitalism are the Marxists'.[21] One of the executives they interviewed waxed ironic, not without a certain bitterness: 'The American
capitalist system is confronting its darkest hour. At this rate business
can soon expect support from the environmentalists. We can get them
to put the corporation on the endangered species list'.[22]

At the risk of exaggerating the real extent of the danger, Powell
also conveyed this idea: 'the ultimate issue may be survival – survival
of what we call the free enterprise system'.[23] The function of this
dramatization is clear: to urge people to act. If we lose the battle, this
is mainly for lack of taking the initiative. 'What has been the response
of business to this massive assault upon its fundamental economics, upon its philosophy, upon its right to continue to manage its
own affairs, and indeed upon its integrity?'[24] Nothing, or not much.
And he portrayed a shapeless mass, unable to mobilize against an
imminent threat. The enemy's advances were taking advantage of this
passivity, which amounted to an 'abdication of the capitalist class'.[25]
It was 'ignoring a major crisis', and this blindness could entail its loss.

The thinkers of the American business world had not read Gramsci.
What their texts described did, however, resemble what that Italian
communist, scribbling stubbornly away in Mussolini's jails, had
called a 'crisis of hegemony'.[26]

Business today needs to engage in a 'war for the minds of men'[27] as
the president of the American Enterprise Institute, William Baroody,
wrote in 1972. The enemy stronghold – both a rearguard base and the
main site of discontent – was academia. But one needed to be aware

that 'idea-germinating and idea-legitimizing institutions' exerted considerable influence over the rest of society. The fact that they are affected by a systematic critical 'bias' poses 'a serious problem for those of us who are concerned for the preservation of a liberal society'.[28]

'One of the priority tasks for the business is to intervene on the source of this hostility in campuses'.[29] And, there as elsewhere, money was the sinews of war. Who after all enables these pools of oppositional ideas to flourish, who finances them? The universities depend mainly on '(i) tax funds generated largely from American business, and (ii) contributions from capital funds controlled or generated by American business. One of the bewildering paradoxes of our time is the extent to which the enterprise system tolerates, if not participates in, its own destruction'.[30]

If we want to stop providing our enemies with rope for them to hang us, all those who, from near and far, propagate critical visions of the capitalist order should have their funding cut. David Packard, former Assistant Secretary of State for Defense and the head of Hewlett Packard, said as much in 1973, urging business leaders to stop blindly subsidizing universities through their donations. He felt that 'such hostile groups of scholars are, to a large degree, responsible for the anti-business bias of many of our young people today. And I do not believe it is in the corporate interest to support them'.[31] Kristol agreed: it is a 'perfectly reasonable suggestion that corporations (. . .) discriminate among friend, neutral and foe in their philanthropy'.[32]

'In the future', prescribes Packard, 'let's focus our money and our energy on those departments which are strong and which also contribute in some specific way to our individual companies, or to the general welfare of our free enterprise system'. Meanwhile, Robert Malott, a big boss in the chemical industry, emphasized the advantage of increasing academia's dependence on private funds: the philanthropic donor could then evaluate the content of the courses before deciding whether or not to take out his cheque book, knowing that it was easy, even without being a specialist, to decide whether a particular economics course 'does or does not also present the conservative views of, say, Milton Friedman'. After all, 'do we have the right to establish a philosophical screen to use in determining how shareholders' money is to be donated? I maintain that we have not only the right and the capability to do so but also that we have the obligation to do so'.[33]

In parallel, new institutions should be created which, according to William Simon, former Treasury Secretary and Director of the

Olin Foundation, 'must serve explicitly as intellectual refuges for the non-egalitarian scholars and writers [. . .]. They must be given grants, grants and more grants in exchange for books, books, and more books'.[34] At the beginning of the 1970s, new think tanks were created with the aim of 'developing the conservative political agenda'[35] in the United States, but also internationally, with the creation of the Davos World Economic Forum in 1971 and the Trilateral Commission in 1973.

'Ideas are weapons', writes Powell, and yet businessmen 'have shown little stomach for hard-nose contest with their critics, and little skill in effective intellectual and philosophical debate'.[36] That's true, Kristol answers, but you have to recognize in their defence that they are not the best placed to do this: 'in any naked contest with the New Class, business is a certain loser. Businessmen who cannot even persuade their own children that business is a morally legitimate activity are not going to succeed, on their own, in persuading the world of it. You can only beat an idea with another idea, and the war of ideas and ideologies will be won or lost *within* the New Class, not against it'. Rather than convert oneself hastily into an intellectual, it is better to recruit defecting counter-intellectuals. But how can they be identified? Well, 'if you decide to go exploring for oil, you find a competent geologist. Similarly, if you wish to make productive investments in the intellectual and educational worlds, you find competent intellectuals and scholars – "dissident" members as it were, of the New Class – to offer guidance'.[37] The project aimed explicitly at shaping a 'counter-intelligentsia', an intellectual community aligned with business interests.[38]

In addition to the places of production of ideas, the channels through which these ideas were broadcast were also of interest. Again, the paradox was that firms 'with their advertising' were sustaining 'the mass media, which today inevitably serve as a national megaphone for every egalitarian crusade'.[39] It would require little effort, for self-aware businessmen, to stop financing these 'media that serve as mouthpieces for anti-capitalist opinions' and to redirect the manna of advertising to a more complacent press. 'Business money must flow [. . .] to media which are either pro-freedom or, if not necessarily "pro-business," at least professionally capable of a fair and accurate treatment of pro-capitalist ideas, values and argument'.[40]

The speaker had warned his peers of an imminent threat. An assault was being launched by the enemies of free enterprise. 'The defense of our society [. . .] must meet the attacks themselves and repulse them.

For this the first requirement of success is to turn to the offensive. Attack may or may not be the best defense in armed warfare. In wars of ideas it always is, simply because an idea on the defensive is already half lost'.[41]

And yet, many entrepreneurs, after having listened politely to this kind of warlike exhortations, returned to hearth and home where they apparently did the complete opposite: they made rhetorical concessions en masse. In the early 1970s, the intransigent and narrow-minded attitude of both neoliberals and the theorists of anti-capitalist conspiracy of the Powell kind was countered by another, subtler approach that did not reject as a whole the adversaries' themes but rather sought, in a strategy of *taking them into account*, to respond to them by appropriating them.

They agreed on one point: there was an urgent need to rise to the challenge. But when it came to knowing how, any unity started to fall apart. How to *react*? For this was a time when fierce debates were tearing apart the dominant classes.

— 11 —

HOW TO REACT?

The traditional ruling class [. . .] may make sacrifices, and expose itself
to an uncertain future by demagogic promises.

Antonio Gramsci[1]

'Businessmen can truthfully say with Sir Winston Churchill that we
have "benefited enormously from criticism and at no point have we
suffered from any perceptible lack thereof!"'[2] With this witticism,
David Rockefeller, chairman of the board of Chase Manhattan Bank,
opened a speech in 1971 to New York advertisers on 'the role of business in an era of increasing responsibility'.

This text could be read as a breviary of the *proper use of criticism*
for the ruling classes, and some general principles extracted from it.
Faced with the protests, what should one do? And first and foremost,
how should it be seen and how should it be heard?

To start with, let me make one remark on the lexicon used. While
at that time some people referred to 'attacks' on free enterprise,
Rockefeller preferred to talk about 'criticisms'. This would give us
a first precept: to translate attacks into criticism. To treat an attack
as a criticism is already to begin the process of disarming it. The difference lies in the way one reacts to hostility. An attack is repulsed,
but a criticism can be taken into account. While an attack calls for
a counter-attack, a criticism also invites self-examination. We start
to wonder what we are learning about ourselves, what flaws the
criticism may enable us to detect. We may be prepared to recognize,
in other words, a truth in negativity, in order to draw lessons for
ourselves. For power, criticism can be an opportunity. You have to
know how to profit from it, as from everything, in fact. This is the
principle of taking advantage of criticism.

Admittedly, 'it is tempting for businessmen to react by striking back at their critics, matching them invective for invective'. But this is not the right tactic, any more than is systematic rejection. To denigrate en bloc the criticisms addressed to us would 'risk compromising our credibility when we need it the most'. Rockefeller here contrasts those who, on the one hand, tend to reduce opposition to an anti-capitalist conspiracy, without understanding that it expresses a social fact, an objective and lasting transformation of the environment in which firms operate, with those who, on the other hand, respond with the conservative reaffirmation of the existing order without seeing that this is a losing strategy.

Defending the status quo is no longer viable. One is faced with the following alternative: either to take part in the ongoing transformations, or to submit to them. 'Businessmen', he continues, 'have no choice but to respond by becoming reformers themselves, making a conscious effort to adapt the operation of the market system to our changing social, political and technological environment. The question really comes down to this: Will business leaders seize the initiative to make necessary changes and to take on new responsibilities voluntarily, or will they wait until these are thrust upon them by law?'

There is no point in resisting change; on the contrary, we should embrace movement so as to guide it. We must not stay as spectators, but climb aboard the train as it sets off and sit in the driver's seat. If Marx's dark predictions have hitherto remained a dead letter, he concludes, it is because of the 'remarkable resilience' of the business world. If we want the system to survive the crisis affecting it, it is necessary to reconnect with that kind of intelligence.[3]

By the end of the 1960s, organizations of the reformist left had taken up the managerial ideology of 'social responsibility' and turned it into the basis for campaigns of a new kind.[4] In 1969, a handful of young lawyers grouped around Ralph Nader founded the 'Project on Corporate Responsibility': 'We want corporate leaders to be accountable to all people affected by corporate decisions'. In February 1970, having bought twelve shares of General Motors, they submitted nine resolutions to the 1.3 million shareholders of the company. Their objective, they announced, was to transform the 'processes of managerial decision making to insure that the wide diversity of interest affected by a firm's decision are considered'.[5]

'We leave this meeting more determined to fulfil our social responsibility',[6] declared James Roche, CEO of General Motors, in 1970, at the closing of the shareholders' AGM. In the brochure that had been

80

distributed to the participants, one could read these words: 'General Motors is committed to solve the problem of air pollution as far as our products and plants are concerned [. . .] in several statements, our executives irrevocably committed General Motors to finding a solution to automotive emission problems at the earliest possible time'.[7] Promises, admittedly, are binding only on those to whom they are made.

On hearing such speeches, the conservatives choked. In 1971 the libertarian journalist and commentator Jeffrey St. John fulminated: 'Giants like GM have faced their growing gaggle of critics intellectually and philosophically disarmed'.[8] And he recapitulated, in dismay, the concessions made by the CEO of the Detroit automobile firm: faced with pressure from activists, had he not gone so far as to accept the appointment to the Board of Directors of a Black director, as well as the creation of a scientific committee for environmental issues? That, he lamented, was what the current response on the part of the business world had come down to: dodges, compromises and concessions.

In the same year, however, in the employers' intimate gathering place, the very elegant Executive Club of Chicago, Roche gave his confreres the key to the interpretation of his public discourse: drawing their attention to the 'serious, yet subtle, threat to our American system of free enterprise',[9] he added that 'corporate responsibility is a catchword of the adversary culture that is so evident today. [. . .] Their philosophy is antagonistic to our American ideas of private property and individual responsibility'.[10] The militant groups that had made this into their watchword were resorting to a 'tactic of divisiveness' aimed at 'trying to make America in the 1970's a society at war with itself'.[11] Still, these themes were meeting with such sympathetic echoes that they could no longer reasonably be ignored: 'we must be ready to accept change. And business today is expected to respond to the new aspirations of the society it serves. This broad public expectation must be recognized'.[12]

The tactic was clear: it involved responding to critics on their own ground, publicly endorsing the discourse of new-style social responsibility by holding your nose and dropping a few crumbs at the margin, so as to change nothing essential. Under pressure, General Motors had indeed appointed the Black priest, Leon Sullivan, to the board of directors of the company, created a vice-presidential position for environmental issues, and formed a scientific committee to study the effects of automobiles on the environment. But these were just peripheral concessions, more symbolic than substantial.

81

In the early 1970s, a wave of commercials touting corporate social responsibility invaded the US media. 'Corporations', explained one CEO, 'are constantly under attack from every quarter. [. . .] Silence by a company in the face of attacks upon its policies and practices is interpreted as an admission of guilt. Corporate advertising provides one avenue of self-defense'.[13] The slogans of these 'greenwashing' or 'fairwashing' campaigns *avant la lettre* – operations of ecological or ethical whitewashing – were eloquent: 'working to keep your trust' was the promise of the oil producer Texaco; 'we are involved', said United States Steel, reassuringly; 'there's a world of things you can do something about' was the carrot dangled in front of you by Dupont, the chemical industrialist. As for the Union Carbide group, whose name later on would remain attached to the Bhopal disaster, its toxic cloud and its thousands of victims suffocated to death in India one night in December 1984, it splashed out on dozens of pages of advertisements in the American press in 1974 to extol its commitment in favour of the 'green revolution'. Its researchers had found a slogan for it that, with hindsight, makes one wince: 'Today, something we do will touch your life'.[14]

'Few things turn my stomach more than watching those companies' television advertising, particularly that of some of the oil companies, which would have you believe that their only purpose for being is to preserve the environment'.[15] The person expressing his disgust in 1972 was none other than Milton Friedman. But what was the reason for his nausea? What repelled the neoliberal economist was not the instrumentalization of ecologist discourse by various firms, but, on the contrary, the way that the spirit of enterprise was distorted by being coated in hippie formulas. Friedman was sickened by the way that companies no longer dared, as if they were ashamed to do so, to publicly endorse the motive that drove them – maximizing profits.

Admittedly, Friedman acknowledges, 'with its widespread aversion to "capitalism", "profits", the "soulless corporation" and so on',[16] advancing in disguise is a justifiable stratagem. Pretending to serve the public interest is certainly, in this context, the most profitable way of pursuing one's selfish interests, and in doing so, management is only doing its job: 'But I really cannot blame the corporate executives for talking this nonsense. In fact, I blame them if they don't. Given the attitude of the public-at-large, one way for an enterprise to promote its profits is to profess to be socially responsible'.[17]

While, on the left, this kind of propaganda was denounced as managerial hypocrisy, Friedman was alarmed by the complete opposite. He feared that these agents would forget to be insincere, that by dint of repeating these fine phrases, they would end up believing what should be just a linguistic façade and get drunk on their own words.[18] Friedman was cynical; he wanted to save hypocrisy. His problem was not that of false speech (insofar as it was a deception for others) but of false consciousness (insofar as it was an illusion for oneself). This phenomenon worried him; we could label it hypercrisy (*hypercrisie*). The hypocrite is the one who wears a mask and who is aware of it. The hypercrite is the one who takes himself for his mask, the one in whom the consciousness of duplicity has vanished. By forgetting itself, hypocrisy switches into hypercrisy, a sort of amnesic profession of faith 'by which a man deceives himself by deceiving others, without having any intention to deceive them'.[19] As Friedman stated, regretfully, 'businessmen often regard themselves as philosophers. They go around in their private capacity talking the same kind of errant nonsense that it may be profitable for them to talk in their business life'.[20] There's the rub: when they stop taking things into consideration, and start to believe in their heart of hearts what they relate in public. But if managers swapped the true spirit of capitalism for this logorrhea of 'responsible' words, they would completely lose their bearings.

This danger is 'ethical' in the sense that it is the very preservation of the capitalist ethos which is thus threatened. But the danger is also political. Will it be possible to continue for any length of time to defend capitalism by non-capitalist values? Is the contradiction tenable?

Perhaps the public, so encouraged by advertising that they believe that the purpose of companies was to serve society, would 'increasingly demand that business perform in accordance with the new business ethic, enunciated not merely by social reformers, but by business leaders themselves'.[21] Thus would start a cycle of politicization of business, fuelled by the rhetorical concessions of its own leaders.

The rage of the neoliberals was all the more intense as they had continued (in the previous phase, while everything was still quiet) to warn against the dangers of this kind of language. When, in the early 1970s, they saw that a whole series of militant movements had seized on the old managerialist themes and turned them against business leaders, they saw their fears being confirmed.

It may be that the adoption of the discourse of social responsibility 'may have started as a purely defensive maneuver', a means to 'maximize the life of capitalism by cutting the grass under the feet of the critics',[22] admitted Levitt, but this is a risky tactic because, as soon as the businessman admits that the fundamental function of business is to 'serve the public', then the critic 'quickly pounces on this admission with unconcealed relish – "Then why *don't* you serve?" But the fact is, no matter how much business "serves," it will never be enough for its critics'.[23] This inevitable failure would inevitably mean that public opinion preferred, to the managers' avowed but impotent goodwill, more restrictive methods – starting with public regulation, for which the way was thus being paved. Hayek predicted the same developments: 'in the long run the effect is bound to be increased control of corporations by the power of the state'.[24]

Those who use the discourse of social responsibility 'to avoid severe government regulation', says Manne in similar vein, claim that 'the very survival of capitalism depends on the adoption of a socially responsible attitude by corporations'.[25] According to them, 'if by these actions the public can be made to believe that business is already operating in a socially responsible way, the political threat may be defused or moderated at a relatively low cost. Better yet, the situation may be turned to positive business advantage if the situation can be used to gain 'self-regulation' for the industry'.[26] This, fundamentally, was the wager of a section of the employers. According to Manne, this strategy was doomed to failure.

But, then, what was to be done? As Friedman quipped, 'it would be inconsistent of me to call on corporate executives to refrain from this hypocritical window-dressing because it harms the foundations of a free society. That would be to call on them to exercise a "social responsibility"!'[27] Beyond the jocular tone, this self-deprecation expresses a fundamental aporia, namely the theoretical inability of the neoliberal economic doctrine to think *within its own framework* of the possibility of collective action, of a coordinated mobilization of the ruling classes to defend their interests.[28] It predicts – wrongly – that this will prove impossible. And yet this was what they now absolutely needed to be able to think.

If business is in trouble politically, said Jeffrey St. John in 1971, this is 'because intellectual bromides have been a substitute for a sound intellectual exposition of its point of view'.[29] But 'business civilization is doomed if it is unable to consistently and intellectually explain its function. [. . .] What men do not understand they will not justify. What they cannot justify they will not defend. And what they will not defend they cannot maintain'. If the process of justification is of strategic importance, this is not only for others, but also for oneself. It is not a matter of propaganda alone, but also of self-conviction. And for that, St. John says in a recursive loop without ever providing this formula with the slightest bit of conceptual content, it is necessary to have a *philosophy*, because if we give in to the groups of radicals, it will be 'for lack of such a philosophy'. But where will we find it?

In 1970, Manne showed where to begin, and what needed to be destroyed in order to re-erect an apologetic discourse on new foundations. 'The most important intellectual source of current attacks on big business is Berle and Means' classic'.[30] As the political vulnerability of business had theoretical roots, it had to be remedied by theoretical means. For those who saw this as a mortal danger, any questions about its foundations, its power and its aims had to be made intellectually inexpressible.

— 12 —

THE CORPORATION DOES
NOT EXIST

Both historically and analytically, the corporation seems to be (. . .) a
power nexus.

Lee Loevinger[1]

Nexus: embrace, hug, knot, link [. . .] to contract
an engagement [. . .] to fall into servitude.[2]

The man who has been nicknamed the 'godfather of American neoconservatism', Irving Kristol, was still lamenting this fact in 1975: 'The
trouble with the large corporation today is that it does not possess a
clear theoretical – i.e., ideological – legitimacy within the framework
of liberal capitalism itself. [. . .] By what right does the self-perpetuating oligarchy that constitutes "management" exercise its powers? On
what principles does it do so? To these essentially political questions
management can only respond with the weak economic answer'.[3]
This represented the very alarming realization that power lacked a
theory, was intellectually deprived and, therefore, politically exposed.
Soviet analysts who were then carefully scrutinizing American intellectual life noted with interest Kristol's ponderings, while noting soberly
that he was clearly 'unable to propose any constructive solution for
this particular problem'.[4] As Stuart Hall remarked, using some of
Gramsci's terms, when 'the crisis is deep – "organic" (. . .) [p]olitical
and ideological work is required to disarticulate old formations, and
to rework their elements into new configurations'.[5] But this takes time.
In addition, things had been slow to kick off in this particular case.
'The attacks on large corporations', noted Manne, 'both popular and
intellectual, came long before there was a defense'.[6] As a result, at the
beginning of the 1970s, there was still not 'a single scholarly theory
defending the American corporate system'.[7]

86

But things were changing, and quickly. It is true that the extent of protest had made the task pressing. Neoclassical economists were going all out, in those years, to develop new theories of business – a 'fascinating field', at last, suggested Manne in 1979, and 'welcome news for a business community long concerned about anti-business attitudes and its own ability to mount a popular defense'.[8]

Economists are now familiar with these 'new theories of the firm'. Students learn them in class and from textbooks, with their endless procession of scholastic nitpicking – but the historical context and the policy that presided over their development are often left out. Thus, doctrines are presented as neutral even though their authors themselves explicitly conceived them as intellectual weapons for the defence of a contested capitalism. This is regrettable; such an omission makes it impossible to grasp the political stakes behind these theories, or their fundamental meaning.

'Can the corporation survive?' This was the question raised in 1978 by the future Nobel Prize winner Michael Jensen and his mentor William Meckling. They would not bet on it – not, in any case, if current trends continued. 'The corporate executive's power [. . .] is becoming more constrained every day'.[9] The CEO had once been so free, but was now hindered by a mass of new government regulations. Under the assaults of ecologists, several toxic products, including DDT, had been banned – in defiance of the freedom of trade. In response to the activism of various 'pressure groups', anti-racist and feminist organizations, measures of positive discrimination had been imposed on employers – in defiance of the freedom to hire. By thoughtlessly caving into these demands, 'government is destroying the system of contract rights [. . .]' on which depends the very existence of the system of 'free enterprise'[10] – a 'highly vulnerable organizational form',[11] they emphasized. At the rate things were going, 'even if they survive in some form the larger corporations as we know them are destined to be destroyed. Indeed in a few industries we believe their demise is imminent! [. . .] Some firms will simply go out of business [. . .] Other firms will take different organizational forms. Some will be nationalized, some will become labor managed'.[12]

But while this 'attack on corporations'[13] was being conducted in the social and political field, it was based on two great conceptual premises: the 'separation of ownership from control' on the one hand, and 'corporate social responsibility' on the other. These were, in the theoretical field, the two big targets that needed to be shot down. If the opponent was scoring points, this was, inter alia, because the public debate had been riddled with 'semantic ambushes'.[14] The ground thus needed to be cleared of mines, in a patient effort of reconceptualization that should not be disdained as a mere empty 'semantic quibbling'.[15] Defining words is a political act. Whoever fixes their meaning gains a strategic asset.

In order to elaborate the theory of the firm that was so cruelly lacking, at the end of the 1960s an article was unearthed that had been published in 1937 by the economist Ronald Coase. He used an evocative metaphor borrowed from a British author: in relation to the market, businesses are 'islands of conscious power in this ocean of unconscious co-operation, like lumps of butter coagulating in a pail of buttermilk'.[16] The firm, theoretically, is a fat – a fat that floats.

Neoclassical economics thereby rediscovered the existence of businesses, those amazing entities. Up until then, they had been schematically conceived of as individual economic agents, as points linked together by transactions, in short as black boxes: their entrances and exits were noted, but not much interest was shown for what might be going on inside them. As soon as you opened the box, one thing was all too apparent: a firm is not a market. In it, other methods of coordination are in force. 'If a workman moves from department Y to department X, he does not go because of a change in relative prices, but because he is ordered to do so'.[17] A company does not work internally by following price mechanisms, in a form of unconscious coordination, but by following commands, by being consciously ordered; it was directed not by exchange, but by hierarchy, not automatically, but by authority, not by the market, but by the plan.

From the neoclassical point of view, this was a surprise, but also a puzzle: even though the market was generally considered to be the only efficient mode of coordination, how were you to explain that such heretical forms could even exist? It was necessary to provide a reason for the firm. To put it in Leibnizian terms: why was there a firm rather than nothing at all? Or rather, more precisely, why was there private economic authority rather than just a pure market?

Coase proposed an explanation that had the advantage of preserving the coherence of the orthodox theory: 'The main reason why it is profitable to establish a firm would seem to be that there is a cost of using the price mechanism'.[18] 'In order to carry out a market transaction it is necessary to discover who it is that one wishes to deal with, to inform people that one wishes to deal and on what terms, to conduct negotiations leading up to a bargain, to draw up the contract, [. . .] and so on. These operations are often extremely costly'.[19] These are the costs, the transaction costs, which are avoided when the activity is coordinated within a firm: 'forming an organization and allowing some authority (an "entrepreneur") to direct the resources, certain marketing costs are saved'.[20] So people discovered that, in the functioning of the capitalist economy, there were two prodigies instead of one: besides the invisible hand of the market, there was the visible hand of corporate management.[21]

What was the basis of the corporation's own mode of coordination, that which was not available to the market? On 'fiat', replied Coase – that is to say on authoritarian decision, hierarchical command – a power relationship irreducible to market relationships, a discretionary power exercised in a relation of subordination of the 'master/servant' type.[22]

But while neoclassical economists who reused this text in the years 1960–70 for the purposes of their theoretical updating were seduced by the concept of transaction costs, a notion they found very fruitful, they were equally embarrassed by this second aspect – by this, let us say, somewhat overly rough and ready shaping of the employers' power. In the political context we have just sketched out, this reluctance can mainly be understood by taking into account tactical considerations. Recognizing so openly that capitalist enterprise is structured by an authoritarian power relationship would be to make life too easy for critics and those who preferred self-management – the very same critics who needed to be disarmed. In that period, neo-Marxist economists fully realized this. When, prompted by these hostile re-elaborations, they in turn re-read Coase's article, they saw right away that they could turn it to their own advantage, eagerly pointing out, not without a certain malice and providing chapter and verse in support, that, as a result, 'neo-classical economic theory recognizes that the capitalist enterprises exists *precisely* as a system of authority within a system of markets'.[23]

So these new theories of the firm were also going to need, not just to offer an external rebuttal, but to struggle with a conceptual obstacle within their own way of thinking. They would need to find a way to renew Coase's problematic while amputating it from his unfortunate confession. This would be a delicate operation. The same power that they sought to perpetuate in practice would need, for this very purpose, to be denied in theory. This involved a certain amount of mental gymnastics, albeit of a kind quite common in everyday life, since it involved practising denial: perpetuating actions for which you are criticized by claiming that they do not exist.

So when Armen Alchian and Harold Demsetz wrote the article

that, in 1972, would relaunch neoclassical reflection on the theory of the firm, their aim, from the very first paragraphs, was to challenge Coase even if this meant flying in the face of common experience; they questioned the idea that business was characterized by a 'power to settle issues by fiat, by authority, or by disciplinary action superior to that available in the conventional market'. This, they said, was a 'delusion'.[24]

The power that your boss exercises over you was, in their view, no different from the 'power' you have over your grocer: admittedly, your boss can fire you, but cannot you, too, 'fire your grocer' by not buying from him?[25] That will not make him unemployed, you might retort, but that is not the point. For them, this wobbly analogy was enough to show that a contract of employment is absolutely of the same nature as any other commercial transaction, and that no *specific* form of power is exercised in enterprise.[26]

They thus went completely against the previous consensus. Until the early 1970s, in fact, it was widely recognized that not only did business exist, but that it existed as a 'managerial structure of power' – as a 'nexus of power', some even dared to say. Their theory of the firm was an attempt to destroy this conception, which admittedly came with the annoying inconvenience that it set power relations in the centre of the picture.

Managerialism had made the fatal mistake of politicizing the theory of the firm. The first task was to depoliticize it, and for that, they would strive to *de-realize* it. In place of a 'private government', there would be nothing of the kind, not even an institution, not even an entity. Long before Margaret Thatcher declared 'There is no such thing as society',[27] some people had already applied this formula to the corporation. They lavished huge amounts of ingenuity on propping up this counter-intuitive thesis.

In retrospect, in 1983, Michael Jensen believed that the great merit of his work from the previous decade was that 'foundations are being put in place for a revolution in the science of organizations'.[28] This new science was still in its infancy, but soon, he promised, would come the sturdy stage of maturity. The seminal article on the 'theory of the firm' that he had co-authored with Meckling in 1976 in the *Journal of Financial Economics* currently occupies third place on the metric podium of the most cited contemporary references in economics.[29] In this text, they made an ontological decision heavy with implications. What is a firm as a firm? 'One form of legal fiction which serves as a nexus for contracting relationships'.[30] Not very clear. What does this mean? Let us take another look.

1) The firm is a legal fiction, that is to say an 'artificial construct under the law which allows certain organizations to be treated as individuals'.[31] A firm can be considered as owning, for example, a building. We can file a complaint against it. In short, we can treat it as a legal person although it is not a human individual. Jensen and Meckling interpret this phenomenon in a nominalist fashion: under the name 'firm', a fictitious person, there is nothing real except the agents of which it is composed.

2) The firm serves as a nexus, that is to say, in Latin, as a 'connection, tie, or link between individuals of a group'.[32] When people enter a contract with it, by doing so, say Jensen and Meckling, they are actually entering relationships with each other. The firm is therefore conceived as a great interweaving of contracts connecting individuals to each other by or under the fiction of a legal entity.

Thus conceived, the firm is no longer a real entity, just the misleading name given to a set of 'contractual relationships', by which we do not necessarily have to understand explicit contracts, but any 'voluntary exchange'.[33] While the criterion of authority proposed by Coase could set out the limits of the firm (it stops where managerial authority ceases to prevail), it is equally true that the criterion of contractual relationship – understood, moreover, as synonymous with transaction in general – erases any demarcation. The nexus-firm encompasses not only employees but also suppliers, creditors, shareholders and consumers as they also play a part to varying degrees in this great interweaving. So this definition also casts uncertainty over the question of belonging to the firm (who is a member? who is not?) and over the question of its borders (when are you inside it? when are you outside it?).

We may criticize the elasticity of the definition, but this defect is deliberate. Rather than a process of definition, we are here dealing with an operation of *indefinition*, which dissolves its object rather than making it more specific. These economists had initially sought to open the 'black box' of the firm. They did not just lift its lid: they also blew up its walls. Finally, all that was left was the blurred image of a continuous interweaving of relationships. And the box no longer exists. This enabled them to conclude, at the polar opposite to Coase, that business is merely a 'pure creature of the market'.[34] The goal was to *reprivatize* the firm, conceptually[35] – the very same firm that managerialists described as 'quasi-public'.

Therefore, ultimately, any criticism of corporations was no longer possible – as there were no real corporations, just a fiction. The protesters were victims of a mirage. They were fighting shadows. You criticized the corporations, you made demands on it, you wanted to question its existence, but all this presupposed that it actually existed as an entity to be questioned; but this was absolutely not the case. The new theorists of the firm were conjurers. They practised sleight of hand, the art of spiriting objects away from under the spectators' very eyes.

From their philosophical readings, Jensen and Meckling had taken the idea that 'the definitions are what is most important, and what most deserves the reader's prolonged attention'.[36] This is a wise precept. Let us apply it to their own definitions.

On analysing them, one realizes that these authors are playing on an ambiguity between two close but different formulations. In the first formulation, employees, suppliers and customers enter into 'unilateral contracts with the legal entity that serves as the contracting nexus'.[37] It is like the feathery ball of a dandelion: the firm as nexus is the equivalent of the white base, round and convex, in the form of colander, where the seeds are stuck through which the egrets each relate individually to the stem without being directly connected to each other.

In the second formulation, still taken from Jensen: the firm is 'the nexus of a set of contracting relationships among individuals'[38] – which Fischel translates as follows: 'we often speak of the corporation as a "nexus of contracts" [. . .] This reference, too, is shorthand for the complex arrangements of many sorts that those who associate voluntarily in the corporation will work out among themselves'.[39] This other definition, which seems to be equivalent to the first only if you read it too quickly, says something different: the firm is no longer simply defined as this common bond with which each unilaterally enters into a contract, but as the collective name of a set of multilateral relations between agents. It is as if the dandelion's egrets were starting to connect to each other, the *analogon* of the firm being then the whole ball of down.

However, strictly speaking, these two conceptions exclude one another: if indeed the firm is defined as a contracting entity, a legal artefact used to make contracts, it must by definition remain distinct from the contracts concluded by means of it, which is exactly what is denied by the second formulation which identifies it instead with all the contracts it serves to establish. The absurdity becomes obvious when Jensen writes: 'independent individuals coordinate their actions through contracts with the legal fiction that serves as the firm's nexus' – the firm that is itself defined as a nexus,[40] which amounts to saying that the legal fiction serves as a nexus for a nexus, or that the firm serves as a nexus for the firm. By failing to make conceptually necessary distinctions, this theory inevitably falls, as Eisenberg has shown, into a logical circle: 'Surely the corporation cannot consist of all the reciprocal arrangements that are linked to the corporation, because that would make the nexus-of-contracts conception circular: It would be like saying that a zebra is a nexus of stripes linked to a zebra'.[41] In short, the firm is a tangle of knots.

To avoid falling into such confusion, they should – even though this would have made the sleight of hand impossible – have started by recalling the elementary distinction between the notion of the *corporation* (*entreprise*) as an *organization* (the flesh-and-blood collective that works there) and the concept of the *society* (*société*) as a legal form (that paper being with which the law associates certain capacities and obligations).[42]

When you sign your employment contract, with whom do you enter into a contract? Even if he signs the document, you do not do so with your CEO as a private person. Through him, *by his hand*, it is with the society as a subject in law that you are entering into contract. You contract with the *society*, but not with the corporation as an organization, not with the other employees, who also have a contract with this same third party. Nor do you enter into a contract with the customers, suppliers or creditors, even though they too are on their side bound by contract with the society with which you are contracting. Jensen and Meckling can only suggest the opposite idea because they are playing on a misunderstanding between *society* and *corporation*. If indeed, thanks to their sleight of hand, you confuse these, then you will imagine that when you contract with the society, a legal being, you are doing so with the corporation, understood as a set of social relations.

Eliminating this crucial difference allows Jensen and Meckling to surreptitiously make a set of category errors that, by domino effect, entails the conclusion, as absurd as it is opportune, that the firm *as a social organization is merely a legal fiction*,[43] and therefore, they decide, a being without the least real consistency – which is doubly false. On the one hand, the corporation as an organization is not reducible to the legal entity that serves it as both a framework and an instrument: a corporation cannot be reduced to the corresponding society any more than a married couple can be reduced to its marriage contract or a sports team to the statutes of its club – the two are linked without being the same. On the other hand, the fact that a *society* is a legal fiction certainly means that it is an artificial being, a creature of law, but – precisely because of this – it still has a reality, a specific mode of existence which comes with very concrete effects. The law may well be an artifice, but it is no less effective.

These new theories of the firm, by resorting to such sophisms, have thus changed their object 'from a leviathan to a paper tiger', except that, paradoxically, these two descriptions, far from excluding each other, are true at the same time: as Gerald Davis puts it, 'corporations are mere legal fictions with "no body to kick, no soul to damn," as Baron Thurlow put it. They are also social facts [. . .]. They may not *have* a body, but their very name comes from the Latin word for body, *corpus*. And corporations may not have a soul, but their participants – and sometimes the law – expect them to act as if they do'.[44]

Jensen, in an article that to some extent constitutes his own *Discourse on Method*, insists on this: in his eyes, the virtue of a definition is above all to be 'productive'.[45] It is especially valuable insofar as it produces useful effects. But what exactly are these effects in this case?

'The nexus of contracts view of organizations also helps to dispel the tendency to treat organizations as if they were persons',[46] say Jensen and Meckling. 'The corporation is not an individual. It does not feel; it does not choose'.[47] What they here present as an important theoretical asset is in reality nothing more than a trivial critique of anthropomorphism, which has no need of the 'theory of the nexus' to be stated, and also rests, by the way, on a conceptual confusion that an authentically pragmatic approach would have cleared up. As the philosopher John Dewey had already warned us in the 1920s: 'the doctrine of "fictitious" personality has been employed, under the influence of the "individualistic" philosophy [. . .] in order to deny that there is any social reality at all back of or in corporate action'.[48]

The main purpose of this redefinition, insisted Jensen and Meckling, was of a political nature: 'Viewing the firm as the nexus of a set of contracting relationships among individuals [. . .] serves to make it clear that the personalization of the firm implied by asking questions such as "what should be the objective function of the firm?" or "does the firm have a social responsibility?" is seriously misleading'.[49] It was about de-realizing and depoliticizing the firm in order to rule out the huge number of critiques of these organizations and those who ran them. The great advantage of the contractualist approach, as noted by two other leading figures of this approach, Frank Easterbrook and Daniel Fischel, 'removes from the field of interesting questions one that has plagued many writers: what is the goal of the corporation? Is it profit (and for whom)? Social welfare more broadly defined? [. . .] Our response to such questions is: "who cares?"'[50]

Reactionaries of all tendencies who in those years engaged in an intense activity of intellectual re-development kept on repeating: you have to have a theory. Yes, but why? The obvious answer, the one most frequently given, albeit inadequate, was formulated in terms of justification. A bare domination was not enough. It needed lawyers to plead on its behalf.[51]

But there was another aspect, more strategic, more offensive. The following anecdote bears witness: a young man, excited by his reading of *The Road to Serfdom*, went to find Hayek in the late 1940s to tell him he was going to take up politics. To which the master apparently replied: 'No you're not! Society's course will be changed only by a change in ideas. First you must reach the intellectuals, the teachers and writers, with reasoned argument. It will be their influence on society which will prevail, and the politicians will follow'.[52]

As for specific theories of the firm as a nexus, they provided a partial answer to the problem posed by Kristol, who was worried that there was a gap when it came to this issue; but their technicality, their jargon, their stylistic aridity, and, even more, their ethical dryness made them unfit to actually serve as a popular defence.

Their very first target was the academic field. They sought to reconquer it. The reconfiguration of scholarly modes of interrogation of economics had been accompanied since the 1970s by tireless efforts to evict, discursively and institutionally, the 'heterodox'; to ensure control of what could be formulated intellectually; to exclude the opponent from the academically sanctioned capacity to 'tell the truth'.

These 'new theories of the firm' were new only in comparison with the old consensus that they were working to eradicate. It was an attempt – historically successful – to bring about the intellectual liquidation of the previous vision, for the purposes of a political counter-offensive. The philosophical operation was radical in that it touched on the very definition of the firm. Here, the fight was on ontological ground, repudiating just about all previous managerialist assumptions. Where power and authority relationships had been admitted, there were now only contracts and problems of agency. Instead of a truly existing organization, there was now only a fiction covering a network of exchange relations. This was a bold manoeuvre, but it also opened the door, by its very reformulations, to new difficulties.

— 13 —

POLICE THEORIES OF THE FIRM

Who 'owns' this new leviathan? Who governs it – and by what right, and according to what principles?

Irving Kristol[1]

How is the 'primacy of shareholder value' to be justified? To this question, in the early 1970s, some stubbornly sought to answer in accordance with outdated schemes, with a philosophy of personal private property, as if nothing, or hardly anything, had changed since Locke. 'In answer to [such] questions [as] "Who 'owns' this leviathan?"' wrote Robert Hessen, a researcher at the Hoover Institution, '[we maintain] that the shareholders own it, the officers make major decisions without consulting the owners, and [. . .] this relationship is perfectly unobjectionable because it rests upon the principles of [. . .] contractual authorization'.[2] Absolutism had also, in its day, made the mistake of believing that it was enough to say 'because such is our good pleasure' to stay in power. This defence was a little laconic, and besides, it was based on a huge counter-truth. Contrary to received ideas, indeed, the shareholders *are not* 'owners of the corporation'.

When I own something, what do I have a right to? This good which is mine, I can use it as I wish, including, if I so desire, destroying it; I can exclude others from its use; I can lend it, rent it, or sell it; I can mortgage it and it can eventually be used to repay my debts if I am insolvent.[3] This is the *bundle of rights* conventionally covered by the category of private property inherited from Roman law.

Does a shareholder have such rights in relation to the assets of the company he owns shares in? No. Having bought Apple shares does not give me the right to go and help myself for free to the electronic gadgets in the Apple stores.[4] But what, then, do shareholders actually own? As their name suggests, merely shares, securities issued by the company, which give them the right to vote at the general meeting and *possibly* receive dividends.[5] A shareholder owns a title deed that he can resell, but not the least fraction of the company's buildings, machinery or stock.

But then, if the shareholders do not own the assets of the company, who does? 'No one [. . .], shareholders no more than anyone else, by the way'.[6] One of the essential features of the company-form, indeed, is 'that it owns most of the productive assets';[7] 'corporations are independent legal entities that own themselves'.[8]

Shareholders do not own the company, but this is no tragedy as far as they are concerned; quite the opposite, in fact, as it is very beneficial for them not to do so. The invention of the shareholder company has historically made it possible to drastically reduce the risks attached to traditional private property. Among these benefits is *limited liability*. Previously, in a partnership, each member was co-responsible for the debts of the shared business. There is nothing of this kind in a joint stock company. If the company has debts, they are *its* debts: nobody will draw on the personal fortune of the shareholders to repay the creditors. If the company makes a profit, on the other hand, this has every chance of becoming *their* profit, falling into their wallets in the form of dividends. This asymmetry of risk is a big incentive: there is no limit to what you can pocket without ever losing more than your initial stake. It is this kind of (highly inventive) reorganization of the rights of ownership that explains the craze for shareholding, its extraordinary development from the middle of the nineteenth century onwards, and the birth of giant corporations, concentrating capital on a scale hitherto unknown, and indeed nigh impossible within previous forms of property.[9]

Shareholder ownership has little to do with the private ownership of the means of production as conceived in the first half of the nineteenth century. But people long continued to think of it in accordance with those outdated categories.[10] Some 'defenders of free enterprise', having become aware of this hiatus, were worried: 'it has, for lack of a new rationale, retained the old ideology – and finds itself trapped by it'.[11] If one was to escape, it was pointless to restate the old, largely outdated justification: it was necessary to invent another.

When it came to new theories of the firm, Eugene Fama explicitly took a big step in 1980, dismissing a category that had run out of steam: 'In this "nexus of contracts" perspective, ownership of the firm is an irrelevant concept'.[12] To the question 'who owns this leviathan?', the theory of the nexus eventually replied: there is no leviathan. There are only contracts, a 'set of contracts among factors of production',[13] relations which constitute no separate entity, nothing that can be possessed like a thing.

Fama thus took note – but *only partly* – of the transformation. For while he admitted that a shareholder company is the property of nobody, he failed to take note of the fact that a company owns itself and wrongly inferred that all the factors of production that it brings each remain 'owned by somebody'.[14] Thus, rather than fully recognizing the originality of the shareholder form, the very one which had historically allowed its growth – the fact that it is related, as Marx wrote, to 'the overtaking of capital as private property within the limits of the capitalist mode of production itself'[15] – he anachronistically drew on an outdated conception of the company as an association of proprietary subjects.

Among the factors of production, there is capital. The sale of shares in the primary market has provided an 'amount of initial money that was used to buy capital and technology'; Fama felt he could conclude from this that the shareholders own the 'capital and technology'.[16] In other words, he freed himself from the illusion that shareholders 'own the business' only to replace this illusion with another, namely that they owned its *capital* – amalgamating under this word the *assets* (*actifs*) of which only the company is the owner and the *shares* (*actions*) which shareholders possess.[17]

Besides capital, there is labour. But employees, he claims, are also bearers of a certain type of 'capital': they 'rent a substantial lump of wealth – their human capital – to the firm'.[18] This metaphorical extension of the term 'capital' played a role in the attempted moral refoundation of shareholder capitalism on the basis of a new form of possessive individualism. In this confusing presentation, which denies the relations between classes, labour is no longer the 'other' of capital, just a form of capital like any another. Whether this capital be human or financial, we are all its bearers, all capitalists, in short. This rhetoric no longer specifically sets out to justify the privileges of property owners as opposed to non-owners, but rather to put forward the interests of the 'bearers of capital', acting as if all of us were included in this category – even when the said 'capital' is reduced, more or less, to your body.

Except that there was a problem, a significant one: if indeed the firm is this nexus of contracts, this entanglement of horizontal relations whose praises are sung to us, what, yet again, justifies the pre-eminence of shareholding interests? Why should the shareholder, one contributor among so many, be any different? It is far from clear. 'Since the enterprise is considered as a nexus of contracts, notably contracts with the different suppliers of inputs, there is, *a priori*, no reason to attribute preferential treatment to the shareholders [. . .]. This appears to strip all legitimacy from the central hypothesis of agency theory, [. . .] [according to which] the managers are the agents of the shareholders alone'.[19] What the theory of the nexus gained on the one hand, it apparently lost on the other: by levelling out everyone's positions, it undermined the foundations of the primacy accorded to some.

Why should there be a 'central agent' who collects the initial stake? This is the stubborn question that will always have to be faced by those who seek to 'legitimize the existence of a profit-based social organization'.[20]

In their 1972 article, Alchian and Demsetz formulated a 'theory of shirking' that would serve as a basis for the general argument. In any labour collective, they stated, there would inevitably be shirkers. Some would shirk their tasks, unburdening their work onto others, thus pocketing the fruits of the common labour without having duly contributed to them. To eradicate this kind of behaviour, they continued, these shirkers must first be identified; this involves an entire inspection, which itself comes with a cost. Hence this question: how to reduce these costs of detection? One good way would be for a member of the team, specializing in this task, to spend his time watching his former comrades.[21] Yes, but what was to ensure that he in turn did not turn out to be a shirker, merely pretending to keep a zealous watch on the others while in fact turning a blind eye? An old question arose: 'But who will supervise the supervisor'?[22] The neoliberals thought of Juvenal, not without reversing the terms of the initial problem: while the classic formula pointed to the threat of an abuse of power on the part of a controller who himself evaded control, it was the opposite risk that was now feared: the risk that the supervisor would not watch closely enough, that he too would start to skimp on his work. So how would they be able, not to limit his power of supervision, but to maximize it, to impel this agent to spy as diligently as possible on the least little deed of the team members?

Answer: with money. The solution which the team was rationally going to adopt, Alchian and Demsetz tell us, would be to pay the supervisor, in exchange for his faithful and true services, the residue of the profits generated by the activity of all of them, after deduction of wages, operating expenses and other production costs. The chief supervisor, the recipient of the remaining share, would therefore have the status of 'residual claimant'.[23] His income, his personal gain, would depend on the total profit generated by the team, so it would be in his personal interest to discipline that team to make it as profitable as possible.[24]

But he would still need to have the means to do so, which implied that he could at his discretion hand out rewards and penalties.[25] If it was essential that the supervisor be endowed with such powers, including, in the first place, power of dismissal, as another author recommending this approach suggested, it was because such a character must always be able to threaten, if he so wishes, 'the workers with a divine terror'.[26] Hence this definition: the firm, as Alchian and Demsetz conclude, must be conceived as 'the particular policing device utilized when joint team production is present'.[27] One could not put it better.

Instead of the self-managing theories that flourished at the time, therefore, they recommended *a police theory of the firm*. The presupposition behind this rational reconstruction was that a team could not cooperate effectively without a chief supervisor, and that he himself could not fully play his role without appropriating a share of the profits. Here we have a police genealogy of the capitalist business, which basically says this: any team needs a cop, prison warden or foreman, and to fulfil his task effectively, he must have the right to take payment in kind.

So here is the little fairy story, the Idiot's Guide to the birth of the boss. Alchian and Demsetz reverse the old logic, that of the employer-based justification of authority. Control no longer derives from the right of ownership; on the contrary, it is appropriation that is presented as arising from the requisites of control. From then on, the appropriation of profits appears as a process guaranteeing the zeal of the central agent by an incentive mechanism. It is a simple matter of governance.[28]

The reinterpretation put forward by these two authors, however, is less based on historical truths than on hypothetical and contingent arguments. Rather than this imaginary account of the origin of the firm, we can put forward another genealogy, just as fictitious, but more likely. Here it is: within the original team, one shirker who is smarter than others ponders the matter and realizes that he could do even less work. Instead of just discharging part of the effort on his teammates, could he not just stop participating in productive tasks altogether? He addresses his team mates, who are rough and ready men, easy to persuade, resorting to an equivalent of the language of Alchian and Demsetz, and succeeds in bringing them round to his own aim: rising above the team and personally pocketing, on the pretext of carrying out indispensable functions of surveillance, a large part of the common benefits.

Under the guise of novelty, this way of presenting the appropriation of profit as the fair reward for supervising labour was actually re-using certain very old apologies for domination, a trope that Marx had long ago mocked by quoting an American defender of slavery who considered it perfectly reasonable that the 'Negro' should be compelled to pay by his labour 'just compensation for the labour and talent employed in governing him and rendering him useful to himself and to the society'. 'Now,' continues Marx, 'the wage-labourer, like the slave, must have a master who puts him to work and rules over him. And assuming the existence of this relationship of lordship and servitude, it is quite proper to compel the wage-labourer to produce his own wages and also the wages of supervision, as compensation for the labour of ruling and supervising him.'[29] The common postulate here is the basic heteronomy of workers, who are known by nature to be incapable of conducting their productive activities by themselves. Hence the conclusion: the need for a master, and the merits of his profit-grabbing.

This genealogy of employers' power, however, conceals an essential dimension of this same activity. Our economists act as if surveillance existed solely in order to flush out the 'shirkers'. But this is to forget that this police apparatus is very useful in at least one other way, about which Marx was less modest: 'this supervision work necessarily arises in all modes of production based on the antithesis between the labourer, as the direct producer, and the owner of the means of production.'[30]

The paradox is also that these economists put forward an apology for hierarchical supervision in the name of economic efficiency at the very same time as, in the real world of American enterprise, many people (including, as we have seen, a good number of management theorists) concurred in diagnosing a crisis in the disciplinary control of labour, its costs, its counter-ends and its inefficiency.

Despite its weaknesses, the arguments put forward by Alchian and Demsetz also served, when moved up a level, to legitimize the position of the shareholders. If the latter were justified in receiving dividends, it was no longer as 'owners of the firm', they now said, but as 'residual suitors'. As they came last, after the other 'assignees' had been served, their balance might well be rather insignificant once the workers had been paid their wages, the suppliers had been paid for the raw materials, and the creditors' bills had been settled, etc. If profits were small, they thus risked pocketing less than hoped, or nothing at all. It was precisely this uncertainty, these economists claimed, which meant that these 'residual risk bearers' were the best guarantors of managerial 'efficiency'.[31]

This marked the emergence of the theme of risk – one that would, by renovating traditional possessive individualism, provide one of the key discourses of legitimation of contemporary shareholder capitalism. If the shareholder has to be well rewarded, it is as a 'risk bearer'. But what risk, exactly? We have already indicated that the shareholder form, unlike the current myth of the 'risk-averse' investor, was, in fact, historically constituted as a very attractive type of *risk limitation* related to speculative investment. To give a clearer sense of the tremendous inversion of reality that comes from contemporary ideology, it will be useful to recall the reception given in the nineteenth century to the then new notion of the 'limited liability' of the shareholders. This privilege struck some eyewitnesses, whose ethos was still marked by a traditional ethics of ownership, as a real scandal. In every civilized nation, as one British lawyer indignantly pointed out in 1856, 'to pay debts, perform contracts, and make reparation for wrongs' is a 'moral obligation' imposed by the law; but 'limited liability' allowed 'a man to avail himself of his agent's acts if advantageous to him, and not to be responsible for them if they should be disadvantageous; to speculate for profits without being liable for losses'.[32]

As for the portrait of the shareholder as an 'investor', this too rests largely on an abuse of language. As Berle remarked, correcting Manne on this point:

> When I buy AT&T or General Motors, I do not remotely 'invest in' either concern. I have bought from Nym, who bought from Bardolph, who bought from Pistol, who bought through ten thousand predecessors in title from Falstaff, who got the stock when originally issued. Let us assume Falstaff was a genuine investor – that he bought the stock directly from the corporation, [. . .] This contribution, the only real 'investment' in the chain, was probably an infinitesimal fraction of the price I paid to Nym. [. . .] By folklore habit we say the buyer of stock of AT&T or General Motors has "invested in" these companies; but this is pure fiction.[33]

By buying back shares on the secondary market, the shareholder provides no new funds for the company. Trying to make out that such a character *is investing* in the company or is a 'provider of capital' while his actions are limited to depositing money on a title deed and drawing his money from the society is a pure sophism.

The basic argument, however, was that the shareholder's reward stimulated productive efficiency. The profit-grabbing that these new 'apologies for the rentier' had ceased to justify as an expression of the owners' natural right was something they now found a different way of justifying – as an indispensable spur to efficient management: 'Producing outputs at lower cost is in the interests of residual claimants because it increases net cash flows, but lower costs also contribute to survival by allowing products to be delivered at lower prices'.[34] So it was a win-win situation. Yielding to the interests of shareholders would not be beneficial only for them, but also for 'the company itself', which was encouraged to increase its competitiveness by cutting back costs. But at whose expense? We know the answer all too well. 'The paradox is that transformations in management methods, directly inspired by the shareholder view, have had the intentional effect of *reducing the risks borne by the shareholders*, and in parallel, increasing the risks borne by the other major stakeholders in the enterprise [. . .]: the employees'.[35] This form of profit-based organization is justified in that it is efficient, but how? 'Efficient' ecologically? Socially? No. It is efficient in that it can make short-term profits for others. It is efficient because it is 'efficient'.[36]

These theories of shareholder value have provided the basis for the current ideology justifying the favours granted to the shareholders, fraudulently presented as 'investors', whom we should, in the name of economic efficiency, reward again and again for their 'risk taking'. But when this new discourse emerged in the 1970s, in phase, then, with that period of intense social conflict and the growing rejection of capitalism, nobody believed it. Including among those who should have been its immediate supporters, the critics were harsh. The neo-conservatives, in particular, did not pull any punches. Kristol was worried, and stated: 'liberal capitalism [. . .] has precious little chance for survival'.[37] Finally, what were the neoliberals proposing? An apology for capitalism that corresponded in every respect to the repellent image brandished by its opponents. But 'who on earth wants to live in a society in which all [. . .] are fully engaged in the hot pursuit of money, the single-minded pursuit of material self-interest? To put it another way: Who wants to live in a society in which selfishness and self-seeking are celebrated as primary virtues?'[38] Such a society, as almost all philosophical and religious traditions have warned us, would be 'unfit for human habitation'. How can you, he retorted in short, seriously think about defending capitalism by admitting that it is consistent with what has always been perceived as its main failing? If you start out like that, you are sure to lose. For example, to recognize blithely, as Hayek does, that the social order resulting from capitalist competition is in principle foreign to any principle of justice, is ideologically inept: 'Professor Hayek's rationale for modern capitalism is never used outside a small academic enclave', wrote Kristol, and continued: 'I even suspect it cannot be believed except by those whose minds have been shaped by overlong exposure to scholasticism'.[39]

Milton Friedman himself recognized as much in his own way: neoliberalism – and this is not the least of the paradoxes – does not really *sell*: 'it is much easier to sell simple-minded, collectivist ideas than it is to sell sophisticated, free enterprise ideas'.[40] So, he comforts himself, somewhat complacently: if our ideas are not popular, this is probably because they are too subtle.

Too subtle? You be the judge: 'do corporate executives, provided they stay within the law, have responsibilities in their business activities other than to make as much money for their stockholders as possible? And my answer to that is no, they do not'.[41] But the neoconservatives had another explanation: if the neoliberal theses are so unattractive, this is not so much because of their alleged intellectual refinement as due to their ethical dryness. 'Make as much money as possible for your shareholders' is admittedly not really a slogan to set you dreaming.

As Kristol wrote in 1974: 'Every day, in every way, the large corporation looks more and more like a species of dinosaur on its lumbering way to extinction'.[42] The environment is hostile. If it does not adapt, it will die. What has changed? Mainly this: given their gigantism, and the implications of their decisions for the lives of all, big companies are no longer seen as simple private economic affairs, but as powerful institutions with a public dimension. That is why they are asked for more than economic profitability. That is also why confining oneself to answering on this basis is notoriously inadequate. Business leaders 'have to learn to govern, not simply to execute or administer. And to govern is to think politically, as well as economically'.[43]

'Governing' can no longer just mean, as Ruml said in the 1950s, 'enacting rules'. Governing involves something else: tactics and strategy. And for this, other types of know-how are required. Business leaders had a pressing need for operative concepts to grasp a new conflictuality that had taken them by surprise. Neoliberal theories of the firm, busy as they were denying the existence of power relations, were unable to provide any. They had to turn to other providers of concepts.

Part IV

A world of protesters

— 14 —

CORPORATE COUNTER-ACTIVISM

> Business itself, since it is engaged in a competitive struggle, is at war.
> Arthur Fürer, Managing Director of Nestlé Group[1]

Throughout the 1970s, employers' calls for a counter-offensive continued. There was the same martial tone, the same threadbare military metaphors, the same spitefulness. In 1979, Donald Kirchhof, CEO of Castle & Cooke, maintained that what was taking place was a 'direct assault on our economic system. [. . .] We are at war, but it is a guerrilla war [. . .] Let's revitalize our corporate leadership and take the offensive, in the best tradition of American capitalism'.[2]

Business, they kept on repeating, was war. Capitalist enterprise is an institution that is continuously sparking upheavals, so it is vital for its leaders to learn to manage the conflict. Producing such conflict is part of its DNA, not only internally, with its own employees, but also externally, with the 'social environment' that its operations impact on.

Faced with the challenge, new forms of know-how develop. There is a shift from a warlike rhetoric to a real strategic rethink. At the overlap between public relations, military intelligence and counter-insurgency tactics, something new was developing in this decade: the elements of a counter-activist doctrine of business.

In 1974, British activists published a booklet called *The Baby Killer*.[3] They denounced the health effects of the breast milk substitute marketed by Nestlé in Third World countries. Sold to populations that could often not read the instructions for use and that lacked access to drinking water, powdered milk was all too often toxic for infants.[4] Ignoring the alerts issued by nutritionists, Nestlé conducted marketing campaigns that involved, for example, getting female representatives of the company to distribute samples; dressed in nurses' suits, they deterred African mothers from breastfeeding.[5]

This militant text might have remained confidential if the company's managers had not made the mistake of overreacting. In 1974, this behemoth of agribusiness sued a Swiss group that had translated the brochure into German, thus giving a global resonance to the accusations in it.[6] In July 1977, American activists called for a boycott of Nestlé.[7] Four years later, more than seven hundred organizations had joined their cause worldwide.

This was one of the first boycott campaigns to be launched on such a scale. Faced with a multinational, on issues of life and death, the struggle was internationalized; consumers in the North were encouraged to act in the face of corporate actions carried out in the South. In this fight, says Bryan Knapp, 'biopolitics converged with geopolitics [. . .] within what we might call bio-capitalism'.[8]

Nestlé managers were initially completely taken aback by a movement they did not understand.[9] In November 1980, a Swiss executive from Nestlé landed in Washington. 'Relying on what was generally being said in Vevey [at the firm's headquarters], he was sure that the boycott involved only a tiny minority of over-excited protesters. No sooner had he landed than he spotted a bumper sticker on a car saying "Boycott Nestlé". He was shocked, and exclaimed: "Ah! the bastards, the bastards!"'[10]

Business leaders became aware of a hitherto unsuspected vulnerability. To their bitter surprise, small networks of activists could, despite the radical asymmetry in their material means, exert considerable pressure on big industrial groups. This was just the beginning: 'the activist movement is approaching internationalization [. . .] In the future, there may be other concerted attacks against multinationals by united activist groups'.[11]

The costs of the boycott were soon felt, 'not only through the hours that Nestlé bosses were forced to waste addressing it, but also because of the dejection into which it sometimes plunged them and their subordinates. It was mostly "psychologically, emotionally," that it affected the corporation'. Nestlé 'had even approached a psychoanalyst to deal with the despondency into which the controversy plunged the staff'.[12]

With its back against the wall, the firm decided to change approach. It recruited a special advisor who had already started to make a reputation for his expertise in crisis management:[13] Rafael Pagan, a man of the hard right and a former military intelligence officer. He had been an advisor on these issues to Presidents Kennedy and Johnson, and in the late 1970s became a business advisor.[14] He joined Nestlé in January 1981 to set up a task force to fight the activists for every inch of the ground.[15]

Members of this team, composed in part of former military men, would later be found sitting on the board of Pagan International in the mid-1980s,[16] then at Mongoven, Duchin & Biscoe, and finally, in the 2000s, at 'Stratfor'. If the name of this outfit rings a bell, this may be because the hacker Jeremy Hammond exposed it in 2011, posting thousands of electronic messages that he had hacked from its servers on WikiLeaks. In the meantime, for three decades, these experts in counter-activism had been selling their services at a high price to multinationals that were about as commendable as Shell in the face of the anti-apartheid boycott, or Union Carbide, or Monsanto.

Management traditionally had two major ways of thinking about antagonism: social conflict within business and competition in the market. Internal tension with subordinates, external competition with rivals. With the eruption of an activism targeting multinationals, a third case, strange and unexpected, was now presenting itself: an external social conflict, against which traditional tactics proved inadequate. Firms which had first thought they could treat this new challenge in the same way as labour disputes eventually realized that 'these new stakeholders also *do not want to be managed* within the corporate defined operational parameters'.[17] If those external forces over which they no longer had any hold were to be fought off, they had to adapt, by developing a completely different repertoire of countermeasures.

If the 'anti-business activists' managed to keep multinationals in check, thought Rafael Pagan at the time, this was not because they were 'smarter than the men and women of Nestlé', but because they, at least, 'know they are in political combat, while business people – even today – do not'.[18] Business management might well be able to draw on colossal resources, but until they actively organized for political struggle, they would suffer setbacks: 'I don't think we will ever be loved or popular [. . .]. But we can, if we learn to think and act politically, defeat our activist critics'.[19] It was time for corporations, added his colleague Arion Pattakos, to 'meet activism with activism'.[20]

In October 1985, after the boycott had ended, one of the main organizers of the campaign against Nestlé, Douglas Johnson, met one of his old opponents, Jack Mongoven, Pagan's right arm, in São Paulo. They dined together, drank wine and spun the conversation out into the small hours. Johnson wrote a report on this interview, today preserved in the archives of the Minnesota Historical Society in Saint Paul.[21]

> This may sound self-serving, but Ray and I were the strategists. We are very different; I come out of political campaigns, and he out of the army [. . .] The very first day, we were filling up the room with analysis, Ray left the room, and I just wrote up on the wall the nine principles of Clausewitz. I had studied him in college, and found him always useful in developing political campaigns. [. . .] Ray came into the room, looked at me and asked if I had gone to the War College; I said no, I'd never been in the Army. And he said, but you know those are the principles of Clausewitz. That's part of how we discovered how well we could work together and complement one another. Sun Tzu's work was very important to how we developed our campaign. The difference for you was in the early years, while you all developed strategy, you were up against people in Switzerland who had no idea of strategy, and never developed one.[22]

'It was like planning for a major combat mission',[23] he still remembers. 'We looked at all of the important conditions: our strengths and vulnerabilities, your strengths and weaknesses, including your base of support'.[24] This was an application to the activist question of the 'SWOT' model ('Strengths, Weaknesses, Opportunities, and Threats'), a market analysis method based on the cross-examination of the strengths and weaknesses of the organization and its rivals, as well as the opportunities and threats in the environment. The anti-activist know-how that was pieced together in this way borrowed from several sources: the hybridization of military strategy, party strategy and market strategy.

As Mongoven said to the activist Douglas Johnson, 'your weakness was resources, your strength was lots of committed people. Our strength was resources; our weakness was people. So we had to design tactics to upset your strengths. A lot of time we adopted tactics, not because they directly helped our strategy, but because they could disperse your efforts'.[25]

How is it that small, poorly funded militant groups, overworked and always on the verge of burnout, could represent a menace for economic empires with incomparable resources? The answer of these analysts was that their trump card, with its many knock-on effects, lay in their 'ability to mobilise legitimacy'[26] – something that the firms on the other side cruelly lacked. 'Your legitimacy, and your strength, came from others: from the churches, from the teachers, from a small group of scientists, from some health organizations. What we did was identify targets and develop tactics to deprive you of their support or legitimacy, so then we could deal with you on our terms'.[27] This meant breaching the adversary's defences so as to deprive him one by one of his 'blocks of credibility'.[28]

Throughout the many campaigns they conducted, Pagan and his colleagues developed a typology of activists. This simplistic scheme allowed them, at each new confrontation, to place their opponents in small stereotypical psycho-tactical boxes.[29] Another member of the gang, Ronald Duchin, set out this house typology one day at a congress of the American Association of cattle farmers, and his intervention was then printed in the organization's bulletin: 'I am also a cattleman', he began as a *captatio benevolentiae*. 'My wife and I run a good-sized Limousin and Charolais cow and calf operation in the Kentucky Bluegrass [. . .] one way or another *we* all are activists. However, the activists we are concerned about here are the ones who want to change the way your industry does business'.[30] Take the case of the BST growth hormone (bovine somatotropin) produced by Monsanto: 'Most of you know it very well. So do I because we work for Monsanto on the issue [. . .] BST is a synthetic hormone produced by biotechnology. It has been shown to increase milk production in dairy cows by 10 to 25 percent. Yet it is under attack by a plethora of public interest groups'.[31]

But who are these groups? If you want to defeat them, you need to know them. But this is not complicated: they fall, invariably, into four main categories:

1) *The radicals.* These want to change the system, they have underlying socio-economic/political motives, are hostile to enterprise as such, and may be extremist or violent. With them, there is nothing to be done.

2) *The opportunists.* These offer visibility, power, followers and, perhaps, even employment.[32] The key to dealing with opportunists is to provide them with at least the perception of a partial victory.

3) *The idealists.* These people are usually naive and altruistic. They apply an ethical and moral standard. The problem with them is that they are sincere, and, as a result, very credible. Except they are also very credulous. If it can be shown that their opposition to an industry or its products causes harm to others and cannot be ethically justified, they are forced to change their position.

4) *The realists.* These are a godsend. They can live with trade-offs; they are willing to work within the system and want to work within the system. They are not interested in radical change, but are pragmatic.[33]

111

Faced with protest, the way forward is always the same: to negotiate with the realists, knowing that in most issues, it is the solution agreed upon by the realists which is accepted, especially when business participates in the decision-making process. Also, the idealists need to be re-educated into realists – an educational process, according to Duchin, which requires great sensitivity and understanding from the educator.[34] If you can manage to work with the realists and re-educate the idealists, they will switch over to your position. Once these critics of conscience have been turned, the radicals will lose the broad credibility that the support of these moral authorities had conferred on them. Without support from the realists and the idealists the positions of radicals and opportunists are seen to be shallow and self-serving.[35] At this point you will always be able to count on the opportunists to accept the final compromise.[36]

The premise is that the 'radicals' derive their strength only by drawing closer to more moderate blocks. Without this link, they are negligible. Radicals isolated in their niche of radicalism are harmless, and pose no threat: a bit of minority folklore without any impact. Such, then, is the general strategy: to cooperate with the realists, to converse with the idealists so as to convert them into realists, to isolate the radicals and to gobble up the opportunists.

In Nestlé's boycott, the activists' medium-term goal was to impose a 'code of conduct' on firms in the sector. Rather than rejecting this prospect, Pagan made it his own and engaged in endless negotiations on the terms of the code. It was a matter of formally embracing the principle so as to better sabotage the content. Faced with what he decided was an *ethical critique* of multinationals, Pagan believed that rejecting the lexicon of social responsibility was no longer a viable strategy: 'The choice for industry is no longer *whether* it will be "responsible," but *how*. Are we going to act according to our own or to a negotiated agenda, or are we going to be dictated to?'[37]

This tactic of acquiescence had the advantage of giving new lustre to the firm's brand, a veneer of credibility, while plunging protesters into tedious talks. This meant forcing activists to engage in long palavers; and shifting 'the debate into the field of interpretations had been a deliberate strategy':[38] busying the opposing leaders with matters other than boycotting Nestlé, and exhausting them in endless meetings – all this in order to divert the movement from the vital task of building up a deeply-rooted protest. This was a new tactic, based on *dialogue*.

— 15 —

THE PRODUCTION OF THE DOMINANT DIALOGY

At the same time, Socrates, our use of rhetoric should be like our use of any other sort of exercise.

Plato[1]

It is not part of the official CSR ('corporate social responsibility') story as it is taught in business schools, but one of the first publications on the theme of the 'social responsibilities of management' was sponsored, in 1950, by the great theorist of 'public relations' Edward Bernays, the author of the famous *Propaganda*.[2]

A few decades later, however, his heirs saw that the public had learned to be wary of 'defensive advertising' and forms of communication inherited from 'partisan propaganda'. Taking note of the wear and tear that the old formulae had sustained, the 'mad men' made their self-criticism: 'the Bernays paradigm defined the public relations role [. . .] as the "engineering of consent" among a malleable public. [. . .] Translated into unscrupulous communication practices, such a paradigm now looks both ethically untenable and ineffective, as the public has learned to receive this type of PR effort with suspicion'.[3] The old propaganda no longer worked as well as before, and something else was needed. Advertising, of course, would not disappear, but an effort would be made to add other, subtler ways of bamboozling people.

The goal was to regain control of an order of expression that was out of control. But what would be the alternative, or rather the necessary complement to the old model? The new key word was *dialogue*. New 'public relations dialogues'[4] praised 'dialogic communication as a theoretical framework to guide relationship building between organizations and publics'.[5] Instead of propaganda, they recommended participation, instead of the vertical, the horizontal, instead of the

113

unilateral, the reciprocal, instead of the symmetric, the asymmetrical.[6] In the early 1980s, managerial ideologues, adopting a philosophical pose, sang the praises of dialogic reason, 'ethical' in essence.[7] And Habermas came along at just the right time – his 'distinction between monological and dialogical rationality' fitted in nicely with this new approach.[8] In this model, transmitter and receiver swap places to become, in a beautiful communicative symmetry, 'equal participants in a communication process that seeks mutual understanding'.[9] Now the time of 'ethical communication' had come, of 'communication' as 'conversation' or 'neutral dialogue' as a 'a precondition of legitimacy in any corporate initiative'.[10] The time of overarching truths was over, promised these devotees of communication, these new converts to a respectable postmodernism: intersubjective agreement must now be co-constructed through a dialogue between stakeholders.

According to one management manual: 'Philosophers have agreed that dialogue can enhance the ethics of communication because it reinforces the dignity and respect of both parties. [. . .] The philosophical notion of *dialogos* can be traced to Plato's rejection of sophism as mere rhetoric, in which monologue was the style'.[11] Plato contrasted 'sophism', we learned from our business philosophers (who got themselves into something of a tangle in the process) with the 'dialogue where participants treated each other as means rather than ends [sic], and did not engage in a war of words'.[12] Philosophers are always good for soundbites. Still, you need to take the trouble (or pleasure) of actually reading them before quoting them, which might perhaps stop you mixing everything up (sophism and sophistry, Plato and Kant, means and ends, etc.). Not to mention that the said philosophers were far from being as angelic as people would like us to believe when it came to the practice of dialogue – starting with that pugnacious, corrosive, implacable dialoguer Socrates, who harried his opponent mercilessly.

Anyway, the contrast was seized on: there was monologue, an old idol that communicators now seemed to be trampling in the dust, with all its manipulation, pretence, dogmatism, insincerity and mistrust; and, on the other side, there was dialogue, with its concern for others, authenticity, open-mindedness, frankness, and trust. Instead of one-way persuasion, that detestable practice of the past, people now preferred reciprocal listening, mutual understanding, relational, empathetic communication based on consensus, the 'co-creation of a shared understanding' between 'stakeholders', horizontality, 'recognition', the relationship to the other, and so on, ad nauseam. *'Enough! Enough! I can't bear it any longer. Bad air! Bad air! This workshop where ideals are fabricated – it seems to me just to stink of lies.'[13]*

Except that there are two sides to the coin of these celebrations of dialogue, not one. Heads is ethics; tails is strategy. For a full view of the situation, we need to set the ethico-philosophic gloop against its double, namely the strategy of dialogue theorized at the same time by the experts of corporate counter-activism. Some quote Habermas, while others refer to Clausewitz, but it makes no difference: both – the philosophical version and the secret agent version – are the complementary faces of the same set of practices.

During their counter-campaign in the service of Nestlé, Pagan and his colleagues were convinced that 'the resolution of the boycott would come about through long-term dialogue and one-on-one discussions with the critics'.[14] 'For them, the dialogue was not a way to open up to another, it was a strategy, [. . .] another way of conducting the fight'.[15] On their side there was no dialogue, no willingness to negotiate: the discussion was aimed only at convincing 'sensible' people that the firm was sincere and making them withdraw from the campaign. The purpose of this kind of discussion was not to 'exchange' ideas but 'to convince people of your point of view and motivate them to act for you'.[16]

Whereas traditional public relations sought to drown their opponents' discourse under a torrent of justificatory advertising, this new tactic was based on the observation that 'destruction of the adversary simply isn't possible in an age in which anti-establishment dissidents command at least as much and sometimes more public attention and support than the corporations they attack'.[17] So you have to play your cards more carefully. 'When an emerging issue threatens to become critical, the issue manager doesn't instinctively "put up his dukes" to fight the invader [. . .] Rather, he or she reaches out to leadership of adversarial groups and philosophies to explore rationally with them the possibility that they have interests in common which can be eliminated from the adversarial agenda'.[18]

Updating the theory of the production of the dominant ideology would these days involve a critique of the *dominant dialogy*. What are the virtues of dialogue as a strategy of power? We have already begun to glimpse some of them. Let us complete the inventory here.

1) The *function of intelligence*. Dialoguing with opponents makes it possible to identify the perils that crop up as soon as possible, to identify 'potentially controversial issues before they reach the public arena'.[19] It is essential to find out what the opponent has in mind, not only to learn what his plans are, but to understand how he thinks.

Keep your friends close to you, but your enemies even closer – good fatherly advice. Try to establish channels of communication with the enemy's groups, including those that 'may even seem destructive – at least in the short run'.[20]

2) A *function of confinement*. Without his actually being asked for anything, one Nestlé executive in the early 1980s wrote a set of rules of conduct for activists, including this: 'Contacting the targeted corporation and attempting to establish a dialogue [. . .] before mounting a public media campaign'.[21] The main advantage of this tactic of 'non-governmental, intergroup resolution of emerging policy issues'[22] was of a topographic order: relocating confrontation in a private forum, confining it far away from 'public space'.[23] In doing so, activists were deprived of their main resource, namely the publicizing of the problems; their leaders were also freed from the social constraints which generally prevented them from overly compromising themselves in broad daylight. In circumstances where 'leaders [. . .] are not too eager for the people to take the upper hand', wrote Montesquieu, 'those who have wisdom and authority intervene'.[24]

3) A *function of diversion*. Chuck opponents a bone to gnaw on so as to divert them from offensive tasks. When, in the late 1980s, Pagan tried to break the boycott against South Africa, he stressed this point: 'A key aspect of this strategy is to ensure that the Shell companies can counter that unbalanced situation by establishing their own meaningful dialogue with these crucial church groups so that churches perceive their anti-apartheid options in a more positive, creative sense than simply joining the Shell U.S. boycott'.[25] It was all quite clear: 'To engage the ecumenical institution, churches and critical spokespersons in post-apartheid planning should deflect their attention away from boycott and disinvestment efforts'.[26]

4) A *function of co-optation*. But dialogue, if properly conducted, means above all that you can co-opt certain of the opponents' 'pressure groups'.[27] In 'the classic corporate co-optation strategy', writes Bart Mongoven, corporations 'seek out the loudest organization that can be identified as realistic. They sit down and offer the power, glory, and money of solving the problem to the loud realist. When the loud realist accepts, it convinces the public that the larger issue is resolved. The entire activist movement, therefore, get swallowed up (mostly involuntarily) by the single deal. Anyone who says the issue isn't resolved looks radical or lacking credibility'.[28]

Activists often have an exaggerated picture of their opponents, say our experts; thus, it is not difficult to surprise them by presenting them with a completely different face from the one they expect.

116

Adopt a humble, open, listening attitude. Coax them by speaking their language, flatter them by treating them as a responsible organization, grant them recognition, dangle before them the image of a 'constructive' action poles apart from 'negative' or 'sterile' opposition. Among the psychological manipulation techniques that Pagan advocates in order to turn the moderate detractors, there is this one: transmit to them sensitive documents that could harm – but not too much – the company if they were divulged, making them promise to keep them to themselves. In his experience, he says, such a pledge of confidence 'was never betrayed'.[29]

5) A *function of discrediting*. One important point: these dialogues, thought to be a way of lobbying opponents, are *selective*.[30] At the same time as they are working to include some groups, they also attempt to exclude others.[31] Stressing 'consensus' as the goal of 'dialogue', the point is to discredit any dissensual policy, implicitly labelling 'groups who do not engage in consensus-oriented direct discussions with industry as "confrontational," "incapable of dialogue" and ultimately as "unworthy" of participating in democratic decision-making processes'.[32] This means drawing a line of demarcation between those who are willing to dialogue and the rest – making some your satellites and discrediting others. They can be repressed all the more easily when they have been presented as being outside the *logos*.

6) A *function of legitimation*. By dialoguing with NGOs that enjoy a great aura of respectability, firms additionally benefit from 'image transfers'.[33] Big companies relatively devoid of reputational capital can hope to acquire this from their detractors, especially as the latter are in a completely different position, one which favours synergies: low economic capital but a high degree of the power to bestow symbolic approval. On the basis of this asymmetry, relations of cross-co-optation can be created. From dialogue, people will move onto collaboration and partnership, the objective being to form coalitions under corporate dominance.[34]

Thus 'new corporate strategies to deal with turbulence created by critics' are developed.[35] Over and above the reactive manoeuvres aimed at the immediate management of overt crises, it will increasingly be a matter of anticipating, of developing a 'systematic and proactive approach to criticism'.[36]

— 16 —

ISSUE MANAGEMENT

> They had to stop being companies to become strategists.
>
> Andre Gorz[1]

'Ever since the civil rights movement, the Vietnam War and the ecological efforts of the 1960s and 1970s, activist organizations have become major participants in the public policy development process. [. . .] If business does not engage the activists, they will have the say in what our public policy is and on their own terms'.[2] Beyond their challenge of this or that particular corporate practice, these troublemakers seemed to be the true instigators of 'excessive government regulation' against which the world of business was then rebelling – especially in environmental matters.

Beyond the face-to-face encounter between firms and activists, there was a three-player game going on, with one of the players being state power, and 'taking' the legislator as the objective. If corporate bosses needed to be militant in their turn, this was not only to repel the enemy assaults, but also to impose their own agenda and ensure that 'public policy choices [were] influenced by the views of the private sector in general'.[3]

This was the explicit ambition of a new branch of managerial knowledge, which, in 1977, W. Howard Chase baptized as 'issue management'. He said he wanted to finish with the 'Maginot line' mentality,[4] with the defensive attitude too often adopted by business, and finally go on the offensive.

The undisguised goal was for businesses to be capable of 'managing public policy'. As Chase openly stated: 'We have no hesitation in speaking about corporate public policy management. Public policy is *not* the exclusive domain of government. In our pluralistic society,

118

public policy is the result of interaction between public and private points of view. The corporation, as an institution, has every moral and legal right to participate in *formation* of public policy – not merely to react, [. . .] to policies designed by government'.[5]

Likewise, David Rockefeller argued: 'Participation in public policy is both a basic responsibility of corporate executives and a management function which, like any other, must be approached with systematic business discipline. Corporations must establish public policy objectives, set priorities, implement a working plan and set guidelines for measuring their success. In the world of today, the diverse activities we call government and public relations, lobbying and issue advertising, must all be part of an integrated management strategy'.[6] Under cover of 'pluralism', the real goal was to impose the political pre-eminence of the interests of capital.

All this involved acquiring new skills. It would of course be necessary to systematize lobbying with the government, but the range of tactics was wider. Public policies turn *ideas* that pre-exist into concrete realities. These ideas, their production, and their spread – these were all things that they had to learn to *manage*.

How are ideas formed? How are 'problems' born? In the long confidential report written in 1987 for Shell by Pagan International – the so-called 'Neptune strategy' designed to allow the multinational oil company to circumvent the boycott of the apartheid regime – a large diagram was included in an annex, illustrating the genesis of a political problem.[7] Before becoming a loudly debated issue, an idea follows a long and much more discreet process of maturing. A 'problem' has a whole 'life cycle' that it goes through, from its first formulations to its critical stage. According to this simplistic and blandly diffusionist view, the 'process of diffusion and adoption of ideas in the public domain' comprises three major steps. (1) A phase of creation: the idea, born of an interaction between activists and intellectuals, is first incubated in restricted academic circles. (2) A period of impregnation: it then spreads into the intellectual sphere, conveyed by articles, reports, books, courses and seminars. (3) A moment of wide dissemination: the mass media spread it and it reaches the general public. Activists who seize on it then have the assurance that their message will enjoy a strong social resonance. The question is ripe to be put on the political agenda. Public action will soon follow.

The tragedy is that business leaders do not generally discover the 'problems' until the end of the cycle, once these latter have hit the headlines – when it is already too late, because by this stage, 'the most

119

business can do is to fight a rear-guard action',[8] one that is expensive, and most of the time unsuccessful. Aware that they could not 'afford to wait until others [had] defined and legitimized the problems before entering the arena',[9] it was necessary to develop strategies of 'proactive neutralization'. According to this new approach, 'the organization does not wait for things to happen around it; it does not wait until the problems become critical, current, or imminent' in order to act.[10]

Business's inability hitherto to respond effectively to its critics lay, it was felt, in the fact that it 'did not fully appreciate the importance of academia in supplying the intellectual fuel for the activist fire'.[11] In a situation where the business world suffered from a severe 'erosion of its societal and intellectual legitimacy',[12] it was imperative to form close relations with the academic world.[13] This was mainly true for the biological and medical sciences, given the crucial role they play in assessing the health and environmental effects of industrial production. It was necessary to flatter researchers; to bribe people to provide 'scientific' opinions; to spread the seeds of doubt.[14] For this, too, was part of 'issue management': a *politics of truth* that seeks to influence the formulation of problems as much as the establishment of the facts.[15] A kind of approach, in Peter Ludlow's analysis, which is not just about 'hiding the reality, but producing it', even if this means resorting to massive 'epistemic attacks'.[16]

Large companies were also advised to acquire strategic intelligence capabilities allowing them to identify emerging problems and follow their 'trajectory' so as to intervene at the right moment.[17] In this respect, the golden rule was the following: 'issues that *threaten* a corporation's survival and growth are never allowed to reach crisis stage'.[18]

On the organizational level, the problem-managing tasks should be left to the strategic planners rather than the public relations officers. The specialist in management S. Prakash Sethi, drawing inspiration from the crisis unit set up by Pagan for Nestlé, suggested that large companies create within themselves 'units of strategic business', officially and more presentably called 'social responsibility centres'.[19]

As well as intelligence from the outside world, internal forecasting was necessary, to spot beforehand any problems that might arise from the business's own activities. A firm that develops new technologies must question in advance their potential effects on society, anticipating the ways these technologies might be rejected. As Pattakos writes: 'Long range corporate planning requires more than the broad, traditional "will it sell?" marketing approach. [. . .] Today's business strategists must consider and assess the impact of their plans on the general socio-political environment as well'.[20]

One of the first multinationals to systematically adopt this kind of pro-active strategy was Monsanto in Saint Louis. At the end of the 1970s, one expert in social responsibility recruited by the firm, Margaret Stroup, implemented an approach directly inspired by Chase's theory of 'issue management'. Convinced that 'analyzing the total environment' was as vital a task for the firm as analysing the market, she established a research unit responsible for 'scanning the environment' and 'identifying problems'.[21]

In August 1982, Christopher Palmer, head of the Audubon Society, one of the oldest organizations for the conservation of nature, published a piece in the *Washington Post* entitled 'Business and Environmentalists: A Peace Proposal'.[22] 'One of our problems', he conceded, 'is that we tend to assume a tone of arrogance when talking to business – this tendency is matched by a tendency to be rigid, unwilling to compromise or negotiate. Environmentalists sometimes are afraid to bend or be flexible'. But surely it would be advantageous 'to diffuse the destructive animosity and mutual misunderstanding – and even make common cause' with the business world, when possible?

Louis Fernandez, the head of Monsanto, was quick to respond to him in the columns of the same newspaper: 'Business must get beyond thinking of environmentalists as obstructionist enemies. [. . .] The way toward a more amicable relationship, in my judgment, lies in greater trust of one another's motives and in more frequent dialogue between us – before an environmental question deteriorates into a battle-lines-drawn controversy'. And Fernandez invited environmental organizations to 'sit down around the table' to discuss the matter. 'We have plenty of extra chairs at Monsanto'.[23] Palmer has handed us an 'olive branch', he said; we accept it willingly. (Good heavens what a 'realist', co-opting his enemies so readily!) 'Let's give the olive branch some additional nourishment and see if we can make it bear mutually beneficial fruit'. In this way the industrialist and the defenders of the birds got into bed with each other.

Monsanto immediately forged several partnerships with NGOs: projects on the protection of wetlands, on the treatment of toxic waste and on the financing of the Environmental Protection Agency. One sign of the importance with which the firm's management treated the question was the way the president of the company in person oversaw the coalition-building strategy with the environmental groups. In fact,

121

many 'environmental' NGOs have flourished since the beginning of the 1980s on the basis of this kind of deal with industry.[24]

At the time, Monsanto had decided to turn to biotechnology. Its leaders knew full well that their new products could come up against strong social resistance. The challenge was to secure the reorientation of their industrial strategy by adopting, very early on, a preventive approach of 'issue management'. As early as 1984, Monsanto's 'committee for emerging issues' identified several key questions for its strategy of influencing public policy, including 'the regulation of bio-technologies', 'intellectual property rights', 'agricultural policy', and compensation arrangements for pollution.[25] These questions were considered so decisive for the future of the firm that each of them had been placed directly under the supervision of a senior officer of the company: 'we must manage, as businessmen [. . .] the delicate task of bringing these issues to the public arena', said Fernandez.[26]

It was not just a simple operation of greenwashing, as it went well beyond that. The aim was to implement the pre-emptive strategy whose principles I have just traced. 'If we are bold, if we continue battling for our interests with determination and creativity, we will emerge ahead of the pack in terms of our ability to operate smoothly and successfully'.[27]

In the historico-philosophical fresco that I am here endeavouring to sketch, we have encountered three major conceptions of the private governance of corporations. The first, that of the managerialists of the 1950s and 1960s, thought of it by analogy with state power. The second, that of neoclassical economists of the 1970s, denied any relationship with government and reduced the issue of governance to an 'agency problem' that consisted in aligning managerial conduct with the value in terms of shares. This marked a shift from ethical manageriality to neoliberal governmentality in its financial aspect. But there was a third aspect to the story: economic governance was, in practical terms, complemented by an art of the strategic management of the social environment.

What thus emerged was another notion of the private government of business, in a sense that differed both from that of the managerialism of previous decades and of the shareholder governance of business that was being formulated in parallel at the same time.

While ethical managerialism proposed to govern business in the shape of an enlightened despotism, this new *strategic manageriality* was an attempt to govern the surrounding social world by deploying an art of 'manipulation of [the] external environment

– physical, social, and political – to make it more receptive to corporate activities'.[28]

The paradox is that at the very moment when neoliberal theories of the firm were denying power relations and totally rejecting the concept of corporate social responsibility, the advisors from these same companies were doing the complete opposite: while the former were depoliticizing the firm in theory, the latter were working to repoliticize it in practice; while the former rejected CSR as a dangerous illusion, the latter, on the contrary, embraced it as a useful subterfuge; while the former conceived the firm as a pure contract, the latter saw conflict everywhere. Different sectors of the ruling class, although defending the same interests, thus began to develop contradictory conceptions of their object.

We often tend to reduce the big reaction, that which was beginning in the 1970s before deploying itself more concretely in the 1980s, to its neoliberal economic component. This is a mistake. Intellectually, the movement was much more composite. There was a diffuse counter-attack, with everyone striving to plug the breaches on their own terrain, without central coordination or doctrinal unity. The result was discrepancies between the different facets of this counter-movement, and, first and foremost, between the economic theory of the firm and the strategic thinking of the company.

In many ways indeed, the approach in terms of the strategic management of the social environment that I have just described represented 'the antithesis of economic liberalism. [. . .] The new paradigm [. . .] required corporations to develop political expertise at the societal level (e.g., IM), a capability that was not addressed by liberal economic theory'.[29] Some people noted the huge gap and endeavoured to make a rapprochement. This attempt at a conceptual synthesis – or rather, the creation of a theoretical mayonnaise – was based on what has been called 'stakeholder theory'.

— 17 —

STAKEHOLDERS

So, as long as the combatants have friends and patrons, so long as they are reasonably well known, we see dilettanti of the kind who pick up tickets to a wrestling match trotting along to the stakeholder's. They grow heated, as bets are laid. (*L'Illustration*)[1]

For a long time, in English, the word 'stakeholder' had just one meaning, that of 'third party depositary' or 'depositary of stakes'. What does this mean? Players, betting on the outcome of a boxing match or a dog fight, entrusted their bets to a third party, the 'stakeholder', who took them on deposit and then handed out the prize to the fortunate winners.[2]

In the early 1960s, researchers from the Stanford Research Institute took this obsolete term and gave it another meaning: stakeholders were defined as these 'those groups without whose support the organization would cease to exist'.[3] This word had been chosen mainly for its phonetic proximity to another which it seemed to echo: 'stockholders'. There were not just 'stockholders', they were basically saying, but also a whole set of 'stakeholders' that management must also take into account.[4]

In parallel with the ideas of the Stanford group, a Swedish management theorist, Eric Rhenman, had in 1964 proposed his own stakeholder theory – 'Intressenterna' in his native language – understood as 'individuals or groups dependent on the company for the realisation of their personal goals and on whom the company is dependent for its existence'.[5] Instead of social conflict, something that Rhenman imagined as a snowball fight or alternatively as a battle fought with stones that business leaders, everywhere under siege and clearly inferior in numbers, seemed very unlikely to win, he held up

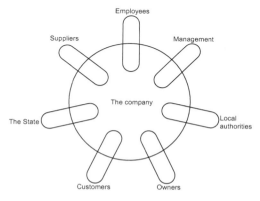

Figure 1 The company and its stakeholders according to Rhenman

Source: Eric Rhenman, *Industrial Democracy and Industrial Management:
A Critical Essay on the Possible Meanings and Implications of Industrial
Democracy*, Van Gorcum, London, 1968

the well-ordered scheme of a harmonious synthesis of interests more
in line with the Scandinavian ideal of a pacified social world (see
figure 1).

In 1966, pointing to the close relationship between Rhenman and
the local bosses, one of his compatriots, the sociologist Marxist Göran
Therborn, was already criticizing what seemed to him an 'ideology
for business leaders', a 'typical example of those ideological relationships of power which we call hegemony'.[6] Rhenman's business theory
was tantamount to 'pretending that power simply does not exist', that
there is no relationship of domination, just 'pressure groups, stakeholders'. In subsuming heterogeneous social relationships under one
blurred category, Rhenman was ultimately merely stating a truism:

'no decision is taken in a social vacuum, it is instead conditioned by factors from the social environment'. This did perhaps have the merit of injecting a little conflict and a certain social aspect into the theory of the firm, thereby escaping from the narrow paradigm of *homo oeconomicus*, but the result, concluded Therborn – and this was a euphemism – 'was far from amazing'.

In the United States, stakeholder theory opted for an assumed strategic direction. We need now, observed William Dill in 1975, to cope 'with an active, intrusive environment [. . .] made up of individuals and organizations [. . .] seeking direct influence on enterprises' strategic decisions. Each enterprise has a broad aggregation of people outside, call them *stakeholders*',[7] who keep asking troublesome questions on topics such as 'environmental protection, overseas investment policies, and employment practices'.[8] Stakeholder theory presents itself as an answer to this broader challenge, to this 'problem of environmentalization' which then affects the company.[9] Faced with a multi-sectoral challenge, management can no longer ignore its social and political environment. It now lives in a 'world of protesters', and it needs to get used to it.[10]

In 1984, R. Edward Freeman, an erstwhile philosophy student who had changed to management theory, published what has become the main reference work in this field: his *Strategic Management: A Stakeholder Approach*.[11] Business, he pointed out, was under unprecedented attack due to 'the increase in pressure from key external groups such as consumers, environmentalists, stockholders, employees, unions, governments, and so on'.[12] It was under siege. To react was a question of survival.[13] It was a familiar story.

To cope, according to Freeman, business executives needed first and foremost a 'new conceptual framework', a new way of conceiving the relationship between the firm and its outside.[14] Traditionally, they were represented as a productive chain, with different links: at one end, providers who brought resources, then the business, which turned them into products, and finally, at the end of the chain, the customers who bought them. Input/output. See figure 2.

On the edge of this first schema, there was admittedly some mention of 'this dark and dangerous area that we call "the environment"', but this was still, noted Freeman, merely a 'convenient label to hide our ignorance'.[15] But if people wanted to respond to new challenges, it was time to survey this terra incognita, to map it out prior to mastering it.

Freeman undertook to 'redraw our picture of the firm',[16] to draw a new 'conceptual map': in the middle, a rectangle, 'the firm', and,

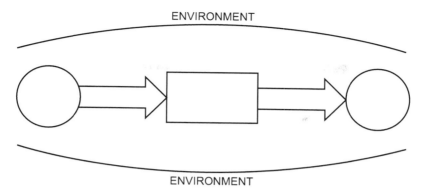

STAKEHOLDERS

ENVIRONMENT

ENVIRONMENT

Figure 2 The firm viewed according to the model of production

Source: R. Edward Freeman, *Strategic Management: A Stakeholder Approach*, Pitman, Boston, MA, 1984, p. 5

all around, two-way arrows which included relationships of mutual affection between 'the firm' and a myriad of heterogeneous entities, its 'stakeholders' (see figure 3).

This representation of the firm as a dandelion is similar to that developed at the same time by the 'theory of the nexus'. In parallel to Jensen and Meckling, who define the firm as an interlacing of contractual relations, Freeman conceives it as a 'constellation of cooperative and competitive interests'.[17] As well as there being a link between different 'holders of capital', there seems to be a relationship between various 'stakeholders', all with an interest in the company. So we can start to see two simultaneous images of the business, one cast in economic and the other in management terms, which, despite their differences (we will come back to this), nevertheless have a family resemblance, a certain isomorphy.

In *The Concept of the Political*, Carl Schmitt proposed a schema to analyse the formation of the concepts associated with liberalism. White light, crossing an optical prism, splits into distinct colour ranges. Similarly, the political concepts that pass through this form of thought diffract and project themselves as separate notions. They split into two divergent beams going in opposite directions: economics and ethics. 'So, in liberal thinking, the political concept of struggle is transformed into competition, on the side of the economy, and into debate, on the side of the mind'. The notion of state or society, 'viewed from the angle of ethics and the mind, will be an image of

127

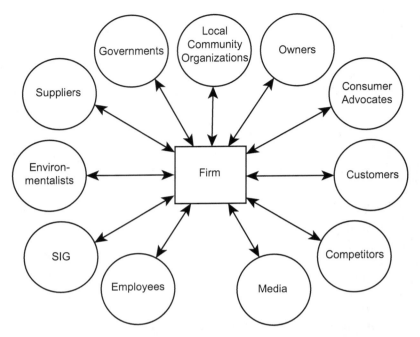

Figure 3 The firm viewed according to the stakeholder model

Source: R. Edward Freeman, *Strategic Management: A Stakeholder Approach*, Pitman, Boston, MA, 1984

Humanity inspired by a humanitarian ideology; viewed from another other angle, it will constitute the economic and technical unity of a uniform system of production and communications'.[18]

This involves not only a process of bursting or splitting but also the eclipse of concrete political concepts, made unthinkable by this very diffraction and replaced by pairs of abstract concepts, ethico-economic doublets of which each element includes only one truncated aspect of the initial notion. Consequently, the 'liberal concepts all move in a highly characteristic way between the ethical (the mind) and the economic (business) [. . .]. Emanating from these opposite poles, they tend to annihilate the political'.[19] Political antagonism thus disappears from the field of the conceivable, to be replaced on one side by the notion of economic competition, and on the other by ethical debate. 'This way, we will end up', he announces, 'with a complete system of demilitarized and depoliticized concepts'.[20]

The business theories we are studying here seem to undergo a similar process of diffraction. Concrete relations are replaced by the abstractions of the theory of nexus (on the economic side), and by the abstractions of stakeholder theory (on the ethical side).

In the 1980s, some authors sought to bring the two sides, economic and ethical, of the liberal view of the firm together into a unified ideology. There were attempts to recast the firm as 'a nexus of contracts between its top managers and its stakeholders'.[21] Given, they said, that all stakeholders incur 'some form of risk as a result of having invested some form of capital, human or financial, something of value, in a firm',[22] they should all have a voice in the management of business. The 'priority of shareholders' defended by the theorists of agency would thus be replaced by another pluralistic or 'multi-fiduciary' norm,[23] according to which management must act in the interest of all stakeholders. This was a warmed-up version of old managerial themes, now served with the dressing of stakeholder language. While, however, managers were describing the business as a private government, our critics now portrayed it as a 'coalition' or a 'partnership', to infer that partners must treat each other with respect, take into account the interests and demands of each party, etc.

So they started saying that it was *because* firms were really nexuses of contracts between free and equal agents that the shareholders' claim to predominance was unacceptable. Except for one thing: the concrete relation was quite different. The priority of shareholders was not a normative claim, it was a fact – a fact of domination, actively constructed, true, but no less real, while the representation of the firm as a coalition, far from expressing the reality of the social relations that constitute it, was a *legend*. By seeing this legend of the firm as its truth, critics contrasted it with a reality that they in turn saw as a simple ideology.

Being effectively devoid of 'concrete political significance', these categories could only lead to inconsistent programmes. If we accept this vision of things, the problem is indeed reduced to knowing, when there is supposed to be a situation not of domination but of horizontal partnership, how management can so systematically favour one of the stakeholders to the detriment of others? This was a mystery. Doubtless, they said, it was because there was lack of dialogue, a failure to listen, a dysfunction in decision-making processes. Hence the cosmetic solutions inevitably served up on the basis of such truncated analyses: let us reform the council of directors, encourage 'participation', appoint 'metaphysical directors',[24] recruit specialists in business ethics who will whisper into managers' ears advice meant for them to balance their decisions more effectively. In terms of a political programme, this discourse on stakeholders never ventured any further than plans to reform business governance, plans whose ultimate horizon, in the most die-hard version, was never anything but German-style co-management. Capitalist property relations, lying at the foundation of an economic absolutism that was, at least on the face of things, cause for regret, were placed out of range. Once these blinkers had been applied, they called, their voices trembling with emotion, for a 'pluralistic' order, a 'stakeholder capitalism', or – why not, while we're on the subject? – a 'Kantian capitalism'.[25]

And yet: when neoliberal economists encountered these reformulations, however timid, of the theory of the nexus, they flew into a rage, considering them to be dangerous hijackings of their own concepts. In this new turn of events, the economic side of liberal theory rejected the synthesis and turned against its double, the ethical side, and denied it.

Jensen thus launched into a virulent critique of the idea that managers should take into account the interests of 'not only the financial claimants, but also employees, customers, communities, and governmental officials, and under some interpretations, the environment, terrorists, blackmailers, and thieves'.[26] If one accepted this thesis, managers would be required to follow multiple, non-concordant, cacophonous obligations, thereby rendering any decision impossible. But above all, the imperative to maximize profit would fall from its pedestal.

In his view, stakeholder theory served as a refuge for the former followers of the 'planned socialist and communist economies'[27] who were now donning this presentable mask to continue the fight. In short, the conspiracy to destroy the foundations of the free world continued, in the shadow of business ethics. Likewise, as the neoliberal ideologue Elaine Sternberg pointed out acerbically, accepting stakeholder theory would be tantamount to 'undermining human rights', that is (because it is actually the same thing), 'it subverts the private property that is essential for defending and exercising fundamental individual liberties': 'When corporations are highjacked from the ends determined by their shareholders, [. . .] owners are denied fundamental rights. In obliging them to serve ends other than those the owners have chosen, champions of conventional business ethics would treat the owners as slaves'.[28] And that is unacceptable because, in this world, masters must remain masters, and slaves, slaves.

However, we must take seriously the answer given by Jensen and his acolytes: shareholders' interest is not one social interest among others, it is the commanding interest, the one which *must* command, and its power is necessarily unshared. In a sense, they were right: there is no real pluralism possible under the dictatorship of capital, no authentic social ethics without some questioning of the property relations that deny that dictatorship. If theories of stakeholders have any merit, it is that they bring out by reaction, as if it were necessary, the tyrannical character of an economic doctrine that will not even tolerate these versions, however soft, of 'pragmatic liberalism'.

It was likely, however, concluded one sociologist returning to these controversies in the late 1990s, that nobody would ever know what this new corporate ethic might have been worth in practice, because 'at about the same time the model was beginning to be discussed seriously, a series of events unfolded that rendered it largely meaningless for many in corporate America'.[29] The neoliberal counter-reformation was in full swing, leading to the ever more entrenched priority of shareholders. What would happen to the theme of 'stakeholders'? 'Beyond generating some academic interest', at least in the view of business leaders, 'stakeholders [. . .] [would] remain a distant second to those holding shares'.[30] They would certainly have to take into account the nuisance power of some of them. 'But this has nothing to do with ethics; it is simple prudence'.[31]

What the dogmatic neoliberals obstinately failed to understand, but what managerial practitioners grasped all too well, was that stakeholder theory was less a moral doctrine than a strategic instrument, an intellectual framework for action.

From where are you talking? was a common question on the left, in the 1970s. My notion of stakeholders, answered Freeman in essence, is one that I formulated by 'taking the viewpoint of the executive, and the claim was that if a group or individual could affect the firm (or be affected by it, and reciprocate), then executives should worry about that group'.[32] This theory was designed to 'allow the analysis of all external forces and pressures whether they are friendly or hostile', so as to 'implement strategies in turbulent environments'.[33]

Until then, management theories had been mainly concerned with 'people inside organizations', in a never-ending quest to make workers more productive. Now that they were facing external challenges, the aim was to expand the sphere of managerial power, to make the social environment of the firm a new object for strategic management.[34] Just as the state has its foreign affairs, a business will have its 'external affairs'. Some at the time even spoke of a 'total environmental management'.[35]

The concept of stakeholders is an amphibious concept, appearing in turn as an ethical notion and as a strategic category. It is this ambivalence that comprises the great interest it holds for management, in that it allows it to play on both senses.[36] But this duplicity also leads to significant conceptual tensions. While, on the ethical side, stakeholders appear as subjects towards whom management has obligations, on the strategic side they are thought of as objects that it must conquer. They are to be respected on the one hand and kept at bay on the other; on the one hand, they are to be recognized, on the other, identified.

Who counts as a 'stakeholder'? It all depends on your point of view. If you put on your ethical glasses, the criterion of recognition cannot be based on power considerations. In the context of a theory of justice, indeed, subjects, even and especially if they are in situation of weakness, must be recognized. And this is exactly what is excluded by strategic consideration, which only has eyes for the strong, for groups likely to constitute a real menace, and treats everyone else as insignificant. In this second perspective, recognizing a stakeholder depends on his *power of affecting others*, on his potential impact on business affairs. The more a social force represents a significant threat, the more consideration must be given to it – regardless of whether or not it is 'legitimate'. Strictly speaking, only its nuisance capacity counts. If you want to be recognized as stakeholders, you have to constitute yourself as risk factors.

There is therefore a dissonance between the criteria for moral recognition and the criteria of strategic identification. A group acknowledged as a stakeholder from a strategic point of view may not be so acknowledged from an ethical point of view, and vice versa. Faced with this problem, some authors in this tradition proposed an ethico-strategic synthesis of the criteria for recognition. Mitchell and his co-authors, for example, suggest combining three factors: the power that groups have over the firm, their legitimacy and the urgency of their claims. Combined with each other, these different traits give birth to a typology. However, one worrying category stands out in the table: that of 'dangerous stakeholders', characterized by the fact that they have power over the whole firm while lacking 'legitimacy', even though they have urgent claims to put forward. These stakeholders, it is predicted, will be 'coercive and possibly violent', 'literally dangerous for the firm'.[37]

Who or what are these stakeholders? A disparate bundle of 'wildcat strikes, employee sabotage, and terrorism'. On the list of these 'stakeholders who resort to coercive tactics' are the workers of General Motors who 'weld cans onto engine blocks to protest company policy', the environmentalists who 'stick long nails into the trees' to make their trunks unusable in sawmills, and 'terrorists' who plant bombs, engage in shootings or organize hostage takings. Any examples? The ANC of Nelson Mandela falls into this 'dangerous category', having used 'coercive power' against the apartheid regime. In fact, under Reagan, Mandela and the ANC were placed by the United States on the list of 'terrorist' organizations – a situation which lasted until 2008.

But our authors have a conscience, a moral conscience, and it pricks them even as they write these lines. Surely it is indecent to reward such actors with the label of 'stakeholders' when they clearly go beyond the 'limits of legitimacy'? Do we not thereby run the risk of legitimizing illegitimate people, the 'violent'? We

> are very uncomfortable with the notion that those whose actions are dangerous [. . .] might be accorded some measure of legitimacy by virtue of the typology proposed in this analysis [. . .] we feel bound to 'identify' dangerous stake-holders without 'acknowledging' them, for, like most of our colleagues, we abhor their practices. We are fully aware that society's 'refusal to acknowledge' after identification of a dangerous stakeholder, [. . .] is an effective counteragent in the battle to maintain civility and civilization. The identification of this class of stake-holder is undertaken with the support of this tactic in mind'.[38]

To identify is not to recognize. If we identify, in general, it is to challenge and put someone away, as in the police sense. But of course, as they take the trouble to specify, police identification does not imply moral recognition – far from it. In fact, quite the opposite, since the tactics to which these ethicists adhere, in full awareness, proceeds by 'identifying stakeholders as dangerous', that is to say illegitimate (and vice versa), refusing to grant them 'recognition' and thereby authorizing against them an exceptional deployment of force in the name of the defence of 'civility and civilization'.

The ANC had used 'coercive power' against the racist police state that ruled by terror in South Africa, and therefore, they concluded, the ANC was 'illegitimate'. As Subhabrata Banerjee comments: 'The breathtaking arrogance of this position not only denies years of struggle against colonial domination, but also serves to justify the "(then) ruling South African culture and government" as legitimate, a flawed and ahistorical argument that displaces attention from the coercive power used by "legitimate" governments to the coercive power used by the ANC in its resistance (the authors are silent on the former but, of course, abhor the latter)'.[39]

But, 'fortunately', continue these authors, 'the ANC, in acquiring legitimacy and abandoning the recourse to coercive power', had gone from the status of 'dangerous stakeholder' to that of 'dependent stakeholder' (that is to say, in their classification, an organization with urgent and legitimate claims but devoid of autonomous power), a position which had won the support of other actors. 'As a dependent stakeholder, the ANC was able to acquire the protection [. . .] of more salient stakeholders (especially investors)'. The organization then became 'a dependent stakeholder of multinationals established in South Africa'. As such, 'The ANC was able to receive protection [. . .] from more prominent stakeholders (in particular investors)'. From then on, 'the worldwide disinvestment movement, *led by the stockholders of multinationals*, was a major force for the transformation' of the regime.[40] According to this interesting rewriting of history, it was thus multinationals and their shareholders, fervent anti-apartheid activists (we saw one blatant example above, in the case of Shell) who, generously taking a 'dependent' liberation movement under their wing, orchestrated a boycott, a disinvestment campaign and sanctions that brought down the regime.

Imagine a 'dangerous group'. What are you to do about it? First identify it, but without recognizing it, that is to say without granting it legitimacy; in this way you will delegitimize it, which will mean it can be repressed. This will involve driving it to give up the use of what they call 'coercive power' (a very broad category which encompasses, beyond physical force, the entire repertoire of 'direct action', any form of extra-parliamentary confrontation) and thereby reduce it to abandoning its strength and falling to the status of 'dependent stakeholder'. So if this group lays down its arms, it will gain recognition from the powerful, who will invite it to their table, legitimize it and eventually go as far as supporting it in its ascent – not without having previously ensured, by taming it if necessary, its docility.

'Dangerous stakeholders', we are told, are illegitimate. But what needs to be understood here is more like this: only the harmless can be deemed legitimate. There is no more legitimate opponent, in the eyes of power, than one that is incapable of threatening it. This is the secret of 'legitimacy' as seen by the masters: they recognize as legitimate only those who have renounced their strength. 'Legitimacy' is the tin medal they get in exchange for their disarmament. Such is the challenge of the struggle for recognition thus conceived. What, indeed, is the condition for obtaining this 'legitimacy' to which some aspire? It comes down to the watchword of the master, that which Malcolm X had already denounced: 'Fight only while respecting the basic rules established by those against whom you fight'[41] – fight only by following these very rules which are made to deprive you of the means of struggle.

The two sides of stakeholder theory, ethical recognition and strategic identification, join to form a double constraint that falls on the actors. If 'stakeholders' manage to build a relationship of force, then they will be recognized at the strategic level, but ethically delegitimized. The false alternative that this *dilemma of recognition* places before protesters is the following: either illegitimate power, or powerless legitimacy. This is the trap.

At first glance, 'stakeholder theory' may seem to be just a smokescreen, a 'simple ideology', but make no mistake, it is much more than that. It is two-sided. It provides management both with the lexicon of an ethical discourse and the operational categories for a strategic management of protest. The notion of stakeholders comes with instruments of analysis, 'sociograms', 'analytical models' that make it possible 'to map meticulously the power and stake of each group'.[42] Behind the false representations, there are real technologies.

At a conference held in Houston in 2011, on 'relations with stakeholders' in the particular case of fracking, a man named Matt Carmichael, 'in charge of foreign affairs' for Anadarko Petroleum, gave some advice on reading to his audience:

> If you are a PR representative in this industry [. . .] I recommend to you three things: (1) download the *U.S. Army/Marine Corps Counterinsurgency Manual* [audible gasps from the audience], because we are dealing with an insurgency. There's a lot of good lessons in there, and coming from a military background, I found the insight in that extremely remarkable. (2) With that said, there's a course provided by Harvard and MIT twice a year, and it's called 'Dealing With an Angry Public.' Take that course [. . .] a lot of the officers in our military are attending this course. It gives you the tools [. . .] (3) I have a copy of 'Rumsfeld's Rules.' You're all familiar with Donald Rumsfeld – that's kind of my bible, by the way, of how I operate.[43]

Another speaker, Aaron Goldwater, CEO of an SME computer firm, closed the day's session. Preaching to the converted, he insisted on the importance of collecting methods and data mining:

> A number of people today [. . .] have talked about having a battle with stakeholders, a bit of a war with stakeholders. So, if you look at the people who are experts at it, which is the military, the one thing they do is gather intelligence [. . .] how do you actually gather intelligence about

your stakeholders? [. . .] because at the end of the day if you are going to deal with them you've got to know about them. [. . .] Stakeholders come with things like geography, they have lots of ways of communicating, [. . .] and they have relationships, they have many relationships [. . .]. I had a father who was an activist, and dad had associations with a lot of other people in his profession [. . .] he was an academic, he called on those relationships to fight a battle.

So it is vital, continues this unworthy son, to get involved in 'tracking and mapping the relationships between stakeholders'. And here too, the military are a model to follow: 'The military doesn't spend billions of dollars on data-mining for the fun of it. They want to know who has relationships with who'. Businesses need to follow suit: the idea is 'having a database that not only has all of your offline conversations recorded in it but all your online conversations, so that you can see that Mary, when we spoke to her about fracking said oh yeah great idea and then she went off on twitter and said these bloody bastards are going to start doing fracking in my area. How do you know that? You should start to combine the data'.

Here we discover, under the reassuring words, something else: the application to those who oppose corporate operations of intelligence methods used by counter-insurgency specialists in Iraq and in Afghanistan, under the name of 'the cartography of the human terrain'.[44] Thus, concepts that had been believed 'demilitarized' become remilitarized.

The schema that Schmitt proposed to account for the concepts behind liberalism needs to be corrected. Between economics and ethics, there is a third, strategic focus, one which mediates between the other two. Between the economic theory of the firm as nexus and the ethical theory of the firm as responsible partnership, there is a third term, the theory of the strategic management of stakeholders.

And when people move from the firm as contract to the firm as conflict, the concepts again split. From the ethical point of view, they speak of the recognition of the other; from the strategic point of view, they practise military/police identification; under the ethical aspect, they glorify dialogue, under the strategic aspect, they wage war. But with this paradoxical caveat: depoliticized categories are used to engage in politics, and demilitarized categories are used to wage war.

On paper, it is true, each of these three visions seems theoretically incompatible with the others. That does not exclude their practical complementarity. Between the conception of the firm as a nexus of contracts, and that of the enterprise as a war machine, between a Jensen and a Pagan, there is no common ground, intellectually speaking. And yet, the triumph of the one conception made the development of the other even more necessary. The neoliberal reorientation of corporate governance, its drastic realignment on shareholder profit, could not fail to entail huge social and environmental impacts which, if Polanyi was right, historically tend to generate powerful social countermovements which management cannot cope with unless it resorts to ad hoc strategic thinking.

Part V

New regulations

— 18 —

SOFT LAW

Where do the rules of law come from? From the social fact itself and the conjunction of ethics and power.

Georges Scelle[1]

The 1970s discovered, among other more pleasant things, the existence of multinationals. The term and the theme, almost absent from the discourses of the previous decade, now entered the public debate. Academics and journalists, activists and politicians started to focus on those giant firms that extended their influence across the world, in many ways rivalling nation states. With multinationals, the 'most important and most visible innovation of the postwar period in the economic field', the most obvious symptom of the 'emergence of a genuine world economy' started to make an appearance: as Peter Drucker notes, 'For the first time [. . .] since the end of the sixteenth century when the word "sovereignty" was first coined, the territorial political unit and the economic unit [were] no longer congruent'.[2] The internationalization of trade came with the increased transnationalization of production, and the old territorial framework of state power no longer coincided with that of private economic power. In consequence, the question of the limits of national legislation and of an *inter*national regulation of multinationals reared its head.[3]

On this point, it was initially the world of labour that went on the offensive. From the end of the 1960s onwards, trade union organizations (including the International Confederation of Free Trade Unions, ICFTU), when faced with multinationals that 'restrict the right of the workers' and 'exploit international labour cost differentials in order to boost profits',[4] argued in favour of a new international law governing their practices. In 1972, the ICFTU called for the drafting

141

of an international treaty under the auspices of the United Nations, a text aimed, beyond the question of workers' rights, to decide on just about all facets of the activity of these firms, including the taxation of capital, the control of investment by host states, technology transfers and contributions to the developing world.

The same year, the Economic and Social Council of the UN instructed a group of experts to study the issue. Should it opt for a binding agreement, or prefer a more flexible form? When questioned by the commission, the CEO of Fiat, Giovanni Agnelli, defended the employers' position: 'We clearly need better rules governing the relations between multinationals and governments. But a binding multilateral agreement [. . .] in the form of a "GATT for investment" does not seem practical at the moment. Instead, the idea of developing a *voluntary* code on the rights and responsibilities of the multinational corporations seems to be an attractive one'.[5]

In Washington, at Congressional hearings, Senator Abraham Ribicoff also asked whether 'an international code of conduct or regulations governing multinationals [might not be] needed?' Finding ways of regulating global capitalism was the big question in the 1970s, he added. 'A code of conduct is what is needed', confirmed the expert Samuel Pisar, 'but how will it be brought into existence [. . .]? I don't believe it is practical to expect the multinational corporations themselves to establish and respect a self-regulatory code'.[6]

In their final report, the UN experts concluded that if the objective was ultimately that of a 'general agreement on multinationals having the force of an international treaty', it would however be 'premature' to open negotiations on this matter. So, rather than a treaty, they would write a code of conduct. Said economist Raymond Vernon, 'there is nothing wrong with an approach of this sort, but it is trivial in comparison with the malaise with which it deals'.[7]

Trivial maybe, but the proposal still worried the business community. In 1973, the *Financial Times* reported: 'the United Nations report is obviously a time bomb ticking in the wings at least as far as the investment future of the multinational corporations is concerned. It looks like the heyday of their growth is past. Multinationals have more danger signs looming on their investment horizon than at any time since World War II'.[8]

At the UN, the international regulation projects led by union confederations then echoed the anti-imperialist agenda of a coalition of 'non-aligned' countries, many of whom had recently won their independence. On the initiative of Algerian President Boumediene, in May 1974 the Assembly General adopted an 'action program for the establishment of a new international economic order'.[9] Six months later, the Charter of Economic Rights and Duties of States reaffirmed state sovereignty over their natural resources and their inalienable right to exercise authority over foreign investment, including law, in exchange for compensation, to 'nationalize, expropriate, or trans-fer ownership of foreign property'. This last sentence was especially unacceptable to the business community.

Action stations! As David Rockefeller wrote in 1975, 'multinational enterprise now finds itself under siege. The battle is still in its early stages'.[10] There were accusations 'from academicians, from writers, from left-leaning economists, and from politicians', accusing this new 'Satan' of relocating production, exploiting developing countries by grabbing their resources, practising tax evasion and eroding the sov-ereignty of nation states. 'We should be doing all in our power to lift the siege that is taking shape around our beleaguered multinational companies'.[11] Otherwise, added Peter Drucker, it was 'entirely pos-sible that the multinationals will be severely damaged and perhaps even destroyed within the next decade'.[12]

The UN had 'declared de facto war on the MNCs and the free enterprise system', said a Heritage Foundation report in 1982.[13] It was the 'poor countries' that were driving it to 'exercise a regulatory authority', to 'govern the global economy' so as 'to increase transfers of resources' that would benefit them. These countries did indeed view technology as '"a common heritage of mankind" – a resource that belongs to no one, to be shared by all countries', as a *right* rather than as 'private property that must be purchased'.[14] And they stigma-tized the very disturbing sub-paragraph where, in black and white, it was written that this might mean the need to 'nationalize, expropri-ate, or transfer ownership of foreign property'. It was the same story the following year, according to Jeanne Kirkpatrick (ambassador, United States representative to the UN, a member of Reagan's cabinet, and a fervent anticommunist): the United Nations, an arena where a 'crude kind of anticapitalist ideology' reigned,[15] a 'version of class war that has been developed by a kind of gross adaptation of Marxist categories to relations among nations',[16] were planning projects of 'paternalistic regulation' which actually, she insisted noisily, were part of a strategy aimed at imposing a 'new world socialism'. Apart from the exaggeration, Kirkpatrick had tangentially identified one of the real issues behind the antagonism: 'Regulation is the instrument for the redistribution of what is called the world's wealth'.[17]

To understand the reason for this persistent dramatization even in 1983, when the neoliberal turn had just started to become entrenched, one must keep in mind that 'many multinational corporations saw the early 1980s not as the dawn of a new era, but as a continuation of the 1970s'.[18] It is important to remember, against the fatalistic illusions of a retrospective narrative, that 'far from the inexorable triumph of free market ideals, the future appeared a contest between the Washington Consensus and [. . .] the prospect of a "new international regulatory order."'[19] Nobody could be sure at the time of winning the battle. The first victories, as we well know, were fragile, far from immune to a reversal. In 1983, Pagan again warned: attempts to create a 'new economic order', and 'efforts to set precedents for the regulation of multinationals' were not dead: they were 'merely awaiting a more opportune moment'.[20]

At the centre of the battle, there was thus a certain type of text, the 'code of conduct', whose meaning, status and scope would be subjected to opposite interpretations: were they mandatory and binding, or optional and voluntary? It was during these debates that some jurists started to thematize the notion, now central in the new capitalist governance, of 'soft law' – a gentle, yielding, flexible law, perhaps even a 'law in the gaseous state'.

In 1975, law theorist René-Jean Dupuy – one of the first to take an interest in this emerging notion – proposed that 'soft law' be understood as the manifestation of a force still unable to establish itself as law, as a law that was still 'unripe', nascent, developing, temporary, transitory or, as he preferred to say, a 'programmatic' law: 'voted in by Third World countries, [these resolutions] are presented in opposition to a positive law which they reject. [. . .] Rather than talk about imperfect laws, it is better to stick to the notion of law as a programmatic statement'.[21] He was visibly seduced by them and surmised that they were an 'attempt to revise law by the way of custom' – an original way, insofar as it aimed to create from scratch, without any previous tradition, a new custom called on to serve as the material source for a law still to come. A kind of 'revolutionary custom' proceeding by the 'factual projection of a political will'.[22]

Other jurists, far from sharing Dupuy's enthusiasm, were worried about the ongoing process. The manoeuvres of the nonaligned, they realized, consisted in exchanging a '"tacit" recognition that the codes must, in fact, if not in name, be voluntary in their legal nature in return for the North's acceptance of more substantive political and economic concessions in the code itself'.[23] In fact, Western diplomats were ready to make important concessions provided they were 'not laid down as compulsory rules but as mere "soft law."' However, 'this tendency is dangerous as "soft law" is something more than "law without any legal obligation" (quite apart from the fact that the concept of a "law without legal obligation" is a logical and semantic impossibility)'. The danger of accepting soft law so as to avoid hard law was that soft law soon started to harden, knowing that the beneficiaries of those 'soft rules' would 'do their best to render them as hard and fast as possible'.[24]

Hardly was an international code adopted than it served as a normative reference. Which meant that in practice, 'the side having first formulated a "code" to its liking enjoys a considerable tactical advantage'.[25] In the fight to constitute the reference point, the firstcomer won the prize; this was well understood by the main protagonists. Hence the race for codification that then began, a 'rush for rival formulations'.[26]

In the rich countries, it was considered that the 'best form of defense against the G-77 onslaught on Western economic interests and values was attack',[27] and this attack took the form of 'apparent concession'. Whereas it would be easier to obtain a consensus among peers, the American administration led the OECD to write its own code of conduct. The arena was changed for one more favourable. If, at the United Nations, the developed countries were in the minority, at the OECD, they were at home. There, they could work fast. The OECD took a year and a half to develop its Guiding Principles for Multinational Companies, non-binding recommendations, with 'broad and sometimes ambiguous' formulations,[28] adopted in June 1976, a full six months before the UN began to work on its own code. In fact, the codes envisaged in New York, mired in negotiations that put irreconcilable positions at loggerheads, never saw the light of day.

'Thus, the race of rival codifications [. . .] was won by the OECD'.[29] This was, as John Robinson summarizes the position, 'a rapid rich world['s] response to the threatened emergence of a much tougher, legally binding code of conduct being negotiated by the United Nations in New York'.[30] A 'pre-emptive strike'.[31] Code against code.

Before being implemented at the OECD by state actors, this strategy, called 'guidance versus regulation',[32] had been initiated by private actors. Alarmed at a very early stage by the initiatives of trade unions in the field of regulating multinationals, the International Chamber of Commerce responded to them in November 1972 with its own Guiding Principles for International Investments. The aim was to 'take the initiative to try to stem a process that threatened to assume alarming proportions if left to the initiative of trade unions and developing countries'.[33]

145

Some big companies, also grasping what was at stake, began to formulate their own home-made codes of conduct. These companies included Caterpillar, which was among the first to write, as early as 1974, its own 'Code of Worldwide Business Conduct'. In 1975, its director of public affairs declared: 'I predict that more companies will venture into this exercise, particularly in a context of growing public scrutiny of multinational corporations'.[34]

It was a classic manoeuvre: make a display of your ethical goodwill in order to avoid legal constraint. As economist Raymond Vernon put it, 'when multinational enterprises begin to feel the breath of governments at their backs, the disposition is to find some formula that relieves the pressure locally'. Thus, '"codes of fair conduct" [. . .] and similar formulas are generally advanced'.[35] Unlike what they would have us believe, far from being a sign of goodwill, this type of voluntary commitment is rather the expression of their *unwillingness* to be regulated.

It would be wrong to see soft law merely as a less stringent version of 'hard' regulation, pursuing similar ends by other means. Its function is fundamentally different. As the authors of a report on the ethical self-regulation of the arms industries blandly put it: 'where laws and regulations are intended to protect the public's interest, company codes and standards are meant to protect a company's interests, especially its reputation for integrity'.[36] By adopting programmes of social responsibility, declared one IBM manager in 1979, firms were 'rising to the defense of the free enterprise system'.[37]

Soft law originated in a lost battle, after which its meaning and political function were reversed: having been a weapon of the South, it now changed into a shield for Northern multinationals. At the polar opposite of Dupuy's optimistic vision, soft law became the major instrument of a strategy for avoiding regulation, aimed at keeping a stillborn norm eternally in the limbo of the law.

The very same people who had viewed with anxiety the arrival of this potential new weapon made it their spearhead, foregrounding the idea that, in economic matters, at the international level there cannot be more than one special legal regime, an 'autonomous branch, less conceptualized and less restrictive, outside the usual processes of law', in which 'the rigid and precise norms of classical international law seem to make room for [. . .] less restrictive rules', and where the rules 'tend to give way to programmes, normativity to forecasting, pure hard law to soft law'.[38]

Proponents of voluntary self-regulation by multinationals these days present it as a pragmatic solution to a problem of which normative regime to adopt: as the legal framework of the nation state is de facto outdated, and the international order lacks a supreme arbitrator, while any attempt to impose binding regulation on this scale is bound to fail, only the flexible and elegant option of the code of conduct remains. In fact, however, when it came to guaranteeing the investments and the property rights of multinationals, this insurmountable obstacle was overcome and binding international agreements reached. In these areas, there was no question of being content with vague recommendations or good intentions. These same hard or rigid normative regimes that are claimed to be lacking when it comes to social and environmental rights are instituted without much difficulty as soon as they are deemed necessary to secure the conditions of accumulation. Here as elsewhere, a double standard is observed.

Business is not hostile to all regulation, only to certain kinds. Typically, when in June 1976 the OECD promulgated its voluntary code of conduct on multinationals, it matched it, on the same day, in the same 'package', with agreements binding on member states relating to the most decisive aspects of the question, including the principle of equal treatment between domestic and foreign companies. In this way they juggled with the conditions. The texture and consistency of the standard were not homogeneous, but varied with the objects under consideration – surfaces that were soft and yielding to social rights, but tough and resistant to property rights.

So soft law is not the name of a new general scheme into which neoliberalism makes us all fall. Against this simplistic picture, César Rodriguez-Garavito is right to emphasize that

> TNCs, for instance, strategically shift among calls for strengthening national and global hard law in matters essential to the profitability of their business (e.g. intellectual property rights), proposals for soft law and self-regulation in other areas (e.g. voluntary codes of conduct for labor), and deregulation in yet other domains (e.g. financial markets). Thus, neoliberal globalization relies neither on 'disciplinary' regulation (Gill 2004) nor on corporate self-regulation or deregulation associated with the 'retreat of the state' (Strange 1996). Rather, neoliberal global governance consists in a mixture of both: hard law to protect corporate rights and soft law to regulate social rights.[39]

Nor should anyone be fooled by the connotations of the vocabulary used. The flexibility of the norm, its apparent softness, means that what will prevail in practice, in the absence of any reliable legal protection, will be the arbitrariness of private power, of really hard and fast relations. A lesser legal constraint (for some) results in greater coercion (for others). So we must always ask ourselves *for whom* soft law is 'soft'. A 'soft' labour law, for example, is hardcore exploitation, a lighter environmental law, and thus worse pollution. Rather than talking about soft law, we would probably be better off talking about 'low law', a law going cheap – something that the political scientist James Rowe expresses more directly: 'the disciplinary underside of voluntary mechanisms like the Global Compact is truncheons, rubber bullets, and tear gas. The consent that business cannot win through voluntary mechanisms will need to be secured with "public regulation" of an overtly violent kind'. In short: 'The truncheon is the code of conduct's telos'.[40]

As defensive weapons in the face of nascent regulations, codes of conduct served, in a third phase, as offensive weapons against existing regulations. It was no longer a matter of 'just defending oneself against a possible law',[41] avoiding regulation, but of actively deregulating – not against the state's will, but driven by neoliberal governments themselves.

Three decades after the events I just mentioned, in 2006, David Cameron delivered a speech to British bosses. He wanted to undeceive those among them who 'still see corporate responsibility as socialism by the back-door'. To the hard of hearing, things had to be said loud and clear. It all came down to a slogan: 'deregulation in exchange for more responsibility'. Or, more clearly: 'the more that companies voluntarily adopt responsible business practices, the more compelling the case for a lighter touch on regulatory inspection and enforcement'.[42]

— 19 —

COSTS/BENEFITS

After all, judgments and valuations of life, whether for or against, cannot be true: their only value lies in the fact that they are symptoms; they can be considered only as symptoms – *per se* such judgments are nonsense. You must therefore endeavour by all means to reach out and try to grasp this astonishingly subtle axiom, *that the value of life cannot be estimated.*

Friedrich Nietzsche[1]

In the early 1970s, the environmental movement and consumer protection had succeeded in establishing themselves as unavoidable political forces in the United States. Their actions sparked an unprecedented wave of government regulations: between 1965 and 1975, more than twenty-five federal legislations were adopted concerning the protection of workers, consumers and the environment. Corresponding budgets quintupled during the period.[2] Various health and environmental agencies were also set up, two of which became the bêtes noires of American employers: the Environmental Protection Agency (EPA) and the Occupational Safety and Health Administration (OSHA).

The lateral pressure of social movements was met with increased government control. This zeal for regulation, as one editorialist on the *Wall Street Journal* fumed, was the direct consequence of a 'concerted attack on business' led by 'public-interest advocates'; and 'this adversary agenda' had been adopted by a new breed of all-powerful government regulatory agencies.[3]

The novelty of these 'new social regulations' lay in their transversal or 'pan-industrial' character[4] – which among other effects rendered inoperable the employers' lobbying traditionally organized by branch or sector of activity. Given, noted David Rockefeller, that companies were undergoing a 'simultaneous assault', the conclusion was that 'all must join in the response. Isolationism can be as disastrous in business as in foreign policy'.[5] The challenge was to go beyond the narrow logics of the competitive struggle to stand up in a common fight.[6] This effort involved the revitalization of former organizations – including the American Chamber of Commerce – and the creation of new ones, including, in 1972, the 'Business Roundtable'. Repeating a tactic previously used by trade unions, it set out to establish 'political action committees' responsible for financing the electoral campaigns of friendly candidates, in order to 'alter the political composition of Congress'.[7]

So battle was now joined with the 'new regulations'. But why exactly were they attacking measures that aimed at reducing pollution, preventing accidents at work, fighting discrimination in the workplace and protecting the health of consumers?

In 1971, Thomas Shepard, co-author of one of the first anti-environmentalist manifestos, targeted what he called the 'disaster lobby', a bunch of alarmist ecologists he regarded as 'the most dangerous men and women in America today'.[8] Immature, uncompromising and diehard, these activists were also shameless liars, who would like to persuade people that air pollution was increasing while the contrary was the case, or that a 'putative black rebellion' was brewing in America while in fact it involved only 'a lunatic fringe – a few paranoid militants who in any other country would be behind bars and whose continued freedom here is testimony to the fact that we are the most liberated and least racist nation on earth'.[9] As for the claim of wanting to save nature by preserving forests, Shepard objected with a knockout argument: 'You don't accuse a beaver of interfering with nature when it chops down a tree to build a dam'.[10] Fortified by such arguments, he concluded: 'The time for surrender and accommodation is past. We must let the American public know that, once free enterprise succumbs to the attacks of the consumerists and the ecologists and the rest of the Disaster Lobby, the freedom of the consumer goes with it. His freedom to live the way he wants and to buy the things he wants without some Big Brother in Washington telling him he can't'.[11] This was the key argument: on the ethico-philosophical level, these regulations hindered the inalienable freedom to consume. After all, if I want to repaint my room with lead paint, insulate my roof with asbestos, buy a car without a seat belt, or force-feed my kids with sandwiches drenched in palm oil, by what right could any 'Big Brother' prevent me?

But that was not all: regulation trampled underfoot not only the customer's freedom, but also the employer's. Health inspectors kept bursting into factories without warning, without having to provide the least authorization – a government intrusion which should surely provoke the indignation of the defenders of human rights, as it represented an 'encroachment on the freedom of individuals as entrepreneurs'.[12] Was the regulatory state a new Big Brother? A 'Big Mother',[13] rather, said Murray Weidenbaum – a suffocating power exercised in the name of care, a benevolent tyranny, the liberticidal expression of a desire for social overprotection.

But the situation was even more serious than people thought, because they had to realize that this 'infringement on the freedom of individuals acting as business executives'[14] actually concealed an insidious change of regime, which led straight towards an exit from capitalism. This 'new wave of government regulation of business' was paving the way, announced Weidenbaum, referring to Berle and Burnham, for a 'second managerial revolution'.[15] Whereas the first revolution had seen control pass from owners to managers, it was now business managers who were gradually being deprived of their prerogatives in favour of those public managers who were the civil servants of regulatory agencies.

The shift in power does not stop there. Behind the bureaucrat hides the leftist activist, who is actually pulling the strings.[16] While some neo-Marxists at the time were proposing, quite against the grain of Engels and Lenin, the thesis of the 'relative autonomy of the state'[17] from the dominant classes, some conservative intellectuals went even further: they were losing control of the state, and its power of constraint was being captured by enemies who, as Jensen denounced, 'are resorting to the political process to invoke the state's police powers in order to take control of corporate assets'.[18] In this hostility to regulation, the desire to preserve intact their power over business management was a decisive motive. It was, in this sense, a fundamentally political revolt. But, more fundamentally, this 'phobia for the state' expressed an intense fear of social movements.

This refusal obviously also had an economic dimension. These new social and environmental regulations appeared as additional cost factors – or even worse, as operators of social redistribution.[19] In fact, insofar as they re-internalized part of the social and environmental costs of private production, insofar as they imposed capital costs previously transferred to others in the form of negative externalities, these measures were redistributive.[20]

Murray Weidenbaum, future president of the Council of Economic Advisors of the Reagan administration and architect of the 1980s wave of deregulation, devoted all his energy, in the middle of the 1970s, to denouncing the 'excessive costs of government regulation'. The new standards enacted by regulators had direct costs for manufacturers – including 'compliance costs' (for example, the purchase of new equipment) – but also indirect costs (for example, the time spent filling out new administrative documents). But these additional production costs, he argued, were paid for by consumers too.[21]

The new safety and environmental standards, he reported, had increased the average price of a new car by $320 between 1968 and 1974.[22] The list of these costly measures included the obligations imposed on carmakers to install seat belts (at an additional cost of $11.51 per vehicle) in 1968, to respect emission standards for exhaust ($6 more), in 1972, and – in the same year – to strengthen the exterior protection of the passenger compartment so as to provide protection for passengers in case of accident ($69.90). 'We must mobilize', he concluded, 'to eliminate the safety measures that generate excessive costs'.[23] If we follow his logic, we realize that seat belts or particulate filters should be optional.

'In earlier periods, when productivity and standards of living were rapidly increasing, the nation could allow itself to applaud the progress of regulations while turning a blind eye to the costs. But these increased federal controls are currently aggravating the slow growth of productivity'.[24] Is it reasonable to worry about health and the environment while our profits and your jobs are at stake? If we dismantled these regulations, the economy would be rid of a heavy burden.[25] The rhetoric of crisis, furthering a 'pedagogy of submission to the economic order', justified revising the social concessions extracted in the previous phase.[26]

However, unlike those obtuse ultra-conservatives who were calling for the pure and simple abolition of social and environmental regulations, Weidenbaum adopted an oblique tactic: rather than dismiss them en bloc, he recommended obstructing them, putting enough spokes in their wheels to block them in practice.

The problem, he claimed, was not regulation in general, but only excessive regulation, *over-regulation*. A certain amount of regulation, of course, was necessary, but there were limits. But how were these limits to be fixed? Where was the line to be drawn? There is over-regulation, said Weidenbaum, when 'the costs for the company exceed the profits'. Hence the golden rule he advocated: 'Government regulation [. . .] should be carried to the point where the incremental costs equal the incremental benefits, and no further'.[27] In the guise of common sense, this principle hid a small revolution. It involved posing the cost/

benefit analysis thus defined as a criterion for decision, a cardinal rule posed as an absolute condition for any regulatory project.

To grasp the scale of the change, we need to compare this new principle with those it was meant to supplant. Take the case of a plant whose toxic fumes are causing disease in the vicinity. Under what conditions can a government agency force it to equip itself with an anti-pollution filter?

One first approach was to give priority to the preservation of health, conceived as a fundamental right. The ultimate aim was then to minimize the emission of pathogenic pollutants, to make it tend towards zero. By this logic, the manufacturer had to be forced to equip himself with the most efficient anti-pollution filter possible.

A second approach, a variant of the previous one, weighted the principle of protection by considerations of feasibility, both technical and economic. Before issuing a standard, make sure that the corresponding technologies exist or can be developed, if need be giving industry enough time; evaluate compliance costs, compare them with the profits, ensure that the measure did not financially jeopardize the activity, even at the expense of public aid to allow the transition. According to this principle, the industrialist would be obliged to equip himself with the most effective pollution control filter possible, given the limits of his capabilities.[28]

If, on the contrary, the cost/benefit approach defended by the deregulators was adopted, the two previous principles were invalidated: it would become impossible to set unconditional health standards (residents' health would be preserved only to the extent that it would not cost the industrialist 'too much'), and even if the company could financially afford it, it would not necessarily have to reduce its toxic emissions (an anti-pollution filter would be considered too expensive once its price exceeded the corresponding 'gains' for the population, even if the expenditure was small compared to the profits generated by the firm). In concrete terms, if it cost the company more to reduce its emissions of fumes than it cost the victims to treat their respiratory diseases, then the industrialist could continue to pollute. The health expenses *for residents* were balanced against the cost *for the industrialist* of avoiding damage to the health of the former. This was the inversion of an old adage: cure is better than prevention.

But, even before knowing if a regulatory project was or was not going to be validated by this kind of test, the question of the conditions of possibility of the test itself arose. What were the requirements for this? In order for the comparison to be made, it must be possible to evaluate first to assess both the costs of regulation and its potential benefits. As for the second part, things were not easy. How could one calculate the 'expected benefits' of an anti-pollution measure?

Regardless of the question of the monetary assessment of these benefits, it would first be necessary to model their likely effects, establishing, for example, a reliable correlation between the reduction of a particulate matter in the atmosphere and its precise impact on the number of associated pathologies. To 'determine the relation between dose and effect, between exposure to the substance and risk of disease'[29] was a difficult task that required 'an array of complex scientific and medical models, with uncertainties multiplying rapidly along the tortuous paths linking pollution sources, atmospheric chemistry, meteorology, materials science, and epidemiology'.[30]

As one senator exclaimed during hearings on the subject in the late 1970s: 'If we waited until we got the information necessary to determine whether or not the cost-benefit balance of building a bag house at Armco was equivalent to that of treatment for the common cold and for every other respiratory ailment, if we had waited for that, we never would have made any regulation. If that had been the standard of evidence, no regulation would ever have been upheld in court'.[31] This was the challenge: by posing the cost/benefit analysis as a decision-making principle, they were seeking to modify the way evidence is weighed in favour of industry. It was an offensive launched on the grounds of evidence – grounds that were at once epistemological and judicial.

In 1977, an epidemiological study published in *The Lancet* showed that workers at a plastic foodwrap factory were exposed to benzene levels that were below the authorized thresholds but they had between five and ten times the chance of developing leukaemia than the ordinary population.[32] The OSHA, the agency responsible for hygiene and safety at work, urgently promulgated a new standard lowering the maximum exposure levels to benzene. It was in compliance with its carcinogenic policy: minimize exposure within the limits of technical and economic feasibility.[33]

But the industry did not interpret it that way. In 1978, a Louisiana Court revoked the new standard on the grounds that 'without an estimate of benefits supported by substantial evidence [. . .]', OSHA did not provide evidence that the effects of the new standard on workers' health were going to 'bear a reasonable relationship to its [. . .] price tag'. The judges added, somewhat deviously: 'The general agreement in the scientific community [. . .] permits the further factual deduction that reducing the permissible exposure limit [. . .] will result in some benefit. This finding and deduction, however, does not yield the conclusion that measurable benefits will result, and OSHA is unable to point to any studies or projections supporting such a finding'.[34] Or, more clearly: the substance is known to be carcinogenic, it is likely that reducing the exposure reduces the risk; but the question which the agency did not answer is 'by how much?' How many cases of leukaemia less for a reduction of so many parts per million of benzene in the atmosphere of the workplace? The agency did not answer because there were no studies to provide figures. But, rather than lowering the standard as a precaution right away, the judges decided that the agency would have to wait for such studies to become available before reaching a decision.

With this judgment, the cost/benefit principle inveigled its way into US jurisprudence. At the time, Weidenbaum hailed this decision as a promising sign which, he commented with undisguised enthusiasm, 'seems to set the high ground to which the public policy debates on regulation could profitably shift'.[35] Trade unionist Anthony Mazzocchi saw things differently: 'The court order leaves us with the body-in-the-morgue method of proof. [. . .] It's a question of who pays. And the courts have placed themselves firmly on the side of the corporation'.[36]

In fact, it was not until ten years later that the standard imposed in 1977 was restored. The expert Peter Infante estimates that this delay 'cost' more than two hundred deaths from leukaemia and myeloma among the workers concerned.[37] This was just one of many examples of the 'human cost' of these obstructive manoeuvres conducted in the name of cost/benefit analysis. Some economists have blood on their hands.

The sword of cost/benefit analysis, however, was double-edged. Even if the first condition had been fulfilled – plausibly indicating the precise extent of the expected effects – there was a second one left: quantifying in cash terms the damage avoided – a sine qua non for relating the social and environmental 'benefits' of a regulatory measure to its costs for the industry.

How could one estimate in monetary terms the damage caused to the environment, health or life?[38] As long as the destruction affects merchant goods, we can refer to their price. But as soon as it affects realities outside the market, the economist is all at sea. For lack of guidance, he will have to invent procedures of conventional estimation. In the 1970s, goaded by the rise of cost/benefit analysis, economists got to work on the issue. They put together various methods, more or less absurd, to estimate what a life was worth.

A first approach, that of Discounted Future Earnings (DFE), suggests that the worth of your life is equal to the total future income of which an early death would deprive you. Income is unequal, so all lives do not have the same value. Measured by this yardstick, the life of an executive is worth more than that of a worker of the same age. The life of an infant is worth less than that of his older brother who is already receiving a salary while his younger brother will still be a burden to his parents. The value of the life of a housewife, a worker without income, is zero. That of an elderly person amounts to almost nothing: in the late 1970s, 'one DFE index placed the value of an 85 year old black woman at $123'.[39] There was also the instructive case of 'loss lives', those which incur expenses (for example, medical care) without generating revenue: 'an auto accident which kills a seriously handicapped child, in this methodology, may produce a net benefit to society'.[40]

Swift, in his famous *A Modest Proposal*, envisaged another method of calculation: 'I have already computed the charge of nursing a beggar's child (in which list I reckon all cottagers, labourers, and four-fifths of the farmers) to be about two shillings per annum, rags included; and I believe no gentleman would repine to give ten shillings for the carcass of a good fat child, which, as I have said, will make four dishes of excellent nutritive meat, when he hath only some particular friend, or his own family to dine with him'.[41] He distinguished two modes of calculation: on the one hand the *value* of the child, determined by its production costs, and on the other hand the *price* of the same child, determined by the willingness of buyers to pay for this type of meat on the market of gourmet foods.

Neglecting the – crucial – issue of the production of life, contemporary economists who had picked up the baton, however, stuck to the second criterion, that of willingness to pay, but with one not insignificant ethical improvement on Swift's text, since they would henceforth take into account not only the desire of the buyers but also that of the individual whose life was the subject of the transaction: for how much would you agree to be eaten? Or, conversely, but it comes down to the same thing, what would you pay *not* to be eaten?

This is the second great method, that of 'Willingness To Pay' (WTP), based on the individuals' own assessments of the 'good' of being alive. At first, economists had considered putting the question directly to people by polling them for their views, but respondents were struggling to answer – many preferring, all things considered, to lose an infinite sum rather than to die. To get around the difficulty, Schelling and Mishan decided to rephrase the question: not 'how much would you pay to avoid dying?', but rather 'how much would you be willing to pay to reduce your risk of premature death by x percent?'[42] But this estimate varied. It was determined by the differentials in ability to pay. The executive officer of a mining company was in a position to pay much more to have the asbestos in his office removed, thereby reducing his risk of cancer from 0.05% to 0.01%, than was a worker of the same company to reduce his risk from 0.5 to 0.1%.[43] In this case, which of these two assessments should prevail, and for whom?

Faced with this kind of aporia, they went down another, more traditional path. To measure the monetary value of things, economic analysis usually relies on the 'aggregated consent of consumers to pay', i.e. on price.[44] Ever since the abolition of slavery, the economist no longer had an official market of human lives to access that kind of truth; therefore, he went in search of 'alternative markets'. Typically, these were trades or positions at risk. By observing for what amount additional workers would accept a higher risk, he hoped to be able to work out the value they assigned to their lives. But here again, several difficulties arose.

Unlike the postulate on which this method was based, it is doubtful that the amount of risk premiums could be adequately interpreted as a self-assessment of the value of life. It more prosaically matches what these workers were able to negotiate in a forced choice situation, dominated by inequalities of qualification, resources and access to information, not to mention unemployment, barriers to mobility and discrimination. People regularly 'consent' to be poorly paid, just as they regularly 'consent' to paying too much, but this does not at all mean that they feel that such a low salary or such a high rent provides a fair standard of value, a price that can serve as a general standard for a public policy.

The company turns to the economist and asks him, as a 'recognized expert on the monetary value of things',[45] what is a life worth – or more implicitly, what is a fair price for a life, the price which one could take as a reference standard to monetarily assess the benefits of reducing risks at work, for example. The economist, placed in a very uncomfortable position, not daring to admit that he is absolutely incapable of answering this kind of normative request, mutters and mumbles, hesitates, goes round and round in circles and ends up asking the same question of the company: let's see, just fill out this questionnaire for me . . . no, actually, in fact I'm not sure I can trust your answers, show me your pay slip instead, starting with your workers at risk, how much will you really accept to lose your shirt? Oh, is that all?' Finally, the economist answers the question 'what is a life worth?' – a question asked, you will recall, in order to find out what it would be rational to spend in order to save a life – by replying: no more than what employers are already ready to pay out to risk one. In short, the snake swallows its own tail.

In 2006, expert economists calculated that one life was statistically worth exactly $1,266,037 in the United States, and just as exactly $5,248 in Bangladesh.[46] Are we to conclude that the 'benefit' of saving a Bangladeshi life is about 241 times less than that of saving an American life? It is estimated that a quarter of Bangladesh could be under water by the end of the century; this country is at the forefront of the current ecological disaster. Will a country-by-country rebate be used to calculate the overall vital 'benefits' of reducing greenhouse gas emissions? Or should we fix an average universal price on human life? But on what 'scientific' basis will we do so?

The truth is that there is no such basis. And not because of technical difficulties, methodological biases or errors in calculation, but because there is no *fair* price for a life, the suppression of which cannot be exchanged for anything without an irreducible loss. The question, in other words, is necessarily aporetic. But this, it must be emphasized, is an integral part of the challenge thrown down by the deregulators. It is the *sphinx's tactic*: put yourself in a position where you can either reply to an insoluble riddle, or jump into the void. There is no other choice.

Questioned in 1979 by a Senate commission, Weidenbaum was grilled by a young Al Gore who persistently kept asking him how much a life was worth: what is the monetary value of a mutilation, a congenital malformation, or the lost life of an asbestos worker? Weidenbaum stubbornly refused to answer, retreating behind his moral values: 'I never have in any of my calculations put a dollar sign on a human life. I think a life is precious'.[47]

But, insisted Senator Gore, if, as you demand, the principle of a cost/benefit evaluation has to be imposed, how can you refuse, even implicitly, to assign a monetary value to life? How for example 'do you quantify the benefits of banning asbestos?'

> Dr. Weidenbaum: The benefit of banning asbestos would be the number of people whose lives are saved or whose length of life is expanded by banning asbestos.
> Mr. Gore: And what dollar value would you . . .
> Dr. Weidenbaum: I would not put a dollar value.[48]

But how can the cost/benefits analysis be applied? In Weidenbaum's view, you would have to compare the number of deaths avoided by banning asbestos with the number of deaths that this banning would itself occasion. And the deaths due to banning asbestos? 'As a motorist who uses asbestos, who gets the benefit of asbestos every time I put my foot on the brake in my car, and the asbestos in those brake linings prevents me from hitting into your car, you and I are both, Mr. Chairman, in effect very well aware of the benefits of asbestos. Any analysis that would just look at the lives saved from banning asbestos without looking at the lives lost from banning asbestos would not benefit this society'.[49]

Weidenbaum fell back on a simplistic dilemma. Ever since brake linings had been made not of asbestos but of fibreglass, he pointed out, there had not been any carnage on the roads, so far as he was aware. But the senator persisted:

> Mr. Gore: You are saying no limitation of exposure to asbestos until we perform this cost-benefit or cost-effectiveness analysis, and I am suggesting to you that it is impossible to come up with a figure that has any kind of accuracy whatsoever that would measure the number of people whose lives would be saved by not limiting the exposure of workers to asbestos in the workplace. [. . .] Do you think that can be accurately calculated?
> Dr. Weidenbaum: That is the challenge that I would put to a regulatory agency.
> Mr. Gore: And you would put that challenge to them and require them to meet that challenge before they could protect the people exposed in the workplace? [. . .]. Even though you are not sure whether they can meet that challenge?[50]

Weidenbaum had just betrayed himself by delivering the key word that summed up his tactics: facing the regulator with impossible *challenges*.

As much as it is relatively easy to estimate the costs of regulation for industry, it is difficult to predict their quantitative effects in an open environment, and impossible, *except artificially*, to evaluate monetarily the 'benefits' for off-market goods. Weidenbaum knew this and his tactics generally exploited this asymmetry to paralyse his adversary – only to be paralysed in turn when the question was turned back on him.

— 20 —

A CRITIQUE OF
POLITICAL ECOLOGY

The profit of a building contractor is sometimes something other than spoliation [. . .]; he does not make a profit because his company produces much more than it costs, but because he does not pay for everything it costs.

J.C.L Simonde de Sismondi[1]

Capital [. . .] is in practice moved as much and as little by the sight of the coming degradation and final depopulation of the human race, as by the probable fall of the earth into the sun.

Karl Marx[2]

In 1950 there appeared an innovative book: *The Social Costs of the Business Enterprise* by William Kapp, a heterodox author whose name has since been stricken from the history of economic thought.[3] This book was an early environmentalist critique of capitalism. Proponents of economic liberalism saw it as a new attack, a new challenge to be met in their intellectual counter-offensive.

Take a factory that is spreading pollution. Its activity has 'private costs' – expenditure on equipment, raw materials, wages – but also 'social costs', costs 'which are not accounted for in entrepreneurial outlays but instead are shifted to and borne by third persons and the community as a whole'.[4] Typically, if the industrialist dumps waste into the nearby river rather than being responsible for reprocessing it, it is others (fish, birds, boaters, residents and so on) who will suffer the 'costs', one way or another.

These social costs of private production are *unpaid* (they cost nothing to the industrialist, nor to his shareholders), *shifted* to others who 'pay' them, if only in kind (it often 'costs' them their well-being, their health and even their lives) and *unrecognized* (they do

160

not appear in the company's balance sheets nor in the national accounts). This outsourcing is in the first place material and physical, but it is also cognitive and epistemological: from the point of view of the capitalist economy, in all senses of the word, these negativities do not *count*.

Werner Sombart argued that this was the 'way of seeing' inherent in modern accounting techniques which, by showing profit as pure quantity, a figure at the bottom of a column, had originally made the concept of capital thinkable.[5] 'The man who devotes himself to transactions on a book-keeping basis', wrote the economic historian Hector Robinson, 'has only one aim – the increase of values comprehended only quantitatively. He does not consider mainly corn or wool or cotton or cloth or the cargoes of ships, or tea or pepper. These (the true realities of commerce) become mere shadows, they become unreal [. . .] – the very conception of capital as "lucrative possessions" practically depends on the analysis of scientific accounting'.[6] According to this hypothesis, capitalist rationality is the product of a certain 'graphic reason',[7] the effect of a writing technology that converts quality into quantity.

But the capitalist definition of value also – and more radically – depended on a fundamental division between what was or was not going to be taken into account. It was founded, as the historian Carroll Quigley noted, on the decision to include only 'economic costs' and not 'social costs'.[8] 'In the new industrial system of the early 19th century, all these costs – transportation of the workers to and from the factory, housing, education, retirement, burial, sickness, care of orphans [. . .] were excluded from the bookkeeping of the enterprise. Is it any wonder that it was a financial success?' Capital benefits from a set of positive externalities only a fraction of which it finances. It also discharges onto its social and natural environment a whole set of negativities the burden of which is assumed by others, both human and non-human. It is only on the hidden condition of this twofold outsourcing of the real costs of production that it can present itself as an economic beneficiary. Capitalism is an *economy of outsourcing, or 'discharge'*.

This vast outsourcing of the social costs of private production, however, triggers countermovements of social self-defence. As Kapp wrote in 1950, extending the analyses of his friend Karl Polanyi:[9] 'The political history of the last 150 years can be fully understood only as a revolt of large masses of people [. . .] against the shifting of part of the social costs of production to third persons or to society'.[10] The modern and contemporary history of social *and* environmental

161

struggles could be read in this light as a *revolt of the outsourced,* whose motives, only apparently heterogeneous, are united by a common root: the same rejection, the same refusal to shoulder the 'social costs' of private production, to pay for capital.[11]

With his concept of social costs, Kapp radicalized a thesis that had been put forward in the 1920s by the economist Arthur Pigou.[12] In some cases, noted the latter, a production, although profitable for the private agent who embarks on it, entails for the company losses that outweigh his own gains. The existence of a discrepancy between 'private product' and 'social product'[13] was the exception that invalidated the argument of the followers of laissez-faire. In such a case, it was clearly false to claim that the pursuit of selfish interest maximized the total value. To correct this kind of dysfunction, concluded Pigou, it was 'necessary that an authority of wider reach should intervene and should tackle the collective problems of beauty, of air and of light'.[14] The state could and should intervene in such cases by 'extraordinary encouragements' or 'extraordinary restraints':[15] subsidies on the one hand, taxes on the other.

Until Kapp's book, however, these negative externalities had been considered as a peripheral problem, a minor aberration in economic theory. He showed on the contrary that the discharge of social costs was a general phenomenon, consubstantial with a mode of decision with 'a built-in tendency to disregard those negative effects (e.g., air and water pollution) which are "external" to the decision-making unit'.[16] This had radical theoretical implications, because as neither company accounting nor prices in general are really able to record the 'destructive off-market effects'[17] shifted onto the social and natural environment, 'the price indicators are not only imperfect and incomplete; they are misleading'.[18]

The liberal economist Frank Knight, who had been one of the very first to criticize, in 1924, the environmental taxation defended by Pigou,[19] wrote in the early 1950s a vitriolic account of Kapp's book, which he denigrated as a pure example of socialist propaganda.[20] Certainly, he answered, the destruction of the environment has its costs, but so does the preservation of the environment, too. For the picture to be complete, the social and economic costs of private production should be weighed against the costs of the alternative, the 'costs of eliminating costs'.[21] In this way, he was stating what would become the central trope of the neoliberal critique of social and environmental regulation, based entirely on this principle of symmetrization of the problem and its remedy. This was the very same principle that we saw in the previous chapter.

Within the previous consensus, it had been agreed that it was desirable, in the case of industrial pollution, 'to make the owner of the factory liable for the damage caused to those injured'.[22] But this was just what Knight and his comrades disputed. It was Ronald Coase who formalized the argument. We commonly think, he said, 'that any measure which will remove the deficiency is necessarily desirable'.[23] But this is a prejudice. We need to remember that, in such a case, to 'avoid the harm to B would inflict harm on A'. If pollution has a cost (for the polluted), anti-pollution measures also have one (for the polluters). Before deciding what to do, you have to put both in balance.

Likewise, as Daniel Fischel says,

> if a firm dumps pollutants in a stream, the firm imposes costs on the users of the stream that may exceed the benefits to the firm. It does not follow, however, that pollution is immoral behavior which should be halted. Consider the reciprocal case in which the firm does not pollute because of concern for users of the stream and instead relies on a more expensive method of disposing wastes. In this situation the users of the stream impose costs on the firm's investors, employees, and consumers that may exceed the benefits to users of the stream. Neither polluting nor failing to pollute is a *priori* the 'ethically' or 'morally' correct course of action.[24]

Rather as if, on the pretext that hurting and caring for someone both incur costs, one could conclude that both acts are ethically indifferent. I have hurt you and that costs you, but to heal you would cost me in turn, so I conclude, says the economist, tapping on his calculator, that neither harming you, nor repairing the damage I have done to you, is a priori 'ethically' or 'morally' correct or incorrect.

It would be wrong, these economists assure us, to pretend that it is always those responsible who should pay. It depends, because penalizing the author of the damage may be less profitable overall than not doing so. We are thus invited to judge the damage in terms of a cost-benefit balance, where only the consideration of the total value counts. If the latter 'might, in sum, be greater if the harmed party is left to bear the damages',[25] then, is it economically rational that the victims take over the costs that others have inflicted on them? 'If we assume that the harmful effect of the pollution is that it kills the fish, the question to be decided is: is the value of the fish lost greater or less than the value of the product which the contamination of the stream makes possible?'[26]

If dead fish are worth less than the production of the chemical factory (which is more than likely), then it is economically rational to let them die.[27] Neoliberalism is, basically, anti-environmentalist.

These economists may present their approach as self-evident, but such calculations presuppose, however, that it is possible (1) to exhaustively record the social and environmental damage linked to a specific activity, and (2) to measure them adequately according to market values. Now these postulates are both problematic. Let's examine them in turn.

In view of the copious examples that can be found in the literature, listing environmental damage looks child's play: the cloud of smoke hypothetically only affects the immediate neighbourhood, the effect of spilling the poisonous substance is limited to killing x fish in the adjacent river. In short, we only envisage situations of finite damage, circumscribed in space and time. But this is to misunderstand the reality of the phenomena of pollution that are characterized by their non-finiteness. In space, first of all: they are not just local, limited to specific areas; they have repercussions elsewhere. And in time, as well: environmental damage is not just instantaneous and immediate, it may persist long after their first manifestation; it may also reveal itself much later, after a long time lag.[28]

Neoclassical economics claims to be able to analyse the phenomena of pollution according to the old pattern of 'mutual reciprocal exchange relationships between micro-economic units'[29] Except that, in an ecosystem, 'the causal process is not, as a rule, bilateral in character, with specific polluters causing damage to specific, identifiable individuals or affected parties'.[30] What we are dealing with, Kapp emphasizes, is more 'a principle of cumulative or circular causation'.[31] Multiple sources of pollution generate combined effects which do 'not necessarily vary proportionately with their amount and frequency. Particularly when critical threshold levels of the assimilative capacity of the environment are reached and when different pollutants combine in chemical reactions and concentrations, the discharge of additional residual waste products may have not proportionate, but disproportionate, that is, nonlinear, effects with possibly sudden catastrophic consequences on human health and well-being'.[32] In addition to their non-finitude and their overdetermination, environmental disturbances have a global character. As Kapp wrote in 1977, 'they are *global* in the sense that certain persistent pollutants and residuals may affect potentially the entire planet by altering the chemical composition of the atmosphere, giving rise to climatic changes, with far-reaching consequences'.[33]

Even as this ecosystemic mode of thinking was emerging, orthodox economics remained in thrall to a serial and linear conception of trade that prevented it from conceiving anything other than simple relations between particular cases of pollution and immediate damages. An emission of greenhouse gas may affect those who breathe

164

it immediately, but it also plays a part in the production of a global hyperphenomenon – a 'hyperobject' that neoclassical economic thinking, dependent on an outdated and pre-ecological epistemology, is unable to grasp other than by fragmenting it and chronically underestimating it.[34] 'To meet this challenge', says Kapp '[. . .] requires even more than quantification and mathematics. It requires a willingness to take account of and evaluate the physical flows and effects in *real* terms'.[35] Doing science differently, going beyond economic rationality by developing a new ecological reason.

In addition to the problem of the aggregation of environmental effects, there is the problem of the commensurabilization of the damage. 'What has to be decided', demands Coase, 'is whether the gain from preventing the harm is greater than the loss which would be suffered elsewhere as a result of stopping the action which produces the harm'.[36] But this kind of balancing exercise presupposes that these two kinds of 'costs' can be adequately expressed in terms of the same accounting unit. We have already discussed these difficulties in the previous chapter: what is a life worth? What will be the common measure between, let's say, Eternit's profits and the number of deaths caused by asbestos? And who will decide this measure?

The moralists may be scandalized perhaps, retort the neoliberals, but regulatory measures, starting with the taxing of polluting industries, already implicitly assign monetary equivalents to such realities that are deemed to be priceless. The problem, they say, is not that we attribute value to a landscape, to an animal species or to human lives. The problem is how we do it. The assessment methods in force, those underlying public policy, they say, 'take as their basis social *prices* (the price of human life, price of prevention against accidents, etc.) that reflect more the idea that certain well organized and particularly highly motivated lobbies [. . .] have of those implicit prices rather than the "optimal" social level that would result from a perfect grasp of the set of individual scales of preference'.[37] In short, what concerns them is the way the current mode of assessment is of a *political* nature: governmental, of course, but above all, too much subject to the 'pressures' of social movements.

But what is the alternative? How else are we to determine 'optimal' price of breathable air or healthy living? 'It's the one that would prevail if we had a market where everyone could compare the price he would be willing to pay to have to put up with less pollution with the price that the polluter would be willing to accept to reduce its pollution'.[38]

165

In one famous example, Coase portrays two neighbours, one a doctor, the other a confectioner. The sound of the craftsmen's machines prevents the doctor, on the other side of the wall, from using his stethoscope. The doctor sues his neighbour. The first possibility is that the court, agreeing with the doctor, will order the confectioner to halt his machines. The confectioner will lose his source of income. But there is nothing to stop him, remarks Coase, once justice is done, negotiating with his neighbour to 'buy' from him the right to continue making a noise. In the second scenario, the court dismisses the doctor's case and authorizes the confectioner to continue to operate his machines. If the doctor still wants to continue practising his profession, however, he too can negotiate with his neighbour to buy the right to some peace and quiet.

Popularized by George Stigler, Coase's theorem has been presented as the paradoxical demonstration of a 'symmetry in relations' between polluter and pollutant and fact that 'the composition of output will not be affected by the manner in which the law assigns liability'.[39] In both cases, it is said, whatever the judge's decision, the agents are able to negotiate a private agreement that satisfies the two parties. As for the rest, knowing who pays is an 'economically indifferent' question to the extent that transfers of money one way or the other do not affect the total value. This is an excellent illustration of the reversibility of social positions, the indifference of economics to the law, the inanity of attributing responsibility, the superfluity of government regulation, and conversely of the self-sufficiency of a private order based on bargaining over rights (the right to pollute, the right not to be polluted).

Except that, when we take a closer look, Coase's argument was far from establishing all of those things. In which cases can negotiation rationally succeed? The doctor cannot buy the silence of the machines unless he earns enough to make the confectioner an offer at least equal to the income that the latter will lose if they are shut down. Similarly, the confectioner cannot buy from his neighbour the right to continue his noisy activity unless he earns at least as much as the latter, otherwise he will be unable to make an offer good enough to compensate for his loss of fees.[40] The constant factor, whatever the deliberations of the court, is that only the man who earns more than the other can hope to bargain for the reversal of an unfavourable court decision. If the judge has ruled in favour of the confectioner but the doctor earns less than him, the doctor will have to endure the noise pollution. Thus, contrary to the interpretations that some people have given of it, this paradigmatic example does not show that the positions of the agents are always reversible, nor that the judicial decision is disinterested in all cases. On the contrary, it establishes that the law makes a difference by recognizing a right not to suffer pollution regardless of the polluted party's income. It also shows that the asymmetry of the power of negotiation, determined by the disparity of income, is generally irreversible in the absence of a binding right. And it shows, finally, that in the absence of a legal rule, the decision is abandoned to the arbitrariness of economic inequalities.

Be this as it may, Coase's major theoretical innovation resided in this bizarre idea of putting the polluted in a position to buy from their polluter their right not to be polluted – to bargain for their rights, to privatize responsibility.[41] This was the signal for a major shift. Before Coase's article, when 'the possibility of a negotiated resolution simply was unrecognized',[42] economists agreed quite generally on the need for corrective action by the public authorities. Instead of the traditional instruments of government intervention against pollution – taxes, subsidies and standards – the neoliberals now, in the 1960s, promoted an approach designed in terms of rights of transferable property. The idea was to set up new markets on which the rights to pollute would be traded – alternative mechanisms to state intervention, but also different from social and political power relations.

First of all, commercial arrangements were envisaged that replicated Coase's scenario, his deal between confectioner and doctor. One could offer polluters the opportunity to buy from the polluter their right not to be polluted. As Stigler stated: 'When a factory spews smoke on a thousand homes, the ideal solution is to arrange a compensation system whereby the homeowners pay the factory to install smoke reduction devices up to the point where the marginal cost of smoke reduction equals the sum of the marginal gains to the homeowners'.[43] The value of health and environmental 'goods' could thus be fixed not by a political decision but through a market mechanism. If you care about your health or this particular landscape, if preserving them is important to you, then you will put a price on them, an amount that will ultimately express, through the objective measure of willingness to pay, the value of the corresponding 'goods'. Thus was invented a strange principle: that of the polluted who pays.

In 1966, Thomas Crocker imagined another type of market: a government agency would establish rights to emit polluting substances, and these rights would be auctioned.[44] Two years later, John Dales proposed a similar model, a system of transferable 'rights to pollute', the total limit of which would be fixed by the government, while the price would be determined by a market that 'automatically ensures that the required reduction in waste discharge will be achieved at the smallest possible total cost'.[45]

The market has failed? Long live the market! Because what better solution is there, faced with the defects of the existing market, than to create a new one, an illusory sticking plaster stuck on the first? Thus was invented a *commercial governance of externalities*. In 1971, Nixon, campaigning for re-election, fleetingly proposed 'selling permits to pollute',[46] but the idea was not politically mature. It was not until the 1990s that such markets for the rights to pollute, well known today, were tried out in the United States.[47] This was a quite new case of 'artificial markets' created from scratch on the basis of economic theory.[48] We all know how successful they proved to be.

The problem, said the environmental critics, is that the social and environmental costs are not taken into account by capitalist economics. If you want us to take them into account, answered the neoclassical economists without losing a beat, we have to assign a price to these realities – without that, they cannot possibly be accounted for. Rejecting the principle of political evaluation, they promoted assessment by market criteria. Markets could be presented as gnoseological solutions to the problem of assessing value, thereby providing a very elegant justification, far from the crass materialism that was after all its essential motive, for a new extension to the domain of private appropriation.

As Kapp clarified: 'I am not denying that it is possible to attribute a monetary value to environmental damages, to human health, human life, or for that matter to esthetic values, just as I am not denying the possibility of placing a monetary value on a piece of art. In fact, in markets such evaluations are made constantly; but [. . .] I am *denying* that monetary values constitute appropriate and responsible criteria for the evaluation of the damages caused by environmental disruption'.[49] The problem was not that these realities were absolutely immeasurable (they were), but that the criteria of commensurability were off beam.

Can a market adequately estimate social and environmental costs? Kapp answered in the negative. Under the fetish of the 'market', there are individual agents who are supposed to be able to determine, through their aggregate choices, the fair price of the environmental realities at stake. But structural limits prevented them from doing so satisfactorily.

The first problem was the limit of the gnoseological capacities of the rational economic agent. Abandoned to himself, 'the individual is not able to appraise the full range of the negative consequences of pollution', as well as 'the full range of benefits resulting from the improvement of the quality of life'.[50] This does not mean that these effects are absolutely unknowable, just that this agent is unable to guess them from market signals. That would need something quite different: a whole activity of socialized information on other bases, and the development of new environmental sciences for which Kapp called – and which the market would not generate by itself.

The second difficulty concerned the temporal horizon in which such agents make their choices. Their decisions affect 'the interests of future generations', but these are not represented in the calculations, 'and therefore will not be reflected in current market prices'.[51] The structural trend therefore consists in choosing an immediate gain at the cost of a loss transferred to others, in a future that will no longer concern us.

The third obstacle is the limits of the principle of the 'willingness to pay'. In the view of neoclassicals, the market shows, by the amount that individuals are ready to pay for certain goods, the state of their subjective preferences. The principle seems plausible: if something counts a great deal to you, you will be ready to commit a large amount to obtain or preserve it. But your 'willingness to pay' is limited in practice by your ability to pay. You *would* probably give everything in the world to save a loved one, but you can only offer what you actually have. The criterion of willingness to pay is structurally distorted by the structure of economic inequalities.[52] If one used this principle to decide, for example, on creating a park either in a wealthy residential area or working-class neighbourhood, it is more than likely that in an auction, with equal subjective preferences, the first group of residents will win. If one had to decide on the location of a discharge plant or cellulose factory, it is equally certain that the latter group would lose again. In an unequal society, giving the market the task of reallocating inalienable environmental rights inevitably results in allowing the wealthiest to offload social costs onto the poorest.[53] It is those who cannot afford to pay (in money) who will pay (in kind). And this is part of a vicious circle where economic inequality attracts to it an environmental inequality that further aggravates the real misery of the dispossessed.

If we want to *take into account* environmental realities, say the neoliberals, we must integrate them into the capitalist logic of value, which implies extending the domain of private property to the common or public goods that had hitherto eluded it. The postulate is that, from the moment a reality becomes private, and gains a market value, so those who benefit from it will have an interest in its preservation. In this conception of the world, the destruction of an environmental reality counts for nothing if it has not been given a quantitative value. The pollution of a lake becomes an economic reality – a reality *tout court* – only if, for example, there is a nautical base that will see its revenues decrease as a result. A non-capitalist lake, on the other hand, *does not exist*. The fundamental thesis is that the market appropriation of nature is the condition of nature's preservation. 'Common goods', on the other hand, are seen as a tragedy.[54]

To understand how the promises of this new 'green capitalism' are not just an imposture but a disaster, it is instructive to reopen an old book. At the beginning of the nineteenth century, a Scottish Lord who had gone to Paris and become radicalized by the French Revolution, James Maitland, Earl of Lauderdale, discovered the economic paradox that bears his name.[55]

What is 'public wealth'? Contrary to what one might think, it is not reducible to the 'sum-total of the fortunes of individuals'[56] – or, as we would say today, to the 'total value produced'. These two notions, public wealth and private value, are not only distinct, but utterly contradictory, as in general the second can increase only at the expense of the former.

'To be qualified to constitute a portion of private riches', Lauderdale says, a thing must, as well as being delightful or useful, exist 'in a certain degree of scarcity'.[57] Conversely, as long as a source of wealth is abundant, freely accessible, it cannot be appropriated with profit. We cannot convert public wealth into private value unless it becomes rare. 'Let us suppose', says Lauderdale,

> a country possessing abundance of the necessaries and conveniences of life, and universally accommodated with the purest streams of water: – what opinion would be entertained of the understanding of a man, who, as the means of increasing the wealth of such a country, should propose to create a scarcity of water, the abundance of which was deservedly considered as one of the greatest blessings incident to the community? It is certain, however, that such a projector would, by this means, succeed in increasing the mass of individual riches; for to the water, which would still retain the quality of being useful and desirable, he would add the circumstance of existing in scarcity, which of course must confer upon it value.[58]

This is the paradox: the increase in private wealth measured by the exchange value presupposes that the corresponding public goods are scarce, or indeed made artificially scarce by deliberately organizing their destruction.

At the time of Lauderdale, this scenario of the destructive appropriation of water resources was still a fiction. It did, however, already echo existing capitalist practices, especially in the colonies. Lauderdale takes the example of the Dutch, who 'were said to burn a considerable quantity of spiceries, whenever mankind was favoured with a fertile season [. . .] they gave to the natives of the several islands premiums for collecting the young blossoms and green leaves of the nutmeg trees, by which means they destroyed them'.[59]

If we want to grasp the true meaning of the current 'ecological crisis', we need to see it in the context of that history of an economic system whose expansion has been essentially based on the destructive appropriation of nature, and see it, as Lauderdale suggested, as part of a continuous tradition of colonial predation and the primitive accumulation of capital.

The difference between these examples of intentional destruction and the hyper-phenomena of environmental disturbance that we have known since is that we cannot, for example, blame global air pollution on the concerted action of a clique of hoarders who have intentionally caused it so as to profit from it directly. The rarefaction of the breathable atmosphere is not surreptitiously orchestrated by bottled air sellers, and global warming is not organized by air conditioning manufacturers even if it so happens that the devices they sell contribute to it in return. The overall effect was not a goal in itself. But that is the only difference. Apart from that, whether the scarcity has been intentionally organized or is produced as a structural side effect of outsourcing the social costs, the result is the same. The environmental damage, insofar as it produces effects of rarefaction, provides the objective conditions for a new market cycle, a conversion of the old *wealth* into a new *value*, in a scheme where, now as before, the extension of private appropriation is preconditioned by the destruction of public wealth.

Once the old public wealth has been denied and integrated into market production, those who benefit from it have no interest – quite the opposite – in returning to states of abundance outside the market. A firm that sells bottled water would have more of an objective interest in seeing public water fountains disappear. It is therefore necessary that the state of scarcity be perpetuated, even accentuated – and this is quite antithetical to a policy of rehabilitation and extension of environmental public goods. 'If land could be had as easily as air, no one would pay rent', wrote the young Engels.[60] He could not imagine that the converse might one day become true: in an era where clean air is becoming scarce, we will soon, one way or another, be forced to pay for it.

The extravagant promise of the dominant economy, as John Bellamy Foster forcibly puts it, lies in claiming to save the planet by expanding that very same capitalism which is in the process of destroying it.[61] In a fantastic reversal of reality, neoliberals present us with private appropriation as being the solution to an environmental disaster when this latter is actually both the product of previous private accumulations and the revitalized condition for wider market appropriation. It is a pseudo-remedy which, as in the case of toxic dependence, extends its grip only by aggravating the damage it claims to relieve.

— 21 —

MAKING PEOPLE RESPONSIBLE

> Directors of the Yorkshire and Lancashire Company take care to advertise on their tickets that in case of accident, whatever the injuries inflicted, whether by the managers' own negligence or their subordinates', they will consider themselves absolved of any legal responsibility. [. . .] it would seem that capital has a particular kind of morality of its own, a sort of superior right [. . .], whereas ordinary morality is supposed to be valid only for poor people.
>
> Karl Marx[1]

1971. Through the window of a car, a hand throws a pouch which bursts open a little further down the roadside. The detritus is scattered at the feet of a majestic figure wearing moccasins. An Indian with a feather in his headdress. Close-up. He faces the camera, looking at you. He is crying. The camera focuses on the tear rolling down his hollowed cheek. Voiceover: 'People start pollution; people can stop it'. Insert on the screen: 'Keep America Beautiful'.[2]

The Indian is nature. You are civilization. He is your bad conscience. The subaltern cannot speak, but his open eyes say what his closed mouth does not. This virgin America, before colonization, has already been soiled, devastated and subjected to genocide, but you are still hurting it, and it is reproaching you for it mutely. Then comes the slogan. The cause of the pollution is you. The remedy, therefore, is also you. Everything is in your hands. You can relieve your guilt. You just have to change your behaviour.

This is a stirring call for environmental awareness and accountability on the part of everyone. But who in fact is hiding behind the signatory of this edifying commercial message? Contrary to what we might believe, 'Keep America Beautiful' is not an environmental organization but a consortium of beverage and packaging manufacturers,

173

including Coca-Cola and the American Can Corporation. This screen organization had been founded in 1953, and it will be instructive to examine its original context.

In the United States, there had long existed a deposit system for the sale of drinks: the customer paid a few cents extra that were returned to him when he brought back the empties. This system of reusing containers – quite different from the recycling of materials (the glass was not melted down, but rather the bottle was refilled) – was effective and durable, and minimized waste.[3]

Things began to change in the 1930s. After prohibition, when business resumed, brewers invented metal cans. The reusable glass bottle to which consumers were accustomed remained the usual form, but the transition to disposable containers opened up enticing prospects: it would remove collection and repackaging costs, eliminate intermediaries (including local bottlers), and concentrate production while extending its diffusion over great distances. Making disposable containers generally available of course involved increasing the production of waste, but manufacturers washed their hands of this. In the early 1950s, soda makers, with Pepsi in the lead and Coca-Cola following, followed hard on the brewers' heels. The changeover was spectacular. Whereas in 1947, 100% of sodas and 85% of beers were sold in reusable bottles, by 1971, the figures had fallen to no more than 50% and 25%.[4] As a result, empty cans and disposable bottles began ever more conspicuously to litter gutters, embankments, riverside pathways and picnic areas. There was an outcry. Petitions were signed. People demanded that the authorities take action. In 1953, the Assembly of the state of Vermont passed a first law making the deposit system mandatory. For firms, this was a serious warning. It was feared that this legislation would create 'a precedent which might someday affect all industry'.[5] It was to stop this movement that, the same year, 'Keep America Beautiful' was created.

In the 1960s, the organization produced adverts featuring a little girl in a white dress, 'Susan Spotless', who lectured her parents when they dropped litter.[6] In 1963, together with an oil firm, Richfield Oil Corporation, the organization co-produced a short film, 'Heritage of Splendor', which praised the natural beauties of the country while denouncing the devastating effects of individual pollution. The narration had been entrusted to an ageing Hollywood actor who had still not yet moved into politics, a certain Ronald Reagan. Environmental incivility was raging, said the voiceover; in some areas, it had even been necessary to ban access to riverbanks because of the 'expensive cleaning up of the litter left by careless fishermen';[7] elsewhere, 'stretches of beach have been closed because of a few people who

174

can't remember their manners'. By the way, this film was released just after the oil spill which in 1962 ravaged the Mississippi and Minnesota rivers downstream from an oil facility that had also apparently forgotten its 'manners'.

But let's talk a bit more about those ill-mannered fishermen whom Reagan's voice was criticizing so severely. In the summer of 1936, when it launched its brand-new beers in cans, the Continental Can Company paid for a big advertising campaign in the American press. It praised the merits of its new and very practical invention, that you could open with a twist of the hand, that retained its taste and freshness, and above all allowed you to 'drink right from the can. No empties to return'. The main selling point for beers in disposable cans was, unsurprisingly, their disposability. No more deposits, no more dead bottles to lug around. A photo provided a picture to flesh out the words and showed two shirt-sleeved fishermen in a boat, their respective postures depicting two moments of one single sequence that was evidently going to be repeated tirelessly over a long afternoon's fishing: one of them has his elbow raised as he drinks, while the other has lifted his arm as he prepares to chuck the empty can into the waters of the lake (see figure 4). Drink, then eliminate.

DRINK RIGHT FROM THE CAN; NO EMPTIES TO RETURN

Figure 4 American Can Company advertisement, 1936 (detail)

Source: 'Continental Can Company, beer in cans,' *Hearst's International-Cosmopolitan*, August 1936, p. 103)

Three decades later, such advertising had become unthinkable. Basically, nothing had changed: the advantage of disposables is that you can throw them away (otherwise there is no real difference). But this could no longer be said so openly. The time had come to correct this first message with a second.

In the 1971 television ad, that of the weeping Indian, the same gesture had been depicted – arm raised and prepared to throw – but this time followed by another image, the native's tear, which, thanks to the Kuleshov effect, retrospectively gave it another meaning (see figure 5). The old manifest content, now repressed, said: 'buy me, it's convenient, once you're tipsy you can throw me in the lake'. Having become latent, it was officially replaced by this one: 'I'm disposable but be careful, if you throw me where you shouldn't (and you've already done so), you're going to feel guilty. What we'd urged you to do, we now enjoin you not only to *refrain* from doing, but also to bear the guilt for it'. The point now was to produce a sense of *penitence*.

'From a social control perspective, appeals to conscience [. . .] are attempts to increase the threats of shame and embarrassment [. . .]. Their function, whether latent or explicit, is to make people feel guilt'.[8] As it happens, the process also serves to redistribute responsibilities, to lay them on some people while relieving others. *You* made that tear fall. And you only have yourselves to blame.

The message was also trying to redefine what the word 'pollution' meant, by reducing it to 'littering', to chucking rubbish on the public highway. The problem was thus reformulated as being due to misconduct, and the solution flowed from the source: it would come from moral re-education. It would be enough for everyone to individually adopt good environmental manners in order to end pollution.

The industry had a problem, which was becoming more and more evident. No matter how much the message was hammered home that 'people' were solely responsible for pollution, the fact is that once these 'people' had left, all that was left, dumped in the middle of the landscape, were things, things in shimmering colours with the brand name written in large letters on them. This pollution was brought to you by, as you preferred, Coca, Pepsi, Ballantine, Pabst or Miller – so this wreckage seemed to proclaim loud and clear. If it wasn't me who threw the can, as the president of the National Soft Drink Association put it in 1970, '[i]t is our trademark on it'.[9] Likewise, the CEO of Coca-Cola proclaimed: 'the packaging for our products is highly visible. As a result, we're criticized more than many other manufacturers'.[10]

Figure 5 Television ad by the 'Keep America Beautiful' campaign (1971). Keep America Beautiful, 'The Crying Indian', first aired on Earth Day in 1971. Created by ad agency Marstellar, Inc.

In April 1970, a few days before the first 'Earth Day',[11] the head of Coca-Cola, J. Paul Austin, gave a speech to a group of bankers. Voicing current ecological concerns, he said he was worried about his own children, who would have reached his age in the 2000s, and were menaced by the 'environmental homicide' in progress. Ultimately, the planet risked being rendered unliveable, perhaps leaving humanity with no other choice than 'interplanetary migration'.[12] While some people lambasted the protests of the younger generation, he publicly praised them: 'The youth of this country know what the stakes are. [. . .] And they're indignant over our apparent unconcern. Whole student populations are engaging in protests and demonstrations'. Now, it was time to *thank* these turbulent youngsters: 'I commend our young people for their awareness and perspicacity. They have done all of us a service by pushing the panic button'. Given that, what now needed to be done? 'The government can't solve our problem. [. . .] The people, though, can do something'.[13] Here, in this two-step formula, was the slogan of industrialists in the face of green protest and the desires for regulation that it inspired: the futility of public intervention was emphasized, and the omnipotence of individual accountability.

Rather than wagging their fingers at those 'negligent fishermen' and other Sunday yobs, as they had been advised to do, environmentalists were now going back to the source, incriminating the industrialists who had gone for disposables and, for the sake of profitability, scuttled a tried and tested system of reusing containers. At the beginning of the 1970s, there was a surge in attempts to force manufacturers to return to the deposit system. A 'law on bottles' to this effect was passed in Oregon in 1972, then in Vermont the following year. The industrialists flew into a rage, sometimes to the point of forgetting to mind their language. 'We must use every tool available to combat bottle referendums this year in Maine, Massachusetts, Michigan, and Colorado, where Communists or people with Communist ideas are trying to get these states to go the way of Oregon',[14] fumed William F. May, who wore two hats, as both director of the American Can Company and president of Keep America Beautiful.

Faced with the threat of regulation, in 1970 the Glass Container Manufacturers Institute (GCMI) launched a big public relations campaign, with a multi-million-dollar budget. The communications agency in charge of operations had had the idea of launching a group of musicians to popularize disposable bottles among teenagers. Originally baptized 'Soda Pop and the One-Way Bottles',[15] its mission was, 'through radio and TV commercials, records, and concerts, to convince the student generation to specify one-way bottles when they buy soft drinks'.[16] 'My one-way bottle keeps me alive and fit [. . .] don't have to go back to town to return it', sang the group in one of the first songs.[17] Faced with the controversy which soon blew up, they back-pedalled a little. 'We erred', admitted the director of the Glass Container Manufacturers Institute, 'we were unprepared for the urgency of the environment as a political issue'.[18] The group was renamed 'The Glass Bottle' and its words toned down. These corporate hippy-like bards with their streaming locks, Indian tunics and headbands round their mops of hair now sang cheesy ditties laden with dreadful puns,[19] celebrating the virtues of soda in bottles (glass is clean, it preserves the taste) rather than insisting too explicitly on the convenient disposability of its container.

But the anti-deposit campaign also took other forms, far more astute than this bottom-drawer, sing-song propaganda. In 1970, two days before the first 'Earth Day', the GCMI launched a recycling pilot programme in Los Angeles: residents, mobilized through associations, partner schools and churches, were asked to take their empty jars and bottles back to special collection centres, for one penny per pound of glass collected.[20] This was intended to demonstrate 'that it is better – ecologically and economically – to recycle no-deposit bottles than to ban or tax them'.[21] Every day the press was kept informed of the number of bottles collected. Participation exceeded expectations. Less than a month later, 250,000 bottles per week were being collected in the metropolitan area. Building on this success, the following year the GCMI set up a full-scale national recycling programme during a 'week against dropping garbage'.

The practice of recycling was thus promoted by the industry as an alternative to mandatory deposit projects and the banning of disposable containers. It was at the end of this successful counter-offensive led by industrial lobbies that 'recycling became the exclusive solution rather than the complement to mandatory source-reduction programs'.[22] At the very moment when the first sorting and recycling practices encouraged by the industry were being set up, the volume of household waste dramatically increased.

This example is paradigmatic of a process of accountability that in the meantime has become, in many areas, one of the main tactics of today's 'ethical neoliberalism'. Its primary function is the avoidance of regulation, governing behaviour by activating goodwill, and stimulating voluntary participation rather than resorting to legal compulsion. Accountability, says Ronen Shamir, is 'an interpellation which constructs and assumes a moral agency', 'a technique of government that sets into action a reflexive subjectivity deemed suitable to partake in the deployment of horizontal authority'.[23]

Accountability calls for subjective autonomy; it addresses individuals who are called upon to take charge of themselves, to govern themselves.[24] In the early 1980s, Thomas Schelling proposed a new word, 'egonomy', to designate *the art of self-management*.[25] Treating yourself as if you were someone else, he remarked, is a 'widespread technique of self-management'.[26] Is accountability an egonomy in this sense? Maybe, but it also seems to be an art of governing others by managing oneself; it is an art of the government of others, founded on activating within them a thoughtful faculty for self-direction – a form of autonomy in heteronomy.

At the very same time as industrialists were dismantling the deposit system, thereby relieving themselves of reprocessing costs, and making structurally anti-ecological decisions, they started calling for ecological responsibility on the part of consumers. A typical case of two-faced morality, where you proclaim a standard that applies to everyone except yourself, and impose responsibility on others so as to relieve yourself of it.

With the help of advertising campaigns, manufacturers managed to frame the issue of waste as 'an individual responsibility, and not one connected to the production process'.[27] It is doubtless flattering to imagine, given the individuals that we are, that everything rests on our own frail shoulders. But, as we busily sort out the packaging in our kitchens, the fact is that – far less evidently – there are other kinds of actors, starting with local governments, which have needed to invest and go into debt in order to finance the necessary infra-structure for coping with the exponential growth in household waste. Ultimately, however, 'consumers did most of the work, subsidizing (both through their labor and through taxes) the beverage industry's packaging-reclamation system, allowing companies to expand their operations without incurring increased costs'.[28]

In the 1970s, industrialists, drawing on the rhetoric of militant movements, called for people to show 'commitment' and to 'continue the fight' with small responsible actions. Beyond the rather coarse hijacking of their opponents' language, their tactical cunning lay in understanding that they would not beat the environmental move-ments without introducing counter-practices able to supplant those of their enemies. The advertising campaign with the weeping Indian was supplemented by a brochure listing the '71 things you can do to stop pollution'.[29] They endeavoured to promote forms of domes-ticated commitment likely to satisfy the emerging desire for action while encouraging this desire to follow a non-antagonistic direction compatible with industrial interests rather than conflicting with them.

The psychological strength of these tactics was that they said some-thing that was very pleasant to hear and also true, so long as it was properly understood: everything was in your hands, you had the power to 'make a difference'. They strove to channel powerful aspirations to change things here and now, including on the level of the practices of everyday life, while confining them to harmless forms of action. Corporate promotion of recycling was one such tactic: cir-cumventing potential oppositions by keeping people in an apolitical state of busy-ness.[30]

This strange ethical neoliberalism dismisses political action, now deemed vain, and promotes instead the accumulation of solitary micro-acts. And yet its own practice immediately negates this: to defeat environmental regulation projects, industrialists actively engaged in politics. Far from acting *in aggregate*, they came together in a *conglomerate*, in a collective body capable of acting in concert.[31]

In the 1960s, for the emerging environmental movements as for feminist movements, 'the personal was the political': it was neces-sary to flush out the relations of domination from the very folds of everyday life, as the revolution also needed to question unthinking habits and so-called private behaviour. The reshaping of the forms of life was thought of as one of the authentic dimensions of a revolution-ary politics. Working to change individual practices and struggling to change the system, composting your waste and being an activist, were not mutually exclusive.

180

It was the talk of accountability promoted by the industry which dissociated and contrasted the two dimensions, promoting a micro-reform of individual behaviour as an alternative to political action. It was this talk which propagated the false antinomy between micro- and macro-transformation; which instead of making demands (now presented as stratospheric, utopian and sterile) for 'systematic trans-formation', encouraged so-called self-sufficiency through the reform of individual practices deemed able to change things purely incremen-tally, without collective action or conflict.

Come to think of it, there is something paradoxical in this history. The deposit system was based on the mobilization of an interest that found expression in hard cash: if I brought back the empty bottle, this was in order to recover, as a good *homo oeconomicus*, my 50 cents. It was a piece of government by interest, fully consistent with the anthropological assumptions of classical economics. It was this motive that they now sought to replace with another, founded on *dis*interested motivation. It is out of pure concern for the general interest that I am now supposed to sort my waste, in the absence of any selfish motive for so doing. Between *homo oeconomicus* and *homo politicus*[32] thus appears a third figure, that of a *homo ethicus*, a 'responsible' subject obliged, on his own level, to deploy micro-virtues against systemic macro-vices.

However, this new ethical governance does not remove the other kind; economic governance is imposed on those same agents. The latter does not eradicate the former, but is added to it. The same indi-viduals, called upon to act as ethical subjects, are still called upon, just as intensely, to act as economic agents. So we all find ourselves having to deal with the tension produced by these contradictory injunctions: to be economically efficient but environmentally responsible.

Accountability is also the way this contradiction is implanted in the psychic life of individuals, in a new figure of the unhappy con-sciousness associated with a form of government by dilemma. In a world where the ethical and economic dimensions of activity are split, wrote the young Marx, the subjects live 'a double existence, earthly and heavenly'. They are torn between their 'earthly' existence as economic agents and their 'heavenly' existence as ethical subjects. 'But whom am I now to believe, political economy or ethics?'[33] It is difficult to say, because 'all of this is grounded in the essence of alienation: each sphere applies to me a different and contrary stand-ard, the moral sphere applies one standard to me and economics another, because each is a definite alienation of man and each retains a particular sphere of alienated essential activity; each is in a relation of alienation to the other alienation'.[34]

What morality calls bad behaviour is nothing other than the most successful expression of what the economy calls good behaviour – a good economic behaviour regulated in practice by an armada of arrangements for aligning interests, encouraging competitive discipline and locking down the relationships of agency. Ethical governance would have us believe that the powerful mechanisms of market governance can be transcended by making depoliticized agents responsible. 'To be obliged to recognize and to punish [. . .] the society of industry, universal competition, private interests that freely pursue their ends, [. . .]; to want, at the same time, to eradicate post factum, for this or that individual, the vital manifestations of this society [. . .]: what a colossal illusion!'[35]

Economic irresponsibility and ethical responsibility, the concrete dissolution of morality and abstract calls to moralization, go hand in hand while forming a contradictory unity. Denouncing duplicity is not enough; the crucial question, in each situation, would rather be one of knowing how to fan the flame of contradiction and convert the moral dilemma into political types of conflict.

Part VI

The ungovernable state

— 22 —

THE CRISIS OF GOVERNABILITY OF THE DEMOCRACIES

[These philosophers], unlike as they are, hold [. . .] that man is 'the hardest of all animals to govern.'

Walter Bagehot[1]

The idea was not new. It had been 'doing the circuit of the cocktail parties for years'.[2] *My dear lady, let me tell you, this country has become ungovernable . . .* But in the mid-1970s, a series of neoconservative intellectuals decided to erect this reactionary commonplace into a theory.

In 1975 the Trilateral Commission published a text which caused a scandal, *The Crisis of Democracy*.[3] Samuel Huntington, who is remembered today especially for his views on the 'clash of civilizations', was one of its co-authors.

Historically, he recalled, democracies have always 'had a marginal population, of greater or lesser size, which has not actively participated in politics'.[4] Greek democracy was based on the exclusion of slaves, foreigners and women, democracy relying on a tax threshold was based on the exclusion of the poor, segregationist democracy was based on the exclusion of Blacks, and patriarchal democracy involved the exclusion of women. These exclusions may well have been inherently undemocratic, but they had, he claimed, 'enabled democracy to function effectively'.[5]

Now, 'marginal social groups' that had previously been 'passive or unorganized' – Blacks, Indians, Chicanos, women, etc. – were taking it upon themselves to be full-fledged political subjects.[6] 'In the family, at the University, in businesses, the discipline relaxed, and the differences in status faded. Each group claimed its right to participate equally – and perhaps more than equally in the decisions which affected itself'.[7]

185

Far from welcoming this 'democratic surge', Huntington worried about it, seeing it as a source of 'problems for the governability of democracy in the 1970s'.[8] The danger lay in 'overloading the political system with demands which extend its functions and undermine its authority'.[9] In this reactionary thinking, as Jacques Rancière has shown, 'what is causing the crisis in *democratic government* is nothing more than the intensity of *democratic life*'.[10] Too much democracy, in short, kills democracy.

Huntington was here updating a classic theme, that political philosophy has never ceased to rehash since the Greeks: democracy is a regime that is perpetually overflowing. But he himself sought less to criticize democracy in general as a form of government that was essentially 'ungovernable' than to examine the situation and find strategies to end the crisis.[11]

As the grammatical twist indicates, raising the problem of the 'governability *of democracy*' was to question the capacity of such a regime not so much to govern its subjects as *to be governed itself*. Far from being paralysed by the crisis affecting it, the state was showing signs of hyperactivity. In response to protest, it intervened, regulated and spent relentlessly. The crisis of governance in democracy was manifested not by withdrawal, but by an expansion of government activity. What was becoming ungovernable, according to this analysis, was the phenomenon of government itself.

Formerly, man had turned to God: 'now he looks to government', said Anthony King in 1975.[12] A government-as-god, from whom he expected everything. The Keynesian policies adopted since the post-war era had 'created more problems than they have solved', especially in that they led people to overstate their rights, to place too much emphasis on equality.[13] In this context, it was easy for 'organized minorities' to try and rekindle the embers. The Keynesian state and social movements: these, for conservative intellectuals, were the 'two endemic threats to liberal representative democracy'.[14] Their combined effects were fuelling an 'inflation of social expectations', a 'claims spiral', which exerted irresistible pressure on political power.[15] The paradox was that this same social unrest, perceived by some on the left as the manifestation of a refusal to be governed, was at the same time interpreted on the right as an infinite demand for government intervention.

However many concessions the welfare state made, it did not calm people's tempers. On the contrary, it was as if every new act of generosity merely whetted the appetite of an insatiable *demos*. 'The generation of excessive expectations',[16] wrote Samuel Brittan of the *Financial Times*, was a danger inherent in representative democracy. However, given the 'disparity between the volume of claims and the capacities of the government', these expectations were bound to be disappointed.[17] This gave rise to a vicious circle: the state, seeking to counter the erosion of its authority by an expansion of its activity, thereby nourished expectations which, when frustrated, resulted in a further loss of legitimacy. It sought to compensate for this loss by the same means, thus relaunching an infinite cycle where, the more government activity grew, the weaker the state's authority became.

The problem, people claimed, lay in the excessive receptiveness of leaders to the demands of 'pressure groups'. But why *were* political leaders so receptive? Some analysts went on to show that this was due to the very way representative democracies worked.

In the wake of Schumpeter, who in the 1940s described democracy as a 'competitive struggle for votes',[18] and of Anthony Downs, who in the 1950s formulated an 'economic theory of democracy',[19] a new trend, the 'school of public choice', proposed in the 1970s to extend the market paradigm to the field of politics. It was a question of 'applying to the state and to all the cogs of public economy the same techniques as those which have been used for forty years to identify the faults and the failures of the market economy'.[20] While the 'constitutionalists' once envisioned the company as a private government, public choice theorists now conversely analysed electoral democracy as a sort of political market.

Seen in this light, the candidate in an election appears as a political entrepreneur exchanging promises for votes in a market where several parties 'compete in periodic elections for control of the governing apparatus'.[21] And of course, 'The easiest way to win votes, both in the political arena and in the marketplace, is to give – or at least appear to give – constituents what they want. A politician who ignores the views of his or her constituents is as rare as a market entrepreneur selling bikinis in the Arctic'.[22] Since politicians can easily win more votes 'by offering new programs than by offering either tax reduction or elimination of existing programs',[23] it is foreseeable that 'coalitions in favour of benefits are, therefore, more efficient than coalitions in favour of tax reduction'.[24] Once these programmes are implemented, the stakes are raised: no government can go back on them without risking losing votes.

What 'public choice' theorists explain is the way that the growing hypertrophy (as they see it) of the welfare state is not a contingent phenomenon but the normal effect of the functioning of the electoral market. So the problem is not the psychological weakness of governors who are too easily influenced, but the fundamental rationality of *homo gubernatorius* in a democratic regime.[25] Ironically, therefore, this theory predicts the likely defeat of its own social and political camp without offering, at least at first, any way out.

It was said that politicians should 'try to educate citizens to seek less from government',[26] but they did not do so: trying to outbid each other electorally, they always preferred to promise more welfare policies rather than to deliver unpopular speeches. Some, however, thought that they had glimpsed the solution. Is not the counterpart of this demagogy the fact that political parties, once elected, will inevitably disappoint expectations? As a result, 'the system as a whole will merely oscillate from one unpopular government to another'.[27] It was the theory of political alternation: the pendulum will swing between the two main parties. It may be, Rose conjectured, that salvation will come precisely from these serial disillusions: 'the failure of first one party, and then another, to give the electorate as much as they want, may have an educative effect upon the electorate, leading them to expect little from government, because they have so often seen it fail'.[28] Parties alternating in power, and repeating the experience of frustration, will convert disenchanted voters to a healthy political realism.

Yes, except that it was also possible, objected James Douglas, that 'at each swing of the pendulum' the whole two-party system would lose 'some of its legitimacy'.[29] How far down could we go? How many alternate governments before we hit rock bottom? And what would happen at the end of this predicted slide? Some envisaged a growing disaffection resulting in mass abstention. Others believed that there was little chance things would stay there. As Claus Offe argued in 1979, 'the disappointments accumulated in this manner may release their explosive force in one of two directions', with a rise to the extremes of the two sides of the political spectrum, or a 'polarization between the party system and social movements operating in a non-parliamentary fashion'[30] – options which can be combined, and would in any case lead to huge political conflagrations.

Such a cycle, people felt, could climax in 'a confrontation like the events of May 1968 in Paris, which did not overthrow a regime but indicated the limits of its authority, or like the successful French coup of a decade earlier'.[31] Anyway, ultimately, there would be only two possibilities left: a situation of pre-insurgency and/or Bonapartism. Because, let's be reassured on this, the 'positive scenario would foresee individuals turning to government to protect them from disorder'.

That would be the path of 'strong government' in the face of any peril.[32]

Anyway, if it is true that the problem is structural, an inherent part of 'the internal dynamics of democracy itself',[33] then there can be no doubt: we cannot be satisfied with superficial countermeasures. We will have to tackle, one way or another, what we have identified as the root of the evil.

According to Brittan, 'representative democracy suffers from internal contradictions'.[34] In those years, right-wing intellectuals active in the 'renaissance of conservative theories of the crisis' started to use a vocabulary which was previously the prerogative of the Marxist style. Some, on the left, interpreted 'the attempt to use neo-Marxist ideas for conservative purposes' as the symptom of a theoretical deprivation, the 'bankruptcy of their own ideas'.[35] Claus Offe read it less optimistically. The discourse of the structural crisis, he said, was changing sides. In the late 1960s, it was the left that was convinced that 'things cannot go on like this'; a decade later it was the opposite side that had inherited the fighting spirit that this feeling inspired.[36] Developing a theory of the crisis was for them the prerequisite for formulating a sensible programme of action.

'A camel is a beast capable of bearing great burdens. But there comes a point at which even one more straw can break a camel's back'.[37] The political scientist Richard Rose used this allegory to illustrate the notion of 'demand overload': the camel was the state; the straws or bales of hay were social demands.[38]

In 1974, Daniel Bell came to a similar conclusion: these grievances, converging on all sides on the state, led to an increase in expenditure, resulting in a budget overload which caused a public finance crisis.[39] The neoconservative intellectual took this idea from a young Marxist economist, James O'Connor, who had just published a big book on the fiscal crisis of the state.[40]

The main idea behind this book, he later said, had come to him one morning when he opened his newspaper and realized that all the information provided on the first page, beneath its apparent heterogeneity, was actually part of the same logic: 'a welfare struggle, a teachers' strike, a new government subsidy to business, a conflict over taxes. This was when I first realized that the class struggle had been displaced (in part) onto the state and its budget'.[41] Who contributes to tax revenue? At what level? What will public expenditure be allocated to? These issues involving competing social interests, and class struggle entails a tax struggle.

The 'new field of class struggle', argued Bell, 'is tax conflict'.[42] While adopting O'Connor's main idea, however, the neoconservatives obliterated a whole tranche of his argument and reduced it to one simplistic, mono-factorial explanation of the budget crisis. As a result, while both sides agreed on the existence of a public finance crisis, explanations for this diverged. For neoconservatives, it was mainly due to the defects of welfare democracy. The neo-Marxist analysis was more complex.

The problem, they showed, is that the capitalist state must 'perform simultaneously two functions that are quite contradictory': an accumulation function – 'helping private industrialists to accumulate more capital [. . .]' – and a legitimizing function – 'obtaining mass loyalty to the system'.[43] Public intervention is not always a hindrance to private economic activity – far from it. On the contrary, they claimed, going against the liberal economic doxa, such intervention played an important role in promoting the development of private activity. By 'social investment' spending – on infrastructure, transport and communication networks, as well as on health, research and education – the state assumes responsibility for a decisive part of the conditions for capital accumulation. However, private accumulation, thus supported and favoured, generates social and environmental costs that trigger countermovements, social conflicts which in turn call for new interventions by a state which, if it wants to maintain its legitimacy as well as consent to the dominant economic order, must 'meet various demands of those who suffer the "costs" of economic growth'.[44] Contrary to the truncated way the neoconservatives presented it, the structural pressure on spending is double, in a dialectical pattern where the consolidation of the first pole entails the equal consolidation of the second.

If this structural contradiction is permanent, in phases of economic recession, it becomes incandescent. The state must then continue to jointly carry out its two fundamental missions at a time when its fiscal resources are dwindling, and it can no longer finance its tasks of legitimation without eating into its tasks of accumulation and vice versa. If it also decides to reduce the taxation on the capital, inheritance and incomes of the wealthiest on the pretext of a policy of supply, its budget situation can quickly become untenable.

But this 'crisis in crisis management' also stems from a deeper contradiction. The problem is that public policy 'must organize the dysfunctional social consequences of private production without being able to infringe on the primacy of private production'.[45] The state must continually save capitalism from its self-destructive tendencies,

190

but without ever affecting the fundamental economic relationships that determine them. Once it ventures to impose measures of social regulation, as essential as they are in a logic of interest properly understood, these measures are felt by capital to be intolerable obstacles to its economic freedom. Here is the dilemma: the state must both guarantee the conditions of accumulation and intervene further down the line to maintain the hegemony that the latter undermines, even when it cannot effectively perform its legitimizing function without encountering immediate opposition from capital. In this respect, Offe concludes, capitalist societies 'are always ungovernable'.[46]

By erasing these contradictions, the neoconservative version of the theory of crisis – a partial and distorted recovery – brought about a major shift from its original formulation: 'What the Marxists mistakenly attribute *to* capitalist economics, however, is, in fact, a product *of* democratic politics', says Huntington, agreeing with Bell.[47] At this point, the problem is no longer the capitalist functioning of the economy but the 'democratic' functioning of politics: 'The difficulties of contemporary societies [. . .] reveal less of the bankruptcy of market economies than the bankruptcy of our political institutions'.[48]

So, despite the apparent similarities, under superficial recuperation, it is not the same problem that is being posed. The question, as rewritten by the neoconservatives, will now be one of knowing how, without affecting capitalist relations, the governability of the state can be restored. The 'crisis of governance in democracy' is the name of a mutilated reformulation of the theory of crisis.

Any criticism of political economy is for them foreclosed in principle, so this discourse necessarily falls back on a critique of government reason. The crisis of governability, say the neoliberals, is due to the existing forms of 'democratic' decision, the 'structural flaws inherent in the current structure of our mechanisms of choice', and the fact that 'western democracies are trapped in an archaic political economy'. As a result, 'the challenge of our time is not economic [. . .], but institutional and political: *how to imagine a new political technology*'.[49] This represents the proclamation of a revolution or rather a counter-revolution in the arts of government. The welfare state as the material basis for hegemony, public intervention as a mode of social regulation, representative democracy as a dialectic of civil society and the state: it was all going to have to be overhauled.

The welfare state in France in the period of recovery and affluence 1945–75 is often presented as a historic compromise that ensured strong growth along with a low level of social conflict. In the mid-1970s, this was not at all how it was perceived among the ruling classes. What had been touted as a regime of stabilization, stifling all struggles, had clearly been transformed into its opposite. André Gorz came to the same conclusion from another point of view: 'contrary to the forecasts of the founders of the welfare state, benefits had not reconciled people with capitalist society [. . .] by intervening, regulating, protecting, arbitrating in all areas, the state had [. . .] pushed itself to the forefront. [. . .] The "crisis of governability" at the level of societies as of companies marked the exhaustion of a model'.[50] A borderline situation had been reached where the state could not hope to 'keep its control of regulatory power and arbitrage except by restricting market activity more than before [. . .]. This meant a showdown with the bourgeoisie'.[51]

Huntington, meanwhile, envisaged two main scenarios, one 'optimistic' where 'the openness and pluralism of democracy allow for constant adaptation to changing circumstances and hence insure the long-term stability of the system'; and another, 'pessimistic' scenario where the depending crisis of governability would lead to 'the over-loading of the system, and eventual polarization and breakdown'.[52]

In the 1970s, right-wing intellectuals had a tendency to melancholia.[53] The crisis was serious. Capitalism was at a loss. Hence the apocalyptic tone often adopted in this literature: 'liberal representative democracy suffers from internal contradictions, which are likely to increase in time [. . .] and [. . .], on present indications, the system is likely to pass away within the life-time of people now adult', predicted Brittan.[54]

'The pessimism of the Trilateral Commission', said people on the left, 'should be the optimism of everyone else. If ruling groups feel they are losing power, it is only because everyone else is gaining it. If their world is crumbling, ours should be being built. Their fears are in reality our opportunities'.[55]

But the Conservatives' alarmism, more than being an expression of real defeatism, marked instead the triggering of a new movement of reconquest. Warning that a slippery slope may lead to ruin does not imply believing in historical fate, or in the futility of political action. It is an argument of *conditional inevitability*: if we do nothing, then such is the fate that awaits us, but we can still act to evade it.

One thing was certain, wrote Huntington, 'No "invisible hand" is going to insure the viability of democratic polities any more than it insures the prosperity of market economies'. In short, 'contrary to any assumption of automatic self-correction',[56] intervention would be necessary. For lack of such a start, the problems already identified 'may accumulate and, eventually, destroy the political order all the more certainly'.[57]

It was now too late, Dahrendorf concurred, to replace one by one the fuses that had blown: no, in actual fact, 'the point is that we need a different system of fuses'.[58] And, in a similar vein, Fritz Scharpf announced: 'What seems necessary are not isolated repairs or improvements of individual parts of the welfare state machinery but a new configuration of [. . .] power'. A 'change of an order of magnitude which is comparable to the transition from laissez-faire capitalism to the welfare state half a century ago'.[59] But in the other direction: a big jump backwards.[60]

— 23 —

HAYEK IN CHILE

Though capitalism and democracy historically have arisen together, and have been commonly justified by philosophical liberalism, there is nothing which makes it either theoretically or practically necessary for the two to be yoked.

David Bell[1]

'The threat to the continued existence of the large corporation is part of a pervasive problem [. . .] – the fundamental conflict between our form of political democracy and the market system. We are convinced that these two systems are ultimately incompatible with each other'.[2] We have to take seriously these words, written in 1978 by Jensen and Meckling. For the radical left, there could be no authentic democracy unless capitalism was left behind. Conversely, on the right, many were starting more and more openly to consider that there could be no salvation for capitalism without somehow shedding 'democracy'.[3]

Some people, wrote Huntington, claimed that 'the only remedy to the evils of democracy is more democracy' – but under the present circumstances, he replied, this would amount to 'adding fuel to the fire'. Given that, in order to function, the political system effectively requires 'some measure of apathy and noninvolvement'[4] on the part of the governed, on the contrary, what was needed was actually 'a greater degree of moderation in democracy'.[5]

Democracy, therefore, is to be taken in moderate doses. But how, in this period of strong politicization, could such sobriety be imposed? The statutory exclusion of a part of the population was no longer a possible option, so it would be necessary for Blacks, women and other minorities to apply 'more self-restraint'.[6] Let them learn to *stand*.[7]

But everyone suspected that they should not count too much on

194

it. 'The tensions likely to prevail in a post-industrial society', warned Huntington, 'are likely to require a more authoritarian and more efficient model of government decision-making'. And he added, chillingly: 'postindustrial politics is likely to be the darker side of postindustrial society'.[8]

As one critic noted at the time: 'The unusual bluntness of *The Governability of Democracies* violates a taboo of American society, which is that no matter how much one may detest democracy, one should never violate its rhetoric in public. Consequently this report has generated a full-scale controversy within the Trilateral Commission itself'. The fact remained that 'Western intellectuals are now calmly discussing hypotheses which they once associated with lunatic fringes'.[9]

During the discussion that followed Huntington's presentation at the meeting of the Trilateral Commission in Kyoto, in May 1975, Dahrendorf implicitly criticized his argument: was he not suggesting that restoring government authority involved a strong state, not only politically but also economically? An interventionist, even *dirigiste* state? Or would it not be better to decide that 'one of the things democracy is about is to enable people and groups to operate in what might be called a market environment rather than an environment which is largely determined by directives issuing from government and political institutions'?[10] The challenge of the debate focused on the nature of the authoritarian turn mentioned by Huntington: would it be economically liberal or not?

In another text, Dahrendorf explained the coordinates of the problem: 'once economic growth – the necessary condition of the ability of governments to respond to expectations the increase of which they themselves had to stimulate – became more difficult, democratic governments were in trouble. If there is, say, the beginning of a Kondratieff cycle which means a quarter-century of low growth or even decline, democratic politics has no way of coping. It is only – thus Huntington's conclusion – by introducing elements of authoritarianism that we can survive the long slump'.[11] Because after all, as Richard Rose quite cynically put it: 'A regime that loses popular consent but still retains effectiveness may use the threat of coercion to carry out its policies'.[12]

In a way, we had already been warned right from the start. I mean the very history of the term 'ungovernability' might have set us thinking. Before being reintroduced into political theory, this word came from the vocabulary of policing; particularly in the context of the 'policing of children' it referred to 'non-criminal misconduct'. Calling a minor 'ungovernable' allowed the administration, even in the absence of an offence or misdemeanour, but merely for repeated misconduct, to submit him or her to measures of coercion or reformation.[13] When the ruling classes complain about the ungovernability of their subjects, thereby recycling in the political sphere a category which also serves to justify putting an incorrigible brat under police supervision, you have to expect them to use similar processes.

In the late 1970s, Nicos Poulantzas warned against the advent of 'authoritarian-social statism'. In this, 'a decisive decline in the institutions of political democracy and the draconian and multifaceted restriction of all of these so-called "formal" freedoms' would entail the state increasingly laying hold of 'all areas of economic-social life'.[14] This hypothesis actually corresponded to what the neoconservatives had in mind at the time: a strong state combining an authoritarian approach to political life, technocratic interventionism in the economy, and the neo-corporatist subsumption of the social.

However, what neither Poulantzas nor Huntington had clearly foreseen was the neoliberal turning point – which, in their defence, they had long seen as just one strategic option among others, a programmatic outlier.

In the ongoing process of restructuring, forms of authoritarian politics would indeed emerge, but they would be decoupled from the economic and social statism which Poulantzas had thought would act as a counterpart: a politically authoritarian but economically liberal state which, in terms of the management of social relationships, would trade the old patterns of corporatist subjugation for more autonomous forms of private governance. To grasp the strange strategic synthesis that was thus outlined – namely, an authoritarian neoliberalism with many faces – other authors would need to be read.

Invited in 1980 to imagine what capitalism might look like in 2000, economist Paul Samuelson described one scenario that worried him. If you want to discern in the present a possible picture of the future, you need to turn, he suggested, not to Scandinavia and its social democratic model, not towards old Europe and its mixed economy, not towards Yugoslavia and its experiments in self-management, but to certain Latin American countries. There, you would come across much less favourable omens.

And he narrated a 'parable', a dismal tale intended to serve as a paradigmatic tale:

> Generals and admirals take power. They wipe out their leftist predecessors, exile opponents, jail dissident intellectuals, curb the trade-unions,

and control the press and all political activity. But, in this variant of market fascism, the military leaders stay out of the economy. *They* don't plan and don't take bribes. They turn over all economics to religious zealots – zealots whose religion is the laissez faire market. [. . .] Then the clock of history is turned back. The market is set free, and the money supply is strictly controlled. Without welfare transfer payments, workers must work or starve. [. . .] Inflation may well be reduced if not wiped out. [. . .] Political freedom aside, there does tend to be a significant increase in the degree of inequality of incomes, consumption, and wealth.[15]

This scenario was in fact quite realistic – it was realized in Argentina and Chile – and it corresponded to the implementation of a certain kind of politico-economic regime which Samuelson described bluntly as 'capitalistic fascism',[16] an unbridled capitalism, imposed and maintained by brute force. 'If the "Chicago Boys" and admirals of Chile had not existed, we should have to invent them as an archetypical case'.[17]

On 2 November 1973, less than a month after Pinochet's coup, a well-informed *Wall Street Journal* was already waxing enthusiastic: 'a number of Chilean economists who studied at the University of Chicago, who are known as the "Chicago School" in Santiago, are champing to be unleashed. That would also be an experiment we would watch with academic interest'.[18]

From a more pragmatic point of view, Amnesty International drew up a provisional report of the experiment in question a few months later: 'Torture has been common practice during the interrogation of political prisoners [. . .] tens of thousands of workers [. . .] have lost their employment for political reasons, many of them apparently being reduced to starvation levels'.[19] Another report, three years later, stated: 'the violations of human rights [. . .] have not stopped: arbitrary imprisonment, executions, systematic use of torture and the "disappearance" of political detainees. [. . .] From 11 September 1973 to date, approximately 100,000 people have been subjected to arrest and detention, more than 5,000 have been executed, and tens of thousands have had to go into exile for political reasons'.[20]

However, this did not prevent the great figures of Western neoliberalism heading off, in full knowledge, to Chile to hail the dictatorship.[21] When Friedman met Pinochet in March 1975, he talked to him, as is well known, about economic policy and 'shock therapy'.[22] When Hayek was in turn received by the dictator in November 1977, he discussed another subject, the thorny question of 'limited democracy and representative government'. 'The head of state', reported the Chilean press, 'listened carefully and asked him to provide him with the documents that he had written on this issue'.[23] Back in Europe, Hayek got his secretary to send Pinochet a draft of his 'model for a constitution', a text which justifies the state of emergency,[24] and wrote to the London *Times* to defend the regime against its critics: 'I have not been able to find a single person even in much maligned Chile who did not agree that personal freedom was much greater under Pinochet than it had been under Allende'.[25] No one, indeed: any person likely to argue otherwise in public had very conveniently disappeared.

During his second visit, in April 1981,[26] Hayek gave a long interview to the daily *El Mercurio*. 'What is your opinion of dictatorships?' asked the pro-Pinochet journalist. A very good question. Thank you for asking. Let's dissect it a little.

> Hayek: Well, I would say that, as a long-term institution I am totally against dictatorships. But a dictatorship may be a necessary system during a transitional period. Sometimes it is necessary for a country to have, for a time, some form of dictatorial power. As you will understand, it is possible for a dictator to govern in a liberal way. And it is also possible for a democracy to govern with a total lack of liberalism. I personally prefer a liberal dictator to a democratic government lacking liberalism. [. . .]
>
> Sallas: Which means that, for the transitional periods, you would propose stronger, dictatorial governments [. . .].
>
> Hayek: [. . .] In such circumstances it is practically inevitable for someone to have almost absolute powers. Absolute powers that they should precisely use to avoid and limit any absolute power in the future.[27]

What Samuelson denounces as fascistic capitalism, Hayek defends as a lesser evil. For the liberals, under such circumstances, dictatorship turns out to be the worst solution with the exception of all the others – first and foremost, socialism. When forced to choose between Allende and Pinochet, as, at other times, between the Republic and Franco, we do not hesitate. Certainly, we do not accept it, we assure our listener, as a form of government destined to perpetuate itself, but as a temporary expedient, a transition phase, a passing state of emergency which, if we believe this theory of the dictatorship of the bourgeoisie, will establish the new order and dissolve itself once the task is completed.

What a head-spinning piece of historical dialectic this liberal defence of transitional dictatorship is! As Lord Kaldor put it at the time: 'Chile is a dictatorship equipped with secret police, detention camps etc. where strikes are ruled out and the organisation of workers in trade unions is prohibited. [. . .] And if we take Professor Hayek literally, a fascist dictatorship of some kind should be regarded as the necessary pre-condition (along with monetarism) of a free society'.[28]

The charge hits home. It should be remembered that, when he made such statements, Hayek was not going off the rails. These positions were in perfect intellectual conformity with what he had been theorizing for decades.[29] However, this apology for a 'transitional liberal dictatorship' does not fit well with what is usually remembered of his doctrine. If, as he says with just as much consistency, liberalism is characterized by the requirement that 'the coercive functions of government [be] strictly limited',[30] how can he affirm the compatibility, however temporary, of liberalism and dictatorship? This remains an enigma only if one sticks to a superficial interpretation of his philosophy. On closer inspection, the contradiction is only apparent.

What is democracy? For Hayek, who understands it in a purely instrumental way, it is merely 'a procedural rule',[31] a method of decision based on the majority rule. A simple means, in no case an end in itself. This political technique has its advantages, especially in that it promotes peaceful transitions from one head of state to the next, but this is not an intangible principle, certainly not the corollary of something like the unconditional political right to self-determination. The absolute value is 'freedom', not democracy. Democracy is just a form of government, while 'freedom' should rather be conceived as a form of life.[32] If by chance the two come into conflict, the second must yield to the first, without any argument. 'I would rather prefer to sacrifice temporarily, I repeat, temporarily, democracy rather than doing without liberty, even if it were temporarily'.[33]

But Hayek, who has a taste for paradox, goes further by claiming that there 'can sometimes be many instances of authoritarian governments under which personal liberty was safer than under many democracies'.[34] Under Pinochet, however, neither political freedoms (including the right to stand for election, but also freedom of expression, assembly and association, not to mention the right to strike and to protest), nor fundamental civil liberties (including that of not being subject to arrest, to arbitrary detention or execution) were preserved. So to argue, as he does, that this kind of regime can safeguard 'personal freedom' presupposes that it be redefined in a wholly different sense. But what content is left in such a truncated notion of freedom? Only 'economic freedom', understood as free disposal of one's property.

'If Mrs Thatcher said that free choice is to be exercised more in the market place than in the ballot box, she has merely uttered the truism that the first is indispensable for individual freedom while the second is not: free choice can at least exist under a dictatorship that can limit itself but not under the government of an unlimited democracy which cannot'.[35] It could not be clearer: economic freedom, the freedom of possessive individualism, is non-negotiable, while political freedom is optional. Now it is 'conceivable, though unlikely, that an autocratic government will exercise self-restraint; but an omnipotent democratic government simply cannot do so'.[36]

Hayek's political philosophy revises established categories and redistributes the relevant oppositions. Thanks to this conceptual redistribution, paradoxical statements can now be formulated: democracy can be denounced as totalitarian, but equally, dictatorship can be praised as liberal.

The difference between liberalism and democracy, he says, 'stands out most clearly if we name their opposites: for democracy it is authoritarian government; for liberalism it is totalitarianism'.[37] In his diagram, the main contrast is between liberalism (understood as economically limited government) and totalitarianism (understood as economically unlimited government). Another, secondary split, this time between democracy and authoritarianism, crosses the main picture and subdivides it. We thus implicitly obtain a quadripartite typology of political regimes, which can be reconstructed as shown in figure 6.

This table of government regimes also works as a map – a means for the neoliberal to orient himself in politics, to make choices in that sphere. This sheds light on the coherence of Hayek's support for the Pinochet regime. In this logic, we will prefer any form of government that is economically 'limited' in any form to any corresponding 'unlimited' form. Given that 'unlimited democracy is probably worse

	Liberalism	Totalitarianism
Democracy	Liberal democracy	Totalitarian democracy
Authoritarianism	Liberal authoritarianism	Totalitarian authoritarianism

Figure 6 Typology of forms of government according to Hayek

than any other form of unlimited government',[38] the conclusion is obvious. Rather Pinochet than Allende.

Asked in 1981 about his position on the totalitarian regimes of South America, Hayek counters that he has none. We should not confuse totalitarianism and authoritarianism. The only 'totalitarian government' to have recently existed in Latin America, he points out, was 'Chile under Allende'.[39] An extreme case of 'totalitarian democracy', to be sure.[40] Totalitarian? But in what sense? A system is 'totalitarian', answers Hayek, when – unlike liberalism and individualism – it wants 'to organise the whole of society and all its resources for this unitary end'.[41]

As Andrew Gamble writes: 'Great play is made in this literature of the distinction between authoritarianism and totalitarianism [. . .], because whilst they interfere with political freedoms, they do not interfere with economic freedom; trade unions are of course disbanded or repressed, but foreign investment is not interfered with and citizens are still free to own [. . .] and to buy and sell'. For neoliberals, 'the destruction of political freedom is always regrettable [. . .] but clearly it is not to be compared to the far more serious loss of economic freedom for capital'.[42]

For Hayek, if we want to avoid sinking into 'totalitarianism', it is absolutely necessary to set limits to parliamentary regimes which, starting out as liberal democracies, tend inexorably to slide towards 'unlimited democracy', and from there to totalitarian democracy. But how does one then proceed? One thing is sure: the transition will not happen spontaneously. It requires an intervention, planning, organization, all things that liberalism had officially forbidden itself. So Hayek finds himself caught in a contradiction: professing, as a rule, respect for spontaneous self-generation as opposed to both social constructivism and political decision-making, he stumbles over a phenomenon that contravenes his views, and to which he sees no other remedy than the very opposite of non-intervention: the imposition by political decision of a limitation of democracy, even if this means resorting, when the danger is imminent, to a state of emergency and a transitional dictatorship. 'After all', concludes Hayek, 'some democracies have been made possible only by the military power of some generals'.[43] This, after all, is where most of them ended up.

Liberalism, Hayek contends, is based on 'the discovery of a self-generating or spontaneous order in social affairs'.[44] The official dogma of this new economic theology affirms that the market would be capable, if only we finally gave it free rein, to generate by itself a harmonious order.[45] As well as the teleocratic order (commanded by ends) there is a nomocratic order (based on general laws). Hayek, however, does not hesitate to support a transitional dictatorship if need be. To avoid the political tyranny of a 'conscious directing' of economic life, he is then ready to endorse the tyranny by the military or the police of a conscious repression of social and political life – as long as it remains 'liberal'.

These contortions are explained more fully by the contradictions constitutive of economic liberalism. Contrary to what its dogma initially claims, the order of the market is not established spontaneously. It must be established and reproduced permanently. As Polanyi wrote, what is presented to us as a natural order actually requires, in order to maintain itself, the artifice of a 'continuous, centrally organized and controlled interventionism'. [46]

Not only is this economic order not self-supporting but, more radically, and contrary to a tenacious understanding, neither does it exist in a separate state. State and civil society, politics and economics, as Gramsci emphasized, are *methodological distinctions*, plotted on the same practical ensemble rather than referring to really separate spheres:

> But since in actual reality civil society and State are one and the same, it must be made clear that laissez-faire too is a form of State 'regulation,' introduced and maintained by legislative and coercive means. It is a deliberate policy, conscious of its own ends, and not the spontaneous, automatic expression of economic facts. Consequently, laissez-faire liberalism is a political programme, designed to change – insofar as it is victorious – a State's leading personnel, and to change the economic programme of the State itself – in other words the distribution of the national income.[47]

If it does not self-generate, however, this order does quite spontaneously generate its own negation, or, as Marx wrote, its own gravediggers. We could, strangely enough, read Hayek's alarmist texts on the fatal slope that leads from unlimited democracy to socialism as a sort of rough translation into the language of liberalism of this famous Marxian thesis. Except that for Hayek, this contradiction, instead of being grasped endogenously on the basis of relations of production, is linked to the intrusion of a reality perceived as external, parasitic, superfluous – politics seen as an alien.

Basically, the question is that of the theory of crisis: if, like the neoliberals, we think that capitalism is essentially stable and self-regulating, then the imbalances and the convulsions by which it is so obviously affected can be due only to something other than itself. The crisis is necessarily external in origin, due to the exogenous politicization of the 'economy'. Theories of the 'crisis of the governability of democracy' are the expression of this denial. Once the internal contradictions of capitalism have been overcome, and their manifestations linked to the effect of interference from democratic politics, the general solution is obvious: as Hayek says, 'limit democracy'.

— 24 —

THE SOURCES OF
AUTHORITARIAN LIBERALISM

As, in his view, government is merely a necessary evil, he concluded that as little as possible of it was needed. This is [. . .] wrong. It is not necessary outside its sphere; but in this sphere, there cannot be too much of it. Freedom gains everything by being severely circumscribed within its legitimate precincts; but it gains nothing, and on the contrary loses out if, within this precinct, it is weak; for there, it must always be omnipotent.

Benjamin Constant[1]

As 'unlimited democracy' slips inexorably towards a 'totalitarian state', it needs to have limits imposed on it. This was the leitmotif of Hayek's political thought, at least after 1944 and *The Road to Serfdom*.

But where does this paradoxical theme of 'totalitarian democracy' come from? Firstly, it repeats a stale commonplace of reactionary thought, and is the classic motif of a long tradition of hatred of democracy which, in the modern period, dates back to the anti-Enlightenment. Hayek is not unaware of this, and on this point he refers to a book by Franz Neumann where we can read the following: 'since the French Revolution, anti-liberal and anti-democratic theories have been propagated which champion the thesis that from democracy there must necessarily emerge the rule of the mob. [. . .] The total state then appears as the necessary fulfillment of democracy. De Maistre, Bonald, Donoso Cortes, Spengler, Ortega y Gasset repeat this idea in one form or another'.[2]

While firmly subscribing to this tradition – which is, properly speaking, 'anti-liberal' – Hayek makes a distinction that dispels the apparent inconsistency of such a position. In his view there are indeed historically two liberalisms, an authentic and Anglo-Saxon version, which he endorses – the liberalism of Smith, but also of Burke, and

another, spurious and continental version, which he hates: 'the tradition of Voltaire, Rousseau, Condorcet and the French Revolution
which became the ancestors of modern socialism'.[3] The opposition between 'liberal and totalitarian democracy' basically simply
expresses 'the antagonism between liberalism and socialism'.[4] But,
in Hayek, this idea also has a closer and more precise source. The
idea that 'the emerging democratic welfare state was destined to
undermine the rule of law' came to him from his youthful readings.
As William Scheuerman puts it: 'For those familiar with Weimar-era
legal debates, much of Hayek's account is surprisingly unoriginal;
his own intellectual socialization, as Hayek notes on many occa-
sions, took place in the shadow of the Weimar debates, and his
argument parallels elements of Carl Schmitt'.[5] As Hayek notes in
Law, Legislation and Liberty, 'This weakness of the government of
an omnipotent democracy was very clearly seen by the extraordinary
German student of politics, Carl Schmitt, who in the 1920s probably understood the character of the developing form of government
better than most people and then regularly came down on what to me
appears both morally and intellectually the wrong side.'[6] So, while
condemning Schmitt's political positions, Hayek adopts his pre-Nazi
critique of democracy.

The key concept in Schmitt's characterization of this form of government is the 'total state'.[7] When Schmitt introduced this formula,
in the early 1930s, it immediately evoked the fascist 'stato totalitario'.
We must remember that the adjective 'totalitarian' was then used
positively, for self-celebratory purposes, by Mussolini and his hench-
men.[8] But Schmitt, as usual, shifted the meaning of the terms. Seizing
on this lexicon for his own contrary ends, he initially applied it, dep-
recatingly, to parliamentary democracy. Schmitt supplemented this
new sense with an impressionistic historical idea that Hayek would
make his own. It could be summed up in the proposition that 'the
neutral nineteenth-century liberal state' was in the process of being
transformed into a 'total state'.[9]

Total in what sense? In that it intervenes 'in all areas of life'. As
the welfare state extends its prerogatives to a whole range of social
and economic issues that had not previously been the responsibility
of the public authorities, its sphere becomes total, encompassing all
things. In a situation where state and society become identical, writes
Schmitt, 'it is no longer possible to distinguish between questions
which are political – which, as such, concern the state – and questions
which are social and therefore non-political'.[10] When everything is
political, there is nothing outside the state.

But what causes this phenomenon? It is 'in democracy', answers Schmitt, 'that we find the cause of the contemporary total state or more exactly of the total politicization of all of human existence'.[11] If the state expands, this is because a democratic government is continuously called upon to 'meet the requirements of all interested parties'.[12] If the state intervenes in the economy, it is because society intervenes in the state. Making society an aspect of the state is simply the effect of the 'societalization' of the state.

However, this extension of the field of the state is, paradoxically, far from being a show of force: 'it is not by force and by power, but by weakness that a pluralist party state becomes "total".'[13] A weakness firstly because it grows passively, becoming the plaything of social interests that somehow take possession of it from below; a weakness secondly because the further its sphere extends, the more its strength diminishes. The more omnipotent this state seems, the more helpless it actually becomes. The old Leviathan, fallen from its height, becomes the mere 'self-organization of society'[14] and loses all transcendence; it softens and degenerates.

Hayek, and Schumpeter too, who had first-hand knowledge of Schmitt's analyses of democracy, transmitted these ideas in the post-war period. They comprised, at a distance, one of the intellectual matrices of the discourse on the crisis of governability of democracy that was developed in the 1970s.[15]

On 23 November 1932, on the threshold of Hitler's accession to power, Carl Schmitt spoke at the invitation of an organization of employers, the Langnam Verein.[16] Its title announced the programme: 'A strong state and a healthy economy'.[17]

In this text, Schmitt distinguished between two versions of the notion of 'total state', one that he rejected, the other that he sought to promote. We have just encountered the former: the 'quantitative' total state. This state is not strong, but weak due to its over-extension. 'This kind of total state is a state which extends indiscriminately to all areas, to all spheres of human existence [. . .]. It is total in a purely quantitative sense, in the mere sense of volume and not of intensity or political energy'.[18]

But how do we get away from this total state? 'Only a very strong state', says Schmitt, 'could break this terrible tangle'.[19] The solution lies in cutting the Gordian knot of the state total by . . . the total state, but taken in another sense. Instead of the quantitative total state, he proposes the 'qualitative total state' – a state that is 'total in terms of quality and energy, just as the fascist state is described as a "stato totalitario"';[20] a strong state, which concentrates in its hands the power of modern technology, starting with military means and the new instruments of mass communication; a military-media, war-like and propagandist state, endowed with the ultimate tools for the technological repression of bodies and the manipulation of minds. Mobilizing 'incredible means of power',[21] this state will no longer tolerate 'the emergence within it of subversive forces'.[22] Again able to tell the difference between friends and enemies, it will no longer hesitate to fight those from within.

But there remains a crucial question: what will be the relationship between such a state and the economy? Answer: 'Only a strong state can depoliticize, only a strong state can clearly and effectively decree that certain questions, like transportation or radio, fall in its domain and must be administered by it [. . .], that others are a matter of autonomous economic management, and that everything else must be left to the sphere of the free economy'.[23] So there will be three sectors: public monopolies in certain strategic areas, the free market and, in between, a form of economic self-government through employers' associations.

Schmitt seeks to win over and reassure German bosses. He promises them a strong, propagandist-repressive state capable of muzzling social and political opposition while ensuring that this immense force will respectfully stop at the threshold of businesses and markets. The private self-government of economic affairs will not be called into question, but on the contrary, extended and sanctuarized.

While democratic politics blurs the distinction of state and society, 'authoritarian-total' politics will carefully distinguish them; while the former politicizes society and 'societalizes' the state, the second will depoliticize society and strengthen the state, but within the strict limits of a properly understood distinction between state and economy. As the class struggle has thus been brought under the iron heel of the state, 'the economy' can flourish anew. A strong state, a healthy economy.

This programme implies, however – and Schmitt does not conceal the fact – a series of shifts away from the dogmas of traditional liberalism.

First, as he already noted in *The Guardian of the Constitution*, it must be recognized that 'the old liberal principle of unconditional non-interference, absolute non-intervention', is out of date.[24] In a situation where the masses are agitated and where big parties clash, adopting a laissez-faire position narrowly understood, remaining a spectator, waiting for the best to win (or the worst – but it all depends on where you stand), is not an option.

And, as he warns, 'painful surgery is going to be necessary, which cannot happen "organically" in the sense of slow growth'.[25] So we must also come to see that 'a depoliticization, a withdrawal of the state from non-state spheres [. . .] is a political process',[26] a task which requires much more than a 'minimal' state or a night watchman state: 'A state that could lead to such a reorganization should, as I have said, be extraordinarily strong – the act of depoliticization is a particularly intense political act'.[27]

Finally, the classic liberal vision, which views civil society as atomistic, where the state would have nothing other than economic agents to face it, is outdated. If the state withdraws from a whole series of economic management functions, other bodies must take over. Between the state and the market, an intermediate domain governed by the private self-government of large employers' bodies must insert itself.[28]

In 1932, when he read Schmitt's speech to the German bosses, the social democratic jurist Hermann Heller understood only too well what was at stake. Shortly before taking the road to exile (he died in Spain the following year), he left behind a short text, which is among the most clairvoyant of the period. We are witnessing, he says, the invention of a new political category, a little conceptual monster, the chimera of an 'authoritarian liberalism'.[29]

Schmitt, who had previously concealed his true positions 'under sophisticated denials', writes Heller, recently felt the need 'to express his ideas a little more clearly' before industrialists.[30] 'So far, we had heard Schmitt say that the current state was a weak state, due to its "pluralistic" character'.[31] Schmitt now sees a solution: the strong, authoritarian, 'qualitatively total' state.

But how strong is this strong state? Who will it be 'authoritarian' towards, and who not? The touchstone lies in its relationship to 'the economic order': 'once it is a question of economics, indeed, the "authoritarian" State renounces its authority. Its allegedly "conservative" spokespersons now have only one slogan: freedom of the economy from the state!'[32] It is a strong-weak state, strong with some, weak with others – strong, comments Wolfgang Streeck, 'against democratic demands for [social] redistribution', but 'weak in its relation to the market'.[33] Because this slogan, continued Heller, 'certainly does not imply that the state practise abstinence from the policy of subsidies to big banks, big industrial companies and big farms, but rather that it proceed to the authoritarian dismantling of social policy'. What these supporters of the 'authoritarian' state abominate above all, he notes, is 'the welfare state'.[34]

In 1934 a young German philosopher who had also fled Nazism published, in the review of the Frankfurt School, a long article on 'the fight against liberalism in the conception of the totalitarian state'.[35] He in turn analysed the conceptual shift spotted by Heller. Herbert Marcuse – for this was the philosopher in question – also had Schmitt in his sights.

On the surface, the new Schmittian philosophy of 'the total-authoritarian state' opposes liberalism, a hatred doctrine which it cannot criticize harshly enough. But what, asked Marcuse, is the real consistency of this antagonism? If you examine their programme, you realize that the supporters of the 'total authoritarian state' do not intend to lay a finger on basic economic relations. This new state, insofar as it 'organizes society without modifying its base in any decisive way is only a self-transformation of the liberal state'.[36]

And if the liberals profess a completely different political philosophy from that of the 'stato totalitario' of the fascists, in practice, some are ready to support this option as the last resort. Marcuse quotes von Mises, Hayek's mentor: 'If we were to reduce the programme of liberalism to a single formulation', he wrote in 1927, 'it would be: the private ownership of the means of production [. . .] all other requirements of liberalism derive from this fundamental principle. [. . .] Fascism and all similar impulses towards dictatorship have for the time being saved European civilization. The credit that fascism has derived from this will forever be etched in history'.[37]

Despite their real philosophical differences, these two currents agree on a decisive point, the safeguarding of capitalistic economic relations. 'So we see', writes Marcuse, 'the reason for which the total authoritarian state shifts its fight against liberalism to the field of "worldviews," why it leaves aside the fundamental social structure of liberalism: this basic structure largely suits it. [. . .] It leaves intact the principle which governs the relations of production'.[38]

But Marcuse immediately gives this first interpretation a much less economistic twist than might at first appear. True, 'the transition from a liberal state to a total authoritarian state takes place on the basis of the same social order',[39] but when that happens it is a real political change, not a simple 'ideological adaptation' that it entails. It would be wrong to reduce 'the theory of the total authoritarian state [. . .] to the mere result of an ideological manoeuvre. With the authoritarian state and with the thoughts it arouses for propagandist purposes, forces develop which go beyond its own political forms and which tend towards another state of affairs'.

That there is a final agreement on fundamental economic relations does not mean that both doctrines, economic liberalism and the authoritarian total state, are identical, nor that the gap between their visions of the world is artificial or negligible. That the growth of the liberal state into a total authoritarian state is possible, and that, without being necessary, this phenomenon is not accidental, does not lead us to conclude that liberalism is in essence crypto-fascism, or that fascism is the simple continuation of the liberal economy by other ideological means. A fascist capitalism is not the mere addition of an attribute to a substrate that remains identical despite an incidental modification in taxonomy. It is a worldview, but it is not just a worldview. When that happens, warned Marcuse, who had lived through it, we suddenly find ourselves in *another world*.

In the 1940s, even as the allies were starting to use the expression 'fight against totalitarianism' to designate their military offensive against the Axis Powers, some conservative intellectuals, even inside these 'Western democracies', seized on this formula to criticize their own governments, guilty in their eyes of heedlessly nursing within their bosoms the seeds of rampant totalitarianism.

Hayek in *The Road to Serfdom* (1944), von Mises in *Omnipotent Government* (1944)[40] and Schumpeter in *Capitalism, Socialism and Democracy* (1942) simultaneously denounced the vices of representative democracy, with a message that could be summarized as follows: if you truly want to fight 'totalitarianism', you need to make one more effort, because in spite of yourselves it actually seeps out from you, it is written as a *fatum* into the intrinsic slippages of your democratic system and your welfare state.

Under the Weimar Republic, says Hayek, wagging his finger, 'it was largely people of good will who, by their socialist policies, prepared the way for the forces which stand for everything they detest. Few recognize that the rise of fascism and Nazism was not a reaction against the socialist trends of the preceding period but a necessary outcome of those tendencies'.[41] This is the heart of his argument: welfare democracy fuels a socialism that leads straight to fascism. Mussolini is thus the necessary result of Gramsci, and Hitler in turn the necessary result of Rosa Luxemburg. This coarse genealogy is as false intellectually as it is politically, and it can only be stated at the cost of a denial of real political relations. However much Hayek may quote authors who, in the 1920s and 1930s, 'identif[ied] liberalism as

210

national socialism's main enemy', he still fails, notes Andrew Gamble, 'to prove that German democratic socialism was inherently totalitarian, since it did not fuse with Nazism, but was crushed by it'.[42] Heller and Marcuse were not mistaken: far from interpreting the nascent regime as an outgrowth of the welfare state, they understood it on the contrary as its negation, a reaction based on a new synthesis between liberal economy and political authoritarianism of the worst kind.

In the middle of World War II, Hayek et al. found nothing better to do than criticize the excesses of democracy and to call for a break with the welfare state. But they lost. To their dismay, the post-war era would be Keynesian. And they would be reduced to preaching in the desert (or almost) for three long decades.

When the social and political turmoil of the late 1960s suddenly broke out, they were both worried and reassured, because while the political crisis was serious, it also seemed to prove them right. The Cassandras puffed themselves up. We told you so, they said. This is where it leads. In this crisis, they saw an opportunity. Their old diagnoses would finally be able to regain credibility, and with them their 'heroic remedies'.

Hayek had always made it clear that while he praised the clairvoyant views of the pre-Nazi Schmitt on 'unlimited democracy', he disapproved of his subsequent political stances.[43] Duly noted. We have to give him credit. Hayek therefore believed that Schmitt had got it right in his examination of parliamentary democracy, but that he 'morally and intellectually' often took 'the wrong side'. As if the two were unconnected, as if the fall were accidental. But is this the case? Are we to say that, despite his astute analysis of the situation, Schmitt drew the wrong conclusions? This would mainly mean reproaching him for inconsistency. But can we, especially with such a sharp-minded thinker, draw such a convenient distinction between analysis and decision? On the contrary: it could be that, having seen things wrongly, he really did quite logically draw the corresponding conclusions. But there would be another interpretation, which would have the merit of doing justice less mechanically to the unity of diagnosis and therapy, placing less emphasis on logic than on *will*. To put it more directly: when you want to drown your dog, you say he has rabies. The same goes for that bitch democracy and her socialist offspring.

Notwithstanding the repeated criticisms he addressed to him, Hayek remains very close to Schmitt when it comes to depicting the flaws of parliamentary democracy. What he takes from his analysis is far from superficial. But there are conceptual frameworks which do not allow themselves to be borrowed with impunity.

Schmitt therefore, according to Hayek, was right (he saw that democracy was rampant totalitarianism), even if he frequently fell (as one can stumble, accidentally, even on a very good road) on the 'wrong side'. But what about Hayek, who therefore sees clearly too – since, in order to examine the question of democratic government, he has borrowed Schmitt's glasses – what side does he fall on? Salazar seizes power in Portugal. Hayek sends him his plan for a constitution, with a flattering message. The generals quell Argentina, he goes there to make speeches. Pinochet sheds blood in Chile: ditto. A boycott is launched against South Africa; Hayek takes up his pen to defend the regime, and so on.[44] Each time, or almost, that he finds himself in a historic situation where 'in reaction against socialist trends' a dictatorial regime prevails, he hastens there to lavish his advice on it.

Foucault's celebrated course on *The Birth of Biopolitics* has mainly given us a vision of neoliberalism as a governmentalization of the state, as the dissolution of the old frameworks of sovereignty into market forms.[45] This is true, but only in part. To better understand the ambiguity of neoliberal politics in its relations to state power, we need to study the other side too. As Wolfang Streeck remarks, 'Foucault might have gone back further, to Schmitt and Heller, where he would have found the basic figure of thought that informed and still informs liberal ideas about the economic role of state authority under capitalism – the idea, in the words of the title of a 1980s book on Margaret Thatcher, that one needs a "strong state" for a "free economy".'[46]

— 25 —

DETHRONING POLITICS

What is the throne, anyway? Four pieces of gilded wood covered with velvet.

Napoleon[1]

What shape was the solution to the 'crisis of governability of democracy' going to assume? Among the options available were what Samuelson called the 'devil's fix':[2] dictatorial power versus democratic surge; in order to depoliticize society, it was necessary to militarize politics. It was the strategy of total preventive war on the enemy within, as theorized in Latin America under the name of 'national security doctrine'.[3]

Democracy, Hayek had warned, is not possible everywhere,[4] but the converse was also true: Pinochet could no longer be exported to all countries. To establish a neoliberal order, military dictatorship is a means of last resort, not a universally generalizable model. Chile, Milton Friedman insisted, was 'an exception, not the rule'.[5] There were many other forms of 'transitional government' possible. 'Limiting democracy' can be achieved by stepping lightly rather than marching in to the tramp of jackboots. In other parts of the world, a Thatcher or Reagan could do the trick.

Hayek says that he wanted, with his latest books, to provide 'intellectual stand-by equipment for the time' capable of saving the system other than by desperately appealing to some form of dictatorship.[6] The attention was commendable, even if it could also be read as a veiled threat: if you refuse the gentle approach, you will leave us no other choice than force.

Echoing the language used about the crisis in the governability of democracy, Hayek further argued in 1978 that 'the epidemic of acute governmentitis which is taking on ever more frightening forms is the

213

unintended consequence of our current system of unlimited democracy'[7] – and, incidentally, using the words 'unlimited democracy' to describe the United States of Carter, the France of Giscard or the Italy of Andreotti says a lot about the limits of Hayek's own concept of democracy, but never mind . . . Since this trend, he continues, is 'inherent in the particular form that we have given to democratic governments, we cannot prevent this explosive growth [. . .] unless we transform our institutions from top to bottom'.[8]

Democracy, he writes, 'can only be preserved under the form of a limited democracy. Unlimited democracy necessarily destroys itself'.[9] If therefore it is doomed to self-destruction, one may as well seize the initiative and solve the problem oneself: amputate the limb to prevent gangrene. But what is lurking in the tool kit? What kind of scalpels? What techniques of de-democratization?[10]

The treatment followed the diagnosis. If indeed 'there is a crisis because of excessive vulnerability of government to popular demands, then means must be found of insulating governments, of putting a whole range of issues beyond the reach of democratic politics'.[11] The point was to 'control the government itself'.[12] Might it not be possible, faced with the sirens of social demand, to resort to an ancient trick and tie the captain of the ship to its mast? This, people thought, might be the way governability would finally be restored.

To this end, Hayek envisioned several processes, all of which would contribute to the realization of the same programme: 'dethrone politics'.[13] And this formula expressed the strategy of neoliberalism as a power of deposition.

The overall goal – to drastically limit government's margins for manoeuvre in social and economic matters – applied to any type of regime, but 'in a democracy', its implementation came up against a specific difficulty: could a way of imposing it be found that would not break too openly with the forms of the representative regime? 'The problem seemed insoluble, however', noted Hayek, 'only because an older ideal had been forgotten, namely that the power of all authorities exercising governmental functions ought to be limited by long run rules which nobody has the power to alter or abrogate in the service of particular ends.'[14] The sole solution was the constitution.

'Democracy', he argued, 'needs even more severe restraints on the discretionary powers government can exercise than other forms of government, because it is much more subject to effective pressure from special interests.'[15] To obviate the 'defects that characterize political regimes where legislative majorities have a practically unlimited ability to legislate',[16] salvation required restricting a priori the field of governmental power, forbidding it, once and for all, by prohibitions set in the stone of the fundamental law, to encroach on the flowerbeds of 'the economy'. Rather than allow too much latitude in democratic decision-making, he promoted the model of a 'constitutionally limited government' in matters of economic decision.[17] The old favourite theme of liberalism was thus taken up by an economic neoliberalism now free to manoeuvre on the field of the *jus politicum*. To dethrone politics, therefore, by constitutionally turning the economy into a sanctuary. Here lay the paradox: either the constitution was ousted, or it ousted its rivals.

As Buchanan points out, we can completely maintain the principle of 'free' elections provided that we initially restrict the decision-making field of the rulers who will emerge from them. It is important, he professes, to distinguish 'between *choices among rules* (constitutional politics) and *choices within rules* (ordinary politics)'.[18] What if 'ordinary politics cannot balance the budget'? All hope is not lost: we can always short-circuit the process by formulating a higher rule that which will compel it to do so. This constitutional strategy sees itself as a meta-politics, as a depoliticizing intervention in the rules for taking political choices.

Note that Buchanan's formulations are more conservative, in terms of public relations, than Hayek's: what we are going to limit, insisted Buchanan in his speech to the members of the Mont Pelerin Society gathered in the charming seaside resort of Viña del Mar in Chile in 1981, is not at all 'democracy', just 'the government' – an important nuance.[19] 'If voting made any difference they wouldn't let us do it', as the saying goes. But likewise, if care is taken to ensure that elections are powerless to change anything, there is nothing to stop us keeping them.

Hayek makes no bones about it: in this way, he agrees, we would pass to a regime of 'limited democracy'. But in what sense? In this sense, he specifies, 'in order to avoid misunderstandings': the legislator's activity should 'be limited to the adoption of general and abstract rules of conduct'.[20] General and abstract – exactly like this clarification. But what does this mean, more precisely and more concretely?

Apparently, this limitation in no way concerns the content of possible laws, only their *form*: a parliament can only adopt *general laws*, which also apply to everyone, but no more *particular* measures, applying specifically to distinct social groups. But – without here going into the details of the model of the constitution imagined by Hayek, the effect sought is much more substantial: 'A constitution like the one here proposed would of course make all socialist measures for redistribution impossible.'[21] Without even going that far, 'any market intervention to correct income distribution will become impossible'.[22] Thus, beneath the juridical formalism, the real social content of limitation soon resurfaces. What is lurking in the prohibited area? The panel explains it all in capitals: under our new constitution, the redistribution of wealth is prohibited, it is strictly forbidden to mess with the 'spontaneous' order of social inequalities.

One of the keys to the corresponding institutional strategy consists of playing on the scales of power: stretching, quartering and ultimately breaking the unity of traditional territorial sovereignty. While final constitutional control would be shifted upwards, to federal authorities, a whole section of the old functions of the state apparatus would be decentralized, transferred to lower rungs. 'Most government service activities could then be advantageously delegated to local or regional authorities, entirely limited in their binding powers by the rules laid down by a higher legislative authority'.[23] These two movements are complementary: they correspond to the two inverse vectors of a cross-*devolution* strategy that cuts away at the form of state sovereignty to replace it with other arrangements for making public policy 'governable'. The construction of Europe would provide a case study for a more detailed study of this strategy. Imagining, as early as 1939, the establishment of a federal system, Hayek was already presenting it as the royal road to a 'restriction of the power and scope of government' by means of the economic constitutionalization of politics at the supranational level.[24]

These plans for constitutional limitation certainly opened up promising prospects for the dethroning of democratic politics, but there still remained a practical problem. How to 'impose limits on the enforcer? How is Leviathan to be chained?' This was, according to Buchanan, 'the critical question of our time'.[25] If there were no providential dictator, how else could democracy be chained unless a gun were placed to its head? Could we reasonably hope that 'unlimited democracy' would limit itself, when it had been specifically criticized for decades as being structurally incapable of this? Here was a new puzzle to solve.

According to analyses of 'public choice', the political programmes favourable to public spending tended, as we have seen, to be 'more efficient than coalitions in favour of tax reduction'.[26] Economist Allan Meltzer nevertheless sought to be reassuring: 'Nothing about the process is inevitable. The growth of government could be brought to an end by constitutional limitation'.[27] Except that the difficulty remained, because if the dynamic of the electoral field is structurally opposed to austerity, it is a safe bet that it will also be opposed to setting them in constitutional stone. So one would need to resort to trickery.

'Conservatives who dislike how democracy works out are unwilling to follow their logic to the fascist conclusion these days and use constitutional limits on taxation as their form of imposed capitalism'.[28] 'To begin to appreciate this new theory you don't have to go below the equator [. . .] If democracy cannot be trusted, write once and forever into the constitution that capitalism must be the law of the land'.[29] Samuelson was referring to a proposed bill submitted to referendum in Massachusetts in 1980 which provided for capping municipal taxes to a maximum of 2.5 per cent of taxpayer resources.[30] This new electoral tactic consisted in relying on the latent tax revolt of the middle classes, intensifying and instrumentalizing it in order to establish binding standards for limiting public spending. What people were starting to say in the conservative camp was that if the political coalitions in favour of the maintenance of the welfare state tended to be stronger than those that promised the mass of those benefiting from them that they would sugar the pill, it might nonetheless be hoped, with a bit of window dressing, that programmes promising the middle classes that their taxes would be reduced would form the basis of new alliances likely to defeat the opposing position.

It was also at this time that a great ideological offensive on the theme of 'balanced budgets' and the 'fight against deficits' was launched. All our ills, according to Buchanan and Wagner's *Democracy in Deficit* (1977), stemmed from 'the Keynesian destruction of the balanced-budget'.[31] The state had swollen, the deficits were abysmal, the public sector literally 'out of control'.[32] 'Budgets cannot be left adrift in the sea of democratic politics'; what was needed was 'an external and "superior" rule',[33] a restrictive and 'sacrosanct' 'constitutional norm' of budgetary balance.

This, at least, was the official anthem. In small groups, however, the neoliberals were humming another tune. In 1982, at a conference organized by the Federal Reserve Bank of Atlanta, Milton Friedman let the cat out of the bag: 'It's a good idea to have a balanced budget but not at the expense of higher taxes. I would rather have a federal government expenditure of $400 billion with a $100 billion deficit than a federal government expenditure of $700 billion completely balanced'.[34] Contrary, therefore, to what we are forever being told, balance is not a value in itself. The overriding objective is the *reduction* of the state budget. But why insist so much, if the goal is elsewhere?

217

'The reason a balanced budget is important', Friedman continues, 'is primarily for political, not economic, reasons; to make sure that if Congress is going to vote for higher spending, it must also vote for higher taxes'[35] – something that parliamentarians, attached to their electoral capital, will baulk at doing.

So it's all about containing expenditure. But what lies in turn behind this goal? Under this question of expenditure, according to Friedman's interpretation, there are others: that of 'taxing, including in particular the real time bomb in Social Security, Medicare and Medicaid programs', and above all, behind this, 'concealed taxes in the form of mandated expenditures on private business'.[36] This is the crux of the matter: if people care so much about the 'overload' of the state budget, it is actually because they are rebelling against the 'overload' of capital, the other camel which is also crumbling under the weight of taxes and social contributions.[37]

But Friedman goes further. On closer inspection, he adds, the much-maligned budget deficit is not a calamity, but a blessing, a great opportunity for his side: 'the deficit has been the only effective restraint on congressional spending. We would much prefer a constitutional amendment that requires a balanced budget and limits spending. Relying on the deficit to check spending is admittedly a second-best solution – but it is better than nothing'.[38] For lack of a golden budgetary rule enshrined in the basic law (this would be ideal), the same objective can be reached by conducting an empty coffers policy while setting up debt as an ideological scarecrow.[39]

But a new economic phenomenon was emerging, opening up other perspectives. To face the growing public finance crisis, noted one political scientist in the late 1970s, 'governments have increasingly relied for financing on private financial markets'.[40] Now you have to understand, he warned, that this 'dependence of governments on private financial markets – which is to a great extent the result of increases in oil prices – creates additional pressures for conservative economic policies that are deferential to the interests of capital. It becomes more difficult to follow egalitarian polices of income distribution'.[41]

This was another form of limitation of government policy, doubtless more effective than all those we have discussed so far. It was neither military, nor constitutional, nor electoral, nor ideological, but technically geared to a public decision about to become financially dependent on the assessment of its policies by the market of sovereign obligations. The norm was instantiated in a different way. It had other agents, more discreet, more dashing, no doubt, than a bedridden old soldier with decorations. The dictatorship of the markets, in short, was higher than that of the generals.

'It is striking', observed Bernard Manin barely ten years after the publication of the Trilateral Report, 'that this theme of the governability of democracies has gone out of intellectual fashion. It's out of the question, no one cares about this problem anymore'.[42] Why not? 'In one way, a solution has been found';[43] located at the heart of monetarist regulations, 'the market provides [. . .] a very effective principle of limitation of power, because it is a regulatory body that lies outside the control of different agents'. This was 'the overall solution to the crisis in governability: the rule of the market'.[44]

One of the major innovations of neoliberalism, said Manin, was to think of the market as a political technology: no longer simply 'as what provides the optimal allocation of resources' in the allegedly autonomous sphere of the economy, but as a 'political principle, as a principle of order and governability'.[45] The market was no longer just what politics should not intrude on, but also what it now needed to yield to. The market thus moved, as far as government policy was concerned, from being an object-limit to the limiting-subject of its action.

The solution was ultimately to apply to state managers an equivalent of the catallarchic formula previously discovered in order to ensure the loyalty of business managers: an agency report sanctioned by markets which, at the same time as they tirelessly fulfilled their speculative function, simultaneously exercised – without its agents even needing to want this – a policing function. In other words, the financial markets, as operators of government governability.

And yet the famous 'crisis of governability of democracy' had two floors, not just one. Besides the fact that this political form was too permeable to 'social expectations', there were those expectations themselves, too much mobilization, too much politicization of society, the 'democratic surge' which alarmed Huntington so much. Besides the problem of democracy-as-government, there was the problem of democracy-as-movement.

Now if neoliberal locking tactics aimed to adjust democracy-as-government by a multidimensional limitation of public decision-making, democracy-as-movement remained intact. To stem its fighting spirit, it was felt, it was necessary to attack the conditions of the power relationship that underpinned it, but this involved going to war, at the risk of melting the minimal consent on which this kind of regime continued, in spite of everything, to depend. The problem, Brittan lamented, is that 'liberal democracy inhibits governments from tackling coercive groups [i.e. social movements] either by an abnegation of the full employment commitment, or by the effective restriction of union monopoly power, or by the enforcement of an "incomes policy".'[46] Rose, who was also considering a whole host of offensive measures, including the privatization of entire sections of the public sector, said he was pessimistic about the chances of achieving it, as resistance was so strong. Ultimately, he ventured, 'only a measure such as the suspension of free elections would substantially and immediately reduce the pressures of expectations upon government'.[47] So the question of resorting to dictatorial power, thrown out through the front door, came in through the back.

The ship's captain is being tied to the mast, but the sirens are still there. It may be that one day, tired of huffing and puffing in vain, they will climb on board. They could be harpooned, perhaps, to clear a route for the vessel, but ship's regulations prohibit doing this properly – and even if the risk is taken, those sirens can be expected to counter-attack.

In 1977, the OECD released the McCracken Report on inflation and slowing growth.[48] The recommendations of this group of economists, still marked by the ambient Keynesianism, remained eclectic, but certain passages especially attracted the attention of the critics – a few pages where experts, albeit still timidly, recommended monetary discipline, the reduction of public spending and a flexible labour market. These new directions were interpreted by some as the harbinger of a possible turnaround, the announcement of a conversion in the dominant economic policy to the neoliberalism that was looming.

In the acerbic account he gave of this report, the political scientist Robert Keohane wondered about the *political feasibility* of the economic project that he suspected lurked within it. The McCracken Commission, he said, advises governments to 'exert more discipline on their economies while resisting the temptation to confer short-term benefits on their citizens through large-scale public spending'.[49] This position, he argued, is neither that of the minimum state of laissez-faire, nor that of the Keynesian welfare state, but an intermediate formula, a 'disciplinary state', which would keep a role in regulating the economy while cutting back on its social policy.[50]

The report's authors naively imagine, he claims, that such '*democratic disciplinary states* [. . .] will be able to persuade their citizens to accept greater economic restraint, and fewer benefits, than they have enjoyed in the past',[51] while retaining 'a substantial legitimacy within their societies'.[52] Personally, he very much doubted it. If the OECD experts seem unable to see where the problem lies, it has not escaped the attention of others. The 'radicals', reports Keohane, the very same people who since the war have faced the boasted prowess of the 'contemporary welfare state [. . .] viewed [. . .] as a refutation of Marxist theories about the crisis of capitalism', have derived the following conclusions from its defeat: 'If the managers of the economy were to renounce their commitment to full employment with price stability, one of the key justifications for capitalism (from the viewpoint of the working class) would be undermined. Could one then blame workers for reconsidering their endorsement of political and economic arrangements that had failed to fulfill their expectations?'[53]

What was being sketched out here, I think, was a new version – even if Keohane does not use the formula – of the crisis of governability, extending this motif to a new kind of political-economic regime in the making. So far, this crisis concerned only welfare democracy. It was said to be this disastrous combination of Keynesianism and representative democracy that had made state policy untenable. But what about maintaining the latter without the former? If the welfare state ended up being affected by a severe crisis of legitimacy despite its good works, what would happen if they pulled the plug on it? The question would then be: is a post-Keynesian democracy possible?

If there are indeed 'structural conditions of ungovernability',[54] said analysts on the left, they actually lie even deeper than the neoconservatives and the neoliberals will admit: 'Capitalism has become dependent on the legitimizing function of social spending. The "embarrassing secret", the contradiction of capitalism is that, while capitalism cannot coexist with, neither can it exist without, the welfare state'.[55] If you think Keynesian 'democracy' is ungovernable, try neoliberal 'democracy' instead.

The authors of the McCracken report, says Keohane, have merely swept the problem under the carpet. They postulate that their 'disciplinary state' will, in principle, as an article of faith, be democratic, but without wondering for a second about the conditions of political viability of such a form in these conditions. They are basically too naive: they think that 'democracy and capitalism are, and can remain, fully compatible with one another' – which, Keohane reminds them (quoting Marx and Schumpeter simultaneously), is not at all obvious.[56]

Can a 'disciplinary democracy' remain 'democratic'? Keohane doubts it, but he refuses to answer in absolute terms. It all depends.

'In Germany, Japan, and perhaps the United States', yes, given that 'the wealth, economic vigor, and political stability of these societies may allow them to take their economic medicine without suffering allergic political reactions'. In other OECD countries, it is less sure. 'Calling for more sacrifices by ordinary people in order to increase profits and thus preserve capitalism hardly constitutes a brilliant rallying cry for a new majority. It is difficult to imagine French socialists, Italian communists, or British trade unionists joining readily in a "consensus on the need for higher profits"'. His conclusion: 'It is unlikely that these states will be established democratically throughout the OECD area'.[57] So back to square one. It is striking to see how, in this still uncertain transition phase towards neoliberalism, the spectre of dictatorship is lurking.

And yet, at least in the language used, the 1980s were going to be the years of a great triumph of 'democracy'. In April 1981, Norman Podhoretz published an article in the *Harvard Business Review* on 'the new defenders of capitalism'. Businessmen, he advised his readers, would do well to take more interest in intellectual life and 'tak[e] ideas seriously' because they are of great political importance. However, announced this neoconservative analyst, there were 'signs of a reversal of the traditionally hostile attitude toward capitalism now beginning to appear within the intellectual community'[58] – especially in France where, he reported, the 'new philosophers' had 'renounced Marxism altogether'.[59] Rediscovering the 'virtues of capitalism', many intellectuals now thought that there was a fundamental political antagonism between 'democracy' and 'totalitarianism'.[60]

Reading these lines, his neoconservative colleague Daniel Bell grimaced. He felt he need to react in the reader's letters column. Podhoretz, he wrote, tells us that 'capitalism [. . .] is conducive to liberty and democracy. Is it?' Not necessarily: 'few serious political philosophers jumble together "liberty" *and* "democracy." Most, in fact, would argue – as did nineteenth-century theorists such as Alexis de Tocqueville – that there is an inherent tension between liberty and democracy, and that often the tyranny of the majority, derived from the *demos*, threatens liberty'.[61] In other words, we'd better stay on our guard, and the nonsense spouted by the 'new philosophers', even if they *were* French, should not make us lose sight of the fundamental principles of a reactionary politics properly understood.

Either way, the tide was indeed turning in the dominant ideology: while in the previous phase, defenders of the system had pointed fairly unanimously to the tensions, even the incompatibility between capitalism and democracy, a new way of talking was starting to present them as synonyms, promoting one in the name of the other.

How is this reversal to be explained? If people were now singing the praises of a democracy that was still abhorred yesterday, this was, of course, on the strict implicit condition that what was being celebrated under this name was merely what some today call 'post-democracy' – an empty residue, a form without substance. But this U-turn can be properly understood only if related to a new political strategy which was then carrying out a pivotal movement, of which this discursive transformation was at once both the sign and the instrument.

'The crisis of the welfare state and the popular frustration that accompanied it', wrote Chantal Mouffe in 1986, 'lay behind a series of anti-state reactions that the right quickly translated into the terms of neoliberal criticism. A chain of equivalence was established between politics = public = state = bureaucracy. This allowed conservatives to present their offensive against democracy as a struggle for democracy, the latter being defined from the angle of a recovery by the "people" of the "rights" that the state had confiscated from them'.[62] While the word 'democracy' was thus reinterpreted as the name of a liberal individualism opposed to state collectivism, the corresponding *demos* was at the same time redefined or reimagined in a neo-traditionalist fashion as an *ethnos* whose identity was threatened by the 'permissive society', another name for the social, racial, sexual and generational emancipation that was then vigorously underway. The strange ideological unity of this liberal-conservative populism was inseparably individualistic and authoritarian, entrepreneurial and traditionalist. Economic neoliberalism, entering the sphere of politics, was thus associated with a kind of national-democratism with sexist, homophobic and racist overtones. It was in this contradictory, slow-burning unity that one of the major sources of the current political pathologies of Western liberal democracies undoubtedly lies. When, in 1979, Andrew Gamble sought to characterize the programme of Thatcherism, he summed it up with this formula: 'The free economy and the strong state'.[63] In this way he repeated almost word for word the title of Carl Schmitt's speech.

Authoritarian liberalism comes in many varieties. But, we must insist, they are *different* versions. As Stuart Hall warned, this was not the return of 'fascism' to the political scene, not the 'awakening of familiar ghosts and spectres' of the left, but the advent of something else that needed to be grasped specifically. So people needed to beware a knee-jerk reaction, a miscognition: 'What we have to explain is a move toward "authoritarian populism" – an exceptional form of the capitalist state – which, unlike classical fascism, has retained most (though not all) of the formal representative institution in place, and which at the same time has been able to construct around itself an active popular consent'.[64]

Thatcherism presented itself as a strangely syncretic ideology, that of a 'new right' that could 'appear by turns libertarian and authoritarian, populist and elitist'.[65] This lay, beyond the apparent inconsistencies, in the way it synthesized 'a traditional liberal defence of the free economy with a traditional conservative defence of state authority'.[66] Beyond an ideology, it was a strategy – a redeployment of the state, called upon both to withdraw almost completely from certain areas and to intensively move into others, in a way that was simultaneously non-interventionist and interventionist, centralized and decentralized. But these seemingly contradictory movements were closely united. If the state is to be strengthened, it is so that it will grow weaker: 'firm and decisive action is necessary to cut public spending programmes and taxes, to privatise public assets and public services, and to abolish interventionist and regulatory agencies'.[67]

And yet, under 'the abstraction called "spending"', said Alan Wolfe, eager to demystify the phenomenon, there are always 'the real needs of real people'.[68] But they were unlikely to be robbed without saying anything. In the early 1980s, neoliberals knew this and were preparing for confrontation.

But in order to win this battle, it would not be enough to lock down policy from the top and show firmness in the central clashes. More subtle, more capillary tactics for neutralizing politics also needed to be perfected.

— 26 —

THE MICROPOLITICS OF PRIVATIZATION

In short, everything is political, but every politics is simultaneously a *macropolitics* and a *micropolitics*.

Deleuze and Guattari[1]

The analysis of micro-powers is not a question of scale, and it is not a question of a sector, it is a question of a point of view.

Michel Foucault[2]

At the end of the 1970s, the main lines of the neoliberal programme had been laid out. The ruling elites of the 'free world' were converted to it at top speed, repudiating the previous Keynesian orthodoxy. Everything was going well. But there was still one shadow to darken the picture. Given the radicalism of the break envisaged and its array of socially harmful implications, implementing it would inevitably come up against strong opposition. People knew only too well that a government which attempted to introduce 'such changes by conventional means would have had to face a hostile crowd'.[3] They had to prepare intellectually and politically for confrontation, rediscover 'the cohesion and the political nerve required to ride out the confrontation with the left in the trade unions that appeared inevitable'.[4]

Hence also the dark strategic ruminations in high places. Some 'speculated on the need for a sacrificial government which would come in to do what was necessary without any hope of re-election afterwards. Others toyed with the idea of a government which would not need to be re-elected'.[5] This was the alternative: kamikaze government or autocratic government. Either find politicians ready to bring in reforms at all costs – defying their unpopularity, at the risk of squandering their electoral capital or forcing their own party to commit political suicide; or else establish some form of caesarism or Bonapartism which would tidy things up by restricting or suspending the usual way representative democracy functioned.

To get out of the impasse, some imagined a third way. 'It was onto this political scene', says Madsen Pirie, 'that the central ideas of *micro politics* were introduced'.[6] Having apparently not heard of Foucault, Deleuze or Guattari, this British neoliberal was firmly convinced that he had invented a new word: 'micropolitics', the name of an original method that 'enabled a government to start on such a programme of reform without paying the electoral price widely predicted'.[7]

Pirie was one of the leaders of the 'St Andrews group', after the name of the Scottish university where its members had earned their spurs.[8]

> We knew we were making revolution. In the late 1960s it was in the air. There were huge marches in London, and all over Britain universities were occupied by student sit-ins. In France the government of Charles de Gaulle tottered under a wave of strikes and protests. But the revolution we were making in St Andrews was different. Their gods were Karl Marx, Che Guevara and Herbert Marcuse; ours were Friedrich Hayek, Karl Popper and Milton Friedman. [. . .] That was it, really, except that we won.[9]

Advisers to the British Conservatives and the Reagan administration, members of this trend actually developed some original political tactics that are still very much in force today.

What does this neoliberal 'micropolitics' involve? Pirie defines it rather abstrusely as 'the art of generating circumstances in which individuals will be motivated to prefer and embrace the alternative of private supply, and in which people will make individual and voluntary decisions whose cumulative effect will be to bring about the desired state of affairs'.[10]

Let us take up the different points of this definition: (1) Micropolitics is an art, a political technology. (2) Its goal is privatization. (3) Its object is individual choices, which need to be reoriented. (4) Its main method relies on neither persuasion by speech, nor coercion by force, but on a social engineering that reconfigures situations of choice through mechanisms of economic incentive. (5) Its cunning (which we could, in tribute to Adam Smith, call 'invisible manipulation') lies in ensuring that individual micro-choices involuntarily manage to bring about by retail a social order that most people probably would not have chosen if it had been presented to them wholesale.

This approach, formulated in terms of political technology, was opposed to another strategy, that of the 'battle of ideas' into which many, on the right, had flung themselves in the early 1970s, and one characteristic example of which we studied above in the form of the Powell memorandum.[11] According to this simplistic model inspired by counterinsurgency doctrines, the main task, faced with what was analysed as an ideological attack on the system of free enterprise, was to win back hearts and minds by a massive counter-attack carried out on the battlefield of 'ideas'. As reinterpreted by this armchair Gramscism, the struggle for hegemony was reduced to a contrary form of brainwashing.

For the St Andrews group, this was barking up the wrong tree. As recent experience had shown, even if a majority of people – enough in any case to win the elections – had been convinced, the fact remained that society was still resisting, and reforms were not gaining ground. And there was no use, in the face of such 'blockages', repeating that more 'pedagogy' was needed. Supporters of the 'battle of ideas' committed a fundamental methodological mistake, due to their misconception of the relationships between theory and practice. Postulating that once people's minds had been conquered, behaviour would follow, they viewed ideological victory as a prerequisite for reform, and in this respect they were seriously mistaken. It was this schema, both idealistic and piecemeal, which Pirie questioned. He suspected that it reflected a typical illusion of intellectuals, those who, by their social position, tend to attribute a primary role to 'ideas', and behind the scenes to intellectuals themselves, deemed to be the instigators of such ideas. 'It comes naturally to such people to suppose that ideas are the ultimate determinants, and that to win the battle for ideas is to win thereby the battle for events'.[12] But this is clearly not true.

If you want to win, he continues, you have to reverse the relationship. If you want to understand, he advises his comrade chums, take a break from your soporific reading of Hayek and have a quick look at something by Che Guevara, a 'hero', and above all Lenin, an authentic 'man of action'. It was Vladimir Ilitch who showed the way: 'Instead of applying Marxist theory, he found from practical experience how a small but ruthless and dedicated band could seize control of a mighty nation and hold that power'.[13] In short, if there is one lesson to be learned from the enemy, it is that 'the action precedes the theory'.[14] This entailed the recuperation, not of this or that theme in the critique of capitalism, but of a revolutionary attitude. It marked the curious birth of a Bolshevo-liberal style in reactionary politics.

The specificity of this trend in neoliberalism lies in its careful attention to practical devices. 'The result was the concentration of some groups in the 1970s', writes Pirie (he often talks about himself and his friends in the third person), 'not on the battle for ideas, but on policy engineering. Instead of simply waving free market flags and shouting the traditional battle cries, attention [. . .] turned instead to the technical and mechanical details of policies'.[15] These intellectuals saw themselves less as tribunes or propagandists than as 'policy engineers' who 'constructed machines which worked'.[16] The task did not lie so much in convincing people as finding the technical means of 'changing the choices people make, by altering the circumstances of these choices'.[17] Let the conditions of practice change, and the rest will follow. 'Many of the successes of micro politics have preceded the general acceptance of the ideas on which they were based. In several cases the success of the policy has led to the victory of the idea, rather than the other way round'.[18]

How was is it, these authors wondered at the end of the 1970s, that conservative governments, despite being comfortably elected and determined to 'reform', had not succeeded, at least not as much as they had promised?[19] Not out of ill will or pusillanimity on their part but for objective reasons, because they came up against the counter-dynamics of 'demand overload' written into the very cogs of welfare democracy – without having the slightest hint of an effective strategy to set against it.

By clumsily trying to prune public expenditure, they inevitably gave rise, on each attempt, to an outcry on the part of the social groups concerned. Their mistake was to want to reduce the government *supply* by removing benefits to which their beneficiaries were attached without first worrying about stemming the social *demand* that the welfare state had structurally concentrated on itself. You might as well try to stop water from boiling by pressing hard on the lid of the pot.[20]

The solution to this problem was to be 'privatization' – a neologism that was still used in quotes in the early 1980s. Quite evocatively, the cover of the book Pirie published in the United States in 1985, *Dismantling the State: The Theory and Practice of Privatization*,[21] was illustrated by the drawing of a giant hand, equipped with a crowbar, smashing the dome of Congress in Washington. Defined as 'the shifting of government functions to the private sector',[22] this 'strategy to cut the budget' had the advantage, in contrast to the previous ones, of not making the service disappear overnight, but of transferring it to other providers. Trade union officials would not fail to oppose privatization in the name of defending their jobs and their status, but the wager was that the users, not seeing immediately how they were going to lose from the exchange – especially as public services would have been allowed to deteriorate beforehand – would not react as vigorously as if they had been immediately informed of the suppression of unprofitable activities.

Privatization is certainly an ingenious way of cutting the budget but, added the neoliberals of St Andrews, it would be wrong to reduce it to that, because its potential was even more promising. What lay behind all this, of course, was the lure of big money, as it was true that the privatization of public services was part of that round of grabbing that David Harvey called 'accumulation by dispossession'.[23] But its promoters preferred to insist on another aspect – also very important, and not just a pretext – depicting it as a properly political strategy, centred on issues of governability.

By taking 'the service into the purely economic world and out of the political world',[24] you do not only change ownership, but also the mode of government. As long as a service is governed by the logic of the political world, it's very difficult to control its costs and limit its expansion, but 'if such a program can be moved to the private sector it automatically becomes subject to market-based disciplines'.[25] What governments are struggling to do voluntarily, the discipline of competition will impose mechanically. Privatization, therefore, is not so much a plan for deregulation than for *re-regulation*: moving from one mode of regulation to another, different in its procedures, but even more drastic, since 'the regulation which the market imposes on economic activity is superior to any regulation which men can devise and operate by law'.[26]

Privatization had promised to solve at the same time the problem of demand overload: 'Rather than trying to frustrate political demands for spending, it means *deflecting* that demand into the nongovernment sector',[27] redirecting demands 'addressed to the welfare state' towards relations of monetary exchange,[28] redirecting claims 'into extra-political "market" domains'[29] so as to neutralize the 'underlying political dynamics of spending'.[30]

By converting old political demands into a market demand, they hoped to relieve the state from the pressure of the public, not only in budget terms but also in political terms. 'The more the state withdraws from the economic process, as by privatizing public services, the better it can escape the legitimation demands that arise from its general responsibility for the burdens resulting from a crisis-ridden capitalism'.[31] They thus intended to kill two birds with one stone: to simultaneously solve the state's financial crisis and its legitimacy crisis – the twin sources of the 'crisis of governability of democracies'.

The vital message, insisted sociologist Paul Starr, was that 'privatization needs to be understood as a fundamental reordering of claims in a society'.[32] While the dissatisfied user turned to the government and loudly asked it to explain itself, the dissatisfied customer confined himself to taking his custom elsewhere. By privatizing the supply, an attempt was made to depoliticize demand, to make it choose, in Hirschman's terms, 'exit' to 'voice': voting with your feet while making for the exit rather than protesting by actually voting (and thus making sure your voice was heard).

In 1987, in a sign of the times, Stuart Butler, one of the privatizers of St Andrews, amused himself by hijacking the old slogan of the radical left, 'Power to the people' and using it for one of his articles, with the following subtitle: 'A Conservative Vision for Welfare'.[33] It was a matter of 'taking the rallying cry of the 1960s – "empowerment" – and giving it real meaning'.[34] Rather than funding social services, he recommended distributing vouchers to beneficiaries so that they could spend them on a market open to competition. While militant empowerment aimed at intensifying a collective and political power to act, neoliberal empowerment aimed instead to promote the agency of individual consumers, 'empowered' against a background of privatization and competition between providers. Give them the choice, but to stop giving them a voice. Market empowerment versus political empowerment.[35]

In the early 1980s, some neoliberals encouraged conservative governments to 'advocate biting the bullet and undertaking to end the state service'. But this meant running the risk, Pirie noted critically, that by 'taking the issue head on', it would 'meet all the enemies head on, and all of them together'.[36] Denationalization en bloc was admittedly possible in certain sectors, but it was a 'highly visible technique',[37] and therefore politically risky. In general, you have to adopt other methods, less showy and more progressive. Micropolitics is 'micro' first and foremost in its mode of action, in that it proceeds little by little. These kinds of recommendations provoked astonishment, including in the conservative camp. Some welcomed the approach of the micropoliticians who, 'instead of seeking the immediate replacement of the public sector by private alternatives [. . .] appeared to look for more modest progress'. But it was nonsense to see it as a lack of ambition, a policy of compromise or a half measure: those neoliberals, far from behaving like timid reformers, were seeking, rather, as consistent revolutionaries, to imagine processes of long-term social transformation.

Nothing illustrates this philosophy better than the procedures they included under the label of 'micro-incrementalism'.[38] One of them was method number 15, 'repealing monopolies to let competition grow'.[39] In this case, we 'leave the public supply intact, while growing an alternative alongside it in the private sector. [. . .] Circumstances are created in which people have an effective alternative choice'.[40] No need to denationalize at once. The state may well remain the sole shareholder – once things have been opened up to competition, a process begins which will ultimately result in roughly the same result. Pirie cites the example of the 1980 liberalization, by a newly elected Mrs Thatcher, of intercity bus transport – a prelude to the privatization of the British railways.[41]

The strength of the procedure lies in this: once liberalization has been enacted, it is the individuals themselves, by their micro-choices as consumers, who become the drivers of change. 'An attractive feature of this type of privatization is that it permits the gradual change from public to private, without the need for a bruising battle to privatize the whole service. [. . .] As far as the general public is concerned, they vote with their pocketbooks for the rate at which they wish the private services to expand'.[42] So 'the choices are made gradually by individuals, and over months and years they cumulatively produce the new reality. The most secure revolutions are ones which people make for themselves over time'.[43]

Unspectacular in its mode of action, this micropolitics of privatization is no less formidable. It is what we could call, by reference to the wood-boring insect of the same name, *the politics of the longhorn beetle*: there is no need to take an axe to the beams to trim them when, lurking in the wood, a thousand small mouths are inexorably gnawing away the frame.

With this method, it is not necessary to persuade everyone to support the overall project of a market society for everyone to endeavour to bring it into being. In reality, it is even crucial never to ask people the question on this scale: you are not going to sell it to them wholesale, only retail. The big question of the choice of society can be evaded by dissolving it into the tiny questions of a society of choice. The cunning of micropolitical reason is that, in these micro-choices, we are also deciding, without knowing it, on something other than their immediate object, with the volitions of each person contributing to building a society that they might not have chosen if it had been depicted right from the start as the expected result. This micropolitics is micro or small, therefore, in the sense of meanness too. It involves narrowing the horizon. You can no longer look at the world except through the small end of the telescope. You will be able to survey the whole landscape only later, maybe finally taking a step back. One by one, the tiniest relations will have been altered and, as far as the eye can see, the whole scene will have become unrecognizable.

Analyses of public choice, when they focused on the welfare state, referred to a 'ratchet effect' in public spending: once certain social programmes had been granted, not only was it difficult to go back, but they tended to extend to new beneficiaries. The privatizers theorized about a 'reverse ratchet effect', a 'private sector ratchet effect' – the idea being that it would be enough to start the process of privatization to set in motion 'a chain of events whose process gradually but inexorably' leads to the desired goal.[44] The most attractive aspect of this solution, from a political point of view, was 'its permanence. It needs to be done only once'.[45]

But we need to be clear. To start this kind of process, it is essential to break down certain legislative obstacles. This can involve central conflicts, macropolitical battles that must be won on this scale. In this respect, far from excluding a showdown, micropolitics requires it often enough to engage its micro-cogs in their micro-trimming. But, for each sector, they promised, it would need to be imposed just once – opening up to competition, changing status, etc. Then there would be no need to guide the movement from above, it would all run by itself. And the termites, that is, you and I, will do their job.

It was this vision of history, the idea that only one single decisive victory would need to be won each time to release the dissolving energies of the market into the sector concerned, which motivated the tenacity of neoliberal governments in this type of conflict: they read them as battles that took place ratchet by ratchet.

They claimed to have discovered the missing link of neoliberalism. Until then, explains Pirie, there was, between its economic methodology and its political recommendations, an astonishing discrepancy: 'economists [. . .] might recognize the prime importance of microeconomic factors, but do not extend this to the political arena. It is not uncommon to hear economists whose analysis derives from microeconomic study calling for such things as "the end of state industries" or [. . .] to "abolish the National Health Service".' But on their side, 'political leaders know that they cannot achieve these things simply by wanting to do so, and regard such cavalier advice as out of touch with political reality'.[46]

It was a question of harmonizing the mode of action with the method of analysis, of rethinking political strategy on the scale of microeconomic analysis: 'Microeconomics considers the behaviour of individuals and groups in economic markets; micropolitics looks at it in political markets'.[47] In a way, it meant extending the approach of 'the school of public choice',[48] except that people were no longer satisfied by *criticizing* the functioning of the electoral market; they wanted to find ways of *changing* the choices that were shaped in it. 'Once the political market is understood, devices can be introduced to redirect the forces that operate within it. This is all that micropolitics seeks to do'.[49]

But the major obstacle identified by analyses of 'choice public' still blocked the path. Those who benefit from the 'largesse' of the welfare state (the famous 'interest groups', but more broadly the general public) formed, with those who provide this largesse (the civil servants) a powerful coalition for their continued existence. Given this, it was difficult to see what could encourage anyone to do anything different.

If this challenge seems impossible to meet, Pirie admits, it is because one would need to find ways 'to make people work directly against their own interest'.[50] The 'fundamental problem of political philosophy', wrote Gilles Deleuze and Félix Guattari, boils down to the famous question raised by Spinoza: 'Why do men fight *for* their servitude as stubbornly as though it were their salvation?'[51] According to them, the answer was to be found in the analysis of the 'machinery of desire',[52] a task that could only be carried out by 'micro-mechanics'.[53]

Neoliberal micro-politicians ask a similar question, but from another angle, and with antithetical political aims: no longer *why* do men fight for their bondage as if it were their salvation, but *how can we ensure that they do so?* Their answer had a spurious family resemblance with that of the authors of *Anti-Oedipus*: deploy a micro-engineering of rational choice to this end. How to get people to do what we want them to do? Not by repressing their big desires but rather by reorientating their smallest choices.[54]

But how were they to proceed, more precisely? The privatizers wrote manuals listing available tactics. Pirie enumerates no fewer than twenty-two major privatization methods, with their variants. Like the Ancients, therefore, he lists the ruses of war – but he neglects to apply to himself what was the first of the stratagems according to Frontinus: 'to hide one's designs'.[55]

Let's take one procedure among others: to successfully privatize, always 'offer something in return for the loss', that is, 'buying out existing interest groups'.[56] In 1983, the Thatcher government decided to privatize British Airways. Twenty thousand jobs were in jeopardy, or nearly one in three employees. If you decide to fire on this scale, you are going to have to face strong opposition. What should you do? 'They were offered generous terms for voluntary redundancy' (a cheque worth two years' salary).[57] It is therefore possible, comments Pirie, to persuade people to 'give up a long-term and continuing gain' in return for 'a substantial and immediate gain'.[58] To torpedo a lasting interest, dangle the carrot of an immediate advantage.

Not everyone will be fooled, but never mind that. The mere fact that a fraction of employees swallows the bait helps destroy unity. You can thus '*buy*' key portions of the opposing coalition. At British Airways, the legal appeals launched by the trade unions 'repeatedly delayed the date of sale', and so 'the employees threatened strike action if it were not hurried forward and completed. The workers were, as so often in other companies, taken aboard as partners on the privatization'.[59] 'It is doubtful to say the least', as Pirie nonetheless admits, 'if any of these reforms could have taken place in a public sector operation without the prospect of privatization at the end of the day'.[60] It is true that, without the stick, the carrot looks much less appetizing.

This tactic has many variations. Rather than buying people's futures from them, we can promise them that they will retain their long-term benefits provided that they sacrifice new entrants. So, 'when existing special interests have the power to thwart a move to the private sector, it may be possible to use a technique which alters the pattern for the future, even while continuing to benefit the present beneficiaries'.[61] Why then would you mobilize to defend a status that will not be taken from *you*? Why worry since you are not personally concerned?

This method of 'blocking future entry, while guaranteeing the benefit of those who are already in' has, besides the obvious case of the status of civil servants, many other fields of application. Take the case of rent controls. The logic is the same: if you suddenly try to deregulate the real estate market, tenants who benefit from capped rents will revolt. Another, more cautious, approach is to refrain from changing existing leases while changing the terms of new rental contracts. 'This method sets in motion a chain of events whose process gradually but inexorably diminishes the publicly-controlled supply, and gradually enhances the proportion covered by the private market. It culminates in the extinction of what may seem another intractable part of the public sector'.[62]

This same method can also be very useful for launching an assault on pension plans. Nothing is gained, here again, by arousing opposition through too explicit an attack on the social rights of workers still active. To pass your reform, take particular care to specify, recommends Pirie, that 'the proposed changes will not apply to promised benefits and will not affect anyone reaching retirement age before the end of the century'. 'Such proposals', he summarizes, 'in a sense "buy out" the present generation in order to phase in a new system'.[63] Sell us the future generations and you will be spared. The message is the same as before: given that you will not be affected *personally*, why would it concern you *politically*? Why fight for others than yourself, be they your children or your grandchildren? Look no further than the tip of your nose. What does it matter after all, since you yourselves – it's a promise – will be able to dodge the raindrops. And *après vous le déluge*.

Neoliberal micropolitics thinks long term and can take its time.[64] Even if it sometimes needs to make rapid breakthroughs in order to take key positions, the overall campaign is not and cannot be a blitzkrieg. Strategic calculation here operates over several generations. In fact, we are still in the same position. Several decades after these principles were first formulated, their topicality is still striking. This is a sign that the process is not completed. I mean there is still time to derail it.

Micropolitics is also micro because of the scale it favours: subdivide the territory, conduct a 'policy (. . .) of the small-scale experiment',[65] create free zones, etc. Consequently, micropolitical arrangements will not all be alike. 'Because each individual case is different, and each case requires a separate politics'.[66] In short, a diversity of tactics is needed. Decentralize, delegate – as much as you can – decisions to multiple local agents at discordant rhythms. Diffract and desynchronize power relationships. This will prevent the opponent not just massing, but also *going down in history*.

This tactic of fragmentation is not only territorial, it is also social. For the sake, above all, of not having to 'confront all the enemies together', micropolitics prescribes a strategy of 'subdivision of classes':[67] 'separating off some groups for different treatment by status'[68] so as to achieve 'a reduction in the size of the opposition'.[69] Divide and conquer; even if it's been done before.

235

The micropolitician devotes 'considerable ingenuity and effort' into turning some groups into friends, and 'into using alliance with some groups to outweigh the opposition of other ones'.[70] This is *method number 11*: set up 'counter groups'[71] To liberalize the health system, for example, it is advisable to rely on 'groups who turn to private medicine'. This tactic is all the more effective in that it is aimed at 'middle classes, of high visibility and effective at applying pressure to the system to secure their ends'.[72] Another case involves the same actors: education. Only a minority of parents – 'those who can afford a choice'[73] – can afford to 'pay twice',[74] by registering their offspring in the private sector. Twice? Yes, because they pay directly, in cash, to enrol their own children in private schools when they have already paid indirectly, through taxes, but for the public education *of other people's children*, since they have given up this service for their own. This is a great opportunity for the creation of a counter-group on the battlefront of the public education service: mobilize parents of private students so that 'their' taxes will stop funding public education.

One important remark: what the tacticians of neoliberal micropolitics have fully grasped is that the political power of market relations does not just lie, despite the misleading image of them that some people convey, in their alleged ability to *automatically* regulate society. Their importance lies also in that they produce and strengthen social interests whose energies can be politically mobilized for the defence and consolidation underlying markets. For the neoliberal project to prevail, it is not enough to economize politics; it is also necessary to politicize the economic interests likely to support the movement, to build up, from market positions, mobilizable socio-political groups. Otherwise, a neoliberal programme cannot win its essential victories on the electoral market nor a neoliberal government long resist, in the event that it is devoid of any social basis other than the oligarchic one, large-scale confrontations. If we want to 'turn the political flank of the spending coalitions',[75] it is essential to build political counter-coalitions. The point is not to completely dissolve politics in market mechanisms, but to activate market interests capable of serving as social foundations for the constitution of political support groups for the liberalization programme.

The core target of neoliberal micropolitics is the 'middle classes'. In the 1980s, the political strategy of the American 'new right', that of Reagan, rested on this social base. Stagflation, unlike other periods of economic depression, had not levelled but on the contrary accentuated, as Mike Davis has shown, 'intra-class differentiation',[76] polarizing social structure not just between classes, but inside the social classes themselves, widening the gap between the haves and the have-nots in each, with the consequence of fostering the prosperity, at the peak of the middle classes, of a grouchy stratum composed of managers, the liberal professions, new entrepreneurs and rentiers. The 'fragmentation of the class structure facilitated the recomposition of politics around the selfishly "survivalist" axis favoured by the New Right'.[77] A neo-populism which, as Mike Davis puts it, exacerbated 'white working-class *ressentiment* against welfare recipients'[78] in order to better promote 'redistributive strategy victimising minorities, public sector employees and low-wage workers'.[79]

If neoliberalism has won its victories, this is less as ideology than as political technology. At the very beginning of the twentieth century, a forgotten anthropologist, Arsène Dumont, proposed a notional distinction between 'ethography, the description of customs' and 'ethonomy, the art of making customs what they should be'.[80] In this sense, neoliberal micropolitics appears as a political ethonomy, a technology for changing ways of behaving both alone and with others. The general spirit of this ethonomy transpires all too clearly in the examples reported here: encourage everyone to follow their most unsociable inclinations, even if it means dissolving the most elementary forms of what Hegel called *Sittlichkeit*, the 'morality of customs'. Neoliberal micropolitics aims to produce effects on people's consciences and on their actions – to radically alter their capacity to think and the ways they act, on an anthropological level. This is the radicality we face. We need to take full measure of it.

CONCLUSION

The seduction that neoliberalism has nevertheless been able to exercise lies in its twofold promise of individual autonomy and social self-regulation. Against the old forms of supervision, against the corsets of discipline, it dangles before us the glittering image of an emancipated subject, enjoying 'the autonomy of an entrepreneur of his life' – someone that it can 'empower in this capacity'.[1] Against the vertical rigidities of command and control, against the interventionism of a bureaucratic state, it offers the utopia of a 'cybernetic regulation of the market economy', where profit would serve as the 'transcendent instrument of a global regulation from which everyone benefits, even if, temporarily, some are benefiting more than others'[2] . . .

If you are looking for an 'art of not being governed', in short, turn to Hayek and others. There you will find a 'form of government rationality that allows the desires of individuals to unfold, that takes note of the fact that it is more effective to let them get on with things, at least partly, rather than to try and control, fix, suppress everything'.[3]

This enchanted, almost libertarian vision of neoliberal governmentality is misleading.

The strategies developed to avert the 'crisis in the governability of democracy' converge, rather, on an *authoritarian liberalism* which we now need to define more clearly.

Authority, it is usually said in political science, is not enough by itself to characterize authoritarianism. Certainly. But what, then, does define it? The abuse of authority? The more or less imposed encroachment by 'authority' over 'liberties'? Doubtless. But also, more fundamentally, something else, which forms the heart of the concept: a power

238

is authoritarian power when it asserts itself as the *only real author of political will*. The supporters of the authoritarian state thus extol the virtues of a sovereign will 'autonomous and responsible towards itself',[4] 'neutral' as it is independent of Parliament and political parties. In practice, however, the erection of an autonomous sovereign will, detached from the *demos*, implies that the subordinate means of pressure on political decision-making be restricted. The weakening of parliamentary powers, the repression of social movements, the reduction of trade union rights, of press freedom, of judicial guarantees, etc., are all part of the same process of the insularization and verticalization of sovereign decision-making.

If the defenders of a 'strong state' do not all take the same view of what this force covers, how far it actually can go from a simple demonstration of firmness to the systematic repression of opponents, they agree, however, that the authority of the state must, in order to be enhanced, be relieved of pressure from the 'popular will'.

But to this first aspect of the concept, the liberal side adds a second dimension which paradoxically implies restricting this same authority that was initially to be strengthened. Even if the authoritarian liberal state seems all-powerful in its sphere, this sphere will have been severely limited. Under an explicit rejection of 'interventionism', this economic demarcation of the field of political decision-making actually covers – Hayek made no secret of it – the fundamental prohibition on changing the order of social inequalities, the repudiation of any redistribution policy. As Heller warned us, authoritarian liberalism is a socially asymmetric authoritarianism. It all depends on who it is dealing with: it is strong with the weak, and weak with the strong.

Far from being reduced to the extreme case of liberal dictatorship, the concept of authoritarian liberalism thus defined applies to all situations where, as well as the scope of political decision-making being restricted by economic prohibition (its *liberal* side), the subordinate means of pressure on the political decision-making is also restricted (its properly *authoritarian* side).

There is no simple accidental conjunction between a certain type of economic programme and a certain style of government, but, more deeply, a functional and strategic connection between reducing the state's field of intervention and the strengthening of its authority in this limited field – in a reciprocal relationship. For if, as one of the founding fathers of ordoliberalism, Alexander Rüstow, put it, the self-limitation of the state is 'the condition and expression of its independence and strength'[5] in that it allows it to evade the 'interest

239

groups' to which it is otherwise 'prey'; if, therefore, it is in order to strengthen itself that the state must limit itself, the fact remains, as Schmitt noted, that it cannot perform this ablation without first having reinforced itself both in political and policing terms, since this operation involves confrontation with the subordinate social interests inseparable from it.

However, just as there may be authoritarian regimes which are not economically liberal, it is hard to conceive of a neoliberal policy which does not, in principle, proceed to the first limitation (the economic restriction of politics), and, by strategic necessity – unless you imagine a people composed of bosses and rentiers – to the second (a more or less pronounced strangulation of the political demonstration of subordinate interests). It has often been said that authoritarian liberalism is an oxymoron. In fact, it is a pleonasm.

But the authoritarian dimension of neoliberalism goes beyond the sphere of state power. What the business world defends tooth and nail – for this is the meaning of its political mobilization – is the autonomy of its private government. If there is a social actor that does not want to be governed, it is this world: it seeks to make itself ungovernable, but only so that it can govern others.

By organizing the ungovernability of the markets, neoliberalism elevates them to the rank of arrangements for governance. We have indicated by what means the conduct of managers was aligned with shareholder values. While the leaders have seen their decision-making leeway limited by their increased subordination to the stock markets, their authority, one which they exercise on their subordinates, has not withered away. The intensification of market disciplines goes hand in hand with strengthening the power of big and small leaders in organizations.

Neoliberal politics practises deregulation, including in labour law, strengthening the power of the employer in the contractual relationship, making the status of workers casual and insecure, weakening their strength, reducing their ability to refuse and their freedom, promoting the accumulation of wealth, widening inequalities and thereby further increasing the opportunities for subjugation of all kinds. In all these ways, it implies a strengthening of private authoritarianism. It is in this sense also that economic liberalism is authoritarian – in the social sense, not just that of the state.

Neoliberalism has been presented as the expression of a 'phobia about the state'. In reality, it accommodates state power very well,

240

including in authoritarian forms, as long as this state remains liberal economically.

What then is it 'phobic' about? We saw from the example of the ecological question that it has a fear of regulation and its costs for capital, its encroachments on managerial prerogatives, and behind that, it is horrified by social movements, of 'democracy-as-movement' and its demands, rightly perceived as tending to be contradictory to the capitalist organization of production and the primacy of the value on which it rests.

For the economists who in the 1970s strove to rebuild new theories of the firm, just as for the management specialists who in the same period were questioning the limits of disciplinary power in the company, there was a more specific object, if not of its phobia, at least of its concern. Not the state, but *self-management*.

This latter was the great theme of the radical left of the time. Nourishing its reflections with a multitude of alternative experiments such as cooperatives, factory occupations with worker control and Yugoslav self-managed companies, the left saw self-management (*autogestion*) as a promising new path, a possible alternative both to the capitalist firm and to state bureaucracy.[6]

It has been forgotten, but the defenders of 'free enterprise', in a situation – at least at the start of the period – that was close to intellectual bankruptcy, were also very interested in self-management theories.[7] The idea that 'individuality in cooperation' can prove socially and historically superior to 'competition in individualism', as French singer-songwriter Colette Magny sang in those same years, appeared to neoliberals as a credible enough hypothesis for them to spill a lot of ink on a lot of paper in an attempt to refute it. And for good reason.

The anti-statism of the self-managing trends, their thought of immanence, autonomy and self-organization exercised an undeniable attraction for them. Self-management, insofar as it was an attempt to break with economic statism and an endeavour both to get beyond managerial government and pseudo-regulation by the market, appeared to them as a real challenge. This was the main enemy, on the theoretical ground. It might represent a danger for the future, much more dangerous, deep down, than a dying Keynesianism. The great reaction that took place in the 1970s was not so much conceived as an alternative to the welfare state but as an alternative to challenging it. It was an alternative to the alternative. Perhaps this provides a good indication for today. Reworking the contested meanings and radical prospects of social autonomy may still be the way to break with authoritarian liberalism.

NOTES

Notes to Introduction

1 Louis Barré, *Complément au Dictionnaire de l'Académie française*, vol. 2 (Brussels, 1839).

2 Willis W. Harman, 'The Great Legitimacy Challenge: A Note on Interpreting the Present and Assessing the Future', in *Middle- and Long-Term Energy Policies and Alternatives, Appendix to Hearings Before the Subcommittee on Energy and Power* (Washington, DC: US Government Printing Office, 1976), pp. 25–31 (p. 27).

3 Michel Foucault, 'Entretien avec Michel Foucault', in *Dits et écrits*, vol. 2 (Paris: Gallimard-Quarto, 1994), p. 94.

4 Eve Chiapello, 'Capitalism and its Criticisms', in Paul du Gay and Glenn Morgan (eds.), *New Spirits of Capitalism?: Crises, Justifications, and Dynamics* (Oxford: Oxford University Press, 2013), p. 63.

5 André Gorz, *Misère du présent, richesse du possible* (Paris: Galilée, 1997), p. 26.

6 Michael Hardt and Antonio Negri, *Empire* (Cambridge, MA: Harvard University Press, p. 240).

7 Michel Foucault, 'Qu'est-ce que la critique? Critique et Aufklärung' (1978), *Bulletin de la Société française de philosophie*, 84, no. 2, April–June 1990, pp. 35–63 (p. 38).

8 Lenin, '"Left-Wing Communism": An Infantile Disorder', in Vladimir I. Lenin, *'Left-Wing Communism': An Infantile Disorder* (Chippendale, Australia: Resistance Books, 1999), pp. 27–99 (p. 83).

9 Foucault sometimes uses the two terms interchangeably. See Michel Foucault, *The Birth of Biopolitics. Lectures at the Collège de France, 1978–79*, edited by Michel Senellart, translated by Graham Burchell (London: Palgrave Macmillan, 2008), p. 70. On this notion, see Jean-Claude Monod, 'Qu'est-ce qu'une "crise de gouvernementalité"?', *Lumières*, no. 8, 2006, pp. 51–68.

10 Michel Foucault, *Security, Territory, Population. Lectures at the Collège de France, 1977–78*, edited by Michel Senellart, translated by Graham Burchell (London: Palgrave Macmillan, 2007), p. 196.

11 Foucault, *The Birth of Biopolitics*, p. 318.

12 Ibid., p. 320.
13 Barthélémy Prosper Enfantin, *Oeuvres d'Enfantin*, vol. XI (Paris: Dentu, 1873), p. 125.
14 Karl Polanyi, *The Great Transformation: The Political and Economic Origins of Our Time*, 2nd edn (Boston, MA: Beacon Press, 2001), p. 136.

Notes to Chapter 1

1 Michel Bosquet (a pseudonym of André Gorz), 'Les patrons découvrent "l'usine-bagne"', *Le Nouvel Observateur*, no. 384, 20 March 1972, p. 64.
2 Bennett Kremen, 'The New Steelworkers', *New York Times*, 7 January 1973, special issue on 'Business and Finance', p. 1.
3 Agis Sapulkas, 'Young Workers Are Raising Voices to Demand Factory and Union Changes', *New York Times*, 1 June 1970, p. 23.
4 Quoted by Emma Rothschild, 'Automation et O.S. à la General Motors', *Les Temps modernes*, nos. 314–15, September–October 1972, pp. 467–86 (p. 479). In the industry, according to the *Wall Street Journal*, 'morale in many operations is sagging badly, intentional work slowdowns are cropping up more frequently and absenteeism is soaring' (*Wall Street Journal*, 26 June 1970), quoted in Jeremy Brecher, *Strike!* (San Francisco, CA: Straight Arrow Books, 1972), p. 252.
5 Michel Foucault, *Discipline and Punish: The Birth of the Prison*, translated by Alan Sheridan (New York: Vintage, 1995), p. 138.
6 Judson Gooding, 'Blue-Collar Blues on the Assembly Line', *Fortune Magazine*, July 1970, reprinted in Lloyd Zimpel, *Man Against Work* (Grand Rapids, MI: Eerdmans, 1974), pp. 61–75 (p. 62).
7 Emma Rothschild, *Paradise Lost: The Decline of the Auto-Industrial Age* (New York: Vintage, 1974), p. 124.
8 Gooding, 'Blue-Collar Blues on the Assembly Line', p. 63. According to one union member, 'the young worker feels he's not master of his own destiny. He's going to run away from it every time he gets a chance. That is why there's an absentee problem' (ibid., p. 66).
9 According to a GM executive cited by Ken Weller, *The Lordstown Struggle and the Real Crisis in Production* (London: Solidarity, 1973), p. 2.
10 Quoted by Ken Weller from the *Sunday Telegraph*, 2 December 1973 and *Newsweek*, 7 February 1973 in Weller, *The Lordstown Struggle*, p. 2.
11 Quoted by Stanley Aronowitz, *False Promises: The Shaping of American Working Class Consciousness* (New York: McGraw-Hill, 1973), p. 26.
12 Gooding, 'Blue-Collar Blues on the Assembly Line', p. 63.
13 Quoted by Aronowitz, *False Promises*, p. 36.
14 Quoted by Studs Terkel, *Working: People Talk About What They Do All Day and How They Feel About What They Do* (New York: The New Press, 2011; first published in 1974), p. 38.
15 John Lippert, 'Shopfloor Politics at Fleetwood', *Radical America*, no. 12, July 1978, pp. 52–69 (p. 58).
16 Ibid.
17 Agis Sapulkas, 'Young Workers Disrupt Key GM Plant', *New York Times*, 23 January 1972, p. 1.

18 See Michel de Certeau, *L'Invention du quotidien, vol. 1: Arts de faire* (Paris: Gallimard, 1990), p. 45.

19 Quoted by Aronowitz, *False Promises*, p. 41.

20 Gooding, 'Blue-Collar Blues on the Assembly Line', p. 68. According to the *New York Times*, today's workers 'are better educated and want treatment as equals from the bosses on a plant floor. They are not as afraid of losing their job as the older men and often challenge the foreman's orders. And at the heart of the new mood [. . .] there is a challenge to management's authority'. See Agis Sapulkas, 'Young Workers Are Raising Voices to Demand Factory and Union Changes', *New York Times*, 1 June 1970, p. 23.

21 Richard Armstrong, 'Labor 1970: Angry, Aggressive, Acquisitive', *Fortune*, October 1969, reprinted in *Compensation & Benefits Review*, vol. 2, no. 1, January 1970, pp. 37–42.

22 Jefferson Cowie, 'That 70's Feeling', *New York Times*, 5 September 2010, p. 19.

23 Bill Watson, 'Counter-Planning on the Shop Floor', *Radical America*, no. 5, May–June 1971, pp. 77–85 (p. 79).

24 Quoted in Milton Snoeyenbos, Robert F. Almeder and James M. Humber (eds.), *Business Ethics: Corporate Values and Society* (Buffalo, NY: Prometheus Books, 1983), p. 307.

25 Aaron Brenner, 'Rank-and-File Rebellion, 1967–1976', PhD dissertation, Columbia University, 1996, p. 37.

26 Weller, *The Lordstown Struggle*, p. 8.

27 Aronowitz, *False Promises*, p. 23.

28 Weller, *The Lordstown Struggle*, p. 3.

29 Quoted in ibid., p. 9.

30 Ibid.

31 Sapulkas, 'Young Workers Disrupt Key GM Plant', p. 1.

32 Jefferson R. Cowie, *Stayin' Alive: The 1970s and the Last Days of the Working Class* (New York: New Press, 2010), p. 46.

33 Cowie, *Stayin' Alive*, p. 7. The Lordstown strike was 'one of the most sustained campaigns of informal in-plant resistance ever to have been documented' in American social history (Weller, *The Lordstown Struggle*, p. 8).

34 Malcolm Denise quoted in Weller, *The Lordstown Struggle*, p. 4.

35 Rothschild, 'Automation et O.S. à la General Motors', p. 469.

36 Ibid.

37 Aronowitz, *False Promises*, p. 35.

38 Rothschild, 'Automation et O.S. à la General Motors', p. 469.

Notes to Chapter 2

1 Karl Marx, *Economic and Philosophic Manuscripts of 1844*, translated by Martin Milligan (Moscow: Progress Publishers, 1959), p. 30.

2 Daniel Bell, *The End of Ideology: On the Exhaustion of Political Ideas in the Fifties* (Glencoe, IL: Free Press, 1960), p. 246.

3 Ibid., p. 247.

4 André Gorz summed up the volte-face as follows: 'The thirst for consumption, throughout the 1950s, remained intense, and seemed to confirm the managers in their deep conviction: [. . .] there is nothing a man will not

agree to do for money; he will sell his labour force, his health, his youth, his nervous equilibrium, his sleep, his intelligence. This lasted for a while. Then, by the mid-1960s, disturbing murmurs started to be heard in the big factories' (Michel Bosquet, 'Les patrons découvrent "l'usine-bagne"', *Le Nouvel Observateur*, no. 384, 20 March 1972, p. 64).

5 Gooding, 'Blue-Collar Blues on the Assembly Line', p. 65.

6 Malcolm Denise, quoted in Weller, *The Lordstown Struggle*, p. 4.

7 Gooding, 'Blue-Collar Blues on the Assembly Line', p. 62. They enter the world of work after experiencing 'rebellion in their school lives and in the military' (Stanley Aronowitz, *False Promises*, p. 35).

8 See Abraham Harold Maslow, 'A Theory of Human Motivation', *Psychological Review*, vol. 50, no. 4, 1943, pp. 370–96. According to Maslow, human beings have several strata of different needs, from the most basic to the most elaborate, from the need to find food to the need for spiritual fulfilment. Economic 'progress' thus corresponds to an elevation on the pyramid of needs, from the bottom (very materialistic) to the top (very ethereal). However much satisfaction we provide the rebel with, he will always want, not necessarily something more, but something *better*.

9 Richard E. Walton, 'How to Counter Alienation in the Plant', *Harvard Business Review*, November/December 1972, pp. 70–81 (p. 72).

10 Max Weber, *The Protestant Ethic and the Spirit of Capitalism*, translated by Talcott Parsons (London: Routledge, 2001), p. 33.

11 'Who Wants to Work? Boredom on the Job', *Newsweek Magazine*, 26 March 1973.

12 Among the models offered at the time by the American social sciences was the famous 'J-curve' put forward by James C. Davies: revolts or revolutions are most likely to occur when a prolonged phase of economic and social development is followed by a sudden stalling of the economy. In this diagram, it is not poverty in itself which is a factor in rebellion, but the mismatch between the subjective expectations generated by a phase of relative prosperity and their actual level of satisfaction when this latter suddenly drops below the expected level. See James C. Davies, 'Toward a Theory of Revolution', *American Sociological Review*, vol. 27, no. 1, 1962, pp. 5–19. A psycho-sociological variant of this socio-economic theory of rebellion has been proposed by Ted Robert Gurr, on the basis of a concept of 'relative deprivation', defined as the perceived gap between people's expectations on the one hand, and their abilities to obtain and to maintain the 'values' to which they think themselves entitled. 'Frustration' then tends to turn into 'aggression' and social violence. See Ted Robert Gurr, *Why Men Rebel* (Princeton, NJ: Princeton University Press, 1970). In the sphere of the political sciences, Walter Korpi criticizes this model; for him, the power relation is essential. 'Relative deprivation explains nothing by itself: it tends merely to lead to open conflict only when the power differential has swayed in favour of the least powerful actors, who may be all the more inclined to engage in struggle as they have seen their "resources of power" grow'. See Walter Korpi, 'Conflict, Power and Relative Deprivation', *American Political Science Review*, vol. 68, no. 4, 1974, pp. 1569–78. For a discussion of these theories and some more finely-nuanced hypotheses, see Edward Shorter and Charles Tilly, *Strikes in France 1830–1968* (Cambridge: Cambridge University Press, 1974), pp. 337ff.

13 Walton, 'How to Counter Alienation in the Plant', p. 71.

14 Ibid.

15 Ibid.

16 James O'Toole, *Work in America. Report of a Special Task Force to the Secretary of Health, Education, and Welfare*, Special Task Force on Work in America, Department of Health, Education, and Welfare, Washington, DC, December 1972, p. 19. 'The acts of sabotage and other forms of protest are overt manifestations of a conflict between changing employee attitudes and organizational inertia. Increasingly, what employees expect from their jobs is different from what organizations are prepared to offer them' (O'Toole, p. xi).

17 See *Worker Alienation, Hearings Before the Subcommittee of Employment, Manpower, and the Poverty of the Committee on Labor and Public Welfare, U.S. Senate, 192nd Cong.* (Washington, DC: Government Printing Office, 1972).

18 Leland M. Wooton, Jim L. Tarter and Richard W. Hansen, 'Toward a Productivity Audit', *Academy of Management Proceedings*, 1975, pp. 327–9 (p. 327).

19 O'Toole, *Work in America*, p. 16. 'General Motors had calculated that if every worker at Lordstown worked for an extra half-second every hour, the company would save a million dollars per year'. Except that, of course, 'productivity – in other words, production per hour of work – has decreased due to worker agitation arising from their dissatisfaction' (John Zerzan, *Un conflit décisif: les organisations syndicales combattent la révolte contre le travail* (Echanges: n.p., 1975), p. 22).

20 Zerzan, *Un conflit décisif*, p. 14. See also Harold Wilensky, 'The Problem of Work Alienation', in Frank Baker, Peter J. McEwan and Alan Sheldon, *Industrial Organizations and Health* (New York: Tavistock Publications, 1969), pp. 550–70 (p. 556).

21 Note, however, that this was a minimum definition of alienation at work which, while superficially drawing on a Marxist notion, surreptitiously proceeded to excise its most problematic aspects. For the young Marx, wage alienation was not characterized solely by a situation of heteronomy, by the fact of being subjected to the command of a foreign will, but also by a process of dispossession at the end of which the worker saw his own activity escape his control and become objectified in the property of another. This aspect (i.e. appropriation) disappeared from the managerial reinterpretation of the concept in the early 1970s. This semantic restriction set the political limits of the problematization adopted, since it was thereby forbidden by definition to extend the question of workers' alienation to the question of the property relationships that conditioned it. Provided with this intellectual equipment, one could certainly admit that alienation was 'inherent in pyramidal, bureaucratic forms of management and taylorized technology', but it could also be claimed that the problem had been fixed without wage exploitation ever being questioned; all one had done was move away from certain worn-out forms of hierarchical management.

22 Richard E. Walton, 'Quality of Working Life: What is it?', *Sloan Management Review*, vol. 15, no. 1, Autumn 1973, pp. 11–21 (p. 13).

23 Alfred J. Marrow, 'Management by Participation', in Eugene L. Cass and Frederick G. Zimmer (eds.), *Man and Work in Society* (New York: Van

Nostrand Reinhold, 1975, pp. 33–48 (p. 35). In the late 1950s, the labour psychologist Douglas McGregor drew a contrast between a *managerial theory X*, which 'places exclusive reliance upon external control of human behavior', and a *theory Y* resting on 'self-control and self-direction'. Douglas McGregor, 'The Human Side of Enterprise' (1957), in Harold J. Leavitt, Louis R. Pondy and David M. Boje, *Readings in Managerial Psychology* (Chicago, IL: University of Chicago Press, 1989), pp. 314–24 (p. 322).

24 Richard E. Walton, 'From Control to Commitment in the Workplace', *Harvard Business Review*, March–April 1985, pp. 77–84 (p. 79). Several commentators, quick to announce a paradigm change, interpreted such statements as the sign of a real break, as the shift from one modality of power to another: from 'direct control' to 'autonomous responsibility'. But this kind of argument, relying on large schematic changes, and the quest for *the* new form of control (the new strategic panacea that would take over from one whose reign was coming to an end), neglects the fact that, as John Storey showed, management is not fully dependent on a single mode of control. Contrary to what is claimed by 'monistic' approaches to the history of managerial techniques, many different means of control persist and coexist, and their modalities experience cycles and oscillations. See John Storey, 'The Means of Management Control: A Reply to Friedman', *Sociology*, vol. 23, no. 1, February 1989, pp. 119–24 (p. 122).

25 O'Toole, *Work in America*, pp. 16 and 23. This was the promise of 'human resources management': a better use of 'the capacities of a major natural resource – the labour force' (Walton, 'How to Counter Alienation in the Plant', p. 81).

26 This 'participation' allowed subordinates to wield a certain influence over the decisions affecting them, even if 'upper-level managers continue[d] to run the company [and] handle major financial transactions' (O'Toole, *Work in America*, p. 85).

27 Walton, 'How to Counter Alienation in the Plant', p. 74.

28 O'Toole, *Work in America*, p. 84. Walton also concluded that this model had 'economic superiority' (Richard E. Walton, 'Work Innovations at Topeka: After Six Years', *Journal of Applied Behavioral Science*, Vol. 13, no. 3, 1977, pp. 422–31 [p. 423]). See also Richard E. Walton, 'Explaining Why Success Didn't Take', *Organizational Dynamics*, vol. 3, no. 3, Winter 1975, pp. 3–22.

29 See William S. Paul, Keith B. Robertson and Frederick Herzberg, 'Job Enrichment Pays Off', *Harvard Business Review*, March–April 1969, pp. 61–78. As André Gorz puts it: 'Wherever an enlargement or enrichment of tasks has been tried out, the results have almost always been convincing. Does this prove [. . .] that the abolition of factory despotism and the introduction of "industrial democracy" might become possible in the interest of capital itself? [. . .] Put this way, the question does not make much sense. There are controlled experiments of this kind, carried out *in vitro*. But there is no example of a workers' rebellion being recuperated by this kind of procedure. On the contrary, where (as at Fiat), struggle leads to forms of autonomous organization, management does all it can to destroy them. The meaning of new forms of non-despotic labour organization therefore depends – as does the meaning of any reform – on the power relationship that presided over their introduction. When imposed from above, on the

employers' initiative, to defuse resistance, they can be profitable for capital and consolidate its hegemony. Imposed from below, through actions organized by the workers, they are irreconcilable with employers' authority. The ambiguity of the "democratization" of the labour process is therefore that of any reform: it is capital's reformist recuperation of worker's resistance if it is instituted from above; it opens a breach in the system of capital domination if it is imposed from below during a show of force' (André Gorz, 'Le despotisme d'usine et ses lendemains', in *Critique de la division du travail* (Paris: Seuil, 1973), pp. 91–102 (pp. 99ff.).

30 John Storey, *Managerial Prerogative and the Question of Control* (London: Routledge & Kegan Paul, 1983, p. 138). In this virtuous circle, we are promised, it will be possible to 'simultaneously enhance the quality of work life (thereby lessening alienation) and improve productivity' (Walton, 'How to Counter Alienation in the Plant', p. 70).

31 It is necessary to distinguish here between the position of certain reformist *theorists* of management and the position of the ordinary *practitioners* of management, who are not generally ready to give in when it comes to their prerogatives.

32 Watson, 'Counter-Planning on the Shop Floor', p. 84.

33 Ibid.

34 'Stonewalling plant democracy', *Business Week*, 28 March 1977, pp. 78–82 (p. 78).

35 Bosquet, 'Les patrons découvrent "l'usine-bagne"', p. 64.

36 Stephen A. Marglin, 'Catching Flies with Honey: An Inquiry into Management Initiatives to Humanize Work' (1979), in William H. Lazonick (ed.), *American Corporate Economy: Critical Perspectives on Business and Management*, vol. 3 (New York: Routledge, 2002), pp. 280–93 (p. 289).

Notes to Chapter 3

1 Joseph Townsend, *A Dissertation on the Poor Laws, by a Well-Wisher to Mankind* (Berkeley, CA: University of California Press, 1971; first published in 1786).

2 Judson Gooding, 'Blue-Collar Blues on the Assembly Line', *Fortune Magazine*, July 1970, reprinted in Lloyd Zimpel, *Man Against Work* (Grand Rapids, MI: Eerdmans, 1974), pp. 61–75 (p. 66).

3 'Adam Smith', *Supermoney* (New York: Random House, 1972), p. 274. He also writes: 'The "sacrifice consensus" is breaking down'. These days, nobody is going to think: 'I am doing this for my family, I am working so that my son has a better life than I do' (p. 280).

4 'Adam Smith', *Supermoney*, p. 275.

5 Gooding, 'Blue-Collar Blues on the Assembly Line', p. 66.

6 Malcolm Denise, quoted in Weller, *The Lordstown Struggle and the Real Crisis in Production*, p. 4 (my emphasis). He wrote: 'Employees in the 1970's are (1) even less concerned about losing a job or staying with an employer; (2) even less willing to put up with dirty and uncomfortable working conditions; (3) even less likely to accept the unvarying pace and functions on moving lines; and (4) even less willing to conform to rules or be amenable to higher authority' (Malcolm L. Denise, 'Remarks by Malcolm L. Denise,

Vice President, Labor Relations, Ford Motor Company at Ford Management Conference, The Greenbrier, White Sulphur Springs, November 10, 1969', pp. 5–6, quoted in B.J. Widick, 'Work in Auto Plants: Then and Now', in B.J. Widick (ed.), *Auto Work and its Discontents* (Baltimore, MA: Johns Hopkins University Press, 1976), pp. 1–17 [p. 10]).

7 Saul Rosenzweig, 'A General Outline of Frustration', *Character & Personality*, vol. 7, no. 2, December 1938, pp. 151–60 (p. 154).

8 Ibid., p. 154.

9 Earl Bramblett, quoted in Gooding, 'Blue-Collar Blues on the Assembly Line', p. 65.

10 See Gérard Duménil and Dominique Lévy, *Crise et sortie de crise, Ordre et désordres néolibéraux* (Paris: PUF, 2000), pp. 32ff.

11 The formation of this line of argument has been studied in detail by John David Truty, 'Ideas in Disguise: Fortune's Articulation of Productivity 1969–1972', PhD dissertation, Northern Illinois University, DeKalb, 2010.

12 Truty, 'Ideas in Disguise', p. 141.

13 See Brenner, 'Rank-and-File Rebellion, 1967–1976', p. 32.

14 'Adam Smith', *Supermoney*, p. 276. Note, however, that neoliberals were divided over the decisive factor in inflation. While the Friedmanians concentrated 'on the immediate causes of inflation – the injection of newly printed money into the economy', the Hayekians insisted on 'the capacity of trade unions to exert a causal influence on the process of monetary creation' (Gilles Christoph, 'Du nouveau libéralisme à l'anarcho-capitalisme: la trajectoire intellectuelle du néolibéralisme britannique', PhD dissertation, Université Lyon 2, 2012, p. 368).

15 In 1975, Raford Boddy and James Crotty, echoing the arguments in the *Wall Street Journal*, wrote: 'We view the erosion of profits as the result of successful class struggle waged by labor against capital' (Raford Boddy and James Crotty, 'Class Conflict and Macro-Policy: The Political Business Cycle', *Review of Radical Political Economics*, vol. 7, no. 1, 1975, pp. 1–19 [p. 1]). Their thesis was immediately criticized for its monocausal character by other authors of the same general tendency. See Howard Sherman, 'Class Conflict and Macro-Policy: A Comment', *Review of Radical Political Economics*, vol. 8, no. 2, summer 1976, pp. 55–60.

16 Christian Parenti, *Lockdown America: Police and Prisons in the Age of Crisis* (New York: Verso, 1999), p. 37. See Robert Brenner, *The Economics of Global Turbulence* (London: Verso, 2006); Harry Magdoff and Paul Sweezy, *The Deepening Crisis of U.S. Capitalism* (London: Monthly Review Press, 1981); and, in particular, John Bellamy Foster, 'Marx, Kalecki and Socialist Strategy', *Monthly Review*, vol. 64, no. 11, April 2013, pp. 1–14.

17 Quoted in Brenner, 'Rank-and-File Rebellion, 1967–1976', p. 65. As *Life Magazine* reported in 1972, 'much of the fear of being unemployed has disappeared, along with the notion that hard work is a virtue in itself' ('The Will to Work and Some Ways to Increase It', *Life Magazine*, 1 September 1972, p. 38).

18 'The U.S. Can't Afford What Labor Wants', *Business Week*, 11 April 1970, p. 106. Quoted in Kim Phillips-Fein, *Invisible Hands: The Businessmen's Crusade Against the New Deal* (New York: Norton, 2010), p. 156.

19 'Adam Smith', *Supermoney*, p. 275.

20 Michael Perelman, *The Pathology of the U.S. Economy Revisited: The*

Intractable Contradictions of Economic Policy (New York: Palgrave, 2002), p. 40. See also Alan S. Blinder, *Economic Policy and the Great Stagflation* (New York: Academic Press, 1981), pp. 107ff.

21 Arnold Weber, head of the 'Cost of Living Council' under Nixon, in *Business Week*, 27 April 1974, quoted in Perelman, *The Pathology of the U.S. Economy Revisited*, p. 41.

22 Armstrong, 'Labor 1970: Angry, Aggressive, Acquisitive', p. 40.

23 Horst Brand, of the Bureau of Labor Statistics, quoted in Armstrong, 'Labor 1970', p. 40.

24 In the early 1980s, the trio of Marxist economists Weisskopf, Bowles and Gordon proposed the notion of the exit cost, defined as the proportion of the standard of living that an employee can expect to lose in the event of dismissal or resignation: 'the higher is the cost to workers of losing their jobs, the more cooperative they are likely to be at the workplace. The lower is the cost of losing their jobs, in contrast, the less responsive they will be to employer efforts to boost productivity' (Thomas E. Weisskopf, Samuel Bowles and David M. Gordon, 'Hearts and Minds: A Social Model of U.S. Productivity Growth', *Brookings Papers on Economic Activity*, no. 2, 1983, pp. 381–441 [p. 387]). Their calculations show that the cost of losing a job, after increasing in the 1960s, fell in the early 1970s. The low unemployment rate, the rise in real wages, and benefits, among other factors, lowered the cost of exit, mitigated the risks associated with dismissal, and made the balance of power more favourable for workers: 'conservatives', they noted, 'propose to restore work intensity through intensified labor market discipline (and, we might add, assaults on unions) and to revive business innovation by unleashing private enterprise from the collar of government regulation' (Weisskopf et al., 'Hearts and Minds', p. 438). Some mainstream economists have adopted this idea, but from the opposite angle, explicitly crediting the neo-Marxists: 'In a provocative recent Brookings paper, Weisskopf, Bowles, and Gordon (1983) have used the presence of the unemployment benefit [. . .] to explain the [. . .] decline in productivity in the United States' (George Akerlof and Janet Yellen, 'Introduction', in George Akerlof and Janet Yellen (eds.), *Efficiency Wage Models of the Labor Market* (Cambridge: Cambridge University Press, 1986), p. 5). At that time, Carl Shapiro and Joseph Stiglitz discussed 'equilibrium unemployment as a worker discipline device'. Their argument was based on treating 'the threat of firing a worker' as a 'method of discipline' and concluding that much of the slowdown in productivity stemmed from a lowering of the costs of losing work (Carl Shapiro and Joseph E. Stiglitz, 'Equilibrium Unemployment as a Worker Discipline Device', *The American Economic Review*, vol. 74, no. 3, June 1984, pp. 433–44 (p. 434).

25 George Gilder, *Wealth and Poverty* (New York: Basic Books, 1981), p. 69, and Phillips-Fein, *Invisible Hands*, p. 178.

26 Townsend, *A Dissertation on the Poor Laws*, p. 23.

27 In the formation of the living conditions of the 'voluntary worker', commented Polanyi, 'the final stage was reached with the application of "nature's penalty," hunger. In order to release it, it was necessary to liquidate organic society, which refused to let the individual starve'. He added: 'the white man's initial contribution to the black man's world mainly consisted in introducing him to the uses of the scourge of hunger. [. . .] [W]hat the white man may still occasionally practice in remote regions today, namely, the smashing

up of social structures in order to extract the element of labor from them, was done in the eighteenth century to white populations by white men for similar purposes' (Karl Polanyi, *The Great Transformation. The Political and Economic Origins of Our Time*, 2nd edn (Boston, MA: Beacon Press, 2001), pp. 173 and 172).

28 John Kenneth Galbraith, *The Affluent Society* (Boston, MA: Houghton Mifflin, 1958), p. 65.

29 Ibid., p. 75.

30 Gilbert Burck, 'Union Power and the New Inflation', *Fortune*, February 1971, pp. 65–70 (p. 65).

31 Marglin, 'Catching Flies with Honey', pp. 284–5.

32 John Lippert, 'Fleetwood Wildcat', *Radical America*, vol. 11, no. 5, 1977, pp. 7–38 (p. 36). The unemployment rate in the United States was 3.5 per cent in 1969, and rose to 8.5 per cent in 1975.

33 It should be added that the complement to this economic and social insecurity was a policy of police insecurity and prison, a 'discipline of the lash' imposed upon the poorest. This represented a dual phenomenon: both a withdrawal from the charitable state and a deployment of the criminal state, which Loïc Wacquant described as a 'state policy of criminalizing the poor' (Loïc Wacquant, *Punishing the Poor: The Neoliberal Government of Social Insecurity* (Durham, NC: Duke University Press, 2009), p. 99). See also Frances Fox Piven and Richard A. Cloward, *Regulating the Poor: The Functions of Public Welfare* (New York: Vintage, 1993); Samuel Bowles, David M. Gordon and Thomas E. Weisskopf, *After the Waste Land: Democratic Economics for the Year 2000* (New York: Routledge, 2015; first published in 1990); Geert Dhondt, 'The Relationship between Mass Incarceration and Crime in the Neoliberal Period in the United States', PhD dissertation, University of Massachusetts Amherst, 2012.

Notes to Chapter 4

1 Adam Smith, *An Inquiry into the Nature and Causes of the Wealth of Nations* (Metalibri Digital Editions, 2007), pp. 105–6 (available at https://www.ibiblio.org/ml/libri/s/SmithA_WealthNations_p.pdf).

2 'The U.S. Can't Afford What Labor Wants: New Union Militancy Could Skyrocket Wages and Trigger Runaway Inflation', *Business Week*, 11 April 1970, p. 105.

3 Ibid., p. 107.

4 Gilbert Burck, 'Union Power and the New Inflation', *Fortune*, February 1971, pp. 65–70 (p. 65).

5 Richard Armstrong, 'Labor 1970: Angry, Aggressive, Acquisitive', *Fortune*, October 1969, reprinted in *Compensation & Benefits Review*, vol. 2, no. 1, January 1970, pp. 37–42 (p. 37).

6 Ibid., p. 41. And: 'The blue-collar worker is in the crosscurrent of social change, disgruntled about his bosses and "the system"; and sensitive to the black-power revolution within the ranks of labor' (p. 37).

7 Ibid., p. 41.

8 Quoted in ibid., p. 41.

9 Murray J. Gart, 'Labor's Rebellious Rank and File', *Fortune*, November

1966, quoted in Brenner, 'Rank-and-File Rebellion, 1967–1976', PhD dissertation, Columbia University, 1996, p. 26.

10 Rejecting, too, stark a difference between economics and politics, he sought to theorize a 'politics of production'. 'The term "internal state" refers to the set of institutions that organize, transform, or repress struggles over relations in production and relations of production at the level of the enterprise' (Michael Burawoy, *Manufacturing Consent: Changes in the Labor Process Under Monopoly Capitalism* (Chicago, IL: University of Chicago Press, 1979), p. 110.

11 Ibid., p. 109.

12 See Michael Burawoy, 'Manufacturing Consent revisited', *La Nouvelle Revue du travail* [online], no. 1, 2012, http://journals.openedition.org/nrt/143.

13 See Armstrong, 'Labor 1970', p. 38.

14 See Thomas Byrne Edsall, *The New Politics of Inequality* (New York: Norton, 1984), p. 155.

15 Douglas Fraser, 'Letter of resignation from the Labor-Management Advisory Committee', 19 July 1978, quoted in Samuel Bowles, David M. Gordon and Thomas E. Weisskopf, *After the Waste Land: Democratic Economics for the Year 2000* (New York: Routledge, 2015; first published in 1990), p. 30. Almost unconsciously, comments Covey, Fraser produced an interpretation that tells us a great deal about the said compromise which, if we are to believe him, rested less on the power of labour and more on the tactical and temporary tolerance of capital. See Jefferson R. Cowie, *Stayin' Alive: The 1970s and the Last Days of the Working Class* (New York: New Press, 2010), p. 297.

16 A.H. Raskin, 'Big Labor Strives to Break Out of Its Rut', *Fortune*, 27 August 1979, quoted in Cowie, *Stayin' Alive*, p. 298. The contradiction, explains Michele Naples, lies in the fact that the 'truce' between capital and labour provided the institutional setting for relative economic prosperity, a prosperity which itself provided the economic context in which workers could struggle for their interests, and thereby undermine the truce (Michele I. Naples, 'The Unraveling of the Union-Capital Truce and the U.S. Industrial Productivity Crisis', *Review of Radical Political Economics*, vol. 18, nos. 1&2, 1986, pp. 110–31, [p. 116]).

17 See Fritz Machlup, 'Monopolistic Wage Determination as a Part of the General Problem of Monopoly', in *Wage Determination and the Economics of Liberalism* (Washington, DC: Chamber of Commerce of the United States, 1947).

18 Henry C. Simons, 'Reflections on Syndicalism', *Journal of Political Economy*, vol. 52, no. 1, March 1944, pp. 1–25 (p. 5).

19 Quoted in Yves Steiner, 'The Neoliberals Confront the Trade Unions', in Philip Mirowski and Dieter Plehwe (eds.), *The Road from Mont Pelerin: The Making of the Neoliberal Thought Collective* (Cambridge, MA: Harvard University Press, 2009), p. 190.

20 Burck, 'Union Power and the New Inflation', p. 65.

21 John Davenport, 'How to Curb Union Power', *Fortune*, vol. 84, no. 1, July 1971, pp. 52–6 (p. 52).

22 See John Logan, 'Employer Opposition in the US: Anti-Union Campaigning from the 1950s', in Gregor Gall and Tony Dundon (eds.), *Global Anti-Unionism* (London: Palgrave Macmillan, 2013), pp. 21–38.

23 Quoted in Robert A. Georgine, 'Statement of Robert A. Georgine. President of the Building and Construction Trades Department, AFL-CIO', in *Pressures in today's workplace: oversight hearings before the Subcommittee on Labor-Management Relations of the Committee on Education and Labor, House of Representatives, Ninety-sixth Congress, first session, hearings in Washington, D.C. on October 16, 17 and 18, 1979*, vol. 1 (Washington, DC: US Government Printing Office, 1979, pp. 408–35 [pp. 411ff]). I am here putting together a composite narrative that draws on different texts.

24 Ibid., p. 412.

25 Ibid.

26 Ibid.

27 Quoted in ibid., p. 419.

28 Quoted in ibid., p. 423.

29 Quoted in Georgine, ibid., p. 421.

30 These words were recorded by journalist Nancy Stiefel, who, armed with a tape recorder, managed to infiltrate a meeting organized by the law firm Jackson Lewis, Schnitzler and Krupman on the art of fighting unionization. Quoted in James Farmer, *The hired guns of de-unionisation, Keynote Address by James Farmer Public Sector Labor Law Conference Spokane. Washington March 10 1979*, reprinted in *Pressures in today's workplace: oversight hearings before the Subcommittee on Labor-Management Relations of the Committee on Education and Labor, House of Representatives, Ninety-sixth Congress, first session, hearings in Washington, D.C. on October 16, 17 and 18, 1979*, vol. 2 (Washington, DC: US Government Printing Office, 1979, pp. 269–80 [p. 274]).

31 Quoted in Georgine, 'Statement of Robert A. Georgine', p. 433.

32 Ibid., p. 415.

33 Alfred T. DeMaria, *How Management Wins Union Organizing Campaigns* (New York: Executive Enterprises Publications, 1980), p. 15.

34 Ibid., p. 209.

35 Ibid., p. 95.

36 Ibid., p. 96.

37 Ibid., p. 153.

38 Ibid., p. 126.

39 Ibid., p. 130.

40 Ibid., p. 148.

41 Quoted in Georgine, 'Statement of Robert A. Georgine', p. 408.

42 Martin Jay Levitt, *Confessions of a Union Buster* (New York: Crown Publishers, 1993), p. 1.

43 Georgine, 'Statement of Robert A. Georgine', p. 408.

44 Quoted in ibid., p. 414.

Notes to Chapter 5

1 Joseph A. Schumpeter, *Capitalism, Socialism and Democracy* (London and New York: Routledge, 1976), p. 142.

2 David T. Bazelon, 'The Scarcity Makers', *Commentary*, XXXIV, October 1962, pp. 293–304 (p. 293).

3 Adolf A. Berle and Gardiner C. Means, *The Modern Corporation and Private Property* (New York: Routledge, 2017; first published in 1932).

4 Paraphrased by Robert Hessen, 'The Modern Corporation and Private Property: A Reappraisal', *Journal of Law and Economics*, vol. 26, no. 2, 1983, pp. 273–89 (p. 273). See John Kenneth Galbraith, 'Books review: Berle and Means, "The Modern Corporation and Private Property"', *Antitrust Bulletin*, vol. 13, no. 4, 1968, p. 1527.

5 Adolf A. Berle, 'Modern Functions of the Corporate System', *Columbia Law Review*, vol. 62, no. 3, March 1962, pp. 433–49 (p. 434).

6 Hessen, 'The Modern Corporation', p. 280.

7 Berle and Means, *The Modern Corporation and Private Property*, p. 64.

8 Thorstein Veblen, *Absentee Ownership: Business Enterprise in Recent Times – The Case of America* (New York: Routledge, 2017; first published in 1923), p. 66.

9 Berle and Means, *The Modern Corporation and Private Property*, p. 8.

10 Ibid., p. 65.

11 Ibid., p. 113.

12 Ibid., p. 6.

13 Walther Rathenau, *In Days to Come* (London: G. Allen & Unwin, 1921), p. 121, quoted in Berle and Means, *The Modern Corporation and Private Property*, p. 309.

14 James Burnham, *The Managerial Revolution* (New York: John Day, 1941). The neologism 'managerialism' seems to have appeared for the first time in a review of this book by Burnham, though the latter did not himself employ it, preferring the term 'managerial society'. See H.S. Person, 'Capitalism, Socialism and Managerialism', *Southern Economic Journal*, vol. 8, no. 2, 1941, pp. 238–43.

15 Note that Orwell was here reporting an idea that he did not share. See George Orwell, 'Second Thoughts on James Burnham' (1946), in *The Complete Works of George Orwell*, vol. 18 (London: Secker & Warburg, 1986), pp. 268–84 (p. 269). Drawing on Rizzi's *La Bureaucratisation du monde* (1939), Burnham reinterprets the separation of ownership and control announced by Berle and Means as a split between two *modes of control*: managers have control in one sense, in that they concentrate the functions of leadership – what he calls 'control over access' – but shareholders always have control in a second sense, in that they carve out for themselves the lion's share in the allocation of profits – 'control over distribution'. But such a situation can, in his view, persist: 'control over access is decisive, and, when consolidated, will carry control over preferential treatment in distribution with it: that is, will shift ownership unambiguously to the new controlling, a new dominant, class' (Burnham, *The Managerial Revolution*, p. 59). In his view, this process is already well underway: it is transnational and trans-regime: Stalinist bureaucracy, fascist *dirigisme* and New Deal interventionism represent, in his view, three versions of one and the same phenomenon.

16 Berle and Means, *The Modern Corporation and Private Property*, p. 8.

17 The rich, 'in spite of their natural selfishness and rapacity [. . .], though the sole end which they propose from the labours of all the thousands whom they employ, be the gratification of their own vain and insatiable desires, [. . .] divide with the poor the produce of all their improvements. They are led

by an invisible hand to make nearly the same distribution of the necessaries of life, which would have been made, had the earth been divided into equal portions among all its inhabitants, and thus without intending it, without knowing it, advance the interest of the society [. . .]' (Adam Smith, *The Theory of Moral Sentiments* (Metalibri Digital Editions, 2005), p. 165 [available online at https://www.ibiblio.org/ml/libri/s/SmithA_MoralSentiments_p.pdf]).

18 Berle and Means, *The Modern Corporation and Private Property*, p. 9.
19 Ibid., p. 304.
20 Ibid.
21 Ibid., p. 9.
22 'The directors of such companies, however, being the managers rather of other people's money than of their own, it cannot well be expected that they should watch over it with the same anxious vigilance with which the partners in a private copartnery frequently watch over their own. Like the stewards of a rich man, they are apt to consider attention to small matters as not for their master's honour, and very easily give themselves a dispensation from having it. Negligence and profusion, therefore, must always prevail, more or less, in the management of the affairs of such a company' (Smith, *The Wealth of Nations*, pp. 574–5). See also Berle and Means, *The Modern Corporation and Private Property*, p. 115.
23 Schumpeter, *Capitalism, Socialism and Democracy*, p. 157, n. 1.
24 Berle and Means, *The Modern Corporation and Private Property*, p. 115.
25 Henry G. Manne, 'Current Views on the Modern Corporation', *University of Detroit Law Journal*, vol. 38, 1961, pp. 559–88 (p. 560).
26 Berle and Means, *The Modern Corporation and Private Property*, p. 302.
27 'The explosion of the atom of property destroys the basis of the old assumption that the quest for profits will spur the owner of industrial property to its effective use. It consequently challenges the fundamental economic principle of individual initiative in industrial enterprise. It raises for reexamination the question of the motive force [. . .], and the ends for which the modern corporation can be or will be run' (Berle and Means, *The Modern Corporation and Private Property*, p. 9).

This does not merely undermine the hypothesis of the maximization of profit as a realistic description of entrepreneurial behaviour, but denies the institutional basis of the traditional profit motive (see Edward S. Mason, 'The Apologetics of "Managerialism"', *The Journal of Business*, vol. 31, no. 1, January 1958, pp. 1–11 [p. 6]).
28 Richard Sedric Fox Eells, *The Government of Corporations* (Glencoe, IL: Free Press of Glencoe, 1962), p. 16.

Notes to Chapter 6

1 Wilbur Hugh Ferry, *The Corporation and the Economy* (Santa Barbara, CA: Center for the Study of Democratic Institutions, 1959), p. 9.
2 Karl Marx, 'British Commerce and Finance', *The New-York Daily Tribune*, no. 5445, 4 October 1858, in Karl Marx and Friedrich Engels, *Collected Works*, vol. 16 (1858–60) (London: Lawrence & Wishart, 1980), pp. 33–6 (p. 36).

3 Charles Fourier, *Théorie des quatre mouvements, Oeuvres complètes*, vol. I (Paris: Librairie sociétaire, 1846), p. 189.
4 Ibid.
5 Ibid., p. 190.
6 Charles Périn, *Le Patron, ses devoirs, sa fonction, ses responsabilités* (Paris: Desclée de Brouwer, 1886), p. 49.
7 What Macpherson writes in another context about the contradictions of modern liberal theory is also valid here: this theory must continue to use the postulates of possessive individualism at a historical moment when the structure of market society no longer provides the necessary conditions for us to deduce a valid theory of political obligations from these postulates (see Crawford Brough Macpherson, *The Political Theory of Possessive Individualism* (Oxford: Oxford University Press, 1962), p. 275).
8 Berle and Means, *The Modern Corporation and Private Property*, p. 312.
9 Ibid.
10 Edwin Merrick Dodd, 'For Whom Corporate Managers Are Trustees: A Note', *Harvard Law Review*, vol. 45, no. 7, May 1932, pp. 1145–63. Tellingly, Dodd had borrowed the title of his article from the speech of a CEO of the period, Owen Young, President of General Electric.
11 Lewis Brown, CEO of the Johns-Manville Corporation, quoted by Edwin G. Nourse, 'From the Point of View of the Economist', in Stuart Chase (ed.), *The Social Responsibility of Management* (New York: New York University, School of Commerce, Accounts, and Finance, 1950), pp. 47–67 (p. 53). 'The manager', we likewise read in 1951 in *La Révolution permanente* [sic], a collective work published by the editors of the magazine *Fortune*, 'is becoming a professional in the sense that like all professional men he has a responsibility to society as a whole' (Russell Wheeler Davenport (ed.), *U.S.A. The Permanent Revolution* (New York: Prentice-Hall, 1951), p. 79).
12 T.H. Robinson, 'Attitudes patronales', in *Bénéfices sociaux et initiative privée* (Québec: Les Presses universitaires Laval, 1959), pp. 65–82 (p. 72).
13 Howard R. Bowen, *Social Responsibilities of the Businessman* (Iowa City, IA: University of Iowa Press, 2013; first published in 1953), p. 17.
14 Ibid., p. 50.
15 Hal Draper, 'Neo-Corporatists and Neo-Reformers', *New Politics*, no. 1, Autumn 1961, pp. 87–106 (p. 91).
16 Sanford Lakoff, 'Private Government in a Managed Society' (1969), in Sanford Lakoff (ed.), *Private Government; Introductory Readings* (Glenview, IL: Scott Foresman, 1973), pp. 218–42 (p. 237).
17 'The manager, in short, is a mediator, as his predecessor was an autocratic entrepreneur' (Lakoff, 'Private Government in a Managed Society', p. 237). Model managers will now behave like model umpires, 'considered able to determine independently the public interest that they are to implement' (Roberta Romano, 'Metapolitics and Corporate Law Reform', *Stanford Law Review*, vol. 36, no. 4, 1984, pp. 923–1016 [p. 938]).
18 Bowen, *Social Responsibilities of the Businessman*, p. 49.
19 Philip Selznick, *Leadership in Administration: A Sociological Interpretation* (New York: Harper & Row, 1957), p. 4. A 1956 study of the new business creed in America concluded that 'managers are assigned a more important and more autonomous role than that of agents for the owners. Theirs is the statesman's function of mediating among the groups dependent on the enter-

prise, satisfying just claims and preserving the continuity of the organization' (Francis X. Sutton et al., *The American Business Creed* (Cambridge, MA: Harvard University Press, 1956), p. 57.

20 Bazelon, 'The Scarcity Makers', p. 304.

21 Quoted in Maurice Zeitlin, 'Corporate Ownership and Control: The Large Corporation and the Capitalist Class', *American Journal of Sociology*, vol. 79, no. 5, March 1974, pp. 1073–119 (p. 1074). The following references are quoted in Zeitlin.

22 John Kenneth Galbraith, *The New Industrial State* (Boston, MA: Houghton-Mifflin, 1971), p. 19.

23 Ralf Dahrendorf, *Class and Class Conflict in Industrial Society* (Stanford, CA: Stanford University Press, 1959), p. 46.

24 David Riesman et al., *The Lonely Crowd; a Study of the Changing American Character* (New Haven, CT: Yale University Press, p. 236).

25 Berle, paraphrased by Zeitlin, 'Corporate Ownership and Control', p. 1076.

26 Carl Kaysen, 'The Social Significance of the Modern Corporation', *The American Economic Review*, vol. 47, no. 2, May 1957, pp. 311–19 (p. 312).

27 Daniel Bell, *The End of Ideology: on the Exhaustion of Political Ideas in the Fifties* (New York: Collier Books, 1962), p. 44.

28 Dahrendorf, *Class and Class Conflict*, p. 47. What the thesis of the separation of ownership and control made possible in political terms was a questioning of control apart from that of ownership: as the capitalist was dead, all that now needed to be settled, here as elsewhere, was the case of the bureaucrat. We can find the trace of this reformulation in the programmatic *aggiornamento* of European social democracy, starting, at a very early date, with the Labour Party. In Great Britain, the managerialist thesis of the separation of ownership and control, said Mason in 1958, had apparently become a flagship argument against any additional wave of nationalization: 'if big enterprises tend to "socialize" themselves, why should the government bother to nationalize them?' (Mason, 'The Apologetics of "Managerialism"', p. 4). In 1957, the leadership of the British Labour Party had published a programme that consecrated the triumph of its right wing. This document was not placed under the auspices of Marx or Ruskin, or even Bernstein, but of Adolf Berle and Peter Drucker. The architect of this 'revisionist metamorphosis' of the Labour Party, Anthony Crosland, had laid out the groundwork of this programme in a book-length manifesto: 'ownership has less and less relevance to the question of control [. . .]: first, because the alienation of the workers is an inevitable fact whether ownership is "capitalist" or collectivist, and secondly because even "capitalist" ownership is increasingly divorced from effective control' (Anthony Crosland, *The Future of Socialism* (Cape: London, 1956), p. 70). Consequently, the outmoded idea of social appropriation could now be forgotten. The American economist Rostow saw the situation clearly: 'In England, socialists say that the managers have already socialized capitalism, so that it is no longer necessary to invoke the cumbersome formality of public ownership of the means of production' (quoted by Hal Draper, 'Neo-Corporatists and Neo-Reformers', p. 106). This was the political correlate of the managerialist theme of the self-management of capitalism, which Draper critiqued: 'Public ownership is no longer necessary for the gradual reform of capitalism into socialism because capitalism is socializing itself in other forms. The transference of power in the corporations to socially responsible

257

managers means that the forms of private property are no longer incompat-ible with our ends. Socialization will now go forward with the inevitability of gradualism in these new corporate forms. Public ownership can now be stored away in the cellar of our program because the development of the new corporate collectivism is adequately doing the job which the socialist movement once thought it was called on to perform'. The road to socialism, concludes Draper, is none other, in this schema, than a process of bureau-cratic collectivization of the capitalist world (Draper, 'Neo-Corporatists and Neo-Reformers', pp. 105-6).

29 Daniel Bell, 'The Coming of Post-Industrial Society', *Business Society Review/Innovation*, Spring 1973, no. 5, pp. 5–23 (p. 23).

30 Michel Foucault, *Security, Territory, Population. Lectures at the Collège de France, 1977–78*, edited by Michel Senellart, translated by Graham Burchell (London: Palgrave Macmillan, 2007), p. 492.

31 Michel Foucault, *The Birth of Biopolitics. Lectures at the Collège de France, 1978–79*, edited by Michel Senellart, translated by Graham Burchell (London: Palgrave Macmillan, 2008), p. 248.

32 In this type of treatise, addressed to a sovereign or future sovereign, the moral qualities of an ideal monarch were set out. By dangling a flattering double in front of him, the hope was that, seduced by this potential projec-tion of himself, he would try to resemble his reflection. Seneca, whom tradi-tion considers as one of the founders of this literary genre, had addressed his *De Clementia* to Nero: may this book, he wrote, 'stand in the place of a mirror that places you face to face with yourself, and makes you see the sublime enjoyment that it has been granted you to attain'. The advice failed. As we know, the emperor, not much inclined to leniency, finally ordered the philosopher to open his own veins. See Seneca, *Oeuvres complètes*, vol. 1 (Paris: Hachette, 1860), p. 281.

33 Adolf Berle, *The 20th Century Capitalist Revolution* (New York: Harcourt, Brace, 1954), p. 178.

34 Ibid., p. 67.

35 When some people objected that this guarantee was quite insubstantial, Berle replied that one needed to trust the powers of the mind: 'priests have usually been able to intimidate the policemen, and [. . .] the philosopher can usually check the politicians. There is a fair historical ground to anticipate that moral and intellectual leadership will appear capable of balancing our Frankenstein creations' (ibid., p. 187).

36 Ibid., p. 180.

37 William W. Bratton and Michael L. Wachter, 'Shareholder Primacy's Corporatist Origins: Adolf Berle and the Modern Corporation', *Journal of Corporation Law*, vol. 34, 2008, pp. 99–152 (p. 131). As the political theo-rist Earl Latham wrote: 'it has been suggested that corporations – anthro-pomorphic corporations, endowed with intelligence, will, personality, and other human attributes – will develop that final testimonial to St. Augustine and Freud, a conscience, the operation of which will curb and control the excesses of corporate power and establish a benevolent regimen: the new "City of God", no less. But one of the lessons of politics is that it is power that checks and controls power and that this is not done automatically and without human hands. [. . .] If the legislative power of the corporation is to be curbed and controlled, the checks will have to be built into the structure of

corporate enterprise, and not just merely laid on from without, nor entrusted to the subjective bias of the hierarchs within' (Earl Latham, 'The Body Politic of the Corporation', in Edward S. Mason (ed.), *The Corporation in Modern Society* (New York: Atheneum, 1972; first published in 1959), pp. 218–36 [p. 228]).

38 Arthur S. Miller, 'The Corporation as a Private Government in the World Community', *Virginia Law Review*, vol. 46, December 1960, pp. 1539–72 (p. 1569).

39 Eells, *The Government of Corporations*, p. 16 (my emphasis).

40 Ibid., p. 20.

41 Ibid., p. 17. Earl Latham also proposed, at the start of the 1960s, 'the reconstruction of corporations in the image of the public government', reorganizing those 'private oligarchies' into republics. A juridical instrument already existed to this end: the charter of incorporation in which the state sets out the conditions under which the creation of a business is authorized (Earl Latham, 'The Commonwealth of the Corporation', *Northwestern University Law Review*, vol. 55, 1960, pp. 25–37 [pp. 26 and 33]). According to Latham, all that would be needed to impose a reform of corporate governance would be to give this document (now a mere formality) its old force, to reformulate it and flesh out its terms. Eells, on the other hand, leans towards a process of self-constitutionalization, in which firms would equip themselves with their own corpus of fundamental laws, knowing that 'the proper forum for working out norms of corporate constitutionalism [. . .] is the corporation itself' (Richard Eells, *The Meaning of Modern Business: An Introduction to the Philosophy of Large Corporate Enterprise* (New York: Columbia University Press, 1960), p. 324). Heald commented: 'Essentially, the alternative he offered was corporate initiative in self-generated constitutional principles. This left the question of managerial legitimacy unanswered' (Morrell Heald, *The Social Responsibilities of Business: Company and Community, 1900–1960* (London: Transaction Publishers), p. 296). This merely created a new aporia: in what way would this managerial autocracy, whose ability to develop a conscience was in doubt, be any more credible when it came to *making its law*?

42 Richard Eells and Clarence Walton, *Conceptual Foundations of Business: An Outline of the Major Ideas Sustaining Business Enterprise in the Western World* (Homewood, IL: Irwin, 1961), p. 381.

43 *The Power of the Democratic Idea. Sixth Report of the Rockefeller Brothers Fund Special Studies Project* (Garden City, NY: Doubleday, 1960), p. 59.

44 Bazelon, 'The Scarcity Makers', p. 297.

45 Heald, *The Social Responsibilities of Business*, p. 307. See also Thomas C. Cochran, 'Business and the Democratic Tradition', *Harvard Business Review*, vol. 34, no. 2, March–April 1956, p. 39. Andrew Hacker resorted to the following analogy: 'a zookeeper does not represent the seals because he responds to their need for fresh fish. A prison warden does not represent the inmates because he consults them on recreational activities. Similarly, the corporation community is not internally democratic' (Andrew Hacker, *Politics and the Corporation; An Occasional Paper on the Role of the Corporation in the Free Society* (New York: Fund for the Republic, 1958), p. 11).

46 Peter Drucker, *The New Society: The Anatomy of the Industrial Order* (New York: Harper, 1950), p. 104.

47 Ibid.
48 Ibid. At this point, Drucker rather strangely starts to sound like the thinkers of Negritude. On the 'immortal principles' of 1789, so vaunted by the French colonialists, Senghor wrote: 'Unfortunately, these principles were not applied fully, without hypocrisy; fortunately, they were partially applied, enough for their virtues [. . .] to bear fruit. As Jean-Paul Sartre puts it, we took up the colonialist's weapons and turned them against him' (Léopold Sédar Senghor, *Liberté: Négritude et humanisme* (Paris: Seuil, 1964), p. 399).
49 Drucker, *The New Society*, p. 282.
50 Milton Friedman, quoted in 'Three Major Factors in Business Management: Leadership, Decisionmaking, and Social Responsibility. Summary by Walter A. Diehm', in *Social Science Reporter: Eighth Social Science Seminar* (San Francisco, CA, 19 March 1958), p. 4.
51 Milton Friedman, *Capitalism and Freedom* (Chicago, IL: University of Chicago Press, 1962), p. 134.
52 Friedman took up these arguments in a celebrated opinion piece (Milton Friedman, 'A Friedman Doctrine: The Social Responsibility of Business is to Increase its Profits', *New York Times*, 13 September 1970, p. 17).
53 Ibid.
54 Geoffrey Ostergaard, 'Approaches to Industrial Democracy', *Anarchy. A Journal of Anarchist Ideas*, no. 2, April 1961, pp. 36–46 (p. 44).
55 David W. Ewing, *Freedom Inside the Organization: Bringing Civil Liberties to the Workplace* (New York: McGraw-Hill, 1978), p. 3.
56 'Cooperative Economics: An Interview with Jaroslav Vanek', *New Renaissance Magazine*, http://www.ru.org/index.php/economics/357-cooperative-economics-an-interview-with-jaroslav-vanek.
57 Karl Marx, *Capital. A Critique of Political Economy*, Volume I, Book One: *The Process of Production of Capital*, translated by Samuel Moore and Edward Aveling, edited by Frederick Engels (Moscow: Progress Publishers, online edition; first English edition, 1887), p. 286, available online at https://www.marxists.org/archive/marx/works/download/pdf/Capital-Volume-I.pdf.
58 See Robert Dahl, 'On Removing Certain Impediments to Democracy in the United States', *Political Science Quarterly*, vol. 92, no. 1, Spring 1977, pp. 1–20.
59 Michael Walzer, *Spheres of Justice: A Defense of Pluralism and Equality* (New York: Basic Books, 1983), p. 296.
60 Ibid., p. 301.
61 Ibid., p. 298. See also Carole Pateman, *Participation and Democratic Theory* (Cambridge: Cambridge University Press, 1970); Iris Marion Young, 'Self-determination as Principle of Justice', *The Philosophical Forum*, vol. 11, no. 1, Autumn 1979, pp. 30–46; Samuel Bowles and Herbert Gintis, 'A Political and Economic Case for Economic Democracy', *Economics and Philosophy*, vol. 9, no. 1, 1993, pp. 75–100. For a synthesis of these discussions, see Nien-hê Hsieh, 'Survey Article: Justice in Production', *Journal of Political Philosophy*, vol. 16, no. 1, 2008, pp. 72–100.
62 Mason, 'The Apologetics of "Managerialism"', p. 6.
63 Theodore Levitt, 'The Dangers of Social Responsibility', *Harvard Business Review*, vol. 36, no. 5, 1958, pp. 41–50 (p. 43).

Notes to Chapter 7

1 Bayless Manning, 'Review: The American Stockholder by J. A. Livingston', *The Yale Law Journal*, vol. 67, no. 8, July 1958, pp. 1477–96 (p. 1488).

2 Gordon Tullock, 'The New Theory of Corporations', in Erich Streissler (ed.), *Roads to Freedom: Essays in Honour of Friedrich von Hayek* (New York: Routledge, 2003; first published 1969), pp. 287–307 (pp. 295ff). Tullock uses their discussions to set out the theory of his friend Manne, who, he said, had never written a general theory of business.

3 Ibid., p. 295.

4 Financial economists and pro-business historians reduced Berle and Means' book to a severely truncated version, sidelining questions of power and bringing everything down to a mere 'problem of agency'. See Kenneth Lipartito and Yumiko Morii, 'Rethinking the Separation of Ownership from Management in American History', *Seattle University Law Review*, vol. 33, no. 4, 2010, pp. 1025–63.

5 Barry M. Mitnick, 'The Theory of Agency: The Policing "Paradox" and Regulatory Behavior', *Public Choice*, vol. 24, Winter 1975, pp. 27–42 (p. 27).

6 Armen A. Alchian, 'The Basis of Some Recent Advances in the Theory of Management of the Firm', *The Journal of Industrial Economics*, vol. 14, no. 1, November 1965, pp. 30–41 (p. 35). See also Eirik G. Furubotn and Svetozar Pejovich, 'Property Rights and Economic Theory: A Survey of Recent Literature', *Journal of Economic Literature*, vol. 10, no. 4, December 1972, pp. 1137–62 (p. 1149).

7 Bayless Manning, 'Corporate Power and Individual Freedom: Some General Analysis and Particular Reservations', *Northwestern University Law Review*, vol. 55, 1960, pp. 38–53 (p. 41).

8 Ibid., p. 42.

9 Ibid.

10 Harold Demsetz, 'The Theory of the Firm Revisited', *Journal of Law, Economics, & Organization*, vol. 4, no. 1, Spring 1988, pp. 141–61 (p. 151).

11 Michel Aglietta and Antoine Rebérioux, *Dérives du capitalisme financier* (Paris: Albin Michel, 2004), p. 47.

12 Paul M. Sweezy, 'The Illusion of the "Managerial Revolution"', *Science & Society*, vol. 6, no. 1, Winter 1942, pp. 1–23 (p. 5). More generally, whether or not managers are directly spurred on by the profit motive as subjective support for a value, as Zeitlin noted, they are objectively constrained, in a market economy, to yield to it. See Zeitlin, 'Corporate Ownership and Control', p. 1097. In his classic *The Power Elite*, published in 1956, sociologist Charles Wright Mills rejected managerialist discourse as 'a curious jumble of notions'. He added: 'These executives, it is held, are responsible for the refrigerator in the kitchen and the automobile in the garage – as well as all the planes and bombs that now guard Americans from instant peril'. However, people venture to ask these powerful men some tricky questions: 'upon what basis does their power rest? [. . .] Maybe the chief executives are trustees for a variety of economic interests, but what are the checks upon how fair and well they perform their trusts?' But these questions, whether flattering or offensive, are usually just 'kindergarten chatter for economic

illiterates' and 'the chief executives and the very rich are not two distinct and clearly segregated groups. They are both very much mixed up in the corporate world of property and privilege' (Charles Wright Mills, *The Power Elite* (Oxford: Oxford University Press), p. 118).

13 Robin Marris, *The Economic Theory of 'Managerial' Capitalism* (Glencoe, IL: Free Press of Glencoe, 1964), p. 46.

14 Ibid., p. 68.

15 Ibid., p. 72.

16 Ibid., p. 73.

17 Michael C. Jensen and William H. Meckling, 'Theory of the Firm: Managerial Behavior, Agency Costs and Ownership Structure', *Journal of Financial Economics*, vol. 3, 1976, pp. 305–60 (p. 353).

18 Frank H. Easterbrook and Daniel R. Fischel, 'The Corporate Contract', *Columbia Law Review*, vol. 89, 1989, pp. 1416–48 (p. 1418).

19 Frédéric Lordon, *Capitalisme, désir et servitude* (Paris: La Fabrique, 2010), p. 54.

20 See Tullock, 'The New Theory of Corporations', p. 288.

21 Ibid., p. 302.

22 Michael C. Jensen, 'Takeovers: Folklore and Science', *Harvard Business Review*, vol. 62, no. 6, November–December 1984, pp. 109–21 (p. 110).

23 Henry G. Manne, 'Mergers and the Market for Corporate Control', *The Journal of Political Economy*, vol. 73, no. 2, April 1965, pp. 110–20.

24 Henri Lepage, *Pourquoi la propriété?* (Paris: Hachette, 1985), p. 185.

25 Manne, 'Mergers and the Market for Corporate Control', p. 112.

26 Ibid., p. 113.

27 Tullock, 'The New Theory of Corporations', p. 300.

28 Jensen, 'Takeovers', p. 110.

29 Armen A. Alchian and Harold Demsetz, 'Production, Information Costs, and Economic Organization', *The American Economic Review*, vol. 62, no. 5, December 1972, pp. 777–95 (p. 788).

30 Henry G. Manne, 'The Myth of Corporate Responsibility – Or – Will the Real Ralph Nader Please Stand Up', *The Business Lawyer*, vol. 26, no. 2, November 1970, pp. 533–9 (p. 535). But these explanations based on the mechanics of the market, notes Williamson, neglect the organizational innovations introduced into business, and its shift to a departmentalized and divisional structure which favours takeovers. See Oliver Williamson, 'Corporate Governance', *Yale Law Journal*, vol. 93, 1984, pp. 1197–230 (pp. 1224ff).

31 Manne, 'Mergers and the Market for Corporate Control', p. 112.

32 Henry G. Manne, 'Review: In Defense of the Corporation by Robert Hessen', *University of Miami Law Review*, vol. 33, 1979, pp. 1649–55 (p. 1654).

33 Paddy Ireland, 'Property and Contract in Contemporary Corporate Theory', *Legal Studies*, vol. 23, 2003, pp. 453–509 (p. 482).

34 Paul P. Harbrecht, 'A New Power Elite?', *Challenge*, vol. 8, no. 6, March 1960, pp. 55–60 (p. 59).

35 Peter Drucker, *The Unseen Revolution: How Pension Fund Socialism Came to America* (New York: Harper & Row, 1976), p. 1. For a critical history of this shift, see Michael A. McCarthy, 'Turning Labor into Capital. Pension Funds and the Corporate Control of Finance', *Politics and Society*, vol. 42, no. 4, 2014, pp. 455–87.

36 Harbrecht, 'A New Power Elite?', p. 59.

37 Ibid.
38 Henry G. Manne, 'The "Higher Criticism" of the Modern Corporation', *Columbia Law Review*, vol. 62, no. 3, March 1962, pp. 399–432 (p. 420).
39 Williamson, 'Corporate Governance', p. 1220.
40 Robert J. Larner, 'Separation of Ownership and Control and Its Implications for the Behavior of the Firm', PhD dissertation, University of Wisconsin, Madison, 1968, p. 114. See also Robert J. Larner, 'Ownership and Control in the 200 Largest Nonfinancial Corporations, 1929 and 1963', *The American Economic Review*, vol. 56, no. 4, September 1966, pp. 777–87.
41 See Neil Fligstein, *The Architecture of Markets: An Economic Sociology of Twenty-First-Century Capitalist Societies* (Princeton, NJ: Princeton University Press, 2002, p. 156).
42 Gerald F. Davis, *Managed by the Markets: How Finance Re-Shaped America* (Oxford: Oxford University Press, 2009), p. 21.
43 Ibid., p. 50.
44 For an analysis of the different reasons behind loss of union power in the 1980s, see Kim Moody, 'Beating the Union: Union Avoidance in the US', in Gregor Gall and Tony Dundon (eds.), *Global Anti-Unionism: Nature, Dynamics, Trajectories and Outcomes* (London: Palgrave Macmillan, 2013), pp. 143–62.
45 That unions had failed to control their pension funds, suggests McCarthy, was a key factor in financialization (McCarthy, 'Turning Labor into Capital', p. 457).
46 Karl Marx, *Capital*, vol. 3, *The Process of Capitalist Production as a Whole*, available online: https://www.marxists.org/archive/marx/works/download/pdf/Capital-Volume-III.pdf, p. 263.
47 Karl Marx and Friedrich Engels, *Das Kapital, III, Werke, vol. 25* (Berlin: Dietz Verlag, [1894] 1964), p. 452 (my translation).
48 Karl Marx and Friedrich Engels, letter of 2 April 1858, in *Werke, vol. 29* (Berlin: Dietz Verlag, 1978), p. 312 (my translation).
49 Karl Marx and Friedrich Engels, *Das Kapital, III*, p. 456.
50 Fourier talked instead of 'industrial feudalism', a secret destiny to which the 'sweet commerce' of economists actually leads in practice. See Charles Fourier, *Publication des manuscrits de Fourier* (Paris: Librairie Phalanstérienne, 1851), p. 312.
51 Karl Marx, 'The French Crédit Mobilier', *New-York Daily Tribune*, 24 June 1856, in Karl Marx and Frederich Engels, *Collected Works*, Volume 15 (London: Lawrence & Wishart, 1975), p. 21.

Notes to Chapter 8

1 Karl Marx, Economic and Philosophic Manuscripts of 1844, available online: https://www.marxists.org/archive/marx/works/download/pdf/Economic-Philosophic-Manuscripts-1844.pdf, p. 11.
2 As John Shad, President of the Securities and Exchange Commission in the early 1980s, remarked: 'The theory that contested takeovers discipline incompetent managements is of limited veracity. [...] contrary to a discipline, the increasing threat of being "taken over" is an inducement to curtail or defer research and development, [...] – which entail current costs for long-term

benefits' (John S.R. Shad, 'The Leveraging of America. New York Financial Writers. Sheraton Center. New York City. June 7, 1984', in *News*, Securities and Exchange Commission, Washington, DC, 1984, p. 4). See also Richard M. Abrams, *America Transformed: Sixty Years of Revolutionary Change, 1941–2001* (Cambridge: Cambridge University Press, 2006), p. 107.

3 Andrei Shleifer and Robert W. Vishny, 'A Survey of Corporate Governance', *The Journal of Finance*, vol. 52, no. 2, 1997, pp. 737–83 (p. 738).

4 Davis, *Managed by the Markets*, p. 20.

5 Ibid., p. 50.

6 See James N. Rosenau and Ernst-Otto Czempiel (eds.), *Governance without Government: Order and Change in World Politics* (Cambridge: Cambridge University Press, 1992).

7 Indeed, 'it would be a great mistake to assume that the separation of ownership and control in a modern large corporation gives anything like that kind of freedom from the normal pattern of market restraints' (Henry G. Manne, 'Corporate Responsibility, Business Motivation, and Reality', *The Annals of the American Academy of Political and Social Science*, vol. 343, September 1962, pp. 55–64 [p. 61]).

8 Henry G. Manne, 'Current Views on the Modern Corporation', *University of Detroit Law Journal*, vol. 38, 1961, pp. 559–88 (p. 586).

9 Hayek was taking up a word proposed at the start of the nineteenth century by Richard Whately to replace the name (inadequate in his view) of 'political economy': 'catallatics' or the 'science of exchanges'. See Richard Whately, *Introductory Lectures on Political Economy* (London: B. Fellowes, 1832), p. 6.

10 Friedrich Hayek, *Law, Legislation and Liberty*, vol. 2, *The Mirage of Social Justice* (London: Routledge & Kegan, 1976), p. 107.

11 Ibid., p. 108.

12 Ibid., p. 185. Hayek distinguishes between *nomos* as a universal rule of behaviour and *thesis* as rules applicable solely to certain persons or for government purposes (Friedrich Hayek, 'The Confusion of Language in Political Thought', in *New Studies in Philosophy and Politics, Economics and the History of Ideas* (London: Routledge & Kegan Paul, 1978), pp. 71–97 [p. 77]).

13 Peter Koslowski, *Ethics of Capitalism and Critique of Sociobiology* (Berlin: Springer, 1996; first published in 1982), p. 28. See also Hayek, 'The Confusion of Language in Political Thought', p. 90.

14 'It is claimed that price affords a privileged access to the truth'. See Gerald F. Davis, *Managed by the Markets*, p. 41.

15 See Manne, 'Mergers and the Market for Corporate Control', p. 112.

16 Eugene F. Fama, 'Agency Problems and the Theory of the Firm', *Journal of Political Economy*, vol. 88, no. 2, April 1980, pp. 288–307 (p. 292). What these authors are trying to grasp are the combined disciplinary effects, not of the *market*, but of the *markets*. There is not, somewhere up there, 'the market', a single all-powerful God, but the combined effects of several markets. So Manne's theory links competition on capital markets with competition on the executive job market: it is the interweaving of these two markets, in connection with a third, the market for votes, which explains the disciplining effect on managerial conduct. As Fama (here following Manne) notes, 'the primary disciplining of managers comes through managerial

labor markets, both within and outside of the firm, with assistance from the panoply of internal and external monitoring devices [...], and with the market for outside takeovers providing discipline of last resort' (Fama, 'Agency Problems', p. 295).

17 Henri Lepage, *Demain le libéralisme* (Paris: Le Livre de poche, 1980), p. 380.

18 Frank H. Easterbrook, 'Managers' Discretion and Investors' Welfare: Theories and Evidence', *Delaware Journal of Corporate Law*, vol. 9, 1984, pp. 540–71 (p. 556). As Manne says, business owners have huge power and control, though not in the way that Berle means, i.e. politically (see Henry G. Manne, 'Controlling Giant Corporations', *Vital Speeches of the Day*, vol. 47, no. 22, 1981, pp. 690–4 [p. 693]).

19 On the distinction between ideology and fantasmagoria, see Marc Berdet, *Fantasmagories du capital: l'invention de la ville-marchandise* (Paris: Zones/ La Découverte, 2013), p. 19ff.

20 As Davis explains, we need to understand 'finance as technology', and the task of governance is to construct institutional *arrangements* that will limit human interactions (Davis, *Managed by the Markets*, p. 45).

Notes to Chapter 9

1 Arthur Fisher Bentley, *The Process of Government: A Study of Social Pressures* (Chicago, IL: University of Chicago Press, 1908), p. 268.

2 Beardsley Ruml, 'Corporate Management as a Locus of Power', *Chicago-Kent Law Review*, vol. 29, no. 3, June 1951, pp. 228–46.

3 Ibid., p. 228.

4 Ibid., p. 229.

5 Ibid.

6 Ibid.

7 Ibid., p. 234.

8 Ibid., p. 233.

9 Thomas Hobbes, *Leviathan* (New York: Touchstone, 2008; first published in 1651), p. 259; William Blackstone, *Commentaries on the Laws of England*, vol. 1 (Chicago, IL: University of Chicago Press, 1979; first published in 1765), p. 456.

10 Carl Kaysen, 'The Corporation: How Much Power? What Scope?', in Edward Mason (ed.), *The Corporation in Modern Society*, pp. 85–105 (p. 91).

11 As Kaysen puts it, management does indeed have significant influence as a 'taste setter or style leader for the society as a whole. Business influence on taste ranges from the direct effects through the design of material goods to the indirect and more subtle effects of the style of language and thought purveyed through the mass media – the school of style' (Kaysen, 'The Corporation', p. 101).

12 Ruml, 'Corporate Management', p. 246.

13 Ibid.

14 Heald, *The Social Responsibilities of Business*, p. 296.

15 Eugene V. Rostow, 'To Whom and for What Ends is Corporate Management Responsible?', in Edward Mason (ed.), *The Corporation in Modern Society*, pp. 46–71 (p. 59).

16 Terry H. Anderson, 'The Movement and the Business', in David R. Farber

(ed.), *The Sixties: From Memory to History* (Chapel Hill, NC: University of North Carolina Press, 1994), pp. 175–205 (p. 181).

17 F.C. Peterson, 'Letter to Midland Location Employees', 3 August, 1966, Folder Youth and Student Protest/Dow Chemical Demonstrations, Labadie Special Collections, University of Michigan. http://michigantheworld. history.lsa.umich.edu/antivietnamwar/files/original/03654a751b016b11e-6a0226ea6ea92e4.pdf. See also Saul Friedman, 'This Napalm Business', in Robert Heilbroner (ed.), *In the Name of Profit* (New York: Doubleday, 1972), pp. 128–53.

18 Howard Zinn, 'Dow Shalt Not Kill' (1967), in Howard Zinn, *The Zinn Reader* (New York: Seven Stories Press, 2009), pp. 314–21 (p. 316).

19 Anderson, 'The Movement and the Business', p. 182.

20 Ibid.

21 David Vogel, *Lobbying the Corporation: Citizen Challenges to Business Authority* (New York: Basic Books, 1978), p. 55.

22 Staughton Lynd, 'Attack War Contractors Meetings', *Guardian* (United States edition), 29 November 1969, reprinted in Henry C. Egerton, *Handling Protest at Annual Meetings* (New York: Conference Board, 1971), p. 5.

23 Eric Norden, 'Interview: Saul Alinsky; A Candid Conversation with the Feisty Radical Organizer', *Playboy*, vol. 19, no. 3, March 1972, pp. 59ff.

24 Ibid. For Alinsky – the proponent of a pragmatic and inventive approach to struggle, where all is grist to the mill – the proxy tactic was just one expedient among many, and in no way involved giving credence to the 'fibs of popular capitalism'. As he put it: 'The basic tactic in warfare against the Haves is a mass political jujitsu: the Have-Nots do not rigidly oppose the Haves, but yield in such planned and skilled ways that the superior strength of the Haves becomes their own undoing. For example, since the Haves publicly pose as the custodians of responsibility, morality, law, and justice [. . .], they can be constantly pushed to live up to their own book of morality and regulations. [. . .] You can club them to death with their "book" of rules and regulations' (Saul Alinsky, *Rules for Radicals: A Pragmatic Primer for Realistic Radicals* (New York: Vintage, 1989; first published in 1971), p. 152).

25 Lynn Taylor, 'Protest Plagues Annual Meetings', *Chicago Tribune*, 4 January 1971, p. 75.

26 National Action/Research on the Military-Industrial Complex.

27 Martha Westover, *Movement Guide to Stockholders Meetings* (Philadelphia, PA: NARMIC, 1970).

28 Egerton, *Handling Protest at Annual Meetings*, p. 2.

29 Ibid., p. 22.

30 Ibid., p. 17.

31 Ibid., p. 18.

32 Ibid., p. 3.

33 Ibid., p. 20.

34 Ibid., p. 23.

35 Robert J. Cole, '"Keep Your Cool", Dow Advises Targets of Antiwar Protesters', *New York Times*, 4 June 1970, p. 59.

36 Ibid.

37 Egerton, *Handling Protest at Annual Meetings*, p. 27.

38 Ibid., p. 31.

39 Ibid., p. 28.

40 Bazelon, 'The Scarcity Makers', p. 294.
41 As David Vogel notes, the political sciences have a regrettable tendency 'to reify politics by identifying it with government' and have largely neglected this original feature of the 1960s 'movement' in the United States: its direct challenge to business, identified with 'a system of power or "private government" – one whose power is comparable, if not greater than, that of the "official" government' (David Vogel, *Kindred Strangers: The Uneasy Relationship Between Politics and Business in America* (Princeton, NJ: Princeton University Press, 1996), p. 15). What then happens is that politicians start to treat corporations as public governments (David Vogel, 'The Corporation as Government: Challenges & Dilemmas', *Polity*, vol. 8, no. 1, Autumn 1975, pp. 5–37 [p. 16]).
42 Philip W. Moore, 'Corporate Social Reform: An Activist's Viewpoint', *California Management Review*, vol. 15, no. 4, Summer 1973, pp. 90–6 (p. 90).
43 See Vogel, *Lobbying the Corporation*, p. 3.
44 As Nace writes: 'Perhaps it could have been foreseen that the successes of the environmental and consumer movements would trigger some sort of backlash by big business, but the scale of the corporate political mobilization proved to be unprecedented' (Ted Nace, *Gangs of America: The Rise of Corporate Power and the Disabling of Democracy* (San Francisco, CA: Berrett-Koehler, 2003), p. 138).

Notes to Chapter 10

1 Karl Polanyi, *The Great Transformation. The Political and Economic Origins of our Time* (Boston, MA: Beacon Press, 2001), p. 151.
2 Lewis J. Powell, *Confidential Memorandum. Attack on American Free Enterprise System* (typescript), 23 August 1971, p. 1. http://law2.wlu.edu/deptimages/Powell%20Archives/PowellMemorandumTypescript.pdf.
3 Lewis Powell, *Political Warfare*, 30 June 1970. http://law2.wlu.edu/deptimages/powell%20archives/PowellWriting-PoliticalWarfareJune301970.pdf.
4 Powell, *Attack on American Free Enterprise System*, p. 2.
5 Ibid., p. 6.
6 Ibid., p. 7.
7 David Rockefeller, 'The Role of Business in an Era of Growing Accountability', reprinted in *Congressional Record*, Vol. 117/36, 13 December 1971–17 December 1971, US Government Printing Office, 1972, pp. 47615–16 (p. 47615).
8 James M. Roche, 'An Address', reprinted in *Congressional Record*, Vol. 117/10, 28 April 1971–5 May 1971, US Government Printing Office, 1972, pp. 13416–19 (p. 13417).
9 Michael Useem, 'Review', *Contemporary Sociology*, vol. 6, no. 5, September 1977, pp. 592–3 (p. 592).
10 Powell, *Attack on American Free Enterprise System*, p. 13.
11 Arthur Shenfield, *The Ideological War Against Western Society*, Rockford College, 1970, p. 4. In the foreword that he wrote for the pamphlet by his colleague Shenfield, who was to succeed him as leader of the Mont Pelerin Society, Milton Friedman drives it home: it is 'crystal clear that the founda-

tions of our free society are under wide-ranging and powerful attack – not by Communist or any other conspiracy but by misguided individuals parroting one another' (Milton Friedman, 'Foreword', in Shenfield, *The Ideological War Against Western Society*, p. 2). Friedman praises Shenfield's 'subtle and penetrating' analysis. This essay, both mediocre and sickening, does indeed contain several 'subtle and penetrating' analyses such as this one, on South Africa: 'The principle of Apartheid is neither dishonorable nor, in the bad sense, racist [sic]' (p. 17).

12 Lionel Trilling, *Beyond Culture: Essays on Literature and Learning* (New York: Viking Press, 1965), pp. xiii ff.

13 Norman Podhoretz, 'Between Nixon and the New Politics', *Commentary*, vol. 54, no. 3, September 1972, pp. 4–8 (p. 5).

14 Irving Kristol, 'Business and "The New Class"', in *Two Cheers for Capitalism* (New York: Mentor, 1979; first published in 1975), pp. 23–8 (p. 27).

15 Ibid., p. 26.

16 Shenfield, *The Ideological War Against Western Society*, pp. 26ff.

17 Robert L. Bartley, 'Business and the New Class', in B. Bruce-Briggs (ed.), *The New Class?* (New Brunswick, NJ: Transaction Books, 1979), pp. 57–66 (p. 58).

18 Ibid., p. 58.

19 Kristol, 'Business and "The New Class"', p. 26.

20 William J. Baroody, 'Toward Intellectual Competition', in *NAM Reports*, vol. 18 (Washington, DC: National Association of Manufacturers, 1973), n.p.

21 Leonard Silk, 'Ethics in Government', *The American Economic Review*, vol. 67, no. 1, February 1977, pp. 316–20 (p. 319).

22 Leonard Silk and David Vogel, *Ethics and Profits: The Crisis of Confidence in American Business* (New York: Simon and Schuster, 1976), p. 71.

23 Powell, *Attack on American Free Enterprise System*, p. 10.

24 Ibid., p. 7.

25 Daniel Bell, *The Cultural Contradictions of Capitalism* (New York: Basic Books, 1978), p. 77.

26 Hegemony is an old notion. It was the 'name that in Greece was given to the political pre-eminence which confederated peoples voluntarily granted to one people because of the prudence, bravery and skill in war that its citizens had shown; as a result of which, this people was invested with supreme leadership of all enterprises related to common affairs'. *Dictionnaire de la conversation et de la lecture*, vol. X (Paris: Didot, 1861), p. 785. First, therefore, in the classical sense, hegemony means a strategic power of managing common affairs. The concept applies properly to the relationships between different cities in a coalition. It is a concept in foreign policy, used as a way of thinking about political alliances that city-peoples and island-peoples form among themselves. If we follow Gramsci in applying the concept of hegemony to internal political relations – to the relations between the different classes within a society – this entails thinking of them as an archipelago of cities, addressing domestic policy and the relationships between classes from, as it were, a geopolitical angle. Secondly, hegemony is 'voluntarily granted' to one people by others. Hegemony is a position that is agreed rather than imposed. But this relationship cannot be reduced to any of the available theories of social contract. There is no transfer or alienation of originating rights, and no pact that would constitute a third entity, a new political body. Thirdly,

hegemony is granted on the basis of what you might call a certain ethical-political status, the ascendancy accorded to the person on whom will fall the functions of community leadership. He must enjoy a certain prestige based on his character, his way of life and his actions. Fourthly, this assent is given or withdrawn based on *actions*. These are acts and ways of acting that lead to a person's gaining support. And there are failures in action that lead to its being withdrawn. So we must not interpret hegemony in ways that are too narrowly 'ideological-symbolic' or 'ideological-discursive'. The texts of the corpus that I present in this chapter tend to be reductive in this way, dealing with the ongoing crisis as a simple loss of ideological influence: this is what constitutes their theoretical and practical limit.

This detour through the traditional interpretation sheds light on Gramsci's concept. A crisis in hegemony arises, he writes, when the dominant groups are no longer able to ensure 'the "spontaneous" consent given by the great masses of the population to the general direction imposed on social life by the dominant fundamental group; this consent is "historically" caused by the prestige (and consequent confidence) which the dominant group enjoys because of its position and function in the world of production' (Antonio Gramsci, *Selections from the Prison Notebooks*, edited and translated by Quentin Hoare and Geoffrey Nowell Smith (London: Lawrence & Wishart, 1971), p. 145). The power of the ruling class suffers a crisis: it is still dominant, economically and institutionally, but this position is no longer magnified by the prestige that it drew from hegemony. The crisis in hegemony is not the loss of all power, but of one of its dimensions, ethical-political in nature – the dimension that ensures consent. For Gramsci, the 'crisis of the ruling class's hegemony' is produced either on the occasion of a failure in one of its major political enterprises, including war; or when huge masses 'have passed suddenly from a state of political passivity to a certain activity, and put forward demands which taken together, albeit not organically formulated, add up to a revolution' (Gramsci, *Selections from the Prison Notebooks*, pp. 450–1). The end of the 1960s combined two factors: the politico-military fiasco of the Vietnam War, and an intense phase of political and cultural protest, which was thought of and lived through by many people as a revolution in the making.

27 William J. Baroody, 'The Corporate Role in the Decade Ahead', 20 October 1972, quoted in Phillips-Fein, *Invisible Hands*, p. 166.
28 Kristol, 'On Corporate Philanthropy', in *Two Cheers for Capitalism*, pp. 131–5 (p. 132).
29 Powell, *Attack on American Free Enterprise System*, p. 15.
30 Ibid., p. 3.
31 Dave Packard, 'Corporate Support of the Private Universities', University Club, New York, 17 October, 1973. https://history.keysight.com/tag/1973.
32 'On the other hand', he adds, 'it does not follow that businessmen or corporations have any obligation to give money to institutions whose views or attitudes they disapprove of. It is absurd to insist otherwise – yet this absurdity is consistently set forth by college presidents, and in the name of "academic freedom," no less' (Kristol, 'On Corporate Philanthropy', p. 133).
33 Robert H. Malott, 'Corporate Support of Education: Some Strings Attached', *Harvard Business Review*, 56, no. 4, 1978, pp. 133–8 (p. 137).
34 William E. Simon, *Time for Truth* (New York: Berkley Publishing Group, 1979), p. 247.

35 See James K. Rowe, 'CSR as Business Strategy', in Ronnie D. Lipschutz and James K. Rowe (eds.), *Globalization, Governmentality and Global Politics: Regulation for the Rest of Us?* (New York: Routledge, 2005), pp. 130–70 (p. 139).
36 Powell, *Attack on American Free Enterprise System*, p. 8.
37 Kristol, 'On Corporate Philanthropy', pp. 134ff.
38 Its mission would be 'to challenge that ideological monopoly: to raise the unnamed issues, to ask the unasked questions, to present the missing contexts, and to place a set of very different values and goals on the public agenda' (Simon, *Time for Truth*, p. 250).
39 Ibid., p. 245. 'This new class has ready access to our leading editorial writers and TV journalists', even though the main media 'are owned and theoretically controlled by corporations which depend upon profits, and the enterprise system to survive' (Thomas Murphy, quoted in Patrick J. Akard, 'The Return of the Market: Corporate Mobilization and the Transformation of US Economic Policy, 1974–1984', PhD dissertation, University of Kansas, 1989, p. 74); Powell, *Attack on American Free Enterprise System*, p. 4.
40 Simon, *Time for Truth*, p. 249.
41 Shenfield, *The Ideological War Against Western Society*. 'In all fairness, it must be recognized that businessmen have not been trained or equipped to conduct guerrilla warfare with those who propagandize against the system [. . .]. The traditional role of business executives has been to manage, to produce, to sell, to create jobs, to make profits' (Powell, *Attack on American Free Enterprise System*, p. 8). But they would need to learn to take on a new role, moving from an ideological to a political counter-offensive. But, for this: 'Business must learn the lesson, long ago learned by Labor and other self-interest groups. This is the lesson that political power is necessary; that such power must be assiduously cultivated; and that when necessary, it must be used aggressively and with determination – without embarrassment and without the reluctance which has been so characteristic of American business' (Powell, *Attack on American Free Enterprise System*, p. 25).

Notes to Chapter 11

1 Gramsci, *Selections from the Prison Notebooks*, p. 451.
2 Rockefeller, 'The Role of Business', p. 47615.
3 Ibid., pp. 47615ff.
4 Luc Boltanski and Eve Chiapello have insisted on capitalism's ability to recuperate criticism. This ability is real enough, but the process does not go in only one direction. We also need to point out the ability of protesters to adopt, for better or worse, capitalism's discourses of legitimation so as to regurgitate them in a modified form. 'Business's passion for CSR' that was noted from the early 2000s onwards was, as Chiapello surmises, the sign that capitalism 'had entered a new cycle of recuperation of criticism of it, one that takes ecological criticism seriously' (Eve Chiapello, 'Le capitalisme et ses critiques', 4th RIODD Congress, Lille, June 2009, https://www.researchgate.net/publication/228592489). But, in this cycle of recuperation, this is only the latest in a longer series. Far from being recent, the discourse on social responsibility appeared in the United States in the early twentieth century as

a managerial ideology. Only later, from the late 1960s, did a reformist activism appropriate this lexicon for polemical purposes. The process was not a way of 'neutering' an originally critical theme. Quite the opposite: a managerial apologetics was diverted by a reformist critique that was itself taken up and reinterpreted in turn. If there was any recuperation, it was caught up in the crisscross games that are the hallmark of any struggle to impose a new meaning. On the notion of 'cycles of recuperation', see Luke Boltanski and Eve Chiapello, *The New Spirit of Capitalism*, translated by Gregory Elliot (London and New York: Verso), p. 425.

5 See Vogel, *Lobbying the Corporation*, p. 74.

6 Quoted in Donald E. Schwartz, 'Towards New Corporate Goals: Co-Existence with Society', *Georgetown Law Journal*, vol. 60, 1971, pp. 57–109 (p. 62).

7 General Motors, 'GM's Record of Progress in Automotive Safety, Air Pollution Control Mass Transit, Plant Safety and Social Welfare', 1970, p. 5.

8 Jeffrey St. John, 'Memo to GM: Why Not Fight Back?', *Wall Street Journal*, 31 May 1971, p. 1.

9 Roche, 'An Address', p. 13416.

10 Ibid., p. 13418.

11 Ibid., p. 13417.

12 Ibid., p. 13418.

13 Letter from Frederick West, CEO of Bethlehem Steel Corporation to Senator Philip A. Hart, 16 July 1974, quoted in S. Prakash Sethi, 'Business and the News Media: The Paradox of Informed Misunderstanding', *California Management Review*, vol. 19, no. 3, 1977, pp. 52–62 (p. 53).

14 On the night of 3 December 1984, thousands of people died, overcome while they slept by the toxic cloud of methyl isocyanate released into the atmosphere by the explosion of the Union Carbide India Limited factory in Bhopal. Slogans quoted in Russell B. Stevenson, 'The Corporation as a Political Institution', *Hofstra Law Review*, vol. 8, no. 1, 1979, pp. 39–62 (p. 59).

15 John McClaughry, 'Milton Friedman Responds: A Business and Society Review Interview', *Business and Society Review*, no. 1, Spring 1972, pp. 5–16 (p. 8).

16 Friedman, 'A Friedman Doctrine', p. 17.

17 McClaughry, 'Milton Friedman Responds', p. 8. If this hypocrisy works to their interest, Friedman cannot criticize them for it – though this does not stop him, in his personal capacity, from reserving his esteem for those who disdain such almost fraudulent tactics (Milton Friedman, 'A Friedman Doctrine', p. 17).

18 Those afflicted by this anxiety could have found reassurance by reading a qualitative survey commissioned in 1974 by an employers' organization, 'The Conference Board'. This had involved a series of interviews with American managers of the time to find out what they were thinking. It emerged that, while business leaders were worried by the general hostility and perceived attacks on the profit motive as 'not only personally insulting but also as threatening the very institution that [had] made America prosperous and free', many had no compunction in ridiculing 'the idea of corporate "social responsibility," attributing the concept to a figment of a sociologist's imagination, and virtually all major efforts to protect the environment, alter hiring practices, and democratize the work place were roundly condemned'. As Michael Useem notes: 'More surprising, however, was the widespread

distrust of the democratic system. [. . .] Enamored with the autocratic efficiency of their own organizations, they have nothing but contempt for the sluggish, irrational administration they see as inherent in a political system subject to the vagaries of public opinion [. . .] "capitalist class authoritarianism" has now reached massive proportions' (Useem, 'Review', p. 593).

19 Pierre Jurieu, *Justification de la morale des reformez contre les accusations de Mr. Arnaud*, vol. I (The Hague: Arnout Leers, 1685), p. 127.
20 McClaughry, 'Milton Friedman Responds', p. 8.
21 Phillip I. Blumberg, 'The Politicization of the Corporation', *Boston University Law Review*, vol. 26, 1971, pp. 1551–87 (p. 1555).
22 Theodore Levitt, 'The Dangers of Social Responsibility', *Harvard Business Review*, vol. 36, no. 5, 1958, pp. 41–50 (p. 41).
23 Ibid., p. 49.
24 Friedrich Hayek, 'The Corporation in a Democratic Society: In Whose Interest Ought It and Will It Be Run?', in Melvin Anshen and George Leland Bach (eds.), *Management and Corporations 1985* (New York: McGraw Hill, 1960, pp. 99–117 (p. 116). 'The years ahead will see a great increase in conscious, collective, governmental controls and of governmental enterprise; [. . .] our giant firms are sitting like fat, delectable ducks, virtually inviting the government to open fire with something more effective than antitrust. The invitation will be accepted [. . .]' (Ben W. Lewis, 'Power Blocs and the Operation of Economic Forces. Economics by Admonition', *The American Economic Review*, vol. 49, no. 2, May 1959, pp. 384–98, [p. 397]).
25 Henry G. Manne, 'The Social Responsibility of Regulated Utilities', *Wisconsin Law Review*, no. 4, 1972, pp. 995–1009 (p. 995).
26 Henry G. Manne, 'The Paradox of Corporate Responsibility', in *A Look at Business in 1990: A Summary. White House Conference on the Industrial World Ahead* (Washington, DC: US Government Printing Office, 1972), pp. 95–8 (p. 96). Despite their differences, managerialists and neoliberals agreed on one fundamental objective: to avoid as much as possible public regulation in social and environmental matters. Their differences were pragmatic, and ultimately came down to this: would CSR stave off government regulation or feed it? For the former, highlighting the social responsibilities of management seemed to be an effective preventive manoeuvre. Management, argued Berle, acted 'as absorbers of the first wave of social shock'. If management did nothing, 'the impact would be such as to force the government to intervene. I rather doubt that Professor Manne would consider that more desirable than assumption of these tasks by the corporate managements' (Adolf A. Berle, 'Modern Functions of the Corporate System', *Columbia Law Review*, vol. 62, no. 3, March 1962, pp. 433–49 (p. 443).
27 Friedman, 'A Friedman doctrine', p. 17.
28 According to Friedman, businessmen have a 'schizophrenic character': they are clear about their short-term interests, but mainly disinclined to consider the broader and more long-term question of the conditions of the 'possible survival of business in general'. Every business individually defends itself by spreading a discourse that is harmful to all other businesses: 'sometimes, I think that businessmen as individuals have a suicidal instinct'. In short, what we have here is a problem of collective action, as the sociologists call it, or of a public good, as the economists say. After the prisoner's dilemma, we have the CEO's dilemma. As Manne says, the tragedy lies basically in the

fact that 'preservation of capitalism is a public good. No profit maximizing corporation would ever invest in such preservation, since the benefits of the investment are external to it'. Here's the rub: the pursuit of individual interest does not in itself ensure the preservation of the system that allows individual interest to be pursued. The logic of the competitive market, left to itself, can paradoxically work against itself, destroying its own properties of existence. See Friedman, 'A Friedman Doctrine', p. 17, and Henry G. Manne, 'The Limits and Rationale of Corporate Altruism: An Individualistic Model', *Virginia Law Review*, vol. 59, no. 4, April 1973, pp. 708–22 (p. 710).

29 St. John, 'Memo to GM: Why Not Fight Back?', p. 1.
30 Manne, 'The Myth of Corporate Responsibility', p. 533.

Notes to Chapter 12

1 Lee Loevinger, 'The Corporation as a Power Nexus', *The Antitrust Bulletin*, vol. 6, 1961, pp. 345–59 (p. 357).
2 Louis Quicherat and Amédée Daveluy, *Dictionnaire Latin-Français* (Paris: Hachette, 1871), p. 753.
3 Irving Kristol, 'On Corporate Capitalism in America', *The Public Interest*, no. 41, Autumn 1975, pp. 124–41 (p. 138).
4 Y.A. Zamoshkin and A.Y. Melvil, 'Neoliberalism and "the New Conservatism" in the USA', *Soviet Studies in Philosophy*, vol. 16, no. 2, 1977, pp. 3–24 (p. 17).
5 Stuart Hall, 'The Great Moving Right Show', *Marxism Today*, January 1979, pp. 14–20 (p. 15).
6 Manne, 'Controlling Giant Corporations', p. 691.
7 Ibid.
8 Manne, 'Review: In Defense of the Corporation by Robert Hessen', p. 1649.
9 Michael C. Jensen and William H. Meckling, 'Can the Corporation Survive?', *Financial Analysts Journal*, vol. 34, no. 1, January/February 1978, pp. 31–7 (p. 31).
10 Ibid., p. 32.
11 Ibid., p. 36.
12 Ibid., p. 37.
13 Michael C. Jensen and William H. Meckling, 'Corporate Governance and "Economic Democracy": An Attack on Freedom', in C.J. Huizenga (ed.), *Proceedings of Corporate Governance: A Definitive Exploration of the Issues*, Harvard Business School NOM Unit Working Paper no. 1983, http://papers.ssrn.com/abstract=321521, pp. 1–23 (p. 2).
14 Michael C. Jensen and William H. Meckling, 'Reflections on the Corporation as a Social Invention', in Robert Hessen (ed.), *Controlling the Giant Corporation: A Symposium*, Center for Research in Government Policy and Business, Graduate School of Management, University of Rochester, Rochester, 1982, pp. 82–95 (p. 86).
15 Ibid., p. 86.
16 Ronald Coase, 'The Nature of the Firm', *Economica*, New Series, vol. 4, no. 16, November 1937, pp. 386–405 (p. 388). Coase borrows this image from Dennis Holme Robertson, *The Control of Industry* (New York: Harcourt, Brace and Company, 1923), p. 84.

17 Coase, 'The Nature of the Firm', p. 387. Marx had established an inverse reciprocal relation between the employers' authority in a business and external market relations.

18 Ibid., p. 390.

19 Ronald Coase, 'The Problem of Social Cost', *Journal of Law and Economics*, vol. 3, October 1960, pp. 1–44 (p. 15).

20 Coase, 'The Nature of the Firm', p. 392.

21 See Alfred D. Chandler, *The Visible Hand: The Managerial Revolution in American Business* (Cambridge, MA: Harvard University Press, 1977), pp. 6 and 515, n. 3 (on Coase). See also Oliver E. Williamson, 'Visible and Invisible Governance', *The American Economic Review*, vol. 84, no. 2, May 1994, pp. 323–6 (p. 324).

22 Coase, 'The Nature of the Firm', p. 403.

23 Samuel Bowles and Herbert Gintis, 'The Power of Capital: On the Inadequacy of the Conception of the Capitalist Economy as "Private"', *Philosophical Forum*, vol. 14, no. 3–4, Spring/Summer 1983, pp. 225–45 (p. 228).

24 Alchian and Demsetz, 'Production, Information Costs, and Economic Organization', p. 777.

25 Ibid.

26 The argument is illegitimate for several reasons, including this one: what the grocer sells is a *thing* distinct from him, while what the employee sells is '*himself*, piece by piece', hours of his life that will henceforth 'belong to the man who buys them' (Karl Marx, *Travail salarié et capital* (Beijing: Éditions en langues étrangères, 1966 [1849]), p. 19). And this makes a big difference in terms of power relations. As Giulio Palermo says: 'When a grocer sells a kilo of coffee, he/she alienates a piece of his/her property and transfers to somebody else his/her power to do with the coffee as he/she likes. When a worker sells his/her labour power, he/she alienates a piece of his/her life and transfers to somebody else his/her power to do with himself/herself as he/she likes. The exchange of labour power involves interpersonal relations directly. The PTA [power to act] that the capitalist obtains in exchange for his/her money is itself a POS [power over someone]' (Giulio Palermo, 'The Ontology of Economic Power in Capitalism: Mainstream Economics and Marx', *Cambridge Journal of Economics*, vol. 31, no. 4, 2007, pp. 539–61 [p. 551]). So, it is wrong to say that this type of exchange does not involve any specific relation of authority. The labour contract does not exclude the power another has over me by mere virtue of the fact that it is a contract – quite the opposite, in fact, because this power relationship in this case forms one of the very objects of the transaction, of this contract of *subordination*: the employer has bought from me the possibility of getting me to make, within certain limits and for a certain length of time, what he requires. This is denied by our authors. See also David A. Ciepley, 'Authority in the Firm (And the Attempt to Theorize It Away)', *Critical Review*, vol. 16, no. 1, January 2004, pp. 81–115.

27 Margaret Thatcher, 'Interview for Woman's Own ("no such thing as society")', September 23, 1987', *Speeches, interviews & other statements*, Margaret Thatcher Foundation. http://www.margaretthatcher.org/document/106689.

28 Michael C. Jensen, 'Organization Theory and Methodology', *The Accounting Review*, vol. 58, no. 2, April 1983, pp. 319–39 (p. 319).

29 Jensen and Meckling, 'Theory of the Firm'. See E. Han Kim, Adair Morse and Luigi Zingales, 'What Has Mattered to Economics Since 1970', *The*

Journal of Economic Perspectives, vol. 20, no. 4, Autumn 2006, pp. 189–202 (p. 192).

30 Jensen and Meckling, 'Theory of the Firm', p. 311.

31 Ibid., p. 310, n. 1.

32 Jensen, 'Organization Theory and Methodology', p. 328. The Latin term *nexus* means a link, an interlacing, a knot. The firm is thus conceived of as an interlacing of contracts. But, in the lexicon of Roman law, this word also meant more specifically a certain obligation, which engaged the freedom of a debtor towards his creditor: in the event of insolvency, the debtor became the creditor's prisoner. So a nexus also designated, by extension, a relation of limitation. This connotation eluded the new theorists of the firm – however, their definition may also be translated as follows: the firm as a contractual prison or limitation.

33 Jensen and Meckling, 'Theory of the Firm', p. 310.

34 David Ciepley, 'Beyond Public and Private: Toward a Political Theory of the Corporation', *American Political Science Review*, vol. 107, no. 1, February 2013, pp. 139–58 (p. 140).

35 See Paddy Ireland, 'Defending the Rentier: Corporate Theory and the Reprivatization of the Public Company', in John Parkinson, Andrew Gamble and Gavin Kelly (eds.), *The Political Economy of the Company* (Oxford: Hart, 2000), pp. 141–73 (p. 163).

36 Jensen, 'Organization Theory and Methodology', p. 330. Jensen is here quoting Alfred Whitehead and Bertrand Russell, *Principia Mathematica to *56* (1910) (Cambridge: Cambridge University Press, 1997), p. 12.

37 Jensen, 'Organization Theory and Methodology', p. 326.

38 Jensen and Meckling, 'Theory of the Firm', p. 311.

39 Frank H. Easterbrook and Daniel R. Fischel, *The Economic Structure of Corporate Law* (Cambridge, MA: Harvard University Press, 1996; first published in 1991), p. 12.

40 Michael C. Jensen, *Foundations of Organizational Strategy* (Cambridge, MA: Harvard University Press, 2001; first published in 1998), p. 125.

41 Melvin A. Eisenberg, 'The Conception that the Corporation is a Nexus of Contracts, and the Dual Nature of the Firm', *The Journal of Corporation Law*, vol. 24, no. 4, pp. 819–36 (p. 830).

42 These terms are often mistaken for synonyms when they are quite different. The status of society (*société*), notes Jean Philippe Robé, serves as a 'legal support for the company (*entreprise*). The legal person holding the rights that allow the company to "function", to "live" (rights of ownership of assets, rights arising from contracts drawn up with suppliers or with distributors or customers) is technically the society'. The society is the name of a legal status, the company designates a socio-economic organization, one 'intended to produce and/or sell on the goods or services market' (Jean-Philippe Robé, 'L'entreprise en droit', in *Droit et société*, no. 29, 1995, pp. 117–36 (pp. 122ff.).

43 Jensen and Meckling, 'Theory of the Firm', p. 310.

44 Davis, *Managed by the Markets*, p. 60.

45 Jensen, 'Organization Theory and Methodology', p. 331.

46 Ibid., p. 327.

47 Jensen and Meckling, 'Reflections on the Corporation as a Social Invention', p. 86.

48 John Dewey, 'The Historic Background of Corporate Legal Personality', *Yale Law Journal*, vol. 35, no. 6, 1926, pp. 655–73 (p. 673). Discussing the ontology of the firm, Dewey proposed, as a way of bypassing false problems, taking the word 'person' as a simple 'synonym for a right-and-duty-bearing unit'. He adds: 'Any such unit would be a person [. . .] What "person" signifies in popular speech, or in psychology, or in philosophy or morals, would be as irrelevant, to employ an exaggerated simile, as it would be to argue that because a wine I called "dry," it has the properties of dry solids; or that, because it does not have those properties, wine cannot possibly be "dry"' (Dewey, 'The Historic Background', p. 656). Applying this minimal category of a personality understood as 'a right-and-duty-bearing unit' to an entity does not involve granting it the additional attributes of a human individual; conversely, applying this category to it does not require it, as a condition, to possess the corresponding anthropological features. So, on this view, nothing stops us giving a personality to an inanimate object or to a collective being. For Dewey, the problem is not knowing if we can (we can decide to do so, precisely as a fiction), but what effects this may have. It does not eliminate the question of capabilities – it is always important to ask what a body, a pebble or a business can do – but it shifts it. Where Jensen wants to ban, a priori and dogmatically, the attribution of social obligations to organizations on the grounds that they are not human individuals, the pragmatic approach starts with the possibility of such an attribution and then ponders what the effects may be. According to this approach, a critical review of 'corporate social responsibility' would proceed in a different way from Jensen: it would not pretend that such an attribution is ontologically impossible (this is not the case), but it would ask what effects it aims for and produces. What are, politically speaking, the 'productive' effects? The economists who consider it to be an enemy would probably be surprised to find in it an unexpected ally. We will be coming back to this.

49 Jensen and Meckling, 'Theory of the Firm', p. 311.

50 Easterbrook and Fischel, 'The Corporate Contract', p. 1446.

51 'The ascendancy of large-scale organizations that dominate virtually all aspects of life [. . .] has made it imperative that the power of these organizations be legitimate – that is, conceded by those affected by this power to be rightful and proper' (Edwin M. Epstein and James Willard Hurst, 'The Historical Enigma of Corporate Legitimacy', *California Law Review*, vol. 60, no. 6, November 1972, pp. 1701–18 [p. 1702]).

52 John Blundell, 'Introduction: Hayek, Fisher and The Road to Serfdom', in Friedrich Hayek, *The Road to Serfdom. The Condensed Version of The Road to Serfdom by F.A. Hayek as it Appeared in the April 1945 edition of Reader's Digest* (London: The Institute of Economic Affairs, 1999), pp. 11–25 (p. 14). See also John Blundell, *Waging the War of Ideas: Why There Are No Shortcuts*, The Heritage Foundation Lecture Series, no. 254, The Heritage Foundation, Washington, DC, 1989, p. 6.

Notes to Chapter 13

1 Kristol, 'On Corporate Capitalism in America', p. 135.

2 Robert Hessen, 'A New Concept of Corporations: A Contractual and Private

Property Model', *Hastings Law Journal*, vol. 30, May 1979, pp. 1327–50 (p. 1330). For a similar argument, see Roger Pilon, 'Corporations and Rights: On Treating Corporate People Justly', *Georgia Law Review*, vol. 13, no. 4, Summer 1979, pp. 1245–1370.

3 Ciepley, 'Beyond Public and Private', p. 146.

4 Lynn A. Stout, *The Shareholder Value Myth: How Putting Shareholders First Harms Investors, Corporations, and the Public* (San Francisco, CA: Berrett-Koehler, 2012), p. 37. They are no longer owners of assets – which become the property of the company itself – but of shares, mere title deeds giving the right to tax a proportion of surplus value, which are properly speaking neither a capital nor a part of capital (Karl Marx, *Capital*, Volume III, *The Process of Capitalist Production as a Whole*, available online: https://www.marxists.org/archive/marx/works/download/pdf/Capital-Volume-III.pdf.

5 As Stout says, 'shareholders are only one of several groups that – at the board of directors' discretion – are residual claimants [. . .]. When a corporation does well, its board may indeed declare bigger dividends for shareholders. But the directors may also decide, in addition or instead, to give rank-and-file employees raises and greater job security, to provide executives with a company jet [. . .]. The corporation is its own residual claimant, and it is the board of directors that decides what to do with the corporation's residual' (Stout, *The Shareholder Value Myth*, p. 41. See also Jean-Philippe Robé, 'À qui appartiennent les entreprises?', *Le Débat*, no. 155, 2009, pp. 32–6.

6 Ibid., p. 33.

7 Benjamin Coriat and Olivier Weinstein, 'Les théories de la firme entre "contrats" et "compétences". Une revue critique des développements contemporains', *Revue d'économie industrielle*, no. 129–130, 2010, pp. 57–86 (p. 71). See also Ireland, 'Defending the Rentier', p. 147.

8 Lynn Stout, 'The Mythical Benefits of Shareholder Control', *Virginia Law Review*, vol. 93, 2007, pp. 789–809 (p. 804).

9 Historically, companies were originally conceived as partnerships, associations of people aggregating their contributions. It is in comparison with the idea of a partnership, from which it takes over, that the specific features of the joint stock company appear most clearly. Besides limited liability, it has two highly advantageous features.

The first is the 'assets lock in': 'A partner really does own a percentage of the partnership, and if she leaves, she removes her portion from the assets of the firm'. If a partner withdraws, this directly affects capital, with a risk of liquidation. In contrast, if a shareholder wants to disengage, he cannot simply withdraw his stakes; he has to find someone who will buy them back, but the stakes remain. Regarding the capital of the company, the 'departure' of a shareholder is in itself a matter of indifference: the deeds change hands, but the corresponding shares are not and cannot be removed from him. Each of the original investors *was* certainly the individual owner of contributions. But these now belong as a whole to the society and no shareholder can recover the corresponding share. They are locked in.

The second characteristic is the *shielding of the entity*. If the shareholder is protected from company debts by the principle of limited liability, the society is also protected from the shareholder's debts. You cannot tap into the assets of the firm to bail out your creditors. Note that this not only protects the company against the debts of its shareholders but also, indirectly, each shareholder against the possible defaulting of others. Shareholding has the effect of artificially limiting the responsibilities and risks previously related to the private ownership of the means of production, according to two complementary vectors: first, due to limited liability, there is a reduction of the risks that might 'fall back' from the company to the shareholder; second, due to both the shielding of the firm as an entity and the locking in of its assets, there is a reduction of the risks that might 'fall forward' from the shareholder to the company. These three privileges make it possible to 'combine strong capital-raising capability with strong liquidation protection' (David Ciepley, 'Neither Persons nor Associations. Against Constitutional Rights for Corporations', *Journal of Law and Courts*, vol. 1, no. 2, Autumn 2013, pp. 221–45 [pp. 226ff]; Lynn A. Stout, 'On the Nature of Corporations', *University of Illinois Law Review*, vol. 2005, no. 1, 2004, pp. 253–67; Margaret M. Blair, 'Locking In Capital: What Corporate Law Achieved for Business Organizers in the Nineteenth Century', *UCLA Law Review*, vol. 51, no. 2, 2003, pp. 387–455; Henry Hansmann, Reinier Kraakman and Richard Squire, 'Law and the Rise of the Firm', *Harvard Law Review*, vol. 119, no. 5, 2006, pp. 1333–403; Jean-Philippe Robé, 'The Legal Structure of the Firm', *Accounting, Economics, and Law*, vol. 1, no. 1, 2011, Article 5).

10 See Ireland, 'Defending the Rentier', p. 170.
11 Daniel Bell, 'The Coming of Post-Industrial Society', *Business & Society Review/Innovation*, no. 5, Spring 1973, pp. 5–23 (p. 20).
12 Fama, 'Agency Problems and the Theory of the Firm', p. 290.
13 Ibid., p. 289. 'This denial of shareholder ownership is critical to the nexus-of-contracts conception, because if the corporation is owned by the shareholders it would not be simply a nexus of contracts' (Melvin A. Eisenberg, 'The Conception that the Corporation is a Nexus of Contracts, and the Dual Nature of the Firm', *The Journal of Corporation Law*, vol. 24, no. 4, pp. 819–36 (p. 825).
14 Fama, 'Agency Problems and the Theory of the Firm', p. 290.
15 See above, p. 56.
16 Fama, 'Agency Problems and the Theory of the Firm', p. 290.
17 See Olivier Weinstein, 'Firm, Property and Governance: From Berle and Means to the Agency Theory, and Beyond', *Accounting, Economics, and Law*, vol. 2, no. 2, 2012, Article 2, p. 39.
18 Fama, 'Agency Problems and the Theory of the Firm', p. 291.
19 Weinstein, 'Firm, Property and Governance', p. 39. Weinstein concludes: 'Logically, the conception of the firm as a "nexus of contracts" should in fact lead one to consider the managers as the agents (or trustees) of several principals' (p. 43).
20 Lepage, *Demain le libéralisme*, p. 351.
21 Alchian and Demsetz, 'Production, Information Costs, and Economic Organization', p. 781.
22 Ibid., p. 782.
23 Ibid.
24 Because the size of his gain will depend on the total profit generated by the team, it will be in his interest to discipline them effectively, since 'the monitor earns his residual through the reduction in shirking' (ibid., p. 782). Here we have two conjoined disciplinary mechanisms: on a first level, in the relation

between supervisor and team, there is the old principle of hierarchical surveillance, while on a second level, concerning the monitoring itself, we have
a process of self-discipline through profit-sharing.

25 'To discipline team members and reduce shirking, the residual claimant must
have power to revise the contract terms and incentives of individual members'
(ibid., p. 782).

26 N. Scott Arnold, *The Philosophy and Economics of Market Socialism: A
Critical Study* (New York: Oxford University Press, 1994), p. 190.

27 Alchian and Demsetz, 'Production, Information Costs, and Economic
Organization', p. 785. There is a paradox in the text of Alchian and Demsetz:
even when they are constructing a theory of authority, they keep denying that
they are doing so. And yet, no sooner have they denied in their introduction
the existence of relations of company-specific powers than they reintroduce
them by describing the firm as subject to hierarchical surveillance intended to
get rid of 'shirkers', making explicit reference to a 'police instrument'. This
incongruity is explained by the fact that they are confusing two ideas. The
first is that in business there is 'no disciplinary action any different in the
slightest degree from ordinary market contracting' (the thesis of the homo-
geneity of power); the second is that the authority that is exercised in the
company is justified (the thesis of the legitimacy of, or the need for, employers'
power). They are mistaken about what they think they are demonstrating:
while building a theory of the legitimacy of employers' authority, they claim
to be proving that this authority does not exist as a specific power. This
confusion becomes even more problematic when we consider the process of
legitimation they set in train. Alchian and Demsetz reinvent by their own
means a theory of the *pact of submission* that is close to that propounded
in seventeenth-century theories of the social contract. For Pufendorf, there
was a first pact by which the citizens bound themselves together, a pact of
association or *pactum unionis* and a second pact of submission or *pactum
subjectionis*, a 'convention by which citizens submit to the authority of the
leaders they have chosen' (Robert Derathé, *Jean-Jacques Rousseau et la
science politique de son temps* (Paris: Vrin, 1974), p. 210). Our economists
are here applying to the case of the firm these two moments: firstly, cooperation, the horizontal association of the subjects forming a productive team
and then their vertical subordination to a third party, to whose authority and
monitoring they submit. The basic idea is also very traditional: it is that pure
association is just not viable. The fundamental presupposition of all the vertical conceptions of power is that association cannot hold together without
submission, that there is no viable union without subjugation. So, paradoxically, even though they set out to conceive of the firm as something other than
a relation of vertical authority, Alchian and Demsetz therefore can find no
better solution than to think of it in line with the reconstituted schema of
contractualist theories of sovereignty. What is worse for them, their theory of
the firm can even in certain aspects be qualified as 'Neo-Hobbesian' insofar
as it is based on the presupposition of an originary 'maleficence' which here,
in the guise of the shirker, renders the initial state of equality non-viable and
forces everyone to submit to an overarching police supervision. See Samuel
Bowles, 'The Production Process in a Competitive Economy: Walrasian,
Neo-Hobbesian, and Marxian Models', *The American Economic Review*,
vol. 75, no. 1, March 1985, pp. 16–36 (p. 16). Thus, they inadvertently place

on the firm an intransigeant theory of sovereignty while imagining that they are thereby demonstrating the complete opposite, namely seeing business relations as homogeneous with those of the market. This is a complete misunderstanding.

28 See Lepage, *Demain le libéralisme*, p. 357.

29 Karl Marx, *Capital*, Volume III, p. 262.

30 Ibid., p. 263. To explain this relation, Marx refers to political domination: 'Just as in despotic states, supervision and all-round interference by the government involves both the performance of common activities arising from the nature of all communities, and the specific functions arising from the antithesis between the government and the mass of the people' (p. 260). This politico-strategic dimension, of course, is not the only function of control, which also has technical aspects, but, as Marx explains, the justification for capitalist control usually relies on the elision of this first aspect and its fallacious reduction to the second. When the economist considers the capitalist mode of production, he identifies the managerial function that emerges from the nature of the process of collective labour with the managerial function determined by the capitalistic and thus antagonistic character of this process (ibid.). This is also true of Alchian and Demsetz: they reduce the contradiction to a problem between the individual and the collective (the problem of the shirker), which has a clear ideological function but weakens their theory by leaving it unable to conceptualize social antagonism – which is, after all, an urgent task when the conflict in question, as was the case at the time, becomes toxic.

31 This reformulation allowed a way out of the central postulate of Berle and Means that the 'separation' of the functions of ownership and control represented a major crisis. On the contrary, recognizing that the holders of shares are not owners, and that the functions, not of ownership and control, but of the 'residual coverage of risks' and the 'management of decision', are analytically separate represented 'a first step toward understanding that control over a firm's decisions is not necessarily the province of security holders'. Shareholders and managers both have their own function, defined independently of ownership: on the one hand, taking the risk of investing and, on the other, taking the responsibility of leading. See Fama, 'Agency Problems and the Theory of the Firm', p. 290.

32 Edward Cox, quoted in Paddy Ireland, 'Limited Liability, Shareholder Rights and the Problem of Corporate Irresponsibility', *Cambridge Journal of Economics*, vol. 34, 2010, pp. 837–56 (p. 844).

33 Adolf A. Berle, 'Modern Functions of the Corporate System', *Columbia Law Review*, vol. 62, no. 3, March 1962, pp. 433–49 (p. 446).

34 Eugene F. Fama and Michael C. Jensen, 'Separation of Ownership and Control', *The Journal of Law & Economics*, vol. 26, no. 2, June 1983, pp. 301–25 (p. 303).

35 Weinstein, 'Firm, Property and Governance', p. 44.

36 See Neil Fligstein, 'The Social Construction of Efficiency', in Mary Zey (ed.), *Decision-Making. Alternatives to Rational Choice Model* (Newbury Park, CA: Sage, 1992), pp. 351–76.

37 Irving Kristol, 'Horatio Alger and Profits', in Irving Kristol, *Two Cheers for Capitalism* (New York: Mentor, 1979; first published in 1975), pp. 79–84 (p. 79).

38 Ibid., p. 80.

39 Irving Kristol, '"When Virtue Loses All Her Loveliness" – Some Reflections on Capitalism and "The Free Society"', *The Public Interest*, no. 21, 1970, pp. 3–15 (p. 9).
40 McClaughry, 'Milton Friedman Responds', p. 16.
41 Ibid., p. 6.
42 Irving Kristol, 'The Corporation and the Dinosaur', in Kristol, *Two Cheers for Capitalism*, pp. 69–78 (p. 69).
43 Ibid., p. 71.

Notes to Chapter 14

1 1 March 1977, RTS, broadcast 'En direct avec': http://www.rts.ch/archives/tv/information/en-direct-avec/3755258-undebat-tres-vif.html.
2 D.J. Kirchhoff, 'Corporate Missionary: Those Who Believe in Capitalism Must Fight Back', *Barrons*, no. 59, 19 February 1979, p. 3.
3 Mike Muller, *The Baby Killer* (London: War on Want, 1974).
4 Charles Vrtis, 'Corporate Responsibility in Developing Countries: Focus on the Nestlé Infant Formula Case', PhD dissertation, Ball State University, Muncie, 1981, p. 17. Doctor Derrick Jelliffe, who brought these charges, spoke of 'commerciogenic malnutrition'. See Derrick B. Jelliffe, 'Commerciogenic Malnutrition?', *Nutrition Reviews*, vol. 30, no. 9, September 1972, pp. 199–205.
5 Jean-Claude Buffle, *Dossier N comme Nestlé* (Paris: Alain Moreau, 1986), p. 30.
6 *Nestlé tötet Babys: Ursachen und Folgen der Verbreitung künstlicher Säuglingsnahrung in der Dritten Welt* (Bern: Arbeitsgruppe Dritte Welt, 1974).
7 In 1977, the INFACT (Infant Formula Action Committee) was set up to call for a boycott.
8 Bryan V. Knapp, '"The Biggest Business in the World": The Nestlé Boycott and the Global Development of Infants, Nations and Economies, 1968–1988', PhD dissertation, Brown University, Providence, Rhode Island, 2015, p. 251.
9 Their first reactions were strikingly amateurish. As just one example, here is one Nestlé executive giving a statement to the senatorial commission in Washington in 1978: Oswaldo Ballarin: 'The avowed goal of this boycott is to put pressure on the Nestlé parent company in Switzerland to end allegedly negative practices of milk marketing for infants in the third world. The US Nestlé company has advised me that their research indicates this is actually an indirect attack on the free world economic system. A worldwide church organization with the stated purpose of undermining the free enterprise system is at the forefront of these activities'. Senator Kennedy: 'Now you can't seriously . . . [laughter and applause]' (quoted in Buffle, *Dossier N comme Nestlé*, p. 90).
10 Buffle, *Dossier N comme Nestlé*, p. 264. Material back-translated from Buffle's French (Translator's note).
11 Richard L. Barovick, 'Activism on a Global Scale', *Public Relations Journal*, vol. 38, June 1982, pp. 29–31 (p. 29).
12 Buffle, *Dossier N comme Nestlé*, p. 257.

13 S. Prakash Sethi, *Multinational Corporations and the Impact of Public Advocacy on Corporate Strategy; Nestlé and the Infant Formula Controversy* (New York: Kluwer Academic Publishers, 1994), p. 220.

14 Having worked for Castle & Cooke, for example, Pagan had specialized in managing the 'conflicts encountered by multinationals seeking to invest and operate in Third World countries' ('Rafael D. Pagan, 67, adviser to 5 presidents', *The Washington Times*, 5 May 1993, p. B6).

15 Pagan set up the 'Nestlé Coordination Center for Nutrition', which shared its offices with the 'Tobacco Institute'. Officially, the Center coordinated Nestlé's 'nutritional activities' in the United States. But Pagan described it more as a 'task force for crisis management' or 'an early warning system and means for analysing political threats' (Judith Richter, *Holding Corporations Accountable: Corporate Conduct, International Codes and Citizen Action* (New York: Palgrave Macmillan, 2001), p. 148). See also Steve Horn, 'Divide and Conquer: Unpacking Stratfor's Rise to Power; Part 1: The birth of the private intelligence firm's strategies for winning on the PR battlefield – for the highest bidder' (https://www.mintpressnews.com/divide-and-conquer-unpacking-stratfors-rise-to-power/165933/).

16 'Pagan International' was set up in 1985. Apart from Rafael Pagan, other people who worked there included Jack Mongoven (a former *Chicago Tribune* journalist and advisor to the Republican Party on electoral strategy) and Arion Pattakos (a former Defense Department analyst, and also a cousin – and admirer – of Stylianos Pattakos, the putschist who was Minister of the Interior in Greece under the dictatorship of the colonels). The firm went bankrupt in 1990.

17 Sethi, *Multinational Corporations*, p. 371.

18 Rafael D. Pagan, *The Future of Public Relations and the Need for Creative Understanding of the World Around Us, Presented at the 35th PRSA National Conference San Francisco Hilton, November 8, 1982*, Nestlé Coordination Center for Nutrition, Washington, DC, 1982, p. 3.

19 'The contest in which we are engaged, however, is a political one'. But 'the activists simply have done a better job in the political arena. They have allied themselves to some of the world's resentments, and have called these resentments on to battle against us'. Thus, the first task is to 'learn to think and act politically; to establish political goals; to develop political techniques and expertise; and, most important, to ally ourselves to some affirmative popular aspirations in the world' (Rafael D. Pagan, 'Carrying the Fight to the Critics of Multinational Capitalism: Think and Act Politically', *Vital Speeches of the Day*, vol. 48, no. 19, 15 July 1982, pp. 589–91 (p. 589).

20 Arion N. Pattakos, 'Growth in Activist Groups: How Can Business Cope?', *Long Range Planning*, vol. 22, no. 3, June 1989, pp. 98–104 (p. 103).

21 Douglas Johnson, *Notes on a Discussion with Jack Mangoven* [sic], *Vice-President, Nestlé Coordination for Nutrition, October 8 & 9, 1985 Sao Paulo, Brasil*, Action for Corporate Accountability Records Collection, Box 25, Minnesota Historical Society. See also Knapp, 'The Biggest Business in the World', p. 168.

22 Ibid., p. 3.

23 Jack Mongoven, quoted in Sethi, *Multinational Corporations*, p. 225.

24 Ibid.

25 Jack Mongoven, quoted in Johnson, *Notes on a Discussion*, p. 10.

26 See Richter, *Holding Corporations Accountable*, p. 196.
27 Jack Mongoven, quoted in Johnson, *Notes on a Discussion*, p. 2.
28 Buffle, *Dossier N comme Nestlé*, p. 280.
29 For Pagan, in 1982, the world of opponents was divided into two: 'fanatic activist leaders', and 'decent people'. 'Our primary goal is survival. Our secondary goal must be to separate the fanatic activist leaders [. . .] from the overwhelming majority of their followers – decent concerned people [. . .]. We must strip the activists of the moral authority they receive from their alliances with religious organizations' (Pagan, 'Carrying the Fight to the Critics of Multinational Capitalism', p. 590). His colleague Channing Riggs puts things in less black-and-white terms, but there is the same dichotomy: 'Our critics easily fell into two distinct groups. One group – the critics of conscience – was honestly concerned with the better health of babies in the Third World. [. . .] In the second critic group were the activists that we felt were more concerned with political objectives' (Channing W. Riggs, *Discours devant la Society of Consumer Affairs Professionals Toronto, Canada, 3 October 1985*, p. 2, in Tobacco Institute Records; RPCI Tobacco Institute and Council for Tobacco Research Records. https://www.industrydocument slibrary.ucsf.edu/tobacco/docs/kqjb0047). This dichotomy, which discredits both parties, also involves a theory of the useful idiot, as is apparent from this remark by Mongoven: 'The weakness and the strength of the church institutions are first and foremost that they have a conscience, and that once they know the truth, the pressure on them to act accordingly is very heavy. It is unlike a political opponent who could know the truth and forget it because he/she does not have the same pressure from his/her own conscience. But we felt that as a collective body, religious organizations would be forced to do what was right even when it was not politically advantageous and even if it meant a hardship for them. Because they are committed to doing that which is ethical, they became our best hope' (quoted in Sethi, *Multinational Corporations*, p. 229).
30 Ronald A. Duchin, 'Take an Activist Apart and What Do You Have?', *CALF News Cattle Feeder*, June 1991, pp. 8–9 and 14 and pp. 18 and 8. Duchin, a former assistant to the Defense Secretary, also had a military training. He had been one of the first members of the Delta commando of the American Army.
31 Ibid., p. 9.
32 The typical example of the opportunist, says Duchin, is Jeremy Rifkin, who may well have 'spent his whole adult life fighting corporations, capitalism and the status quo in general', but is still not a radical (Duchin, 'Take an Activist Apart', p. 9).
33 Ibid., p. 14.
34 Ibid.
35 Ibid.
36 Twenty years later, people had moved on from handouts to PowerPoint, but the same reheated meal was being sold to firms at extortionate prices. In the mass of documents from Stratfor 'leaked' by the hacker Jeremy Hammond, we find a presentation prepared in 2010 by Bart Mongoven, Jack's son, for the Suncor company, facing a movement against its works in oil sands. He used the same diagram: represented by partially overlapping coloured circles, we find the idealists, the radicals, the realists and the opportunists. For this kind of analysis – a mere recycling of the paternal doctrine – Mongoven Jr.

was paid $15,000 by the firm. See Stratfor, 'Oil sands market campaigns': https://wikileaks.org/gifiles/attach/33/33714_Suncor%20Presentation-1210. pdf.

37 Rafael D. Pagan, 'Framing the Public Agenda: The Age of New Activism', *Vital Speeches of the Day*, vol. 55, no. 6, 1 January 1989, pp. 177–80 (p. 180).

38 Buffle, *Dossier N comme Nestlé*, p. 334.

Notes to Chapter 15

1 Plato, *Gorgias* (456b), translated by W. R. M. Lamb, available online: http://www.perseus.tufts.edu/hopper/text?doc=Perseus%3Atext%3A1999.01.0178%3Atext%3DGorg.%3Apage%3D456.

2 In his preface to this collective work on the social responsibility of management, Bernays wrote: 'I hope that this book will help put an end to the social shortsightedness of those who still cannot see the reality of the actual needs in our democratic societies, currently faced by the imperious necessity of continuing to move forward while defending themselves against their enemy' – in other words, Communism and its avatars (Edward L. Bernays, 'Foreword', in Stuart Chase (ed.), *The Social Responsibility of Management* (New York: New York University, School of Commerce, Accounts, and Finance, 1950), pp. 5–7. See also Edward Bernays, *Propaganda* (Paris: Zones/La Découverte, 2007).

3 Priscilla Murphy, 'The Limits of Symmetry: A Game Theory Approach to Symmetric and Asymmetric Public Relations', in Larissa A. Grunig and James E. Grunig (eds.), *Public Relations Research Annual*, vol. 3, no. 1–4 (New York: Routledge, 1991), pp. 115–131 (p. 119).

4 See Shannon A. Bowen and Brad L. Rawlins, 'Corporate Moral Conscience', in Robert L. Heath (ed.), *Encyclopedia of Public Relations*, vol. 1 (Thousand Oaks, CA: Sage Publications, 2005), pp. 205–10 (p. 207). And, for a critical perspective: Judith Richter, *Dialogue or Engineering of Consent? Opportunities and Risks of Talking to Industry* (Geneva: International Baby Food Action Network – Geneva Infant Feeding Association, 2002), p. 2.

5 Michael L. Kent and Maureen Taylor, 'Building Dialogic Relationships through the World Wide Web', *Public Relations Review*, vol. 24, no. 3, Autumn 1998, pp. 321–34 (p. 322).

6 See Urša Golob and Klement Podnar, 'Corporate Social Responsibility Communication and Dialogue', in Øyvind Ihlen, Jennifer L. Bartlett and Steve May (eds.), *The Handbook of Communication and Corporate Social Responsibility* (Oxford: Wiley-Blackwell, 2011), pp. 231–52 (p. 236).

7 'Dialogue in public relations can be regarded as an aspect of ethical communication between an organization and its stakeholders. It is related to the notion of "symmetrical dialogue"' (Golob and Podnar, 'Corporate Social Responsibility', p. 236).

8 'The focal concept for ethical public relations is dialogue', writes Ron Pearson with reference to Habermas. See Ron Pearson, 'Business Ethics as Communication Ethics: Public Relations Practice and the Idea of Dialogue', in Carl H. Botan and Vincent Hazleton (eds.), *Public Relations Theory* (New York: Routledge, 1989), pp. 111–35 (p. 122).

9 Ron Pearson, 'Beyond Ethical Relativism in Public Relations: Coorientation, Rules, and the Idea of Communication Symmetry', in James E. Grunig and Larissa A. Grunig, *Public Relations Research Annual*, vol. 1 (New York: Routledge, 1989), pp. 67–86 (p. 71).

10 Golob and Podnar, 'Corporate Social Responsibility', p. 236.

11 Bowen and Rawlins, 'Corporate Moral Conscience', p. 207.

12 Golob and Podnar, 'Corporate Social Responsibility', p. 233 (my emphasis).

13 Friedrich Nietzsche, *On the Genealogy of Morality* (Cambridge: Cambridge University Press, 2003), p. 31.

14 S. Prakash Sethi, *Multinational Corporations and the Impact of Public Advocacy on Corporate Strategy; Nestlé and the Infant Formula Controversy* (New York: Kluwer Academic Publishers, 1994), p. 226.

15 Jean-Claude Buffle, *Dossier N comme Nestlé* (Paris: Alain Moreau, 1986), p. 310.

16 Jack Mongoven, quoted in Douglas Johnson, *Notes on a Discussion with Jack Mangoven* [sic] *Vice-President, Nestlé Coordination for Nutrition, October 8 & 9, 1985 Sao Paulo, Brasil*, Action for Corporate Accountability Records Collection, Box 25, Minnesota Historical Society, p. 1.

17 W. Howard Chase, *Issue Management: Origins of the Future* (Stamford, CA: Issue Action Publication, 1984), p. 105.

18 Ibid.

19 Stephen E. Littlejohn, 'Competition and Cooperation: New Trends in Issue Identification and Management', *California Management Review*, vol. 29, no. 1, Autumn 1986, pp. 109–23 (p. 114).

20 Sethi, *Multinational Corporations*, p. 374.

21 Henry G. Ciocca, 'The Nestlé Boycott as a Corporate Learning Experience, Speech presented to the Institute of Food Technologists, Northeast Section, March 18, 1980', quoted in Charles Vrtis, 'Corporate Responsibility in Developing Countries: Focus on the Nestlé Infant Formula Case', PhD dissertation, Ball State University, Muncie, 1981, p. 34. Any mention of the support of celebrities for the anti-Nestlé cause was also to be avoided – Ciocca mentions Jane Fonda and Vanessa Redgrave. If stars do decide to get involved, stars should always 'make attempts at dialogue and proposing positive alternatives *before* using their public stature to persuade'.

22 Douglas L. Sanders, 'Issues Management and the Participation of Large Corporations in the Public Policy Process', PhD dissertation, Claremont Graduate University, Claremont, 1998, p. 5.

23 Knapp, 'The Biggest Business in the World', p. 205. 'If private conflicts are brought into the public arena', notes Schattschneider, this is generally so that private interests will not prevail, but will be balanced by a general interpellation. Conversely, 'if the most powerful particular interests seek private resolutions, this is because they are then in a position to dictate the result' (Elmer E. Schattschneider, *The Semi-Sovereign People* (New York: Holt, Rinehart and Winston, 1964; first published in 1960), p. 40).

24 Montesquieu, *De l'esprit des lois*, Book 1 (Paris: Garnier, 1962), p. 62.

25 Pagan International, *Shell U.S. South Africa Strategy, Prepared for The Shell Oil Company*, Washington, DC, [1987], section 'Religious group strategy', p. 3. This document is in the Archives du Conseil oecuménique des Églises, in Geneva.

26 Pagan International, *Shell U.S. South Africa Strategy*, p. 2.

27 Judith Richter, 'International Regulation of Transnational Corporations: The Infant Food Debate', PhD dissertation, Amsterdam School of Communication Research, Amsterdam, 2001, p. 135.

28 Bart Montgoven, 'Re: CLIMATE – Canadian group condemns TckTckTck, Hopenhagen as greenwasher, fraud; accuses allies GP, NRDC, Oxfam, etc.', email of 13 January 2010, https://wikileaks.org/gifiles/docs/40/409761_reclimate-canadian-group-condemnstcktcktck-hopenhagen-as.html. NGO reformists playing that particular game hoped to flip the relationship of co-optation. 'If an NGO wants to flip this, it offers the green seal of approval to a corporation that is realistic in opposition to notion that there is a problem. The louder the corporation (Coke, Nike, Dell) the better. The company gets the power of the deal, the glory of the reputation and ideally profits. It also cracks the "corporate" position on an issue and denying a problem become far less tenable when a big loud company has accepted that a problem exists. [. . .] Once the block is broken [. . .] the blanket denial that there is a problem looks silly [. . .]. The debate is no longer about whether there's a problem but about what the correct resolution is'.

29 Rafael D. Pagan, 'Carrying the Fight to the Critics of Multinational Capitalism: Think and Act Politically', *Vital Speeches of the Day*, vol. 48, no. 19, 15 July 1982, pp. 589–91 (p. 590).

30 'We tried to take the concept of lobbying – in its old British parliamentary sense of persuasion – and apply it to working with groups and organizations'. The aim was '[. . .] to see consumer groups and other organizations in society as real entities which need to be lobbied or persuaded about our point of view' (Jack Mongoven, quoted in Johnson, *Notes on a Discussion*, p. 1.

31 It was a matter of 'inviting carefully selected influential groups and critics to participate in consensus-oriented "dialogues" or to engage in "partnerships" [. . .] while discrediting groups which do not participate as incorrigible "radicals" who are "confrontational" for the sake of it' (Richter, *International Regulation of Transnational Corporations*, p. 126).

32 Richter, *Dialogue or Engineering of Consent?*, p. 15.

33 This process consists in becoming 'identified with symbols, values or institutions which have a strong social base of legitimacy' (John Dowling and Jeffrey Pfeffer, 'Organizational Legitimacy: Social Values and Organizational Behavior', *The Pacific Sociological Review*, vol. 18, no. 1, January 1975, pp. 122–36 (p. 127).

34 Sanders, 'Issues Management', p. 326. 'One way of successfully countering activist pressure involves a company mobilizing its own activists. Take, for example, a pharmaceutical company faced with activists who object to using recombinant DNA techniques [. . .]. Why not get the American Cancer Society involved? Have a cancer victim testify before the appropriate government agencies, "My only hope of living another five years is if these guys find a cure." [. . .] There are people that you can motivate on your side to offset the grassroots support on the other side' (Jack Mongoven, quoted in Ronald Bailey, 'Greenbusters', *Chief Executive*, no. 60, 1990, pp. 37–9 (p. 39). So it is possible to create artificially your own home-made 'supports', or even 'opponents' – the kind of tactic known as 'astroturf'. See John Stauber, Sheldon Rampton and Mark Dowie, *Toxic Sludge is Good for You: Lies, Damn Lies, and the Public Relations Industry* (Monroe, ME: Common Courage Press, 1995), p. 89. One example of this procedure was the establishment, in 1987,

of the 'Coalition on South Africa' (COSA), a puppet collective dreamt up by Pagan to weaken the support of the American churches for the boycotting of South Africa, and financed to the tune of over a million dollars by multi-nationals implanted in the country, including Mobil Oil, Johnson & Johnson and Caltex Petroleum. The employers of the nineteenth century invented the yellow trade unions, those of the twentieth, the yellow NGOs. See Ronen Shamir, 'The De-Radicalization of Corporate Social Responsibility', *Critical Sociology*, vol. 30, no. 3, 2004, pp. 669–90 (p. 671).

35 Robert L. Heath, 'A Rhetorical Approach to Issues Management', in Carl Botan and Vincent Hazleton (eds.), *Public Relations Theory*, vol. 2 (New York: Lawrence Erlbaum Associates, 2006), pp. 55–87 (p. 61).

36 Robert L. Heath, 'Issues Management', in Robert L. Heath (ed.), *Encyclopedia of Public Relations*, vol. 1 (Thousand Oaks, CA: Sage Publications, 2005), pp. 460–3 (p. 461).

Notes to Chapter 16

1 André Gorz, *Misère du présent, richesse du possible* (Paris: Galilée, 1997), p. 29.

2 Quoted in Arion N. Pattakos, 'Growth in Activist Groups: How Can Business Cope?', *Long Range Planning*, vol. 22, no. 3, June 1989, pp. 98–104 (p. 98).

3 S. Prakash Sethi, 'Corporate Political Activism', *California Management Review*, Spring 1982, vol. 24, no. 3, pp. 32–42 (p. 32).

4 W. Howard Chase, *Issue Management: Origins of the Future* (Stamford, CA: Issue Action Publication, 1984), p. 13.

5 Barrie L. Jones and W. Howard Chase, 'Managing Public Policy Issues', *Public Relations Review*, vol. 5, no. 2, 1979, pp. 3–23 (p. 7).

6 Quoted in Jones and Chase, 'Managing Public Policy Issues', p. 9.

7 The authors silently took this from the management theorist S. Prakash Sethi's *Business and Society: Dimensions of Conflict and Cooperation* (Lexington, MA: Lexington Books, 1987), p. 344.

8 S. Prakash Sethi, *Multinational Corporations and the Impact of Public Advocacy on Corporate Strategy; Nestlé and the Infant Formula Controversy* (New York: Kluwer Academic Publishers, 1994), p. 373.

9 Richard E. Crable and Steven L. Vibbert, 'Managing Issues and Influencing Public Policy', *Public Relations Review*, vol. 11, no. 2, Summer 1985, pp. 3–16 (p. 10).

10 Ibid.

11 Sanders, 'Issues Management', p. 26.

12 Sethi, *Multinational Corporations*, p. 334.

13 S. Prakash Sethi, 'A Strategic Framework for Dealing with the Schism between Business and Academe', in S. Prakash Sethi and Cecilia M. Falbe (eds.), *Business and Society: Dimensions of Conflict and Cooperation* (Lexington, MA: Lexington Books, 1987), pp. 331–52 (p. 333). More generally, 'Another key element in the overall strategy is the formation of alliances with [. . .] government, academic, religious and the media. All too often it happens that industry will look to one of those disciplines for help or advice in a crisis without first having laid the foundation for a permanent relationship' (Charles Vrtis, 'Corporate Responsibility in Developing Countries: Focus

on the Nestlé Infant Formula Case', PhD dissertation, Ball State University, Muncie, 1981, p. 33). If these alliances are set up well in advance, in times of calm, they will be solid and will protect the business in stormy times. That way, the firm will build up a stock of strategic resources that will, the day it faces a crisis, allow it to have a bit of 'slack' (Sethi, 'A Strategic Framework', p. 375). So the aim is to accumulate credibility, trust and reputation as a preventive measure – a whole safety net of resources that will deaden any shocks and 'resist demand for change' (Sethi, 'A Strategic Framework', p. 376). In the case of the Nestlé boycott, the polemics over the substitute for mother's milk had started in the medical world, and this had been the main milieu that needed to be won back. Pagan had set up a strategy of 'manipulation through assistance', which consisted in handing out money to researchers to gain their goodwill. See Jean-Claude Buffle, *Dossier N comme Nestlé* (Paris: Alain Moreau, 1986), p. 30.

14 See Naomi Oreskes and Erik M. Conway, *Merchants of Doubt: How a Handful of Scientists Obscured the Truth on Issues from Tobacco Smoke to Global Warming* (New York: Bloomsbury Press, 2010).

15 As Pagan wrote, 'A business choosing to remain in South Africa can lose its legitimacy fast in such a climate if it allows a unilateral definition of reality' (Rafael D. Pagan, 'Framing the Public Agenda: The Age of New Activism', *Vital Speeches of the Day*, vol. 55, no. 6, 1 January 1989, pp. 177–80 [p. 179]).

16 Peter Ludlow, 'The Real War on Reality', *New York Times*, 14 June 2013. Available at: https://opinionator.blogs.nytimes.com/2013/06/14/the-real-war-on-reality/. A note that Jack Mongoven wrote for a group of chlorine manufacturers faced with a Greenpeace campaign will help explain the tenor of this kind of 'psychological operation' launched on the battlefield of truth: 'activists are also using children and their need for protection to compel stricter regulation of toxic substances. This tactic is very effective because children-based appeals touch the public's protective nature for a vulnerable group'. Given that, 'for most substances, the tolerances of babies and children, which includes fetal development, are obviously much lower than in the general adult population', it was clear that '"environmental policies based on health standards that address the special needs of children" would reduce all exposure standards to the lowest possible levels'. How to counter this threat? Mongoven advised, inter alia, creating a 'panel of eminent physicians and inviting them to review data regarding chlorine as a health risk and as a key chemical in pharmaceuticals and medical devices', and stimulating 'peer-reviewed articles for publication in the *[Journal of the American Medical Association]* on the role of chlorine chemistry in treating disease'. He added that it was necessary to 'take steps to discredit the precautionary principle within the more moderate environmental groups as well as within the scientific and medical communities' (Mongoven, quoted in Sheldon Hampton and John Stauber, *Trust Us, We're Experts!* (New York: Putnam, 2001), pp. 146ff. and p. 135).

17 Sethi, *Multinational Corporations*, p. 373.

18 Ibid., p. 376.

19 Ibid.

20 Pattakos, 'Growth in Activist Groups: How Can Business Cope?', p. 98.

21 See Margaret A. Stroup, 'Environmental Scanning at Monsanto', *Planning Review*, vol. 16, no. 4, July/August 1988, pp. 24–7.

22 Christopher Palmer, 'Business and Environmentalists: A Peace Proposal', *Washington Post*, 8 August 1982.
23 Louis Fernandez, 'Business Isn't Perfect Either', *Washington Post*, 14 September 1982.
24 For a contemporary example, see Macdonald Stainsby and Dru Oja Jay, *Offsetting Resistance: The Effects of Foundation Funding and Corporate Fronts from the Great Bear Rainforest to the Athabasca River*, http://www. offsettingresistance.ca/
25 Sanders, 'Issues Management', p. 170.
26 Louis Fernandez, quoted in Stephen E. Littlejohn, 'Competition and Cooperation', p. 122.
27 Ibid., p. 113.
28 S. Prakasah Sethi, 'Dimensions of Corporate Social Performance, An Analytical Framework', *California Management Review*, vol. 17, no. 3, Spring 1975, pp. 58–64 (p. 60).
29 Sanders, 'Issues Management', p. 307.

Notes to Chapter 17

1 'Curiosités de l'Angleterre', *L'Illustration*, vol. 15, no. 367, 9 March 1850, pp. 151–4 (p. 153).
2 By extension, the term designates 'A third person, chosen by two or more persons, to keep in deposit property, the right or possession of which is contested between them and to be delivered to the one who shall establish his right to it', or 'a person having in his hands money or other property claimed by several others' (entry on 'Stakeholder', in John Bouvier, *A Law Dictionary*, vol. 2 (Philadelphia, PA: Johnson, 1843), p. 524).
3 Robert F. Stewart, J. Knight Allen and J. Morse Cavender, *The Strategic Plan, Research Report no. 168*, Long Range Planning Service, Stanford Research Institute, Menlo Park, April 1963. Quoted in R. Edward Freeman, *Strategic Management: A Stakeholder Approach* (Boston, MA: Pitman, 1984), pp. 31 and 49. See also R. Edward Freeman, Jeffrey S. Harrison, Andrew C. Wicks, Bidhan Parmar and Simone de Colle (eds.), *Stakeholder Theory: The State of the Art* (Cambridge: Cambridge University Press, 2010), p. 47.
4 In the early 1960s, Richard Cyert and James March had proposed a theory of 'participants': 'there is a set of potential participants in the firm [. . .] investors (stockholders), suppliers, customers, governmental agents, and various types of employees', not to mention the 'actual or potential participants' such as 'investment analysts, trade associations, political parties, and labor unions' (James G. March, 'The Business Firm as a Political Coalition', *The Journal of Politics*, vol. 24, no. 4, November 1962, pp. 662–78 (pp. 673, 663 and 672). On this view, commented Igor Ansoff in 1965, 'the objectives of the firm should be derived from balancing the conflicting claims of the various "stakeholders" in the firm' (H. Igor Ansoff, *Corporate Strategy: An Analytic Approach to Business Policy for Growth and Expansion* (New York: McGraw-Hill, 1965), p. 34. If indeed the firm views itself as a 'system of socio-political conflict', as a 'political coalition' torn between the diverging interests of many groups, the organization's aims, far from being already set in advance, are the object of endless negotiations between a multitude of 'actual

or potential participants'. See also Russell Lincoln Ackoff, *Redesigning the Future: A Systems Approach to Societal Problems* (New York: Wiley, 1974), p. 62.

5 Eric Rhenman, *Företagsdemokrati och företagsorganisation* (Stockholm: Norstedts, 1964. English translation: Eric Rhenman, *Industrial Democracy and Industrial Management: A Critical Essay on the Possible Meanings and Implications of Industrial Democracy* (London: Tavistock, 1968), p. 25.

6 Göran Therborn, 'Herr Rhenmans omvälvning av vetenskapen', in Göran Therborn (ed.), *En ny vänster* (Stockholm: Rabén & Sjögren, 1966), pp. 169–79 (p. 169).

7 William R. Dill, 'Public Participation in Corporate Planning: Strategic Management in a Kibitzer's World', *Long Range Planning*, vol. 8, no. 1, February 1975, pp. 57–63 (p. 58).

8 By insisting on the hostility of the relationship, comments Freeman, 'Dill set the stage for the use of the stakeholder concept as an umbrella for strategic management' (Freeman, *Strategic Management*, p. 39).

9 Ackoff, *Redesigning the Future*, p. 18.

10 Dill, 'Public Participation', p. 63.

11 In the late 1970s, Freeman took part in a 'stakeholder project' newly set up at the Wharton School, with the explicit aim of developing 'a theory of management which enabled executives to formulate and implement corporate strategy in turbulent environments' (R. Edward Freeman and David L. Reed, 'Stockholders and Stakeholders: A New Perspective on Corporate Governance', *California Management Review*, vol. 25, no. 3, Spring 1983, pp. 88–106 [p. 91]).

12 Ram Charan and R. Edward Freeman, 'Planning for the Business Environment of the 1980s', *Journal of Business Strategy*, vol. 1, no. 2, 1980, pp. 9–19 (pp. 11ff.).

13 Charan and Freeman, 'Planning', p. 10.

14 Freeman, *Strategic Management*, p. 5.

15 Ibid., p. 12.

16 Ibid., p. 24.

17 Ibid., p. 25.

18 Carl Schmitt, *La Notion de politique* (Paris: Flammarion, 1992), p. 117. Thanks to Ivan Segré for bringing this passage to my attention.

19 Ibid.

20 Ibid., p. 116.

21 Thomas M. Jones, 'Instrumental Stakeholder Theory: A Synthesis of Ethics and Economics', *The Academy of Management Review*, vol. 20, no. 2, April, 1995, pp. 404–37 (p. 407).

22 Max B.E. Clarkson, 'A Risk Based Model of Stakeholder Theory', *Proceedings of the Second Toronto Conference on Stakeholder Theory*, University of Toronto, 1994, p. 5, quoted in Ronald K. Mitchell, Bradley R. Agle and Donna J. Wood, 'Toward a Theory of Stakeholder Identification and Salience: Defining the Principle of Who and What Really Counts', *The Academy of Management Review*, vol. 22, no. 4, 1997, pp. 853–86 (p. 856).

23 Kenneth E. Goodpaster, 'Business Ethics and Stakeholder Analysis', *Business Ethics Quarterly*, vol. 1, no. 1, January 1991, pp. 53–73 (p. 63).

24 William M. Evan and R. Edward Freeman, 'A Stakeholder Theory of the Modern Corporation: Kantian Capitalism', in Tom L. Beauchamp and

Norman E. Bowie (eds.), *Ethical Theory and Business* (Englewood Cliffs, NJ: Prentice Hall, 1993), pp. 75–84 (p. 82). See also Norman P. Barry, 'The Stakeholder Concept of Corporate Control is Illogical and Impractical', *Independent Review*, vol. 6, no. 4, Spring 2002, pp. 541–54 (p. 550).

25 See Freeman et al. (eds.), *Stakeholder Theory*, p. 268. For a critique of these approaches, see Paddy Ireland, 'Corporate Governance, Stakeholding and the Company: Towards a Less Degenerate Capitalism?', *Journal of Law & Society*, vol. 23, no. 3, September 1996, pp. 287–320.

26 Michael C. Jensen, 'Value Maximization, Stakeholder Theory, and the Corporate Objective Function', *Business Ethics Quarterly*, vol. 12, no. 2, April 2002, pp. 235–56 (p. 236).

27 Ibid., p. 243.

28 Elaine Sternberg, 'The Need for Realism in Business Ethics', *Reason Paper – A Journal of Interdisciplinary Normative Studies*, vol. 31, Autumn 2009, pp. 33–48 (p. 40).

29 William Beaver, 'Is the Stakeholder Model Dead?', *Business Horizons*, vol. 42 no. 3, March/April 1999, pp. 8–12 (p. 8).

30 Ibid., p. 11. According to Englander and Kaufman, in the mid-1980s the directors of major companies no longer needed to cling to their old managerialist ideology of social responsibility: 'The manager for the new millennium was not an impartial technocrat, but a shareholder partisan. [. . .] For managers to abandon their old technocratic perspective, they had to find shareholder ideology congruent with their interests. Corporate and executive compensation reform brought manager's interests into alignment with agency theory'. At the end of this process, in the early 2000s, the value of the stock options given to the CEOs of big American businesses represented on average 636 per cent of their salary. It was the 'end of managerial ideology'. In 2001, Hansmann and Kraakman likewise concluded that the standard shareholding model had managed to ensure its 'ideological hegemony' (Ernie Englander and Allen Kaufman, 'The End of Managerial Ideology: From Corporate Social Responsibility to Corporate Social Indifference', *Enterprise & Society*, vol. 5, no. 3, September 2004, pp. 404–50 [p. 428]); see also Henry Hansmann and Reinier Kraakman, 'The End of History for Corporate Law', *Georgetown Law Journal*, vol. 89, no. 2, January 2001, p. 439 (p. 468).

31 Norman Barry, 'The Stakeholder Fallacy', Foundation for Economic Education, 2000, https://fee.org/articles/the-stakeholder-fallacy/

32 Freeman et al. (eds.), *Stakeholder Theory*, p. 54.

33 See Freeman and Reed, 'Stockholders and Stakeholders', p. 91.

34 We discover that you need not just to 'manage people in organisations' but also 'manage the organisation's relations with other organisations' (Jeffrey Pfeffer, 'Beyond Management and the Worker: The Institutional Function of Management', *The Academy of Management Review*, vol. 1, no. 2, April 1976, pp. 36–46 [p. 36].) But as Marina Welker suggests, what is more fundamentally at stake is the very distinction between an inside and an outside: 'the question of boundaries lies at the very heart of the issue; stakeholders of different kinds effectively alter the boundary between business and society'. Initially, management feels swamped by groups of outsiders: 'corporations are being "polluted" by society as never before'. In reaction, it realizes that it has to learn to foresee the threat. 'The normative operational task is to

know ex ante who these stakeholders might be and this requires a broader view of the potential boundaries of a business or project'. So there is a second, expansionist movement in which management strategically includes the firm's social environment in its objects of vigilance and intervention. This extension can be read as 'the internalization of previously external relations', but the reconfiguration of managerial power has taken up other aspects in parallel, including the 'externalization of previously internal relations, i.e., by creating chains of suppliers and customers within the production process itself'. As Marina Welker comments: 'Boundary reconfiguring involves both an internalization of what is external (e.g. customer demands, the competitor for benchmarking purposes) and an externalization of what is internal (e.g. the imposition of values, priorities, and standards on entire supply chains)' (Marina Welker, *Enacting the Corporation: An American Mining Firm in Post-Authoritarian Indonesia* (Berkeley, CA: University of California Press, 2014), p. 58). See also Michael Power, 'Corporate Responsibility and Risk Management', in Richard V. Ericson and Aaron Doyle (eds.), *Risk and Morality* (Toronto: University of Toronto Press, 2003), pp. 145–64 (pp. 152ff.).

35 William Van Dusen Wishard, 'Corporate Response to a New Environment', *Law and Contemporary Problems*, vol. 41, no. 3, Summer 1977, pp. 222–44 (p. 239).

36 As Michael Power explains, 'The concept of "stakeholder" is attractive precisely because of its morally ambivalent mixture of strategic and ethical meaning, and the pragmatic bridge it promises between managerial and CSR agendas' (Power, 'Corporate Responsibility', p. 152).

37 Mitchell, Agle and Wood, 'Toward a Theory of Stakeholder Identification and Salience', p. 877.

38 Ibid., p. 878.

39 Subhabrata Bobby Banerjee, 'Corporate Citizenship, Social Responsibility and Sustainability: Corporate Colonialism for the New Millennium?', in Jan Jonker and Marco de Witte, *The Challenge of Organizing and Implementing Corporate Social Responsibility* (New York: Palgrave Macmillan, 2006), pp. 31–50 (p. 41).

40 Mitchell, Agle and Wood, 'Toward a Theory', p. 880 (my emphasis).

41 Malcolm X, *Le Pouvoir noir* (Paris: Maspero, 1966), p. 201.

42 Freeman and Reed, 'Stockholders and Stakeholders', p. 96.

43 Conference on 'Media & Stakeholder Relations: Hydraulic Fracturing Initiative 2011', Houston, 31 October–1 November 2011. I have transcribed the passages quoted below from audio recordings of the conference, initially published on the website http://www.media-stakeholder-relations-hydraulic-fracturing.com/ (site no longer active). See also: Steve Horn, 'Fracking and Psychological Operations: Empire Comes Home', *Truthout*, 8 March 2012: https://truthout.org/articles/fracking-and-psychological-operations-empire-comes-home/, and Brendan DeMelle, 'Gas Fracking Industry Using Military Psychological Warfare Tactics and Personnel in U.S. Communities', 11 September 2011, https://www.desmogblog.com/gas-fracking-industry-using-military-psychological-warfare-tactics-and-personnel-u-s-communities.

44 See Horn, 'Fracking and Psychological Operations'.

Notes to Chapter 18

1 Georges Scelle, *Manuel de droit international public* (Paris: Domat-Montchrestien, 1948), p. 6.
2 Peter F. Drucker, 'Multinationals and Developing Countries: Myths and Realities', *Foreign Affairs*, vol. 53, no. 1, October 1974, pp. 121–34 (p. 1 33).
3 Some people then started to envisage 'public-institutional' solutions for the problems posed by the internationalization of production. See Kees van der Pijl, 'The Sovereignty of Capital Impaired: Social Forces and Codes of Conduct for Multinational Corporations', in Henk Overbeek (ed.), *Restructuring Hegemony in the Global Political Economy: The Rise of Transnational Neo-Liberalism in the 1980s* (New York: Routledge, 2002, pp. 28–57 (p. 31).
4 Quoted in Francesco Petrini, 'Capital Hits the Road. Regulating Multinational Corporations During the Long 1970s', in Knud Andresen and Stefan Müller (eds.), *Contesting Deregulation: Debates, Practices and Developments in the West since the 1970s* (New York: Berghahn Books, 2017), pp. 185–98 (p. 188).
5 Department of Economic and Social Affairs, *Summary of the Hearings Before the Group of Eminent Persons*, UN, New York, 1974, pp. 149–50. See Khalil Hamdani and Lorraine Ruffing, *United Nations Centre on Transnational Corporations: Corporate Conduct and the Public Interest* (New York: Routledge, 2015), p. 80.
6 *Multinational Corporations, Hearings before the Subcommittee on International Trade of the Committee on Finance, United States Senate Ninety-Third Congress, First Session, February 26, 27, 28; and March 1 and 6*, US Government Printing Office, Washington, DC, 1973, p. 229.
7 Raymond Vernon, 'The Multinational Enterprise: Power versus Sovereignty', *Foreign Affairs*, vol. 49, no. 4, July 1971, pp. 736–51 (p. 743).
8 John F. Lyons, 'Multinationals: Reaching the Outer Limits?', *Financial World*, 17 October 1973, p. 39.
9 The corresponding resolution affirmed the principle of a 'full permanent sovereignty of every state over its natural resources' and envisaged the supervision of foreign investment by the subsequent drawing up of two codes of conduct, one providing for technology transfers to developing countries, the other prohibiting, inter alia, the interference of multinationals 'in the internal affairs of the countries where they operate and their collaboration with racist regimes and colonial administrations'. See 'General Assembly Declaration on the Establishment of a New International Economic Order', *The American Journal of International Law*, vol. 68, no. 4, October 1974, pp. 798–801 (p. 799).
10 David Rockefeller, 'Multinationals Under Siege: A Threat to the World Economy', in *Congressional Record, 94th Congress, 1st Session*, vol. 121, section 14, 6 June 1975–13 June 1975 (Washington, DC: Government Printing Office, pp. 18323–6 [p. 18323]).
11 Ibid., p. 18326.
12 Drucker, 'Multinationals and Developing Countries', p. 133.
13 Roger A. Brooks, 'Multinationals: First Victim of the UN War on Free

Enterprise', *The Backgrounder* (Washington, DC: The Heritage Foundation, 16 November 1982), p. 5.

14 Ibid., p. 9.

15 Jeanne J. Kirkpatrick, 'Global Paternalism: The UN and the New International Regulatory Order', *Regulation*, vol. 7, no. 1, January/February 1983, pp. 17–22 (p. 21).

16 Ibid., p. 18.

17 Ibid., p. 22.

18 Paul Adler, 'Planetary Citizens: U.S. NGOs and The Politics of International Development in the Late Twentieth Century', PhD dissertation, Georgetown University, Washington, DC, 2014, p. 126.

19 Ibid.

20 Rafael D. Pagan, 'The Politicalization of Institutions: The Responsibilities of Multinational Corporations', *Vital Speeches of the Day*, vol. 50, no. 1, 15 October 1983, pp. 25–7 (p. 25).

21 René-Jean Dupuy, 'Droit déclaratoire et droit programmatoire de la coutume sauvage à la "soft law"', in Société française pour le droit international, *L'Élaboration du droit international public* (Paris: Pedone, 1975), pp. 132–48 (p. 145).

22 Ibid., p. 135.

23 Ignaz Seidl-Hohenveldern, 'International Economic "Soft Law"', in *Recueil des cours de l'Académie de droit international*, vol. 163, Nijhoff, La Haye 1979, pp. 165–246 (p. 194).

24 Ibid., p. 195.

25 Ibid., p. 197.

26 Ibid., p. 197.

27 John Robinson, quoted in James K. Rowe, 'Corporate Social Responsibility as Business Strategy', in Ronnie D. Lipschutz and James K. Rowe, *Globalization, Governmentality and Global Politics* (New York: Routledge, 2005), pp. 122–60 (p. 128).

28 John M. Kline, *International Codes and Multinational Business: Setting Guidelines for International Business Operations* (Westport, CT: Quorum Books, 1985), p. 46.

29 Seidl-Hohenveldern, 'International Economic "Soft Law"', p. 197.

30 John Robinson, *Multinationals and Political Control* (Aldershot: Gower, 1983), p. 151.

31 Quoted in Francesco Petrini, 'Capital Hits the Road. Regulating Multinational Corporations During the Long 1970s' (draft version), workshop on 'Changes in Social Regulations – State, Economy, and Social Actors since the 1970s', Hans-Böckler-Stiftung, Düsseldorf, 8–9 June 2012, p. 6. http://www.acad emia.edu/1551027/Capital_hits_the_road_regulating_multinational_corpor ations_during_the_long_1970s.

32 Kline, *International Codes and Multinational Business*, p. 29.

33 Francesco Petrini, 'Capital Hits the Road. Regulating Multinational Corporations During the Long 1970s', in Andresen and Müller (eds.), *Contesting Deregulation*, p. 4.

34 *The Multinationals: Their Function and Future, Report on the Sixth Meeting of Members of Congress and of The European Parliament, December 1974* (Washington, DC: US Government Printing Office, 1975), p. 124.

35 Raymond Vernon, 'Future of the Multinational Enterprise', in Charles P.

Kindleberger (ed.), *The International Corporation* (Cambridge, MA: MIT Press, 1970), pp. 373–400 (pp. 394ff.).

36 Ethics Resource Center, *A Quest for Excellence, Appendix, Final Report by The President's Blue Ribbon Commission on Defense Management*, Washington, June 1986, p. 271.

37 Jacques Maisonrouge, quoted in Edward Collins Bursk and Gene E. Bradley, *Top Management Report on Corporate Citizenship: Outstanding Examples Worldwide* (Washington, DC: International Management and Development Institute, 1979), p. 124.

38 Prosper Weil, *Le Droit international en quête de son identité, recueil des cours de l'Académie de droit international*, vol. 237, 1992–6 (The Hague: Nijhoff, 1996), p. 91.

39 César A. Rodriguez-Garavito, 'Nike's Law: The Anti-Sweatshop Movement, Transnational Legal Mobilization, and the Struggle over International Labor Rights in the Americas', in Boaventura de Sousa Santos and César A. Rodriguez-Garavito (eds.), *Law and Globalization from Below: Towards a Cosmopolitan Legality* (Cambridge: Cambridge University Press, 2005), pp. 64–91 (p. 77).

40 Rowe, 'Corporate Social Responsibility as Business Strategy', p. 155.

41 Kline, *International Codes and Multinational Business*, p. 161.

42 David Cameron, 'Speech to Business in the Community', 10 May 2006, reported in the *Financial Times*, https://www.ft.com/content/5f394dcc-e04a-11da-9e82-0000779e2340. See also Daniel Kinderman, '"Free us Up so We can be Responsible!": The Co-evolution of Corporate Social Responsibility and Neoliberalism in the UK, 1977–2010', *Socio-economic Review*, vol. 10, no. 1, 2012, pp. 29–57 (p. 47).

Notes to Chapter 19

1 Friedrich Nietzsche, *The Twilight of the Idols*, translated by Anthony M. Ludovici, available online: https://www.gutenberg.org/files/52263/52263-h/52263-h.htm.

2 See Patrick J. Akard, 'The Return of the Market: Corporate Mobilization and the Transformation of U.S. Economic Policy, 1974–1984', PhD dissertation, University of Kansas, 1989, p. 35. See also David Vogel, 'The Power of Business in America: A Re-Appraisal', *British Journal of Political Science*, vol. 13, no. 1, January 1983, pp. 19–43 (p. 23). The decisive role played by consumer movements is often emphasized as an explanation for this surge in regulation. It was indeed real enough, but we should not forget that one of the first regulations of this type was extracted by the civil rights movement, on the question of racial discrimination in hiring, with the creation of the Equal Employment Opportunity Commission (EEOC) by the Civil Rights Act of 1964.

3 Bartley, 'Business and the New Class', p. 58.

4 See Michael Useem, *The Inner Circle: Large Corporation and the Rise of Business Political Activity in the U.S. and U.K.* (New York: Oxford University Press, 1984), p. 160; David Vogel, *Fluctuating Fortunes: The Political Power of Business in America* (New York: Basic Books, 1989), p. 201; Alejandro Reuss, 'Capitalist Crisis and Capitalist Reaction: The Profit Squeeze, the

Business Roundtable, and the Capitalist Class Mobilization of the 1970s', PhD dissertation, University of Massachusetts, Amherst, 2013, p. 70.

5 David Rockefeller, 'The Role of Business in an Era of Growing Accountability', reprinted in *Congressional Record*, Vol. 117/36, 13 December 1971–17 December 1971, US Government Printing Office, 1972, pp. 47615–16 (p. 47616).

6 As Bartley notes with regret, 'the most important handicap is business' inability to unite in defending its class interests. Macy's does not think it is locked in competition with the New Class – it thinks the enemy is Gimbels' (Bartley, 'Business and the New Class', p. 65; Macy's and Gimbels were two rival chain stores).

7 Reuss, *Capitalist Crisis and Capitalist Reaction*, p. 60. See also Akard, *The Return of the Market*, p. 13.

8 Thomas R. Shepard, 'The Disaster Lobby', Illinois Manufacturer's Association, Chicago, April 1971, p. 1. See also Melvin J. Grayson and Thomas R. Shepard, *The Disaster Lobby: Prophets of Ecological Doom and Other Absurdities* (Chicago, IL: Follett Publishing Company, 1973).

9 Shepard, 'The Disaster Lobby', p. 2.

10 Ibid., p. 3.

11 Ibid., p. 6.

12 Murray L. Weidenbaum, 'The New Wave of Government Regulation of Business', *Business and Society Review*, no. 15, Autumn 1975, pp. 81–6 (p. 81).

13 Ibid. Kim Moody notes that the ideology of American management – based on the 'freedom to control', closely attached to the defence of its prerogatives, and hostile both to government 'interference' and to the whims of the internal democratization of businesses – is rooted in the specific history of capitalism in the United States where, unlike in Europe, a continent where strong states preceded the emergence of big companies, the development of huge business concerns (from railroads to steelworks) preceded the emergence of a strong central state. Kim Moody, 'Beating the Union: Union Avoidance in the US', in Gregor Gall and Tony Dundon (eds.), *Global Anti-Unionism: Nature, Dynamics, Trajectories and Outcomes* (London: Palgrave Macmillan, 2013), pp. 143–62 (p. 145). In the United States, wrote Gramsci, 'hegemony [. . .] is born in the factory' (Antonio Gramsci, *Selections from the Prison Notebooks*, edited and translated by Quentin Hoare and Geoffrey Nowell Smith (London: Lawrence & Wishart, 1971), p. 571).

14 Weidenbaum, quoted in Phillips-Fein, *Invisible Hands*, p. 176.

15 Weidenbaum, 'The New Wave of Government Regulation', p. 85.

16 See Murray L. Weidenbaum, 'The Changing Nature of Government Regulation of Business', *Journal of Post Keynesian Economics*, vol. 2, no. 3, Spring 1980, pp. 345–57 (p. 354).

17 See Nicos Poulantzas (ed.), *La Crise de l'État* (Paris: PUF, 1976).

18 A process of the transfer of control that would lead to 'the destruction of the corporation as we know it' (Michael C. Jensen and William H. Meckling, 'Corporate Governance and "Economic Democracy": An Attack on Freedom', in C. J. Huizenga (ed.), *Corporate Governance: A Definite Exploration of the Issues*, Harvard Business School NOM Unit Working Paper no. 1983, http://papers.ssrn.com/abstract=321521, pp. 1–23 [p. 5]).

19 Vogel, 'The Power of Business in America: A Re-Appraisal', p. 36. See also

Andrew Szasz, 'The Reversal of Federal Policy toward Worker Safety and Health', *Science & Society*, vol. 50, no. 1, Spring 1986, pp. 25–51.

20 This is why David Vogel concludes that the struggle over the question of government regulation was for the first time in American history placed at the heart of class struggle, setting business interests against public interest and most workers' organizations (David Vogel, 'The Power of Business in America', p. 36).

21 Regulations raised a 'hidden tax on sales' (Murray L. Weidenbaum, 'Benefit-Cost Analysis of Government Regulation', in *Use of Cost-Benefit Analysis by Regulatory Agencies. Joint hearings before the Subcommittee on Oversight and Investigations and the Subcommittee on Consumer Protection and Finance of the Committee on Interstate and Foreign Commerce, House of Representatives, Ninety-sixth Congress, first session, July 30, October 10, and 24, 1979* (Washington, DC: US Government Printing Office, 1980), pp. 337–53 (p. 351).

22 Murray Weidenbaum, 'The High Cost of Government Regulation', *Business Horizons*, vol. 18, no. 4, August 1975, pp. 43–51 (p. 46).

23 Ibid., p. 51.

24 Ibid., p. 44.

25 Phillips-Fein, *Invisible Hands*, p. 176.

26 See François Cusset, *La Décennie: le grand cauchemar des années 1980* (Paris: La Découverte, 2006), p. 92.

27 Weidenbaum, 'The High Cost of Government Regulation', p. 51.

28 See Steven Kelman, 'Cost-Benefit Analysis. An Ethical Critique', *Regulation*, vol. 5, no. 1, January–February 1981, pp. 33–40.

29 Ibid., p. 40.

30 Joe Greene Conley II, 'Environmentalism Contained: A History of Corporate Responses to the New Environmentalism', PhD dissertation, Princeton University, 2006, p. 170.

31 Bob Eckhardt, quoted in *Use of Cost-Benefit Analysis by Regulatory Agencies*, p. 104.

32 P.F. Infante, R.A. Rinsky, J.K. Wagoner and R.J. Young, 'Leukaemia in benzene workers', *The Lancet*, vol. 310, no. 8028, 9 July 1977, pp. 76–8.

33 In this policy, 'it is presumed that once a substance has been determined to be a human carcinogen at *any* level of exposure, there is no threshold level at which the substance does not present a cancer risk'. Given that the agency's statutes 'require[s] standards to be as highly protective as is feasible, standards for carcinogens are set at a level of zero exposure if such a standard will not bankrupt the affected industries' ('Supreme Court's Divided Benzene Decision Preserves Uncertainty Over Regulation of Environmental Carcinogens', *Environmental Law Reporter*, vol. 10, no. 6, June 1980, pp. 10192–8 (p. 10193).

34 'American Petroleum Institute v. Occupational Safety and Health Administration', *Environmental Law Reporter*, vol. 8, 1978, pp. 20790–8 (p. 20794).

35 Weidenbaum, 'Benefit-Cost Analysis of Government Regulation', p. 353.

36 Anthony Mazzocchi, quoted in Mark Green and Norman Waitzman, *Business War on the Law: An Analysis of the Benefits of Federal Health/Safety Enforcement* (Washington, DC: The Corporate Accountability Research Group, 1979), reprinted in *Use of Cost-Benefit Analysis by*

Regulatory Agencies. Joint hearings before the Subcommittee on Oversight and Investigations and the Subcommittee on Consumer Protection and Finance of the Committee on Interstate and Foreign Commerce, House of Representatives, Ninety-sixth Congress, first session, July 30, October 10, and 24, 1979 (Washington, DC: US Government Printing Office, 1980), pp. 141–316 (p. 230).

37 Peter F. Infante, 'Benzene: An Historical Perspective on the American and European Occupational Setting', in Paul Harremoes et al. (eds.), *Late Lessons from Early Warnings: The Precautionary 1896–2000* (London: Earthscan, 2002), pp. 35–48.

38 As one critic remarks, Professor Weidenbaum, 'on grounds of efficiency, wants to apply market criteria to the regulatory process. Costs must be carefully calculated and compared with benefits to determine an "optimal" level of regulation. But how does one calculate an optimum number of deaths of miners?' (Daniel R. Fusfeld 'Some Notes on the Opposition to Regulation', *Journal of Post Keynesian Economics*, vol. 2, no. 3, Spring 1980, pp. 364–7 (p. 365).

39 Green and Waitzman, *Business War on the Law*, p. 188.

40 Ibid.

41 Jonathan Swift, 'A Modest Proposal for preventing the children of poor people in Ireland, from being a burden on their parents or country, and for making them beneficial to the publick' (1729), available online at: https://www.gutenberg.org/files/1080/1080-h/1080-h.htm.

42 See Ezra J. Mishan, 'Evaluation of Life and Limb: A Theoretical Approach', *Journal of Political Economy*, vol. 79, no. 4, July/August 1971, pp. 687–705; Thomas C. Schelling, 'The Life You Save May Be Your Own' (1968), in *Choice and Consequence, Perspectives of an Errant Economist* (Cambridge, MA: Harvard University Press, 1984), pp. 113–46. In this way, the daunting question of the value of life was avoided and replaced by the more abstract question of the 'value of statistical life', a life that could be yours – or not. The intimidating question, points out Schelling, 'disappears when we deal with statistical deaths, with small increments in a mortality rate in a large population' (Schelling, 'The Life You Save', p. 127).

43 See Eric Tucker, 'The Determination of Occupational Health and Safety Standards in Ontario 1860–1982: From Markets to Politics to . . .?', *McGill Law Journal*, vol. 29, no. 2, 1984, pp. 260–311 (p. 304).

44 Ibid., p. 298.

45 John G. U. Adams, '. . . and How Much for Your Grandmother?', *Environment and Planning A*, vol. 6, no. 6, December 1974, pp. 619–26 (p. 625).

46 Working Party on National Environmental Policies, *The Value of Statistical Life: A Meta-Analysis* (ENV/EPOC/WPNEP(2010)9/FINAL) (Paris: OECD, 2012), p. 14. http://www.oecd.org/officialdocuments/publicdisplaydocumentpdf/?cote=ENV/EPOC/WPNEP(2010)9/FINAL&doclanguage=en

47 *Use of Cost-Benefit Analysis*, p. 468.

48 Ibid., p. 472.

49 Ibid.

50 Ibid., p. 475.

Notes to Chapter 20

1 Jean Charles Léonard Simonde de Sismondi, *Nouveaux principes d'économie politique*, vol. I (Paris: Delaunay, 1827), p. 92.

2 Karl Marx, *Capital. A Critique of Political Economy*, Volume I, Book One: *The Process of Production of Capital*, translated by Samuel Moore and Edward Aveling, edited by Frederick Engels (Moscow: Progress Publishers, online edition; first English edition, 1887), available online at https://www. marxists.org/archive/marx/works/download/pdf/Capital-Volume-I.pdf, p. 181.

3 K. William Kapp, *The Social Costs of the Business Enterprise* (Cambridge, MA: Harvard University Press, 1950).

4 K. William Kapp, *The Social Costs of the Business Enterprise*, revised and extended edition (Nottingham: Spokesman, 1978), p. 29.

5 Werner Sombart, *Der Moderne Kapitalismus*, Vol. II, part 1, *Das europäische Wirtschaftsleben im Zeitaiter des Frühkapitalismus* (Leipzig: Duncker & Humblot, 1919; first published in 1917), p. 120.

6 Hector M. Robertson, *Aspects of the Rise of Economic Individualism* (Cambridge, MA: Cambridge University Press, 1935), pp. 53ff.

7 See Jack Goody, *The Domestication of the Savage Mind* (Cambridge: Cambridge University Press, 1977), p. 68.

8 Carroll Quigley, 'Marxism: Yesterday and Today', in *Perspectives in Defense Management*, December 1969, pp. 31–40 (p. 32).

9 On the relationship between Kapp and Polanyi, see Sebastian Berger, 'Karl Polanyi's and Karl William Kapp's Substantive Economics: Important Insights from the Kapp-Polanyi Correspondence', *Review of Social Economy*, vol. 66, no. 3, September 2008, pp. 381–96.

10 Kapp, *The Social Costs of the Business Enterprise*, p. 15.

11 This notion of 'social costs' lies at the heart of an eco-socialism that views the exploitation of labour and the exploitation of nature as the two sides of a general economy of despoliation. 'For, if entrepreneurial costs do not measure the total costs of production, the competitive cost-price calculus is not merely meaningless but nothing more than an institutionalized cover under which it is possible for private enterprise to shift part of the costs to the shoulders of others and to practice a form of large-scale spoliation which transcends everything the early socialists had in mind when they spoke of the exploitation of man by man' (Kapp, *The Social Costs of the Business Enterprise*, p. 271).

12 Arthur Cecil Pigou, *The Economics of Welfare* (London: Macmillan, 1920).

13 More precisely, a divergence between 'marginal net private profit' and 'marginal net social profit'. 'In general industrialists are interested, not in the social, but only in the private, net product of their operations [. . .] When there is a divergence between these two sorts of marginal net products, self-interest will not, therefore, tend to make the national dividend a maximum' (Pigou, *The Economics of Welfare*, p. 172). 'Externalities today provide the standard exception to the equation of optimality with universal perfect competition' (Ezra J. Mishan, 'The Postwar Literature on Externalities: An Interpretive Essay', *Journal of Economic Literature*, vol. 9, no. 1, March 1971, pp. 1–28 [p. 1]).

14 Pigou, *The Economics of Welfare*, p. 195.
15 Ibid., p. 192.
16 K. William Kapp, 'Environmental Disruption: Challenge to Social Science', in K. William Kapp, *Environmental Policies and Development Planning in Contemporary China and Other Essays* (Paris: Mouton, 1974), pp. 57–76 (p. 60).
17 Kapp, *Environmental Policies*, p. 86.
18 Ibid.
19 See Frank H. Knight, 'Some Fallacies in the Interpretation of Social Cost', *The Quarterly Journal of Economics*, vol. 38, no. 4, August 1924, pp. 582–606.
20 Frank H. Knight, 'Review: The Social Costs of Private Enterprise by K. William Kapp', *The Annals of the American Academy of Political and Social Science*, vol. 273, January 1951, pp. 233–4 (p. 234).
21 Ibid.
22 Ronald H. Coase, 'The Problem of Social Cost', *The Journal of Law & Economics*, vol. 3, October 1960, pp. 1–44 (p. 1). On the relations between Knight and Coase, see Sebastian Berger, 'The Discourse on Social Costs: Kapp's "Impossibility Thesis" Vs. Neoliberalism', in Paolo Ramazzotti, Pietro Frigato and Wolfram Elsner (eds.), *Social Costs Today. Institutional Analyses of the Present Crises* (New York: Routledge, 2012), pp. 96–112 (p. 103).
23 Coase, 'The Problem of Social Cost', p. 43.
24 Daniel R. Fischel, 'The Corporate Governance Movement', *Vanderbilt Law Review*, vol. 35, no. 6, November 1982, pp. 1259–92 (p. 1270).
25 Harold Demsetz, 'The Core Disagreement between Pigou, the Profession, and Coase in the Analyses of the Externality Question', *European Journal of Political Economy*, vol. 12, 1996, pp. 565–79 (p. 566).
26 Coase, 'The Problem of Social Cost', p. 2.
27 There is a single principle, a single gold standard in this type of thinking: 'the economic problem in all cases of harmful effects is how to maximise the value of production' (Coase, 'The Problem of Social Cost', p. 15). The absolute criterion of decision is a number. A sum. All that counts is the total quantity, independently of its distribution. But why that criterion rather than another? Why take as a reference the total value produced rather than, for example, the sustainable satisfaction of social needs? Neoclassical economics does not really answer this question, but merely repeats, in a circular argument, that it adopts this criterion because it is constitutive of its mode of thought. But someone like Coase was too subtle to ignore the problem completely. Right at the end of his paper, he mentions the elephant that has been in the room ever since the start of the piece: 'In this article, the analysis has been confined, as is usual in this part of economics, to comparisons of the value of production, as measured by the market. But it is, of course, desirable that the choice between different social arrangements for the solution of economic problems should be carried out in broader terms than this and that the total effect of these arrangements in all spheres of life should be taken into account. As Frank H. Knight has so often emphasized, problems of welfare economics must ultimately dissolve into a study of aesthetics and morals' (Coase, 'The Problem of Social Cost', p. 43; see also Knight 'Some Fallacies', p. 161).
28 K. William Kapp, 'Environment and Technology: New Frontiers for the

Social and Natural Sciences', *Journal of Economic Issues*, vol. 11, no. 3, September 1977, pp. 527–40 (p. 532).

29 K. William Kapp, 'Environmental Disruption and Social Costs: Challenge to Economics', in *Environmental Policies and Development Planning in Contemporary China and Other Essays* (Paris: Mouton, 1974), pp. 77–88 (p. 84).

30 Kapp, 'Environment and Technology', p. 531.

31 K. William Kapp, *Social Costs, Economic Development, and Environmental Disruption* (Lanham, MD: University Press of America, 1983), p. 2.

32 Kapp, 'Environment and Technology', p. 530.

33 Ibid., p. 529. The tendency of capitalism to 'socialize the real costs of production' is also a material process in which physico-chemical flows are metabolized by a profoundly disrupted planetary environment. In this sense, socialization is also a 'naturalization'.

34 'What counts is not simply the effects of a specific pollutant of air or water, but the total physical and social effects from multiple sources, including the degradation of living and working conditions, which determine the quality of the human environment and the extent of the damages caused. In short, both environmental damages and the quality of life must be understood as aggregates, that is, in their totality' (Kapp, 'Environment and Technology', p. 530). According to Kapp, classical economic theory is not well adapted to the analysis of such interdependencies. 'In dealing with problems of environmental disruption and social costs we are confronted with direct technological non-market effects which in their cumulative character and consequences make the customary equilibrium approach of conventional economics irrelevant and antiquated' (Kapp, 'Environmental Disruption and Social Costs', p. 83). In such a context, it is difficult to establish a one-to-one relationship between a particular individual pollutant and a particular form of environmental damage. This affects not only arguments in terms of retributive justice (who may be held responsible for a global effect?), but also the classic economic scheme of bilateral exchange which here comes up against the same basic epistemological limit, that of an atomistic conception of agency coupled with a linear conception of causality. In one sense, the neoliberals are right to say that the judicial approach is unsuitable, but they do not provide the right reason. If the approach in judicial terms is insufficient, this is not, as they claim, because there the positions of polluter and polluted are reversible, so that the question of responsibility is irrelevant, but rather because the relation between the damage and its repercussions is increasingly non-linear. On the concept of hyperobject, see Timothy Morton, *Hyperobjects: Philosophy and Ecology After the End of the World* (Minneapolis, MN: University of Minnesota Press, 2013).

35 Kapp, 'Environmental Disruption and Social Costs', p. 88.

36 Coase, 'The Problem of Social Cost', p. 27.

37 Lepage, *Demain le capitalisme* (Paris: Le Livre de poche, 1978), p. 294.

38 Ibid., p. 296.

39 George J. Stigler, *The Theory of Price* (New York: Macmillan, 1987), p. 120.

40 As Coase himself remarks: 'The solution of the problem depends essentially on whether the continued use of the machinery adds more to the confectioner's income than it subtracts from the doctor's' (Coase, 'The Problem of Social Cost', p. 9).

41 As Demsetz emphasizes: 'It was not Coase's observations on the importance of transaction cost but his "privatization" of the externality problem that constitutes the main methodological advance in his work' (Demsetz, 'The Core Disagreement', p. 566).

42 Ibid., p. 572.

43 This idea appeared in 1966, in the third edition of Stigler's manual. See Stigler, *The Theory of Price* (New York: Macmillan, 1966), p. 113.

44 Thomas D. Crocker, 'The Structuring of Atmospheric Pollution Control Systems', in Harold Wolozin (ed.), *The Economics of Air Pollution: A Symposium* (New York: Norton, 1966), pp. 61–86.

45 John H. Dales, *Pollution, Property & Prices* (Toronto: University of Toronto Press, 1968), p. 107.

46 Krystal L. Tribbett, 'RECLAIMing Air, Redefining Democracy: A History of the Regional Clean Air Incentives Market, Environmental Justice, and Risk, 1960–present', PhD dissertation, University of California, San Diego, 2014, p. 51.

47 See Hugh S. Gorman and Barry D. Solomon, 'The Origins and Practice of Emissions Trading', *Journal of Policy History*, vol. 14, no. 3, 2002, pp. 293–320 (p. 309).

48 See W. David Montgomery, 'Markets in Licenses and Efficient Pollution Control Programs', *Journal of Economic Theory*, vol. 5, no. 3, 1972, pp. 395–418 (p. 395) and Cédric Philibert and Julia Reinaud, *Emissions Trading: Taking Stock and Looking Forward* (Paris: International Energy Agency, 2004), p. 9.

49 Kapp, 'Environment and Technology', p. 531.

50 Kapp, *The Social Costs of the Business Enterprise*, p. 314.

51 Kapp, 'Environment and Technology', p. 531.

52 As Kapp shows, 'the use of willingness to pay as the criterion of quantifying and evaluating the quality of the environment has the insidious effect of reinterpreting original human needs [. . .] in terms of criteria which reflect the existing inequalities and distortions in the price, wage and income structure'. If economic units of unequal power can tip their costs onto others, then market costs and prices need to be considered as more or less arbitrary measures. In other words, given economic inequalities, the ability to pay and the agreement to pay are 'as arbitrary as the price and wage structure of which they are the outcome' (Kapp, *The Social Costs of the Business Enterprise*, p. 313).

53 Kapp, 'Environmental Disruption and Social Costs', p. 81.

54 This counter-offensive on ecological terrain is closely linked to the theoretical critique launched at the same period against the 'commons': to accredit the idea that only private appropriation can safeguard natural resources, it was necessary to invalidate the alternative – that is, to depict the communal management of public goods as doomed to failure, hence the theme of the 'tragedy of the commons'. See Garrett Hardin, 'The Tragedy of the Commons', *Science*, vol. 162, no. 385, 13 December 1968, pp. 1243–8.

55 Earl of Lauderdale, *An Inquiry into the Nature and Origin of Public Wealth and into the Means and Causes of its Increase*, 2nd edn (Edinburgh: Archivald Constable & Co., 1819).

56 Ibid., p. 38.

57 Ibid., p. 41.

58 Ibid., pp. 41–2.

59 Ibid., p. 52.
60 Friedrich Engels, *Outlines of a Critique of Political Economy*, translated by Martin Milligan, available online at: https://www.marxists.org/archive/marx/works/1844/df-jahrbucher/outlines.htm.
61 See John Bellamy Foster and Brett Clark, 'The Paradox of Wealth: Capitalism and Ecological Destruction', *Monthly Review*, vol. 61, no. 6, 2009, pp. 1–18.

Notes to Chapter 21

1 Karl Marx, 'Political Movements – Scarcity of Bread in Europe' (13 September 1853), in Marx and Engels, *Collected Works*, vol. 12 (Moscow: Progress Publishers, 1979), pp. 301–8 (pp. 303 and 304).
2 This can be seen online: https://www.youtube.com/watch?v=9Dmtkxm9yQY.
3 For this whole passage, see Joe Greene Conley II, *Environmentalism Contained: A History of Corporate Responses to the New Environmentalism*, p. 95.
4 Andrew Boardman Jaeger, 'Forging Hegemony: How Recycling Became a Popular but Inadequate Response to Accumulating Waste', *Social Problems*, 2017, pp. 1–21 (p. 4), doi: 10.1093/socpro/spx001.
5 'Report of the Vermont State Litter Commission to Governor Joseph B. Johnson' (1956), quoted in Jaeger, 'Forging Hegemony', p. 9.
6 See Finis Dunaway, 'The "Crying Indian" ad that fooled the environmental movement', *Chicago Tribune*, 21 November 2017.
7 This clip can be seen here: https://archive.org/details/Heritage1963.
8 Harold G. Grasmick, Robert J. Bursik Jr. and Karyl A. Kinsey, 'Shame and Embarrassment as Deterrents to Noncompliance with the Law. The Case of an Antilittering Campaign', in Arnold P. Goldstein, *The Psychology of Vandalism* (New York: Springer, 1996), pp. 183–98 (p. 186). Passing from one function to another, from guilt to gratification, the actor in this ad, 'Iron Eyes Cody', was also sometimes responsible for delivering, dressed in ceremonial costume, the 'awards' that Keep America Beautiful awarded to the deserving figures of a new 'green capitalism'. For the record, it turned out that Cody, dressed as an Indian in town as on stage, and presented everywhere as such, was not actually of Cherokee ancestry but Italian-American. See Angela Aleiss, 'Indian Heritage Lives On in Actor', *Indian Country Today*, Oneida, 24 February 1997, p. 5.
9 'Meeting minutes from the State Association Conference, National Soft Drink Association, 10 Nov. 1970', quoted in Bartow J. Elmore, 'The American Beverage Industry and the Development of Curbside Recycling Programs, 1950–2000', *Business History Review*, vol. 86, no. 3, Autumn 2012, pp. 477–501 (p. 493).
10 Ibid., p. 488.
11 Following the January 1969 oil spillage on the shores of Santa Barbara, activists launched the idea of an 'Earth Day', a day of environmental mobilization. The first took place on 22 April 1970. Millions of Americans took to the streets to support reforms in favour of better environmental protection.
12 J. Paul Austin, 'Environmental Renewal or Oblivion – Quo Vadis?', *Congressional Record*, Vol. 116/10 (23 April 1970–4 May 1970), US Government Printing Office, Washington, DC, p. 12814.

13 Ibid.
14 'Clean-up groups fronting for bottlers, critics say', *The San Bernardino County Sun*, 29 August 1976, p. 3.
15 Paul Swatek, *The User's Guide to the Protection of the Environment* (New York: Friends of the Earth/Ballantine Books, 1970), p. 128.
16 *CSA Super Markets*, vol. 46, January–June 1970, p. 67.
17 Conley, 'Environmentalism Contained', p. 98.
18 Richard L. Cheney, quoted in Conley, 'Environmentalism Contained', p. 98.
19 The refrain of their advert, 'it's uncanny', means 'it's strange', but also 'it's not a can'. The clips can be seen online: https://archive.org/details/dmbb01623 and https://archive.org/details/dmbb01622.
20 Conley, 'Environmentalism Contained', p. 96.
21 Ibid.
22 Elmore, 'The American Beverage', p. 493.
23 Ronen Shamir, 'The Age of Responsibilization: On Market-Embedded Morality', *Economy and Society*, vol. 37, no. 1, February 2008, pp. 1–19 (p. 4). See also Nikolas Rose, 'Inventiveness in Politics', *Economy and Society*, vol. 28, no. 3, pp. 467–93; David Garland, *The Culture of Control: Crime and Social Order in Contemporary Society* (Chicago, IL: University of Chicago Press, 2001), pp. 124ff.; Wendy Brown, *Undoing the Demos: Neoliberalism's Stealth Revolution* (New York: Zone Books, 2015), pp. 143ff.
24 As Pat O'Malley notes, 'risk also undergoes a noteworthy transformation, from a technique for providing social security, to a responsibility to be assumed by self-governing individuals aided by an empowering and ena-bling state' (Pat O'Malley, *Risk, Uncertainty and Government* (New York: Routledge, 2004), p. 57).
25 Thomas Schelling, 'The Intimate Contest for Self-Command', in Schelling, *Choices and Consequences*, pp. 57–82 (p. 63).
26 Ibid., p. 64.
27 Don Hazen, 'The Hidden Life of Garbage: An interview with Heather Rogers', AlterNet, 30 October 2005, https://www.alternet.org/story/27456/the_hidden_life_of_garbage. See also Heather Rogers, *Gone Tomorrow: The Hidden Life of Garbage* (New York: The New Press, 2006), p. 25.
28 Elmore, 'The American Beverage Industry', p. 501.
29 *71 Things You Can Do to Stop Pollution* (New York: Keep America Beautiful, 1971).
30 This is what Samantha MacBride calls 'busy-ness'. See Samantha MacBride, *Recycling Reconsidered: The Present Failure and Future Promise of Environmental Action in the United States* (Boston, MA: MIT Press, 2011), pp. 6 and 220.
31 On this distinction, see Peter French, *Collective and Corporate Responsibility* (New York: Columbia University Press, 1984), p. 13.
32 Brown, *Undoing the Demos: Neoliberalism's Stealth Revolution*, p. 87.
33 Karl Marx, *Economic & Philosophic Manuscripts of 1844*, available online: https://www.marxists.org/archive/marx/works/download/pdf/Economic-Philosophic-Manuscripts-1844.pdf, p. 51.
34 Ibid.
35 Marx and Engels, *The Holy Family, or Critique of Critical Criticism, against Bruno Bauer and Company*, available online: https://www.marxists.org/archive/marx/works/download/Marx_The_Holy_Family.pdf.

Notes to Chapter 22

1 Walter Bagehot, *Physics and Politics* (New York: Appleton, 1883), p. 25.
2 James Douglas, 'The Overloaded Crown', *British Journal of Political Science*, vol. 6, no. 4, October 1976, pp. 483–505 (p. 483).
3 Michel J. Crozier, Samuel P. Huntington and Joji Watanuki, *The Crisis of Democracy: Report on the Governability of Democracies to the Trilateral Commission* (New York: New York University Press, 1975). The Trilateral Commission was a private organization founded in 1973 at the urging of the banker David Rockefeller and the political thinker Zbigniew Brzezinski; it comprised eminent figures from the United States, Western Europe and Japan, a transnational elite with the mission of developing political recommendations for the 'developed countries'. See Holly Sklar (ed.), *Trilateralism: The Trilateral Commission and Elite Planning for World Management* (Boston, MA: South End Press, 1980).
4 Samuel P. Huntington, 'The United States', in Michel J. Crozier, Samuel P. Huntington and Joji Watanuki, *The Crisis of Democracy: Report on the Governability of Democracies to the Trilateral Commission* (New York: New York University Press, 1975), pp. 59–118 (p. 114).
5 Ibid.
6 Ibid., p. 61.
7 Ibid., p. 75.
8 Ibid., p. 76.
9 Ibid., p. 114.
10 Jacques Rancière, *La Haine de la démocratie* (Paris: La Fabrique, 2005), p. 13. In *The Class Struggle in France* Marx presented a concise analysis of the (masculine) 'universal suffrage' brought in with the 1848 constitution; its perspicacity surpasses many later conservative accounts of the crisis in governability of democracies: 'The comprehensive contradiction of this constitution, however, consists in the following: The classes whose social slavery the constitution is to perpetuate it puts in possession of political power through universal suffrage. And from the class whose old social power it sanctions, the bourgeoisie, it withdraws the political guarantees of this power. It forces the political rule of the bourgeoisie into democratic conditions, which at every moment help the hostile classes to victory [. . .]. From the first group it demands that they should not go forward from political to social emancipation; from the others that they should not go back from social to political restoration' (Karl Marx, *Class Struggles in France, 1848–1850*, available online: https://www.marxists.org/archive/marx/works/download/pdf/Class_Struggles_in_France.pdf, p. 35). For this type of regime to maintain itself at its peak, the parties involved must all symmetrically respect a taboo that none of them can actually observe. Dominated classes are not supposed to continue, even when they have the opportunity to do so, their movement for political emancipation in the social and economic field; and the bourgeoisie is not supposed to use its colossal economic power to ensure the maintenance of its full social pre-eminence by more or less frontal manoeuvres of political restoration.
11 'Our report', he writes, 'decisively rejected the undiluted pessimism that nothing can save democracy. It provided practical suggestions of what could

305

and should be done [. . .]. It was concerned, as its title suggests, with the "governability" of democracy and how to improve that governability and not with futile lamentations about the "ungovernability" of democracy' (Huntington, 'The Governability of Democracy One Year Later', *Trialogue*, no. 10, 1976, pp. 10–11 [p. 11]). Actually, Huntington does not use the term 'ungovernability' in the Trilateral Report, unlike his colleagues Crozier (pp. 11, 30 and 37) and Watanuki (p. 119).

12 Anthony King, 'Overload: Problems of Governing in the 1970s', *Political Studies*, vol. 23, no. 2–3, 1975, pp. 284–96 (p. 288).

13 Anthony H. Birch, 'Overload, Ungovernability and Delegitimation: The Theories and the British Case', *British Journal of Political Science*, vol. 14, no. 2, April 1984, pp. 135–60 (p. 136).

14 Samuel Brittan, 'The Economic Contradictions of Democracy', *British Journal of Political Science*, vol. 5, no. 2, April 1975, pp. 129–59 (p. 129).

15 See Joachim Heidorn, *Legitimität und Regierbarkeit: Studien zu den Legitimitätstheorien von Max Weber, Niklas Luhmann und Jürgen Habermas und der Unregierbarkeitsforschung* (Berlin: Duncker and Humblot, 1982), p. 214. See also Armin Schäfer, 'Krisentheorien der Demokratie: Unregierbarkeit, Spätkapitalismus und Postdemokratie', *Der Moderne Staat. Zeitschrift für Public Policy, Recht und Management*, vol. 1, 2009, pp. 159–83 (p. 162). 'The essence of "Keynesian democracy,"' says Jean Leca, 'consists in the institutionalization of class conflict by the "politiciza-tion of the economy" (by government intervention) and by the transforma-tion of politics into a market. [. . .] There follows a paradox of the Welfare State: its very success makes its continual intervention more necessary, but more difficult. [. . .] The more it develops, the more its inertia inevitably grows' (Jean Leca, 'Conclusion. Perspectives démocratiques', in Jean Leca and Roberto Papini (eds.), *Les démocraties sont-elles gouvernables?* (Paris: Economica, 1985), pp. 173–95 (p. 182).

16 Brittan, 'The Economic Contradictions of Democracy', p. 129.

17 Claus Offe, '"Ungovernability": The Renaissance of Conservative Theories of Crisis', in Claus Offe, *Contradictions of the Welfare State* (London: Hutchinson, 1984), pp. 65–88 (p. 68).

18 Joseph A. Schumpeter, *Capitalism, Socialism and Democracy* (London and New York: Routledge, 1976), p. 417.

19 See Anthony Downs, 'An Economic Theory of Political Action in a Democracy', *The Journal of Political Economy*, vol. 65, no. 2, April 1957, pp. 135–50.

20 Lepage, *Demain le capitalisme* (Paris: Le Livre de poche, 1978), p. 176.

21 Downs, 'An Economic Theory of Political Action', p. 137. Whence the elec-toralist theorem in which 'political parties in a democracy formulate policy strictly as a means of gaining votes' and 'the government always acts so as to maximize the number of votes it will receive'.

22 James D. Gwartney and Richard E. Wagner, 'Public Choice and the Conduct of Representative Government', in James D. Gwartney and Richard E. Wagner (eds.), *Public Choice and Constitutional Economics* (Greenwich, CT: JAI Press, 1988), pp. 3–28 (p. 9).

23 Allan Meltzer, 'The Decline of the Liberal Economy', *Vie et sciences économiques*, no. 72, January 1977, pp. 1–7 (p. 3).

24 Lepage, *Demain le capitalisme*, p. 211.

25 Just as, according to Berle and Means, managers were rationally inclined to pursue their selfish interests in defiance of the interests of shareholders, bureaucrats will tend, in short, to seek to maximize theirs, even at the expense of the economically dominant classes. For a neoliberal criticism of state bureaucracy, see William Niskanen, *Bureaucracy and Representative Government* (Chicago, IL: Aldine Atherton, 1971).

26 Richard Rose, 'Overloaded Government: The Problem Outlined', *European Studies Newsletter*, vol. 5, no. 3, 1975, pp. 13–18 (p. 16).

27 Douglas, 'The Overloaded Crown', p. 487.

28 Rose, 'Overloaded Government', p. 16.

29 Douglas, 'The Overloaded Crown', p. 487.

30 Offe, '"Ungovernability"', p. 68.

31 Rose, 'Overloaded Government', p. 17.

32 Ibid., p. 16.

33 Huntington, 'The United States', p. 115.

34 Samuel Brittan, 'The Economic Contradictions of Democracy', p. 129.

35 Alan Wolfe, 'Giving Up on Democracy: Capitalism Shows its Face', *The Nation*, 29 November 1975, pp. 557–63 (p. 561).

36 Claus Offe, '"Ungovernability"', p. 65.

37 Richard Rose, *Challenge to Governance, Studies in Overloaded Politics* (London: Sage, 1980), p. 6.

38 'The institutions of government are overloaded, and increasingly so'; this 'threatens to debilitate or disrupt the activities of government' – a slippery slope that can 'even destroy political regimes' (Rose, 'Overloaded Government', p. 13).

39 Daniel Bell, 'The Public Household: On "Fiscal Sociology" and the Liberal Society', *The Public Interest*, no. 37, Autumn 1974, pp. 29–68 (p. 40).

40 James O'Connor, *The Fiscal Crisis of the State* (New York: St. Martin's Press, 1973). See Huntington, 'The United States', p. 73.

41 James O'Connor, *The Fiscal Crisis of the State* (New Brunswick, NJ: Transaction Publishers, 2009), p. 14.

42 Bell, 'The Public Household', p. 34.

43 Wolfe, 'Giving Up on Democracy', p. 560.

44 O'Connor, *The Fiscal Crisis of the State*, p. 8. In brief: 'The socialization of costs and the private appropriation of profits creates a fiscal crisis, or "structural gap," between state expenditures and state revenues' (p. 9).

45 Claus Offe, 'Crises of Crisis Management', in Claus Offe, *Contradictions of the Welfare State* (London: Hutchinson, 1984), pp. 35–64 (p. 61).

46 Offe, '"Ungovernability"', p. 83.

47 Huntington, 'The United States', p. 73.

48 Lepage, *Demain le capitalisme*, p. 40.

49 Ibid.

50 André Gorz, *Misères du présent, richesses du possible* (Paris: Galilée, 1997), p. 26.

51 André Gorz, *Métamorphoses du travail: Quête du sens. Critique de la raison économique* (Paris: Galilée, 1988), p. 229.

52 Huntington, 'The Governability of Democracy One Year Later', p. 10.

53 As Michel Feher writes, 'if we realize that melancholy has not always dwelled in the same place, we can start to think that it may change sides' (Michel Feher, *Le Temps des investis* (Paris: La Découverte, 2017), p. 10).

54 Brittan, 'The Economic Contradictions of Democracy', p. 129.
55 Wolfe, 'Giving Up on Democracy', p. 563.
56 Huntington, 'The Governability of Democracy One Year Later', p. 11.
57 Fritz W. Scharpf, 'Public Organization and the Waning of the Welfare State: A Research Perspective', *European Journal of Political Research*, vol. 5, no. 4, January 1977, pp. 339–62 (p. 345).
58 Ralf Dahrendorf, 'Effectiveness and Legitimacy: On The "Governability" of Democracies', *The Political Quarterly*, vol. 51, no. 4, 1980, pp. 393–410 (p. 406).
59 Scharpf, 'Public Organization', p. 344.
60 See Serge Halimi, *Le Grand Bond en arrière* (Paris: Fayard, 2006).

Notes to Chapter 23

1 Daniel Bell, *The Cultural Contradictions of Capitalism* (New York: Basic Books, 1978), p. 12.
2 Michael C. Jensen and William H. Meckling, 'Can the Corporation Survive?', *Financial Analysts Journal*, vol. 34, no. 1, January/February 1978, pp. 31–7 (p. 32).
3 Wolfe, 'Giving Up on Democracy', p. 558.
4 Huntington, 'The United States', p. 114.
5 Ibid., p. 113.
6 Ibid., p. 114.
7 'Liberal democracy [would] not be saved [. . .] if contemporary egalitarianism were to lose its hold over the intelligentsia' (Brittan, 'The Economic Contradictions of Democracy', p. 159).
8 Samuel P. Huntington, 'Postindustrial Politics: How Benign Will It Be?', *Comparative Politics*, vol. 6, no. 2, January 1974, pp. 163–91 (p. 166).
9 Wolfe, 'Giving Up on Democracy', p. 559.
10 Ralf Dahrendorf, 'Excerpts of Remarks by Ralf Dahrendorf on The Governability Study', in Crozier, Huntington and Watanuki, *The Crisis of Democracy*, p. 188.
11 Dahrendorf, 'Effectiveness and Legitimacy', p. 405.
12 Richard Rose, 'Ungovernability: Is There Fire Behind the Smoke?', *Political Studies*, vol. 27, no. 3, 1979, pp. 351–70 (p. 355). He adds that, in the literature on ungovernability, there is a tendency to underestimate the way a regime might ensure its survival by coercion; and 'the rise of protest and terrorist activities in the past decade has incidentally revealed widespread popular support for harsh anti-subversive and anti-terrorist measures' (p. 369).
13 Incorrigibility and ungovernability, we read in an early 1960s administrative report, 'are interchangeable terms [. . .]. A child falls into one of these categories when he is beyond the control of his parents but has not yet been involved in violation of law' (Richard A. Myren and Lynn D. Swanson, *Police Work with Children: Perspectives and Principles, Children's Bureau Publications, no. 398* (Washington, DC: US Government Printing Office, 1962), p. 69).
14 Nicos Poulantzas, *L'État, le pouvoir, le socialisme* (Paris: PUF, 1978), p. 226. For a productive updating of Poulantzas's concept, see Christos Boukalas, 'État d'exception ou étatisme autoritaire: Agamben, Poulantzas et la critique

de l'antiterrorisme', *Revue Période*, http://revueperiode.net/etat-dexception-ou-etatisme-autoritaire-agamben-poulantzas-et-la-critique-de-lantiterror-isme/. See also Christos Boukalas, 'No Exceptions: Authoritarian Statism. Agamben, Poulantzas and Homeland Security', *Critical Studies on Terrorism*, vol. 7, no. 1, pp. 112–30.

15 Paul Samuelson, 'The World Economy at Century's End', in Shigeto Tsuru (ed.), *Human Resources, Employment and Development*, vol. 1 (London: Macmillan, 1983), pp. 58–77 (p. 75).

16 Paul Samuelson, 'The World Economy at Century's End', *Bulletin of the American Academy of Arts and Sciences*, vol. 34, no. 8, May 1981, pp. 35–44 (p. 44). This text has the same title as the previous one, but the contents are different.

17 Ibid.

18 'Review and Outlook', *The Wall Street Journal*, 2 November 1973.

19 Amnesty International, *Chile: An Amnesty International Report* (London: Amnesty International Publications, 1974), p. 7.

20 Amnesty International, *Disappeared Prisoners in Chile* (London: Amnesty International Publications, 1977), p. 2.

21 Milton Friedman, Gordon Tullock, James Buchanan and Friedrich Hayek, among others, attended and the Mont Pelerin Society held a conference there in November 1981. Hayek himself indicates that, before his visit, in an attempt to dissuade him from going, he had received a mass of documents on the régime, some from Amnesty International. See Friedrich Hayek, 'Internationaler Rufmord. Eine persönliche Stellungnahme', *Politische Studien, Sonderheft 'Chile, ein schwieriger Weg'*, 1978, pp. 44–5 (p. 44).

22 See Naomi Klein, *The Shock Doctrine: The Rise of Disaster Capitalism* (New York: Picador, 2008), pp. 145ff. See also John Meadowcroft and William Ruger, 'Hayek, Friedman, and Buchanan: On Public Life, Chile, and the Relationship between Liberty and Democracy', *Review of Political Economy*, vol. 26, no. 3, 2014, p. 358–67 (p. 363).

23 'Premio Nobel Friedrich von Hayek', *El Mercurio*, 8 November 1977, pp. 27–8, quoted in Andrew Farrant, Edward McPhail and Sebastian Berger, 'Preventing the "Abuses" of Democracy: Hayek, the "Military Usurper" and Transitional Dictatorship in Chile?', *The American Journal of Economics and Sociology*, vol. 71, no. 3, July 2012, pp. 513–38 (p. 520).

24 Ibid., p. 525.

25 Friedrich Hayek, 'Freedom of Choice', *The Times*, 3 August 1978, p. 15.

26 Hayek went to Chile under the dictatorship twice, in November 1977, when he met Pinochet in person, and in April 1981. See Bruce Caldwell and Leonidas Montes, 'Friedrich Hayek and his visits to Chile', *The Review of Austrian Economics*, vol. 28, no. 3, September 2015, pp. 261–309.

27 Friedrich Hayek, interviewed by Renée Sallas, *El Mercurio*, 12 April 1981, quoted in Caldwell and Montes, 'Friedrich Hayek and his visits to Chile', pp. 44 and 45.

28 Nicholas Kaldor, 'Chicago Boys in Chile', *The Times*, 18 October 1978, p. 17.

29 See Andrew Farrant and Edward McPhail, 'Can a Dictator Turn a Constitution into a Can-opener? F.A. Hayek and the Alchemy of Transitional Dictatorship in Chile', *Review of Political Economy*, vol. 26, no. 3, 2014, pp. 331–48 (pp. 332ff.).

30 Friedrich Hayek, 'The Principles of a Liberal Social Order", *Il Politico*, vol. 31, no. 4, December 1966, pp. 601–18 (p. 605).

31 'Democracy has a task that I call of "hygiene," ensuring that political processes are conducted in a healthy way. It is not an end in itself. It is a procedural rule that has the objective of serving freedom' (Friedrich Hayek, interviewed by Lucia Santa Cruz, *El Mercurio*, 19 April 1981, quoted in Caldwell and Montes, 'Friedrich Hayek and his visits to Chile', p. 47).

32 Renato Cristi, *El pensamiento politico de Jaime Guzmán: autoridad y libertad* (Santiago: LOM Ediciones, 2000), p. 11.

33 Hayek, interviewed by Lucia Santa Cruz, *El Mercurio*, 19 April 1981, p. 47.

34 Hayek, 'Freedom of Choice', p. 15.

35 Friedrich Hayek, 'The Dangers to Personal Liberty', *The Times*, 11 July 1978, p. 15.

36 Friedrich Hayek, *Law, Legislation and Liberty, Volume 3, The Political Order of a Free People*, in *Law, Legislation and Liberty* (London: Routledge, 1982), p. 99.

37 Friedrich Hayek, *The Constitution of Liberty* (Chicago, IL: The University of Chicago Press, 1978), p. 103.

38 Hayek, 'The Dangers to Personal Liberty', p. 15.

39 Hayek interviewed by the *Daily Journal* (Venezuela), 15 May 1981, quoted in Alan Ebenstein, *Friedrich Hayek: A Biography* (New York: Palgrave, 2001), p. 300.

40 'It would seem that wherever democratic institutions ceased to be restrained by the tradition of the Rule of Law, they led not only to "totalitarian democracy" but in due time even to a "plebiscitary dictatorship"' (Hayek, *Law, Legislation and Liberty*, p. 4).

41 Friedrich Hayek, *The Road to Serfdom – the Definitive Edition* (Chicago, IL: The University of Chicago Press, 2007), p. 100.

42 Andrew Gamble, 'The Free Economy and the Strong State', in Ralph Miliband and John Saville (eds.), *Socialist Register*, vol. 16, 1979, pp. 1–25 (p. 9).

43 Hayek, 'Freedom of Choice', p. 15.

44 Hayek, 'The Principles of a Liberal Social Order', p. 602.

45 'Absence of domination as opposed to central planning, noninterference as opposed to interventionism, and coordination as opposed to subordination': as Peter Koslowski notes, classical economics 'corresponds theologically to deism and ontologically to the model of preestablished mechanism' (Peter Koslowski, *Ethics of Capitalism and Critique of Sociobiology*, p. 28).

46 Polanyi, *The Great Transformation*, p. 146. See Philip Mirowski, 'Postface', in Philip Mirowski and Dieter Plehwe (eds.), *The Road from Mont Pelerin: The Making of the Neoliberal Thought Collective* (Cambridge, MA: Harvard University Press, 2009), pp. 417–56 (p. 441). See also, for a critique of the rhetoric of the 'free market', Bernard E. Harcourt, *The Illusion of Free Markets* (Cambridge, MA: Harvard University Press, 2011), pp. 240ff.

47 Antonio Gramsci, *Selections from the Prison Notebooks*, edited and translated by Quentin Hoare and Geoffrey Nowell Smith (London: Lawrence & Wishart, 1971), p. 371.

Notes to Chapter 24

1 Benjamin Constant, 'De Godwin, et de ses ouvrages sur la justice politique' (1817), in *Mélanges de littérature et de politique*, vol. I (Louvain: Michel, 1830), pp. 144–52 (p. 149).

2 Franz L. Neumann, *The Democratic and the Authoritarian State: Essays in Political and Legal Theory* (New York: The Free Press, 1966), p. 211. And see Hayek, *The Constitution of Liberty*, p. 421, note 3.

3 Hayek, 'The Principles of a Liberal Social Order', p. 601.

4 Hans Kelsen, quoted in Hayek, *The Constitution of Liberty*, p. 431, note 4.

5 William E. Scheuerman 'The Unholy Alliance of Carl Schmitt and Friedrich Hayek', *Constellations*, vol. 4, no. 2, October 1997, pp. 172–88 (p. 178).

6 Friedrich Hayek, *Law, Legislation and Liberty, Volume 3, The Political Order of a Free People*, in *Law, Legislation and Liberty* (London: Routledge, 1982), pp. 194–5, n. 11.

7 Hayek, on the idea that a 'democracy may well wield totalitarian powers', also quotes Heinz Ziegler, who was one of Schmitt's sources on this theme. Hayek, *The Constitution of Liberty*, p. 442, note 1. See Heinz O. Ziegler, *Autoritärer oder totaler Staat* (Tübingen: Mohr, 1932).

8 See Jean-Pierre Faye, *L'État total selon Carl Schmitt* (Paris: Germina, 2013), p. 9.

9 Carl Schmitt, *Der Hüter der Verfassung* (Berlin: Duncker & Humblot, 1931), p. 79. This passage is quoted in Hayek, *The Road to Serfdom*, p. 190, note 32.

10 Schmitt, *Der Hüter der Verfassung*, p. 78.

11 Carl Schmitt, *Legalität und Legitimität* (Berlin: Duncker & Humblot, 1932), p. 93.

12 Ibid., p. 96. This passage is quoted in Hayek, *Law, Legislation and Liberty*, pp. 194–5, n. 11.

13 Schmitt, *Legalität und Legitimität*, p. 96.

14 Schmitt, *Der Hüter der Verfassung*, p. 79.

15 See William E. Scheuerman, *The End of Law: Carl Schmitt in the Twentieth Century* (Lanham, MD: Rowman & Littlefield, 1999), p. 85.

16 Langnam Verein, the 'long-name association', the sobriquet of the union for the preservation of common economic interests in Rhineland-Westphalia. See Renato Cristi, *Carl Schmitt and Authoritarian Liberalism: Strong State, Free Economy* (Cardiff: University of Wales Press, 1998).

17 Carl Schmitt, 'Starker Staat und gesunde Wirtschaft. Ein Vortrag vor Wirtschaftsführern', in *Volk und Reich. Politische Monatshefte für das junge Deutschland*, 1933, vol. 1, no. 2, pp. 81–94. Schmitt took over and varied the title of a lecture given two months earlier by the economist Alexander Rüstow, one of the founding fathers of ordoliberalism: *Économie libre, État fort*. In it, Rüstow referred to Schmitt's critique of a quantitative total state, concluding: 'The new liberalism [. . .] calls for a strong state' (Alexander Rüstow, 'Freie Wirtschaft – Starker Staat. Die staatspolitischen Voraussetzungen des wirtschaftspolitischen Liberalismus', in Franz Boese (ed.), *Deutschland und die Weltkrise* (Dresden: Duncker & Humblot, 1932), pp. 62–9 [p. 69]). On the history of the theme of the strong state in ordoliberalism, see Werner Bonefeld, 'Authoritarian Liberalism: From Schmitt via Ordoliberalism to

the Euro', *Critical Sociology*, vol. 43, no. 4–5, 2017, pp. 747–61, and Gilles Christoph, 'Du nouveau libéralisme à l'anarchocapitalisme: la trajectoire intellectuelle du néolibéralisme britannique', PhD dissertation, Université Lyon 2, 2012, pp. 119 and 129ff.

18 Schmitt, 'Starker Staat und gesunde Wirtschaft, p. 84.
19 Ibid., p. 86.
20 Ibid., p. 84.
21 Ibid.
22 Ibid. 'Modern technological means', he writes, 'confer such power and influence that the old notions of state power and resistance to that power become blurred. The saccharine images of stones and barricades look like child's play compared to these modern means of power' (p. 83). Apart from armed repression, there is propaganda: 'the rise of technological means does however make it possible to exert on the masses an influence far greater than anything that the press and other traditional means of shaping opinion could accomplish' (p. 83). Schmitt has in mind radio and cinema, 'means of mass domination, mass suggestion and the shaping of public opinion' – means which the state cannot leave in the hands of its opponents.
23 Ibid., p. 90.
24 Schmitt, *Der Hüter der Verfassung*, p. 81.
25 Schmitt, 'Starker Staat und gesunde Wirtschaft', p. 86.
26 Ibid., p. 87.
27 Ibid., p. 90. Carl Schmitt, *Legalität und Legitimität*, p. 93. Hayek quotes this passage from Schmitt as well as Ziegler's short work. See note 7 above.
28 Schmitt, 'Starker Staat und gesunde Wirtschaft', pp. 89 and 90.
29 Hermann Heller, 'Autoritärer Liberalismus', *Die Neue Rundschau*, vol. 44, 1933, pp. 289–98.
30 Ibid., p. 295.
31 Ibid., p. 296.
32 Ibid., p. 295.
33 Wolfgang Streeck, 'Heller, Schmitt and the Euro', *European Law Journal*, vol. 21, no. 3, May 2015, pp. 361–70 (p. 362).
34 Heller, 'Autoritärer Liberalismus', p. 296.
35 Herbert Marcuse, 'Der Kampf gegen den Liberalismus in der totalitären Staatsauffassung', *Zeitschrift für Sozialforschung*, vol. 3, no. 2 (Paris: Librairie Felix Alcan, 1934), pp. 161–95.
36 Ibid., p. 195.
37 Ibid., p. 166. Hayek's mentor added an important codicil to this homage, which Marcuse does not mention: 'But although his policy has brought salvation for the time being, it is not capable of promising an enduring success. Fascism was a temporary expedient: to see it as more than that would be a fatal mistake' (Ludwig von Mises, *Liberalismus* (Jena: Fischer, 1927), p. 45).
38 Marcuse, 'Der Kampf gegen den Liberalismus', p. 166.
39 Ibid., p. 174.
40 Ludwig von Mises, *Omnipotent Government: the Rise of the Total State and Total War* (New Haven, CT: Yale University Press, 1944).
41 *The Condensed Version of The Road to Serfdom by F. A. Hayek as it Appeared in the April 1945 Edition of Reader's Digest* (London: The Institute of Economic Affairs, 1999), p. 31. (I have corrected an error of transcription that occurs in this edition.)

42 Andrew Gamble, *Hayek: The Iron Cage of Liberty* (Boulder, CO: Westview Press, 1996), pp. 88ff.

43 'The conduct of Carl Schmitt under the Hitler regime does not alter the fact that, of the modern German writings on the subject, his are still among the most learned and perceptive' (Hayek, *The Constitution of Liberty*, p. 485, note 1).

44 See Farrant, McPhail and Berger, 'Preventing the "Abuses" of Democracy', pp. 518 and 521.

45 See Michel Foucault, *The Birth of Biopolitics. Lectures at the Collège de France, 1978–79*, edited by Michel Senellart, translated by Graham Burchell (London: Palgrave Macmillan, 2008). But Foucault himself had found in the texts of the ordoliberals, including Röpke, the theme of need for 'a strong state, aloof from the hungry hordes of vested interests' (ibid., p. 262, n. 7).

46 Streeck, 'Heller, Schmitt and the Euro', p. 364. The reference is to Andrew Gamble, *The Free Economy and the Strong State: The Politics of Thatcherism*, 2nd edn (Basingstoke: Palgrave, 1994), first published in 1988.

Notes to Chapter 25

1 Quoted in Pierre François Henry, *Histoire de Napoléon Buonaparte* (Paris: Michaud, 1823), p. 289.

2 Paul Samuelson, 'The World Economy at Century's End', in Shigeto Tsuru (ed.), *Human Resources, Employment and Development*, vol. 1 (London: Macmillan, 1983), pp. 58–77 (p. 75).

3 See Joseph Comblin, *Le Pouvoir militaire en Amérique latine. L'idéologie de la Sécurité nationale* (Paris: Delarge, 1977). In this doctrine, argues Comblin, we find a 'pernicious inversion of Clausewitz's argument: politics is [. . .] the continuation of war by other means' (pp. 13–14). On a lesser scale, similar repressive tactics were deployed in 'Western democracies' against militant movements. In the United States, one example was the 'Cointelpro' programme. See Nelson Blackstock, *Cointelpro: the FBI's War on Political Freedom* (New York: Pathfinder Books, 1988; first published in 1975). See also Ward Churchill and Jim Vander Wall, *Agents of Repression: The FBI's Secret Wars Against the Black Panther Party and the American Indian Movement* (Boston, MA: South End Press, 2002).

4 In 1978, Hayek wrote: 'That a limited democracy is probably the best possible known form of government does not mean that we can have it everywhere, or even that it is itself a supreme value rather than the best means to secure peace, [. . .] our doctrinaire democrats clearly ought to take more seriously the question when democracy is possible' (Hayek, 'Freedom of Choice', p. 15).

5 'The adoption of free-market policies by Chile with the blessing and support of the military junta headed by General Pinochet has given rise to the myth that only an authoritarian regime can successfully implement a free-market policy. The facts are very different. Chile is an exception, not the rule' (Milton Friedman, 'Free Markets and the Generals', *Newsweek*, 25 January 1982, p. 59). See also John Meadowcroft and William Ruger, 'Hayek, Friedman, and Buchanan: On Public Life, Chile, and the Relationship between Liberty

313

and Democracy', *Review of Political Economy*, vol. 26, no. 3, pp. 358–67 (p. 365).

6　Hayek, *Law, Legislation and Liberty*, p. xx.

7　Friedrich Hayek, 'Die Entthronung der Politik', in Friedrich Hayek, *Grundsätze einer liberalen Gesellschaftsordnung, Aufsätze zur Politischen Philosophie und Theorie* (Tübingen: Mohr Siebeck, 2002), pp. 217–30 (p. 217).

8　Ibid.

9　Ibid., p. 226.

10　On this notion, see Wendy Brown, *Undoing the Demos: Neoliberalism's Stealth Revolution* (New York: Zone Books, 2015), p. 18; and Wendy Brown, 'American Nightmare: Neoliberalism, Neoconservatism, and De-Democratization', *Political Theory*, vol. 34, no. 6, December 2006, pp. 690–714. See also Charles Tilly, *Democracy* (Cambridge: Cambridge University Press, 2007), pp. 58ff.

11　Colin Crouch, 'The State, Capital and Liberal Democracy', in Colin Crouch (ed.), *State and Economy in Contemporary Capitalism* (London: Croom Helm, 1979), pp. 13–54 (p. 15).

12　Rose, *Challenge to Governance*, p. 1.

13　See Hayek, 'Die Entthronung der Politik'; see also Hayek, *Law, Legislation and Liberty*.

14　Hayek, *Law, Legislation and Liberty*, p. 129.

15　Ibid.

16　Gwartney and Wagner, 'Public Choice and the Conduct of Representative Government', p. 4.

17　Ibid. Foucault comments: 'the institutional innovation we must now adopt is the application to the economy of what is called the *Rechtsstaat* in the German tradition and the Rule of law in English, or *l'État de droit* in French. At this point the ordoliberal analysis no longer follows the line of the economic theory of competition [. . .]; it follows a line of legal theory' (Michel Foucault, *The Birth of Biopolitics. Lectures at the Collège de France, 1978–79*, edited by Michel Senellart, translated by Graham Burchell (London: Palgrave Macmillan, 2008), p. 168).

18　James M. Buchanan, 'Clarifying Confusion about the Balanced Budget Amendment', *National Tax Journal*, September 1995, vol. 48, no. 3, pp. 347–55 (pp. 349ff).

19　James M. Buchanan, *Democracy: Limited or Unlimited* (Buchanan House Archives, 1981), p. 12, quoted in Andrew Farrant and Vlad Tarko, 'James M. Buchanan's 1981 visit to Chile: Knightian Democrat or Defender of the "Devil's Fix"?', *The Review of Austrian Economics*, vol. 32, January 2018, pp. 1–20 (pp. 14 and 15).

20　Hayek, 'Die Entthronung der Politik', p. 218.

21　Friedrich Hayek, *Law, Legislation and Liberty* (London: Routledge, 1982), p. 150.

22　No constitution, the reader may object, is really invincible. The history of the law is strewn with apparently irrevocable laws that have in fact been revoked. But if radical change really is to be effected, it obviously requires much more energy than a simple change in legislation. The other important point is that any political attempt to emancipate oneself from restrictions written into the constitution will see, hovering over its head, the threat of a legal coup d'état initiated by the person who has been declared the guardian of that constitution.

23 Hayek, *Law, Legislation and Liberty*, p. 133. Thus, 'most services could be and probably should be delegated to regional or local corporations competing for inhabitants' (ibid., p. 103).

24 Friedrich Hayek, 'The Economic Conditions of Interstate Federalism', in Friedrich Hayek, *Individualism and Economic Order* (Chicago, IL: University of Chicago Press, 1948; first published 1939), p. 266. See also Cédric Durand 'Introduction: qu'est-ce que l'Europe?', in Cédric Durand (ed.), *En finir avec l'Europe* (Paris: La Fabrique, 2013), pp. 7–48 (p. 28).

25 James M. Buchanan in 1973, in the *Atlantic Economic Journal*, quoted in Farrant and Tarko, 'James M. Buchanan's 1981 visit to Chile', p. 15.

26 Meltzer, 'The Decline of the Liberal Economy', p. 5. See above, p. 188.

27 Ibid., p. 9.

28 Paul Samuelson, 'The World Economy at Century's End', in Shigeto Tsuru (ed.), *Human Resources, Employment and Development*, vol. 1 (London: Macmillan, 1983), pp. 58–77 (p. 75).

29 Paul A. Samuelson, 'The World Economy at Century's End', *Bulletin of the American Academy of Arts and Sciences*, vol. 34, no. 8, May 1981, pp. 35–44 (p. 44). This text has the same title as the previous one, but the contents are different.

30 'Proposition 2½', voted on in Massachusetts in November 1980, had been preceded by the very similar proposition 13 adopted in California in 1978.

31 James M. Buchanan and Richard E. Wagner, *Democracy in Deficit: The Political Legacy of Lord Keynes* (New York: Academic Press, 1977), p. 131.

32 James M. Buchanan and Gordon Tullock, 'The Expanding Public Sector: Wagner Squared', *Public Choice*, vol. 31, Autumn 1977, pp. 147–50 (p. 147).

33 Ibid.

34 Milton Friedman, 'Supply-Side Policies: Where Do We Go from Here?', in *Supply-Side Economics in the 1980s, Conference Proceedings – 'Conference at the Atlanta Hilton, March 17–18, 1982'* (Westport, CT: Quorum Books, 1982), pp. 53–63 (p. 62).

35 Ibid.

36 Milton Friedman 'Why the Twin Deficits are a Blessing', *Wall Street Journal*, 14 December 1988.

37 See above, p. 189.

38 'Friedman', adds Perelman, 'was not alone in welcoming the deficit. Alan Meltzer, another noted conservative economist, [. . .] credited the Reagan administration with a policy of intentionally building up the deficit as a deliberate tactic to restrict future administrations from adopting spending programs' (Michael Perelman, *The Pathology of the U.S. Economy Revisited: The Intractable Contradictions of Economic Policy* (New York: Palgrave, 2002), p. 68). 'Leaving a large deficit', explains Meltzer, 'may be an efficient way of restricting government spending' (Allan H. Meltzer, 'Economic Policies and Actions in the Reagan Administration', *Journal of Post Keynesian Economics*, vol. 10, no. 4, pp. 528–40 [p. 538]).

39 This 'politics of deficits' or 'politics of empty chests' was aimed, as Sébastien Guex has shown, 'to limit or reduce state receipts, by putting a ceiling on or lowering taxes, preferably those that affect the holders of capital, with the intention of reducing budgetary deficits. In other terms, the objective was

to encourage or even trigger a crisis in public finances. [. . .] The purpose of this strategy was to create what one American writer has called "a climate of austerity", and another a "permanent way of cutting into social budgets" – in short, establishing ideological conditions and policies favourable to social and financial counter-reformation' (Sébastien Guex, 'La politique des caisses vides', *Actes de la recherche en sciences sociales*, vol. 146–147, March 2003, pp. 51–61 [p. 54]).

40 Robert Keohane, 'Economics, Inflation and the Role of the State. Political Implications of the McCracken Report', *World Politics*, vol. 31, no. 1, October 1978, pp. 108–28 (p. 120).

41 Ibid., p. 121.

42 Bernard Manin, 'Les deux libéralismes: marché ou contre-pouvoirs', *Intervention*, no. 9, May–July 1984, pp. 10–24 (p. 19).

43 Ibid., p. 19.

44 Boaventura de Sousa Santos, 'Beyond Neoliberal Governance: The World Social Forum as Subaltern Cosmopolitan Politics and Legality', in Boaventura de Sousa Santos and César A. Rodriguez-Garavito (eds.), *Law and Globalization from Below: Towards a Cosmopolitan Legality* (Cambridge: Cambridge University Press, 2005), pp. 29–63 (p. 34).

45 Bernard Manin, 'Les deux libéralismes', p. 19. He adds: 'It is the return to a certain kind of invisible government in the name of international constraints [. . .]. Thus, monetarist regulations are also regulation of a political type, which have the huge advantage of shifting the crucial variable from something visible to something much more complex [. . .]. On the other hand, this is perhaps even more important, where the place of decision mainly lies beyond the pressures and activities of democracy' (p. 19). 'The same argument', Gorz commented, 'was valid for the "crisis of governability" in businesses [. . .]. There too, it was starting to become a matter of urgency to replace the too visible power of the central source of order by forms of decentralized self-organization, that is to say by the networking of relatively autonomous sub-units that, by coordinating themselves, would also save organizational costs. It was an urgent task to thereby break the fighting spirit of employees, the bargaining power of unions, and the "rigidities" that collective agreements, company agreements and social rights had introduced into the relations of production. In a word, it was necessary to "liberate the labour market" from what was distorting it. The watchword was "deregulate"' (Gorz, *Misères du présent*, p. 26).

46 Brittan, 'The Economic Contradictions of Democracy', p. 130.

47 Rose, 'Overloaded Government', p. 15.

48 Paul McCracken et al., *Towards Full Employment and Price Stability: A Report to the OECD by a Group of Independent Experts* (Paris: OECD, 1977). On the origins and interpretation of this report, see Vincent Gayon, 'Le keynésianisme international se débat. Sens de l'acceptable et tournant neoliberal à l'OCDE', *Annales. Histoire, Sciences Sociales*, vol. 72, no. 1, 2017, pp. 121–64.

49 Keohane, 'Economics, Inflation and the Role of the State', p. 109.

50 Ibid., p. 122.

51 Ibid.

52 Ibid.

53 Ibid., p. 117.

54 Offe, '"Ungovernability"', p. 84.
55 Claus Offe, 'Some Contradictions of the Modern Welfare State', in Claus Offe, *Contradictions of the Welfare State* (London: Hutchinson, 1984), pp. 147–61 (p. 153). See also Thomas O. Hueglin, 'The Politics of Fragmentation in an Age of Scarcity: A Synthetic View and Critical Analysis of Welfare State Crisis', *Canadian Journal of Political Science*, vol. 20, no. 2, June 1987, pp. 235–64 (p. 253).
56 Norman Podhoretz, *The New Defenders of Capitalism* (Washington, DC: Ethics and Public Policy Center, 1981), p. 97.
57 Ibid., p. 104.
58 This is crucial, for, he suggests, 'the very survival of private enterprise in the United States may depend on whether this newly sympathetic view of capitalism ultimately prevails in the world of ideas over the traditional hostility' (ibid., p. 96).
59 Ibid., p. 97.
60 Ibid., p. 104.
61 Daniel Bell, 'Letter to the Editor', *Harvard Business Review*, vol. 59, no. 3, May–June 1981, pp. 60–1 (p. 61).
62 Chantal Mouffe, 'L'offensive du néo-conservatisme contre la démocratie', in Lizette Jalbert and Laurent Lepage (eds.), *Néo-conservatisme et restructuration de l'État. Canada – États-Unis – Angleterre* (Montréal: Les Presses de l'Université du Québec, 1986), pp. 35–47; available online at http://clas siques.uqac.ca/contemporains/mouffe_chantal/offensive_neo_conservatrice/mouffe_offensive.pdf.
63 Andrew Gamble, 'The Free Economy and the Strong State'. Gamble, who seems not to be aware of Schmitt's text, takes this formula from Rüstow. See note 17 on p. 311 above. Thatcher herself declared, in 1980: 'the activities of the State have penetrated almost every aspect of life. Among other things the State has become responsible for huge nationalised monopolies employing hundreds of thousands of men and women. The trouble is that when the State becomes involved in every strike, price or contract affecting a nationalised industry, people tend to associate the State with those things rather than with its higher traditional and necessary role. Consequently its authority is not enhanced, it is diminished. In our Party we do not ask for a feeble State. On the contrary, we need a strong State to preserve both liberty and order' (Margaret Thatcher, 'Airey Neave Memorial Lecture', 3 March 1980, quoted in Gilles Christoph, 'Le libéralisme autoritaire de Friedrich Hayek: un exemple de bricolage idéologique?', in Françoise Odin and Christian Thuderoz (eds.), *Des mondes bricolés? Arts et sciences à l'épreuve de la notion de bricolage* (Lausanne: Presses polytechniques universitaires romandes, 2010), pp. 253–264 [p. 259]).
64 Stuart Hall, 'The Great Moving Right Show', *Marxism Today*, January 1979, pp. 14–20 (p. 15).
65 Andrew Gamble, *The Free Economy and the Strong State. The Politics of Thatcherism* (London: Macmillan Education, 1988), p. 28.
66 Ibid.
67 Ibid., p. 32.
68 Wolfe, *The Limits of Legitimacy*, p. 342.

Notes to Chapter 26

1 Gilles Deleuze and Félix Guattari, *A Thousand Plateaus. Capitalism and Schizophrenia*, translated by Brian Massumi (Minnesota, MN: University of Minnesota Press, 1987), p. 213.
2 Michel Foucault, *The Birth of Biopolitics. Lectures at the Collège de France, 1978–79*, edited by Michel Senellart, translated by Graham Burchell (London: Palgrave Macmillan, 2008), p. 186.
3 Madsen Pirie, *Micropolitics* (Aldershot: Wildwood House, 1988), p. 281.
4 Robert Moss, *The Collapse of Democracy* (London: Temple Smith, 1975), p. 257.
5 Pirie, *Micropolitics*, p. 279.
6 Ibid. (my emphasis).
7 Ibid., p. 284.
8 Keith Dixon, who has traced their political and intellectual itinerary, remarks that 'their proto-Thatcherite student militantism' was combined with the 'defence of the racist regimes of Southern Africa and the struggle to save British (White) identity' (Keith Dixon, 'Le "groupe de Saint Andrews". Aux origines du mouvement neoliberal britannique', in Jacques Guilhaumou, Jean-Louis Fournel and Jean-Pierre Potier (eds.), *Libertés et libéralismes: Formation et circulation des concepts* (Paris: ENS Éditions, 2015), pp. 407–21 (http://books.openedition.org/enseditions/2528)). See also Keith Dixon, *Les évangélistes du marché: les intellectuels britanniques et le néolibéralisme* (Paris: Raisons d'agir, 1998).
9 Madsen Pirie, 'The St Andrews Revolution', *Progressus*, 1999, quoted in Dixon, 'Le "groupe de Saint Andrews"'.
10 Madsen Pirie, *Dismantling the State: The Theory and Practice of Privatization* (Dallas, TX: National Center for Policy Analysis, 1985), p. 29.
11 See above ch. 10, p. 72.
12 Pirie, *Micropolitics*, p. 17.
13 Ibid., p. 26.
14 Ibid., p. 29.
15 Ibid., p. 265.
16 Ibid., p. 271.
17 Ibid., p. 127.
18 Ibid., p. 269.
19 In 1974, the stand-off between the Conservative Prime Minister Edward Heath and the miners' unions drove him to call an early election, which he lost. These unfortunate Conservatives (that was the same year in which Nixon lost office) 'ha[d] been persuaded of the case against big government, but they did not know how to make it smaller'. They lacked the right tactics (ibid., p. 50).
20 See Stuart Butler, 'Privatization: A Strategy to Cut the Budget', *Cato Journal*, vol. 5, no. 1, Spring/Summer 1985, pp. 325–35 (p. 326).
21 Pirie, *Dismantling the State*.
22 Butler, 'Privatization: A Strategy to Cut the Budget', p. 326.
23 See David Harvey, *A Brief History of Neoliberalism* (Oxford: Oxford University Press, 2005), pp. 159ff.
24 Pirie, *Dismantling the State*, p. 24.

25 Ibid., p. 3.
26 Ibid., p. 4.
27 Butler, 'Privatization: A Strategy to Cut the Budget', p. 330.
28 Offe, '"Ungovernability"', p. 69.
29 Ibid., p. 71.
30 Butler, 'Privatization: A Strategy to Cut the Budget', p. 326.
31 Jürgen Habermas, *The New Conservatism: Cultural Criticism and the Historian's Debate* (Cambridge, MA: MIT Press, 1989), p. 26.
32 Paul Starr, 'The Meaning of Privatization', *Yale Law & Policy Review*, vol. 6, no. 1, 1988, pp. 6–41 (p. 38).
33 Stuart M. Butler, 'Power to the People: A Conservative Vision for Welfare', *Policy Review*, no. 40, Spring 1987, pp. 3–8.
34 Ibid., p. 7.
35 In her book *The Will To Empower*, Barbara Cruikshank concludes that between the empowerment of the left and the empowerment of the right, 'the problem and the strategy are the same, however: to limit government intervention by getting people to govern themselves' (Barbara Cruikshank, *The Will to Empower: Democratic Citizens and Other Subjects* (Ithaca, NY: Cornell University Press, 1999), p. 70). The Conservatives, however, were very explicit on this point: their notion of empowerment was not that of the left; it was – and had to be – distinguished from it precisely because it was the name of another tactic, mobilized for opposite goals. Here is a revelatory anecdote: at the beginning of the 1990s in the internal wars of the Bush administration, between the old guard and the followers of a radical reform of the welfare system, the conflict crystallized on the use of the term 'empowerment', with Richard Darman, the Budget Director, prohibiting his colleagues from using it. One of them remembers a phone call: '"let me do you a favour – don't use the word empowerment in any memo you send [. . .]." He said, "You people don't understand the connotations of the word from the 60's." Of course we did. I was going to say that's what's fun about it – stealing one of the Left's words. But I didn't get that far' (quoted in Jason Deparle, 'How Jack Kemp Lost the War on Poverty', *New York Times*, 28 February 1993).
36 Pirie, *Micropolitics*, p. 209.
37 Ibid., p. 206.
38 Ibid., p. 209.
39 Pirie, *Dismantling the State*, p. 81.
40 Pirie, *Micropolitics*, p. 206.
41 Pirie, *Dismantling the State*, p. 82.
42 Ibid.
43 Pirie, *Micropolitics*, p. 209.
44 Pirie, *Dismantling the State*, p. 82.
45 'Once a program is operating successfully outside of the state sector, it can stay there', which does indeed allow a 'reverse ratchet' effect, 'a means of systematically reducing the public, government-directed part of the economy' (ibid., p. 3).
46 Pirie, *Micropolitics*, p. 126.
47 Ibid., p. 127. Pirie adds: 'there is a "micropolitics" just as there is a "micro-economics"'.
48 See above, p. 187.

49 Pirie, *Micropolitics*, p. 255.
50 Ibid., p. 121.
51 Gilles Deleuze and Félix Guattari, *Anti-Oedipus. Capitalism and Schizophrenia*, translated by Robert Hurley, Mark Seem and Helen R. Lane (Minneapolis, MN: University of Minnesota Press, 1983), p. 38.
52 Ibid., p. 184.
53 Ibid., p. 338.
54 This is a strategic principle: 'Micro politics moves down to the micro-scale because it recognizes that it can win on the level at which motivated individuals make decisions' (Pirie, *Micropolitics*, p. 263).
55 Frontin, *Les Stratagèmes*, Livre I (Paris: Panckoucke, 1848), p. 25.
56 Pirie, *Dismantling the State*, p. 65.
57 Pirie, *Micropolitics*, p. 185.
58 Ibid., p. 123.
59 Ibid., p. 185.
60 Ibid.
61 Pirie, *Dismantling the State*, p. 65.
62 Ibid., p. 66.
63 Ibid.
64 Micropolitics triggers a process of profound and long-term change. 'It may take more than a generation before the last of those within the state scheme finally work their way through, but the alternative supply is growing all of this time, and forms an effective interest group long before the final demise of the state supply.' This will lead to the extinction of a model. All things come to those who wait (Pirie, *Micropolitics*, p. 228).
65 Ibid., p. 214.
66 Ibid., p. 205.
67 Ibid., p. 209.
68 Ibid., p. 214.
69 Ibid., p. 210.
70 Ibid., p. 209.
71 Pirie, *Dismantling the State*, p. 69.
72 Pirie, *Micropolitics*, p. 208.
73 Ibid., p. 147.
74 Ibid., p. 145.
75 Stuart Butler, 'Privatization: A Strategy to Cut the Budget', p. 330.
76 Mike Davis, *Prisoners of the American Dream: Politics and Economy in the History of the US Working Class* (London: Verso, 1999), p. 178.
77 Ibid.
78 Ibid.
79 Ibid.
80 Arsène Dumont, quoted in *Bulletins et mémoires de la Société d'anthropologie de Paris* (Paris: Masson, 1902), p. 365.

Notes to Conclusion

1 Jacques Donzelot, 'Michel Foucault et l'intelligence du libéralisme', *Esprit*, no. 319, November 2005, pp. 60–81 (p. 78).
2 Lepage, *Demain le libéralisme*, p. 403.

3 This is how Jean-Claude Monod summarizes the 'underlying admiration' for neoliberalism that Foucault betrays in his lectures of 1977–1979. See Jean-Claude Monod, 'Qu'est-ce qu'une "crise de gouvernementalité"?', *Lumières*, no. 8, 2006, pp. 51–68 (p. 59).

4 Ziegler, *Autoritärer oder totaler Staat*, p. 8.

5 Rüstow, 'Freie Wirtschaft – Starker Staat', p. 68.

6 At the author's suggestion, I have retained the English 'self-management' for the French *autogestion*, though the two words have somewhat different political connotations. (Translator's note.)

7 To give just one example, in 1978 Henri Lepage, who played a major role in popularizing and importing neoliberal theories from the United States into France, wrote a whole book condemning self-management. See Henri Lepage, *Autogestion et capitalisme: réponses à l'anti-économie* (Paris: Masson, 1978).

INDEX

Marxism 21, 202, 222
  see also neo-Marxism
Maslow, Abraham 15
Mason, Edward 47–8
May, William F. 178
Mazzocchi, Anthony 155
Means, Gardiner 35, 37–8, 42, 50,
  53, 54, 85
Meckling, William 51, 87, 90, 91, 92,
  93, 94, 127, 194
media, pro-business 77
Medicare and Medicaid 218
Meltzer, Alan 216, 315n38
merger-acquisition operations 54
meta-government 58, 61
meta-politics 215
micropolitics 225–37
  creation of counter groups 236
  fragmentation strategy 235–6
  middle-class target 236–7
  neoliberal 225–37
  political ethonomy 237
  of privatization 225–37
  tactical diversity 235–6
Mills, Charles Wright 261n12
Mises, Ludwig von 209, 210
Mishan, Ezra J. 156–7
Mitchell, Ronald K. 132
Mitnick, Barry 50
*The Modern Corporation and Private
  Property* 35, 36
  see also Berle, Adolf; Means,
  Gardiner
modernism, oppositional culture of
  73–4
monetarism 199, 219
Mongoven, Bart 116, 283n36,
  286n28
Mongoven, Jack 109–10, 282n16,
  283n29, 286nn30, 34, 288n16
Monod, Jean-Claude 321n3
monologic communication 114
Monsanto 109, 111, 121–2
Mont Pelerin Society 27, 215
Montesquieu 116
Moody, Kim 296n13
Moore, Philip 71
Mouffe, Chantal 223
multinational regulation 141–8
  guidance versus regulation 145

international codes of conduct
  141–3, 144
self-regulation codes 146–7
soft law and 144–8
Murphy, Thomas 270n39
Mussolini, Benito 205, 210
mutiny 2

Nace, Ted 267n44
Nader, Ralph 72, 80
Naples, Michele 252n16
Napoleon Bonaparte 213
NARMIC 69
national security doctrine 213
National Soft Drink Association
  176
Nazism 210, 211
Negritude 260n48
neo-Marxism 89, 151, 189–90
neo-populism 237
neoclassical economics 87, 88, 89, 90,
  122, 164, 168, 169
neoconservatives 6, 22, 74, 86, 103,
  104, 189, 190–1, 196, 222
neoliberalism 3, 4, 43, 45, 49, 58, 60,
  83, 104, 131, 163, 165, 172, 191,
  196, 214, 225
  accommodation of state power
    240–1
  anti-regulation 149–59, 162, 178,
    241
  anti-unionism 27
  authoritarian turn 196, 199–202,
    204–12, 223, 238–9, 240
  construction of political counter-
    coalitions 236
  eclectic and contradictory 4
  economic neoliberalism 43, 50, 84,
    103, 130, 169, 202, 215, 219,
    223, 232, 240
  ethical neoliberalism 179, 180
  governmentality 122, 147, 212
  micropolitics 225–37
  political engineering 61
  privatization and 225–37
  promise of individual autonomy
    and social self-regulation 238
  vision of history 59
Neptune strategy 119
Nero, Emperor 258n32